D0821325

REGGA

Traffic policeman: 'Don't you know the speed limit
on the *autostrada* is 130 kilometres an hour?
You were doing 200.'

Regga: '200? Bullshit! I was doing 250 …'

Christopher Hilton
Foreword by Sir Frank Williams

REGGA

THE EXTRAORDINARY TWO LIVES OF CLAY REGAZZONI

© Christopher Hilton, 2008

Christopher Hilton has asserted his right to be
identified as the author of this work

First published in September 2008

All rights reserved. No part of this publication may be
reproduced, stored in a retrieval system or transmitted,
in any form or by any means, electronic, mechanical,
photocopying, recording or otherwise, without prior
permission in writing from the publisher.

A catalogue record for this book is
available from the British Library

ISBN 978 1 84425 479 8

Library of Congress control no 2008926352

Published by Haynes Publishing,
Sparkford, Yeovil, Somerset BA22 7JJ, UK
Tel: 01963 442030 Fax: 01963 440001
Int.tel: +44 1963 442030 Int. fax: +44 1963 440001
E-mail: sales@haynes.co.uk
Website: www.haynes.co.uk

Haynes North America Inc.,
861 Lawrence Drive, Newbury Park,
California 91320, USA

Page layout by G&M Designs Limited,
Raunds, Northamptonshire

Printed and bound in Britain by
J. H. Haynes & Co. Ltd, Sparkford

CONTENTS

REGGA

FOREWORD

— BY SIR FRANK WILLIAMS —

Clay Regazzoni has a permanent place in the hearts of the Williams Grand Prix team because he gave us our first victory, at Silverstone in 1979. Alan Jones led that race very strongly but suffered a mechanical problem, so Clay took over and when he crossed the line we all felt delighted for him – he was very popular within the team, as he was everywhere – but sadness for Alan, who had done so much for us building up to the victory. He won the next three races and we were on our way, but Clay will always be the first.

He was a charming person, very experienced and part of a generation that would always do outrageous things. If Clay thought it was fun to drive his hire car into a swimming pool he would drive it straight in – and at racing speed if he could. Drivers don't do that any more!

The year after he left us he crashed at Long Beach, which ended his career in racing cars. I saw him several times in his wheelchair. When something like that happens you have to say *right, that's it, it's happened, get on with it –* that or you wither away. I think what Clay did for the handicapped after his crash was outstanding, especially the driving school at Vallelunga and the rallies in which he competed.

He never lost his charm, even in adversity.

I am told that this is the first book about him in English, which seems amazing when you consider the extent of his career, what he achieved and his popularity here – not least at Williams.

The start at Silverstone, 1979, and a glittering future lay ahead for the Williams team. Regazzoni alongside Jean-Pierre Jabouille – Jones (pole) was already away and out of our sight. (LAT)

INTRODUCTION

— REGGA —

'I had the good fortune to live the last years when racing was still an adventure, where the cars – without wings, with smaller tyres – were beautiful and really had to be driven.'

These are the words of Clay Regazzoni and they capture the essence of the man, but if he'd just been that, an old-time, devil-take-the-hindmost character who drove hard and lived hard, he'd have taken his place in the panorama of dangerous derring-do that motor racing was in the 1960s and 1970s – and not much else. Of his 132 Grands Prix he took five pole positions and won five. Two of these wins were genuinely memorable but, in the history of Formula 1, they scarcely amount to a career approaching greatness.

The essence lies elsewhere, most notably in what he did after an horrendous crash at Long Beach in 1980 left him in a wheelchair for the rest of his life. From that he built himself into an inspirational figure for paralysed people, teaching them that they could drive and compete. He went on Paris-Dakar Rallies – he once tried to take a 400km short cut through the jungle in the Congo – and those Dakars were themselves panoramas of dangerous and sometimes lethal derring-do involving the Sahara desert. He drove trucks and cars that he manipulated using hand controls, and, quite naturally, he travelled at racing speed.

It was the only speed he had ever known or ever would know – as, it seems, he carried it all the way to a lorry on the *autostrada* near Parma in December 2006 and the crash that killed him.

He was charismatic, naughty, utterly charming, and had eyes so deep they threw one seasoned old motor racing campaigner, Morris Nunn, into confusion. He had sex appeal, too, plenty of that. He deployed it with conclusive effect regularly and right round the world.

Ponder. Sir Frank Williams, almost completely paralysed in 1986, continues to run one of the most successful Grand Prix teams. Philippe Streiff, almost completely paralysed in 1989 testing in Brazil, created a major world karting event before taking up a senior position in the French government with responsibility for the handicapped. When you add Regazzoni you are forced to conclude that these motor racing people are one breed, and quite a breed.

That is the essence of the man and what you'll be reading.

There is no other book in English on him, itself astonishing when you consider the annual output in motor sport. You'd have needed a cricket scoreboard to keep abreast of the total number on Lewis Hamilton at the end of his first season.

This book began as the third in a sequence called *Memories of* – Ayrton Senna was the first, James Hunt the second. To carry a book involving a host of people giving their memories imposes discipline on your choice of subject: you have to have a multi-faceted personality or all the memories risk being the same. Regazzoni seemed a natural to continue the sequence but, as the research developed, the direction of the book changed: Senna's life story has been recounted in great detail, Hunt's exploits, too, so the memories simply had to bring fresh eyes to received wisdom and known facts. Regazzoni's life story had not, I repeat, been recounted at all for an English readership – except in various précis – and, as a consequence, a more orthodox biography began to emerge.

I soon realised that, all else aside, it ought to embrace all his single-seater races, because imagining that any man could have survived (survival = staying alive) on a repetitive basis most weekends for damn near two decades in an era of unsafe cars, unsafe circuits and unsafe people is extraordinary. The races read like a raw, primitive expression of a man's need to race that entirely subjugates any other considerations. In them you will find death, fire, heroism, politics to make politicians seem innocent, risk, vanity, money, claimed innocence, anger, accusations and all manner of mechanical failures.

No ordinary tale, no ordinary human being.

Because of this, and because races three or four decades ago are largely unknown these days, some are recreated in great detail.

Clay Reggazzoni, a man's man. (LAT)

The Paris-Dakar Rally in 1989, and you can't do this to a vehicle if you're going slowly. (DPPI)

And that's before we've reached the wheelchair and a decade and a half of rallies travelling at that racing speed through Africa, North, Central and South America, tracts of the Middle East, China and Australia. There'll be the co-driver who fled, barrel-rolls (which he discussed quite calmly while they were happening) and a yak barbeque near Tibet – the barbeque made of metal coat-hangers.

There'll be his original approach to driving Italy's *autostrada* at racing speed, and there'll be the quiet, private man at home tending his

garden – pruning his beloved roses – and gazing, lost in thought, at the blue Mediterranean sky.

I have many people to thank at two levels: for assistance and for sharing their memories.

I am indebted to Sir Frank Williams for the gracious Foreword, as well as a lively interview. His eyes still sparkle with delight when the talk turns to motor racing, the ironic asides are delivered as they always have been and he has, I suspect, a more profound understanding of human beings than he is given credit for.

Maddalena Mantegazzi lived with Regazzoni for almost 20 years. She spoke with touching love and tenderness about the joys – and problems – of that. His son Gian Maria spoke with great candour about the problems as well as the joys, and spiced that with some truly wonderful anecdotes. Maddalena and Gian Maria gave freely of their time and I pay sincere tribute to both. Giordano (known as Dodo), Regazzoni's youngest brother, gave precious glimpses and insights into family life. The book would have been infinitely poorer without these three good people and their undisguised affection for Regazzoni.

Apart from Sir Frank, Patrick Head, Frank Dernie and Neil Oatley took me deep inside the 1979 Williams season with Regazzoni. Oatley showed many other kindnesses and, in reading the chapter, corrected my spelling mistakes. Formula 1 is attention to detail – and here it was.

I'm also indebted to the following (in no particular order) for interviews: Mario Poltronieri, Klaus Seppi, Hans Stuck, John Watson, Mo Nunn, Jochen Mass, Franco Gozzi, Craig Burkett, Tim Parnell, Vic Elford, Robin and Alice Widdows, Derek Bell, Brian Hart, Simon Taylor, Sir Jackie Stewart, Brian Redman, Aleardo Buzzi, Giacomo Tansini, Don Nichols, Patrick Tambay, Leo de Graffenried, Professor Sid Watkins, Gary Anderson, Dan Gurney, Martyn Pass, Ricardo Zunino, Malcolm Folley, Andrea Stella, Massimo del Prete, Carol Hollfelder, Stefano Venturini, Rob Hurdman, Gunther Stamm, Heidi Hetzer, Dylan Mackay, Franco Pipino, Graham Bogle, Keke Rosberg, Roger Dixon, Henry and Tina Koster, John Brown, Jim Baynam and Martin Taylor.

Gareth Rees sent a host of photographs and memorabilia and provided the perfect spectator's viewpoint in a sequence of penetrating observations. I have used all these observations.

Rainer Küschall, a quadriplegic who manufactures custom-built wheelchairs, welcomed me into his Basle apartment, gave me a fascinating interview and lent photographs.

The assistance of Monica Meroni played a major role. She did extensive translations and interpreted beautifully, as well as arranging interviews in Italy.

Thanks also to Gordon Kirby, Ken Breslauer the Sebring historian, Liam Clogger of Williams, Reg

He'd take only five pole positions in his career. This is the second of them, at Silverstone in 1971. (Roger Dixon Photography)

Plummer who understands statistics, Marco Ragazzoni of *Autosprint* for finding precious contact details, John Reitman (Regional Executive of the California Club SCCA), Sara Howley (of Broward Health, Fort Lauderdale), Otello Sorato, Agnes Carlier, Nicole Bertellotti, David Hayhoe, Nigel Roebuck for raiding his library (again) and sending cuttings as well as escorting me down memory lane, the amazing website www.formula2.net/F268_Index.htm, which was utterly invaluable, Renaud de Laborderie, Ron Jackson of Trans World Events for permission to quote from four of their rally books – *The Panama-Alaska*, *The Shield of Africa*, *The Carrera Sudamericana* and *The 2000 London to Sydney*; Robert Arndt, editor of *Saudi Aramco World,* published by Aramco Services Co, Houston, Texas, for permission to quote from an article on the Rally of the Pharaohs. Alan Barton sent a wonderful description of events on a rally in Tunisia, and Nino Fiorello sent a video of an historic Targa Florio, a CD of a Regazzoni interview and a Regazzoni baseball-style cap. It suits me (I think).

Juan Carlos Ferrigno sent two of his wonderfully evocative paintings, which are gratefully reproduced.

David Hayhoe kindly provided the Formula 1 statistics and Stuart Dent provided decals to liven up those statistics.

I pay my dues to the two books Regazzoni wrote: *Le Combat* (Solar, Paris, 1982), a translation from the original Italian *È Questione di Cuore* (Sperling & Kupfer, Milan); and *E la Corsa Continua* (Sperling & Kupfer, 1988). Both were written with Cesare de Agostini. I have consulted them for background, particularly Regazzoni's youth, early career, recovery and the 1986 Paris-Dakar. They are doubly invaluable as primary sources since, as you can see, neither was published in English and consequently what is in them will be new to an English-reading audience. That's you.

I've used, directly or indirectly: Niki Lauda's *For The Record* (William Kimber, London, 1978, and Stanley Paul, 1986); *Frank Williams* by Maurice Hamilton (Macmillan, London, 1998); *Flying on the Ground* by Emerson Fittipaldi (William Kimber, 1973); *Driving Ambition* by Alan Jones (Stanley Paul, 1981); *Life at the Limit* by Professor Watkins (Macmillan, 1996); *Ferrari: The Grand Prix Cars* by Alan Henry (Hazleton, Richmond, 1989); and *Against All Odds* by James Hunt (Hamlyn, London, 1977).

Several other publications helped, too: Hayhoe and Holland's *Grand Prix Data Book* (Haynes), the *Autocourse* annuals, the *Marlboro Grand Prix Guide*, and two magazines, *Autosport* and *FI Racing* – Matt Bishop, the former editor of both, was particularly helpful.

I met kindness at every turn, not least in the number of people happy to lend their photographs and memorabilia. Rather than acknowledge them all here I've made sure that the donors are properly thanked with each picture. However, Kathy Ager of LAT deserves a special mention for her care in combing their immense archive to find a superb selection of Regazzoni studies.

THE FIRST LIFE: DANGERMAN

Clay was a driver partly out of time in the sense that he was from the generation for whom it was living the life as much as being the driver. Clay was a man who epitomised, I believe, what people perceive a race driver to be, a slightly dangerous character, slightly bad reputation, a great lothario, great lover, everything.
– *John Watson*

I said 'How's the car?' and he said 'Just the same.' I said 'But Clay, you went two seconds quicker.' I asked where the two seconds had come from. He said 'But I didn't try as hard.' I said 'Clay, the object of racing is to do the fastest time with the least effort.' He looked at me and said 'Morris, that's not racing. I can't drive like that.'
– *Mo Nunn*

We flew to Johannesburg and during the night a young girl ran right down the plane naked with Clay's helmet on – for a bet with a *Playboy* photographer. Clay said 'Give me a couple of hours and I will make that girl do it.' And he did. And she did. Unbelievable.
– *Franco Gozzi*

At meetings Lambert's father would come up and start bloody rowing and carrying on and all that. I personally told Lambert he'd better back off or he'd be in serious trouble, not only legally but he risked getting a thump from somebody. Regga was a bit concerned but he was a pretty tough character.
– *Tim Parnell*

I don't remember him being particularly good at testing and one of the things was that the engineer running the test never knew what percentage of the exploitation of the car he was giving, or whether after lunch he was putting more effort or less effort in than before lunch. He really was a man who only responded to a race.
– *Patrick Head*

CHAPTER 1

WALK ON THE WILD SIDE

Switzerland is mysterious because its constituent parts – the south very Italian, the west very French and the north very German – are exactly the sort which have made so many countries tear themselves apart. Landlocked, so the benefits of seagoing have always been denied it, and dominated by mountains that are useless (except for skiing holidays, walkers and yodellers), the Swiss have created the highest living standard in Europe. They are home to many international organisations, including the headquarters of the Olympic movement, the United Nations' European operations and, since 1863, the International Committee of the Red Cross. The most famous convention on civilising conduct towards prisoners of war is known throughout the world as the Geneva Convention.

A deeper mystery is that the Swiss themselves, who have done all this, are not mysterious but disarmingly straightforward (up to and including accepting bank deposits no questions asked) and there is no mystery about Clay Regazzoni, a *Ticinois*.

'Ticino means mild climate, unique natural contrasts and varied landscapes. The Ticino River, which gives its name to the Canton, begins in the Gotthard Region amid steep gorges and deeply carved valleys. Ticino is divided into four regions: Bellinzona, Lake Maggiore, Lake Lugano and the Mendrisiotto in the very south. Each region offers different and special scenery [...] Ticino's flora is

RIGHT *Nobody knew, but all the early years were leading towards this: an emotional, emotive union with Ferrari. This is the 1970 Austrian Grand Prix, where Regazzoni finished second, and here is what the Ferrari faithful felt about it.* (LAT)

typified by the coexistence of plants of both Alpine and Mediterranean origin. It is the most interesting botanical region in Switzerland because of its subtropical climate – 2,300 hours of sunshine per year promote the growth of cypress, palm trees, camellias, mimosas and magnolias and chestnuts (just to list a few). Spring arrives earlier in Ticino.'[1]

Gianclaudio Giuseppe Regazzoni arrived early on the morning of 5 September 1939 at Lugano, the second son of Pio and Bruna. Pio was in the Army. Bruna felt the contractions begin and set off for hospital on foot at four o'clock in the morning. A passing baker's van gave her a lift. We don't know if the van travelled fast, the contractions increasing, but if it did that would perhaps explain a great deal. If Regazzoni was in a hurry to get here, he was constantly in a hurry when he did get here.

The family were Italian by origin and, as all who knew him are agreed, Regazzoni was *very* Italian in thought, word and deed while, of course, remaining Swiss. It's the mystery again: two potentially conflicting personalities – Italian anarchy, Swiss discipline – coexisting in such perfect harmony that they became a source of strength.

The Regazzonis had been in commerce at Bergamo before emigrating to Switzerland. His parents hadn't decided on a name but, some hours after his birth, his mother was reading a newspaper and saw that a couple had just Christened their first child Jean-Claude. She thought that sounded pleasant enough, rendered it into the Italian and he became Gianclaudio. People said *nice name but it's too long* and there was talk of calling him Clyde instead. She wouldn't be moved and Gianclaudio it remained until the nickname Clay came along.

We don't know whether she approved, but Clay it was, Clay it is and Clay it will always be.

He had an elder brother, Renato, and would have a sister, Vanna, then two more brothers, Mauro and Dodo – so many of them that they seemed more like a region than a family, although, Dodo insists, 'the family was quite normal. My parents were simple people. They taught me to respect others and they taught me hard work. They also taught me to respect money. Life is work – I don't think that when you get to 60 you stop. In the home there was discipline and the man was the leader. My mother was very important to the family, of course, but in second place to my father! The man was in charge of the house, and that was Clay, too.

'He was 15 when I was born, and so there was a big difference. I was only eight when he started racing but he had a young mentality and we had a good feeling together. Was that true of all the brothers and the sister? That's difficult to say because Clay had a different life. He didn't live with us [later] but he was an example to us. He had a good personality but he was a simple man.'

Pio was strong-willed, especially in arguments, and Regazzoni must have inherited some of that. Hans Stuck, who'd become a team-mate in Formula 1, remembers that 'as far as I know Clay had no enemies, although maybe the family had at home in Switzerland because his father was in charge of the ice hockey stadium in Lugano and for some reason – I think there was a quarrel with someone – he switched off the lights during a match and they had to stop it! That's where Clay got it from. I met his father once or twice and he was a pretty funny guy.'

Regazzoni's son Gian Maria feels that the strong-willed aspect 'comes from this: they thought they could do anything they wanted to. My grandfather was the mayor and he used to drive around all the streets with myself following in a little child's car like it was normal [and by implication not the respectable, responsible sort of thing a mayor should be doing]. I was eight or nine. My grandfather was a big man, a tough guy. Everybody respected him. The family are very dedicated people and hard-working.'

Regazzoni wasn't interested in school but preferred wrestling with his chums to prove who was strongest. He played football, which presaged enthusiasm for and accomplishment at many sports, tennis, bobsleighs, canoeing, cross country skiing, cycling ...

His father – evidently an austere man who believed in the primary values we've just heard, the family and hard work as well as the church – had a body shop and a car which, at 12, Regazzoni drove for the first time. 'Nobody taught me, I watched my father doing it.' He followed the exploits of two of the great Grand Prix drivers of the day, Juan-Manuel Fangio and Stirling Moss, but from a distance because, as he said, information about them was sparse. 'There was no television and it was not easy to find magazines.'

In time young Regazzoni went to work in the body shop for, as he'd remember, 700 Swiss francs a month, rising to 1,000. His mother got half for subsistence. He obeyed his father's dictum and worked hard, beginning in the early hours of the morning and staying until everything was done.

There were, of course, cars around although he had no dreams of racing. In Switzerland, as he'd point out, 'we don't have circuit racing and I didn't have any money.' The banishment of circuit

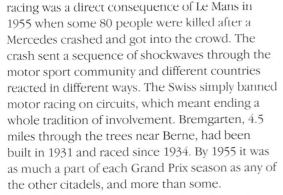

racing was a direct consequence of Le Mans in 1955 when some 80 people were killed after a Mercedes crashed and got into the crowd. The crash sent a sequence of shockwaves through the motor sport community and different countries reacted in different ways. The Swiss simply banned motor racing on circuits, which meant ending a whole tradition of involvement. Bremgarten, 4.5 miles through the trees near Berne, had been built in 1931 and raced since 1934. By 1955 it was as much a part of each Grand Prix season as any of the other citadels, and more than some.

For a Swiss to create a career in motor racing became infinitely harder because the important tributaries into it had been dammed, the infrastructure that would feed youngsters into those tributaries gone. Perhaps it doesn't do to make too much of these things, if only because people who intend to do the creating don't let petty considerations like nationality or absence of opportunity deter them. It might even make them want it more – the forbidden fruit theory – although, as we've just seen, Regazzoni nursed no such dreams. There were, however, good Swiss drivers around, including Silvio Moser. Two years

younger than Regazzoni, he'd begun racing in 1961 with a Jaguar. They'd become firm friends, although Moser was from Zurich and spoke Italian with an accent, which amused Regazzoni a great deal.

Regazzoni began to follow motor racing in a serious way comparatively late, after military service. There, during his four months as a private in the infantry, he confronted the mystery because he couldn't avoid witnessing the intense rivalry between the Swiss Germans, French and Italians. Some of the exercises resembled war itself. Regazzoni, however, drove military trucks and mountain tractors. He made one move so fast on a descent that he was summoned to explain how he'd got to the bottom so early.

After demob he bought a white MG, much to the family's disapproval, and *loved* it. He was 21. A year later he journeyed to Monza to watch the Italian Grand Prix and, with a friend, managed to get a ticket into the paddock. He posed for a photograph beside the Ferrari of Giancarlo Baghetti (and only years later realised that in the background was a very young-looking Mauro Forghieri, who he'd come to know well at Ferrari).

Regazzoni described the first part of his life in a book entitled 'A Question Of Heart'. The cover of the French edition, 'Le Combat', and selection of early photographs offer an insight into the man he would become.

'I was working with my father, going Friday night and back on Sunday night. I never thought seriously about motor racing. That came when I met Silvio Moser. There was a club in Lugano where we met every Thursday night, and just talked about racing.' Moser was now driving the Jaguar with his racing car on a trailer and 'I accompanied him to the circuits. We went through the night and I drove while he slept' – by definition the races were outside Switzerland, necessitating the travel. Eventually Moser said 'Why don't you have a go?'

Yes, he thought, *I will.*

Before we go any further, or rather to appreciate events as we do go further, consider that Clay Regazzoni was a man from another time and mentality, the former spicing the latter. It was 1963, so that as he took his first tentative steps into the career he was already *24 years old.* That alone distances him from the whole of motor racing today. Consider it this way: Lewis Hamilton, given a go-kart at the age of six, was racing seriously at eight. He was *still* younger than Regazzoni's starting point when he reached Formula 1 in 2007. You can argue that the world was not yet obsessed by youth in 1963 and equally argue – as Frank Dernie, with the Williams team when Regazzoni got there, does – that 'guys in

those days [1979!] partied a lot. The only time you ever needed to drive flat out in Formula 1 was qualifying. The Grand Prix was generally a race of attrition and the drivers were big, fat, old and really knackered by lap 10 – but they were all like that.' Dernie is not being unkind and you know what he means.

I've used Hamilton for another reason. He embodies the modern racing driver: a controlled man in a controlled environment, each word measured, each gesture restricted. It's as if the environment has taken him over and obliged him to conform to all its dictates, minute by minute. The other drivers are mostly like that, too, and I'm not criticising them. It's the way the world is.

Once upon a time, within an hour of the start of the Canadian Grand Prix at Mosport, a lady appeared in a fur coat, suspenders and nothing else. Regazzoni did what a man is going to do and, as one who was nearby confides, it took so much out of him that he crashed on the second corner.

Once upon another time, at a race in Spa, Regazzoni and a British driver were due to have dinner. The Briton arrived at Regazzoni's hotel – he was still in his bedroom. The Briton went up, knocked and a voice boomed 'Come in!' He did, and there before him was Regazzoni on the bed with the lady who owned the hotel on one side and her daughter on the other. He'd clearly done what a man is going to do, and seemingly given an encore.

The contrast between this and the modern driver serves a singular purpose: it sharpens the appreciation of Regazzoni, that other time and that other mentality. To reinforce it, we'll be visiting many circuits for many races on his journey towards Formula 1 and along the way we'll be meeting many people, just as he met them. They come at you in great profusion but that can't be helped. It's exactly how they came at him.

Dodo explains that when Regazzoni started racing 'it was very difficult for him because my father wanted him to work in the factory. After two years, when he started to get results, it became very interesting. I told my father I wanted to go racing but he said "No, you must work! Just one son racing is enough in the family!" That made it very difficult for me to start.'

Regazzoni did hill climbs in an Austin Healey Sprite. Hill climbs were still legal in Switzerland and he finished one of the most celebrated – Mitholz to Kandersteg – third in category. It was dangerous and could be deadly. During practice four years later a Swiss called Gody Winzenried

The bon viveur and a period piece at the same time. No driver would dare pose for a picture like this now. (courtesy Gareth Rees)

&BIRELL – the taste of a real drink!

Ace-racing driver Clay Regazzoni enjoys Birell

&BIRELL

lost control of his Triumph on a bend and struck an embankment and a tree. One anonymous witness in 1963, however, describes Regazzoni's Healey Sprite as 'harmless'.

He competed in a Schauinsland hill climb in Germany's Black Forest, although whether this was on 11 August, the fifth round of the European Mountain Championship, is not clear. He was fourth in category. *Autocourse* reported that Schauinsland comprised two ascents with aggregate time counting, and a new record at 13m 26.64s – but no mention of Regazzoni. He was also third in category at a hill climb at Marchairuz, north of Geneva.

That season Moser bought a Brabham for Formula 3.

Meanwhile Regazzoni acquired a Mini Cooper S, a practical choice because he used it for work during the week and raced it at weekends. He spent 1964 doing more hill climbs and slaloms – courses arranged at aerodromes – and his only victory came on one at Monteceneri. He was second in category at Payerne (a major Swiss Air Force base), third in category at, successively, Kandersteg, Marchairuz and Schauinsland. It was all a man at play, and enjoying playing.

One day Moser said 'Why don't you have a go at Formula 3?'

Yes, he thought, *I will*.

Moser smoothed Regazzoni's way into a small team called Martinelli and Sonvico, so that they'd be team-mates. He'd drive a de Tomaso, prepared at Modena, with a Ford engine. Regazzoni journeyed to Modena and drove it on the little circuit there but the car had been modified from the previous season – it had won a race – and was beset by problems. After work on it he tried again, at another small circuit built on 'private land on a mountain plateau in the Jura, near Berne, close to the village of Lignieres. This tiny circuit, which is less than a mile in length, was built in the 1960s in the hope that the government would change its attitude to racing but events can only be held there if there are traffic cones placed on the circuit.'[2] A wet day, snow lying on the rim of the track, and Regazzoni spun so repeatedly he concluded he wasn't made to be a single-seater driver. He created such a modest impression that some observers remembered only the transport vehicles with 'Martinelli & Sonvico' on them.

Moser talked him out of retiring before he'd even really begun.

Instead he went to compete in a minor race at Imola on 11 April, the first time he had driven a major circuit. He was in the second heat and so missed a major crash in the first where the cars went at it 'hammer and tongs from the start'[3] and, with cars and drivers evenly matched, something had to give. It did on the second corner. One car spun and in the chaos seven others were wrecked. Andrea de Adamich, from Trieste and a very promising young driver, avoided all this and won. Moser took the second heat and Regazzoni covered no more than three laps before the de Tomaso expired. 'Geki' – a pseudonym for a wealthy and successful driver, Giacomo Russo – won driving a de Sanctis, a car designed by a successful Rome car dealer and well known in its time. Jonathan Williams, a young Englishman based in Italy – and who would reach Grand Prix racing with Ferrari – came fourth.

This humble race, just one among so many anonymous thousands in the junior reaches of motor sport, deserves to be remembered not just because it marked the beginning of Regazzoni's racing – the hill climbs and airport slaloms were by definition time trials, not races – but because it marked the beginning of a sustained, gargantuan assault on virtually every branch of motor sport lasting four decades. By bitterest irony, only an *autostrada* crash could stop it.

The races would come, and keep coming, in profusion, and the more they came the more he loved it. I've tried to include a little bit on each because, cumulatively, they represent the gathering career. By definition this tended to happen at the same circuits against the same opponents. That's the nature of the beast that is a motor racing career. Here, then, is the gathering, repetitions and all.

At the beginning of May he was at Magny-Cours, the circuit lost in the middle of France near Nevers, and then only four years old. It was his first race abroad, in the sense that anything in Switzerland was home, and anything in Italy felt home.

The engine ran better. The meeting comprised two heats of 20 laps and a final of 30 – a general structure, as we shall see, much favoured in junior formulae. He went in the first heat and finished fifth, a lap down. On race day it rained hard but he found cornering comfortable and concluded that the Lignieres nightmare no longer haunted him. He drove without alarms to sixth place, albeit a lap down again. Another of the promising drivers of the generation, Roy Pike, won, and a certain hail-fellow-well-met, Charlie Crichton-Stuart, came fourth.

Motor racing, a comparatively small community – even at the global level – interweaves and interconnects. In 1977 Regazzoni would drive for a team run by Mo Nunn, who had once been hired to partner Pike at Lotus (and would drive against Nunn in these junior days, something Nunn doesn't remember at all). In 1979 Regazzoni would drive for Williams, and by then Crichton-Stuart was a senior member of the team.

If you're a student of motor sport it's fascinating to watch the youngsters making their entrances, each so anonymous, and to follow the interweaving.

A few days after Magny-Cours he went to Zolder, the Belgian circuit lost in the Ardennes woodlands, which had only just opened. Crichton-Stuart was there, Pike, Moser, Williams and two other young Englishmen, Piers Courage and Peter Gethin. Regazzoni reached the final by coming ninth in his heat (and the usual lap down). Pike won.

In the final, he had his first crash after a mechanical fault on the eighth lap when he turned into a corner and the car went straight ahead to a sand trap. Williams won from Pike, Moser sixth.

At Monza, such a short journey from Lugano, he was too eager and too confident. He spun twice, so that he didn't survive the pruning process – 81 cars were entered – for the heats.

At the end of the month he travelled to what would be his fifth Grand Prix circuit (present or future): Monaco. The Formula 3 race traditionally supported the Grand Prix and assumed a particular significance because the great and the good of Formula 1 were supposed to cast their knowing eyes over it. Regazzoni liked the layout of the circuit immediately. He felt fit and he felt ready. He'd hardly had any sleep but he didn't care about that. In practice, however, he came upon Crichton-Stuart and at the Gasometer hairpin tried to overtake by out-breaking him. He got that wrong and tapped Crichton-Stuart, who continued. He had to stop for repairs.

At Monaco he'd witness another tradition. For as long as anyone could remember, pre-war driver Louis Chiron started the Grand Prix with a highly theatrical waving of the flag and now he did the same for the Formula 3 runners. A huge entry had been pruned to 40 by the practice times and divided, on the Saturday, into two heats of 16 laps followed by a 24-lap final.

Regazzoni lined up on the fifth row of ten in the first heat. Crichton-Stuart was in it. So were Peter Revson (American, and already a Grand Prix driver) and Bob Bondurant (another American, who'd reach Grand Prix racing later in the season). Chiron started it, as a contemporary report describes, with 'immense energy', and we can assume the racers showed the same immense energy during the 16 laps. It finished:

Revson	27m 45.3s
Mauro Bianchi (Belgium)	28m 11.4s
Crichton-Stuart	28m 25.0s
Rob Slotemaker (Holland)	29m 01.6s
Regazzoni	at one lap

Unsurprisingly, Revson won the final with Regazzoni fourteenth.

He entered but didn't attend the race at Chimay, Belgium, did go to La Châtre in the middle of France – and described as 'tiny, tight, twisty' which could 'just about cope with Formula 3 cars'[4] – but didn't qualify, even though he'd sold the de Tomaso and now had a Brabham. He did go to Monza again, the race attracted another huge entry and – again – he didn't survive the pruning process. Frank Williams qualified fourth in the first heat but a mechanical problem halted him in the final.

Regazzoni rounded the season off at Rouen – run on public roads with a downhill cobbled hairpin – where Courage won from Jean-Pierre Beltoise (who'd reach Grand Prix racing the following season), and he came fifth after running with the leaders early on.

Autosport, although a British magazine, kept a watchful eye on the sport around the world and one of its winter issues carried a comprehensive review of the Formula 3 season at home and in Europe. It noted that although there had been 'several nasty accidents' and three drivers had been taken to hospital at least no drivers died.

In all those words it did not mention Regazzoni once.

He felt he had no future, and if Martinelli and Sonvico had walked away from motor racing he'd have whispered *goodbye* to it too, although that wouldn't have been easy. He'd found – his own words – a wonderful world, untainted by professionalism and offering purest pleasure. Deep down he must have known he was going to taste it again and again.

He found the cockpit, you see, an island of solitude and a place where everything else became irrelevant. He'd found his true home.

Martinelli and Sonvico stayed.

If anything, 1966 was busy rather than frenetic as he waited and waited for a new Brabham and uncertainty surrounded Martinelli and Sonvico. An Englishman, Robin Widdows, began in Formula 3 and describes those days as 'remarkable'. They were that. 'We had good, tough races – not always the cleanest. We were trying to make a career of it. There wasn't a lot of money around in Formula 3 but everyone was dead serious on breaking into the big time.' Regazzoni also sampled Formula 2,

which, as Widdows explains, 'started to become serious because you were getting factory teams.'

First, Regazzoni flew to Argentina for the four-race Temporada Series that had developed since the 1940s. He'd not been to the country before and was captivated by it, as well as the fact that he was given a daily allowance of $100 and the hotel rooms cost a trifle, so he was doing very nicely (no doubt the Swiss in him overcoming the Italian). Even the fact that prize money was in pesos, which couldn't be converted into hard currency or taken out of the country, didn't trouble him. Cannily, he bought leather.

The first of the four races was in Buenos Aires on 23 January and it included Jochen Neerpasch (later a senior man at Mercedes who guided Michael Schumacher's career) and Wilson Fittipaldi (brother of Emerson, and who would later run his own Grand Prix team). Regazzoni finished fourth in his heat and twelfth in the final.

They moved to the town of Rosario a week later, the track a narrow road and dangerous. The racing attracted a vast crowd and, despite warning signs and the heavy presence of the police, some spectators sat on the kerb at the most exposed places, risking their feet being run over. Confronted with all this the organisers abandoned the original structure of the meeting, substituting three heats of 10 laps for two of 20. Regazzoni went in heat three and overtook Eric Offenstadt (Lola) for second place then an Argentine in a Brabham for the lead but dropped back. Moser won the final, which Regazzoni didn't finish.

He didn't finish his heat in the third round, at Mendoza, either and consequently didn't qualify for that final, which Crichton-Stuart won. That left Mar del Plata, where, from seventh in the first heat, he reached second place in a couple of laps but again didn't finish. During this meeting one car spun off, killing a spectator and injuring two others.

In Europe in April, he prepared for the Formula 3 season. At Pau – a street circuit so far south in France it was close to the Spanish border – he'd find himself facing an extensive entry, including Brian Hart (who'd go on to make Grand Prix engines), Widdows, Derek Bell, Jean-Pierre Jaussaud, Crichton-Stuart, Gethin and Courage. Pau was a straight 35-lap race and while Courage was winning Regazzoni limped to seventh, five laps down.

From there he went to the Nürburgring, or rather the 4.8-mile *Sudschleife,* which was attached to the daunting full circuit like an umbilical cord and used the same pits, to try Formula 2. Here he encountered an established Grand Prix driver for the first time. Jochen Rindt would be described by Frank Williams as the fastest man God ever put on the earth. He took pole in his Brabham-Cosworth and won the race from a Briton, Peter Arundell (Lotus-Cosworth), Regazzoni sixth a lap down.

Formula 2 had been created to give promising young drivers a chance to measure themselves against such as Rindt, who incidentally, deplored the fact that some of the seniors wouldn't come to the races in case they were beaten. He was not the sort of man to worry about anything like that himself.

After the Nürburgring Regazzoni settled to the rhythm of Formula 3 and although he didn't qualify for the final at Salo, Italy, he did at Vallelunga, the circuit high in the hills above Rome and surrounded by vineyards. He finished his heat third behind 'Geki' and another Italian, Carlo Facetti, but in front of de Adamich. In the 40-lap final he raced Ernesto Brambilla hard:

Brambilla	59m 41.6s
Regazzoni	59m 41.9s

That was 29 May, and at the same circuit on 9 June he finished second in his heat to 'Geki', and third behind Brambilla and de Adamich in the 50-lap final. These two results were significant because, although neither entry was representative of Formula 3's strength that season, the June race – Jonathan Williams and Offenstadt included – was a strong one. Paradoxically, a huge entry went to Monza (89) and Regazzoni didn't even qualify for the heats: the pruning process again.

On 22 August he married Maria Pia from Lugano in a simple ceremony. They went to Crans Montana and then Zermatt on their honeymoon – Crans Montana because there was a hill climb there in which Regazzoni expected to compete. Each day he drove the course in Pai's saloon car while he waited for news of a Brabham from Martinelli and Sonvico. They rang and said it wouldn't be ready and at that moment all interest in the hill climb vanished.

Because the rumours persisted about Martinelli and Sonvico's future, and because Regazzoni still waited for the Brabham, he left his racing to his dreams and rejoined his father's firm as, he insisted, a model worker. He did, however, drive at Monza in September in a support race to the Grand Prix, in an old Brabham. It went well in practice and from the flag in the first heat he seized the lead. He shed the following bunch of duelling slipstreamers so comprehensively that he led by some ten car's lengths crossing the line to complete the lap. He increased this lead on the second lap and by lap 5 had consolidated it, the bunch still duelling and slipstreaming. He completed the 12 laps in 22m 20.4s against Tino Brambilla's 22m 24.0s.

This made him favourite for the 30-lap final and again he seized the lead, Brambilla tracking him and staying close over the opening lap. The slipstreamers were faster here and by lap 10 Regazzoni was running behind Argentine Carlos Pairetti's Brabham. On lap 12 Pairetti spun at Lesmo, clouting the Armco and, two wheels in the air, rebounded. Regazzoni twisted the steering wheel violently to miss him but Pairetti was now in mid-track. Clipping him with his rear wheels Regazzoni went off, striking a tree. He suffered no worse than biting his tongue but he was taken to hospital as a precaution.

By Monza he'd had a phone call on behalf of the owner of Tecno in Bologna. Founded in 1962 by brothers Luciano and Gianfranco Pederzani, they'd progressed from karts to single-seaters in 1964 and were clearly ambitious. Would he like to test one of their cars?

Yes, he thought, *I would*.

He went to the Temporada Series in January 1967, driving a Martinelli and Sonvico Brabham just as his daughter Alessia was being born. His best result was sixth in the second race at Mar del Plata and that, in a sense, marked the end of the first phase of his career. From the moment he returned to Europe he entered the second phase, a season of Formula 3 with Tecno, initially as a paying driver and from the following season as a factory driver.

Robin Widdows says crisply: 'Those Formula 3 days *were* remarkable.'

It began quietly at Vallelunga in April. He didn't finish – but he set the pace in practice at Imola, where Lella Lombardi, one of the few women to reach Formula 1, competed. He won his heat with 28m 38.9s against 'Geki's' 28m 39.3s. The final, in glorious sunshine, produced a three-way struggle between Regazzoni, 'Geki' and de Adamich that lasted the whole race, or rather to the penultimate lap, when Regazzoni's Ford-Novamotor engine failed.

He didn't finish at Monza and was a distant 18th at Caserta – near Naples – in June.

Nogaro – another French circuit in the deepest south, and noted for its inaccessibility (as well as bullfights in the town square) – was, truly, quite different. Nogaro attracted those already moving into serious careers, Henri Pescarolo, Bell, Jaussaud, François Cevert and Jean-Pierre Jabouille. Regazzoni went in the first heat and was eighth

(25m 18.6s against Pescarolo, fastest, 24m 43.8s). Pescarolo did a lap of 57.2s, good enough for pole. Pescarolo won from Bell, Regazzoni seventh.

Some of this illustrious company – Pescarolo, Jaussaud, Cevert – also went to Zandvoort, the seaside circuit in Holland, as did Mo Nunn (Lotus) and a Briton, Mike Beckwith. Regazzoni had what a contemporary report says was a 'very' fast Tecno for the straightforward 24-lap race measuring 100.56km.

The Widdows description 'remarkable' was about to be fully justified. *Autosport* reported that

'drama set in very early on in the proceedings with the race being delayed 15 minutes from flag fall for Regazzoni on the front row to change his battery; this was barely over when all the drivers who were behind him on the grid started waving and pointing at poor Tony Lanfranchi [a Brit] whose car was, unknown to him, pouring out oil. Lanfranchi, thinking the car might be on fire, leapt out of it while the officials pushed the car off the circuit. As if this were not enough Dutch girl Liane Engeman, who was on the back of the grid, suddenly decided she needed something from her

Wild thing. The 'finish' at Hockenheim, 1967, and this is what happened to Derek Bell.
(Julian Kirk)

pits and proceeded to sprint in that direction, much to the delight of the large crowd. Eventually the flag dropped.'

Beckwith led the opening lap, Regazzoni third, and that set the tone: an intense fight for the lead – Regazzoni doing fastest lap with a 'staggering' 1m 35.7s, a new track record. The fight lasted until lap 9 when he spun. That seemed to destroy his rhythm and he ran down the field, finishing eighth, Nunn ninth.

They went to Hockenheim for an event called the *Preis der Nationen.* Bell sets out the background: 'To be honest Regazzoni had more crashes than anyone I have ever known and got away with it, but I think the biggest was in Formula 3. We had a thing at Hockenheim called the World Championship of Formula 3, which basically involved the European drivers, a couple of Americans and a load of South Americans. We all represented our countries.'

This Championship had been born the year before, run at Brands Hatch, and Britain won. Hockenheim seemed a strange choice because – without the chicanes, added later – it was not a test of promise or technique but a great exercise in slipstreaming except for the twisting Stadium Complex before the pits. To compound all this it was not very wide.

Regazzoni (now, incidentally, being called Clay by *Autosport*) and Moser formed the Swiss team.

'I was selected by the RAC with a chap called Charles Lucas and Chris Williams, who sadly died at Silverstone,' Bell says. 'So the three of us were representing Great Britain and I somehow got the old buggy – the Brabham – on pole position. It always surprised me when sometimes I went quicker than Regga.'

Regazzoni was alongside Bell on the front row with a time of 2m 18.1s but he made a poor start and soon enough Bell, who'd fallen back to fifth, slipstreamed his way into the lead. As Bell says, 'Hockenheim was *all* slipstreaming before the chicanes, balls out the whole way round until you got back to the Stadium, when you all outbraked each other and hoped you made it through.' Regazzoni was fourth on lap 2 and by lap 5 the first 14 cars moved in a bunch, the slipstreaming more and more furious. On lap 8 Regazzoni powered past Bell for the lead, then Brambilla powered past Regazzoni ... then Regazzoni fourth ... then Regazzoni third. Lap 19, one to go: Pescarolo leading from Regazzoni, Lucas and Bell.

'By degrees Regga started to eliminate the bloody field, outbraking them and pushing them off the road. It came to the last lap and I wasn't going to win it,' Bell says.

Autosport reported that 'Lucas slipped out of someone's tow along the return straight, taking the lead as the bunch of eight cars entered the fast right-hander that precedes the final section of the circuit [the stadium]. Then Regazzoni came powering round on the outside, carving Lucas up and smashing his way through to the next left-hander. By the time Regazzoni was at this corner he was already minus his nose section, which had gone up in a shower of fibreglass between the two corners. Now he lunged up against Jaussaud's Matra, forcing Jaussaud to ride up on the left side of Jabouille's Matra, tearing off the left-side mirror and part of the windshield.'

Bell remembers being 'fourth coming into the Stadium. Regga came by me, he took out Jabouille in the works Matra. He then went 300 yards all the way down on the grass to the left-hander, came back on and took out Jaussaud in the other works Matra.'

Autosport reported that 'Derek Bell was on the outside and got the brunt of all this, leaving the circuit and finishing up with a wheel torn off and extensive bodywork damage. Jaussaud was unable to continue, while [German driver Kurt] Ahrens, Regazzoni and Pescarolo got clean away from a frustrated Lucas in fourth spot. All round the last long right-hander Ahrens kept ahead of the Tecno, so that when the flag came out the German shot up a hand in victory, 0.2s ahead of his rival. Pescarolo followed them, while Lucas came fourth.'

Ahrens	46m 17.9s
Regazzoni	46m 18.1s
Pescarolo	46m 18.4s
Lucas	46m 23.7s

Bell remembers that Regazzoni 'went over the line with virtually no bodywork on the car. I'd been off the road as well. Afterwards somebody said "We're going to object because he had no bodywork" – which meant he didn't have any wing mirrors, and you had to complete your race with them. They were on my car, not his ...'

Bell also remembers reading differing accounts after the race – *Autosport* described the lap as 'sensational' – because 'it all depended where you were looking which accident you saw because there were so many, so all the journalists had different stories.'

Whatever, Regazzoni held that second place and Moser came eighth, giving Switzerland 10 points at the Championship from France (Pescarolo, Vidal, Jaussaud) on 15, Sweden third, Britain fourth, West Germany fifth and Denmark sixth.

He went to Montlhéry and crashed … then, at Jarama, Madrid, everything came right. There were two ten-lap heats and he won the first from Swede Reine Wisell (16m 43.8s against 16m 49.2s). His fastest lap, 1m 39.1s, brought him pole – Jaussaud in the second heat did 1m 39.8s. The race was no trouble either. He set fastest lap (1m 38.0s, and thus better than pole) and beat Wisell by 11.9 seconds.

Gareth Rees was an authentic motor sport lover who travelled to races for the delight of it. Although highly perceptive, he was an outsider. His recollections are important (and you will be meeting them a lot) precisely because they come from a different dimension.

'The first time I saw Clay Regazzoni was when he arrived at Brands Hatch as one of many Continental Formula 3 drivers for the Motor Show 200 meeting in October 1967. It's difficult to explain why, as an 11-year-old kid, you take a particular liking to some drivers and not others,

but I think the start of it was that fabulous racer's name, Gianclaudio, or "Clay", Regazzoni, coupled with the fact that it was my first sighting of the good-looking Tecno, and his was Italian red, just like a Ferrari Formula 1 car. Last, but not least, he was in the thick of the battle at the front with the established British and French stars of the time, such as Derek Bell, Peter Gethin, Henri Pescarolo and Jean-Pierre Jabouille. Regazzoni was in the second of the then customary two qualifying heats. Imprinted on my memory is an image of his car, in the midst of a slipstreaming bunch, bursting under the bridge towards Hawthorn Bend.

'The 1-litre Formula 3 of the late 1960s was the best racing I have ever witnessed. Unfortunately, the final that day was run in a deluge and was abandoned after all sorts of crashes, including one where a car hit an ambulance that happened to be on the track going to assist at another accident! I don't recall where he finished but it was a strong performance at Brands and part of a strong end of

The start of the 1968 Formula 2 race at Monza, and look for the Swiss cross on the helmet. (LAT)

season for Regazzoni. As a result, Tecno's order book started to fill up with the names of a few other drivers in that same Brands Hatch entry list: people like Reine Wisell, Ronnie Peterson and François Cevert, who would all start their own rise to stardom in 1968.'

Regazzoni felt that his reputation as a kamikaze driver didn't come from the Hockenheim dodgem cars but the following season at Rheims. There were other candidates: Monaco, Monza and Zandvoort. He was regarded as such a kamikaze racer that, as he moved ever nearer Formula 1, many were openly alarmed at what might happen when he got there too. That stemmed directly from the events of this season of 1968 as he contested Formula 3 in the Tecno-Ford and Formula 2 in the Tecno-Cosworth.

Even Formula 2, as Brian Hart attests, was 'generations away from what it is today. You turned up and raced. You'd see Derek Bell with his trailer and his dad – all quite normal. Tecno were a small Italian company who decided to make cars and they were all right. Regga was a very interesting guy and he had the name Clay, a very unusual name which nobody ever forgot. You couldn't. Clearly he was going to do special things and he was a very nice guy, very, very nice. Always had a smile on his face. He'd chat, unlike some others who didn't have the time for you.'

It began well: he won Vallelunga in Formula 3 in March and, at the end of the month, went to Barcelona for the Formula 2 race. *Motor Sport* noted cryptically that 'although Formula 2 has been dropped by all but one British race organiser, on the Continent of Europe the Formula opened at Barcelona with a full entry list and many hopefuls being turned away.'

His son Gian Maria was born, completing the family.

Formula 2 represented a significant rise in the quality of the opposition. Regazzoni would now be meeting Jackie Stewart, Graham Hill, Jim Clark, Jacky Ickx, Chris Amon and Jackie Oliver, who were the backbone of Grand Prix racing.

Simon Taylor covered the Formula 2 season for *Autosport*. 'If you compared it to motor racing today it would seem extraordinarily amateurish but you've got to remember we're talking the late 1960s and *Formula 1* was by current standards wonderfully amateurish. The key to Formula 2 was that all the races tended to be on alternate weekends to Formula 1 and most of the Formula 1 drivers had Formula 2 contracts as well.

'The season always began with the Easter Monday race at Thruxton and there would be Rindt, Hill, Stewart, Jimmy Clark, Bruce McLaren

Franco Gozzi, Ferrari's man who kept a close eye on everything. (Author)

and it was an opportunity for up-and-coming people like Chris Lambert, Robin Widdows – but also an opportunity for the people just coming in to Formula 1. They'd be at the back of the grid there but in Formula 2 – because the cars were pretty similar – they'd find they could mix it wheel-to-wheel with people like Stewart. So Formula 2 had twin aspects: on the one hand, Formula 1 drivers were competing with less pressure than at a Grand Prix so they were all rather relaxed, having a nice time and were much more approachable, while these lesser lights could race against them to try and demonstrate if they were any good.'

That embraced Facetti (in another Tecno), de Adamich, Courage, Widdows and Bell among others. Of Lambert there will be more – alas, much more – soon enough.

'The Formula 2 races alternated with the Grands Prix,' Widdows says. 'That was the great thing about it. You had the drivers who'd been in the Grand Prix the week before and now you were able to gauge whether you were any good at all. It was wonderful: you could improve by watching what they did. You spent a few moments trying to keep up with someone like Jochen Rindt and you realised how good he was.'

The Tecno had a conventional space-frame, although a stronger version of the Formula 3 chassis, and a short wheelbase.

Stewart took pole with a lap of 1m 32.8s, Regazzoni joint 15th on 1m 37.2s. In the race he became embroiled in a bumping-barging bout with Irwin's Lola shortly after the start and the Tecno withdrew, injured, to the paddock where a wishbone was replaced. Regazzoni emerged poised to take them all on again after 11 laps but was disqualified because the repairs had not been done in the pits. Lambert, incidentally, dropped a jack on his foot but refused to have it checked by the doctor in case he wasn't allowed to race. That scarcely mattered because a mechanical problem halted him before the start.

Barcelona was non-Championship. The first round of that Championship – Hockenheim – clashed with a Formula 3 race at Monza, where Regazzoni went (and finished second to Jaussaud, Ronnie Peterson in a Tecno fourth). As a consequence he was spared the sombre day at Hockenheim that nobody can forget, Clark's Lotus swerving off and destroying itself against a tree, Clark dead.

Regazzoni entered the Thruxton round on 15 April but evidently Tecno didn't send their works car and he didn't go. He did, however, go to Pau a week later for a non-Championship round with two Tecnos. A huge crowd, in sunshine, watched Stewart lead from Widdows. Regazzoni clouted some straw bales in the *Parc Beaumont* – a long right-handed loop – and was classified sixth, four laps behind Stewart. Widdows came second and, capturing the era, says 'everybody got together after the race. We went on holiday together. I used to go on holiday with Graham Hill.'

Regazzoni finished fifth in the third round of the European Championship at Jarama – Max Mosley in a Brabham ninth.

Thereby hangs a tale. Franco Gozzi was a Ferrari team manager and, as he says, 'when we were at some tracks in Europe – I remember in Spain, for instance – there was not only the Formula 1 race but also the Formula 2. When I was waiting for us to begin – probably a practice session – I saw Clay in Formula 2 and I asked "Who is he? Who is this young man driving a Tecno?" I was told "He's Swiss." A journalist on the Italian magazine *Autosprint* informed me that Regazzoni was happy in the Tecno Formula 2 team but I said to this journalist "Tell him we have Formula 2 as well as Formula 1 cars." Clay regarded himself as a friend of the brothers at Tecno and could not do something behind their backs.'

Gozzi bided his time.

Regazzoni went to the Formula 3 race at Monaco. As practice began he accelerated the Tecno onto the harbour front, foot hard down, and the car got away from him. It speared into the Armco so fiercely that he risked decapitation as it went underneath. He'd remember afterwards gazing at two photographs – the first with his head poised to smash into the Armco, the second with

his head safely on the other side. He wouldn't remember ducking …

He was, as he realised, extremely fortunate to be alive.

He'd recovered by the fourth round of the European Formula 2 Championship at Crystal Palace, where Rindt won from British driver Brian Redman, Regazzoni third – one of only five cars still running after the 90 laps.

Gareth Rees was there. 'Regazzoni was leader of the still-red works Tecno team. In those days, of course, Formula 2 races formed a fantastic meeting ground for contemporary F1 drivers and aspiring stars still climbing the ladder, and no place had a better entry or atmosphere than Crystal Palace in the heart of South London. Fast becoming a Regga fan, I was not to be disappointed: he put up a strong performance and finished third behind the king of Formula 2, Jochen Rindt, and Brian Redman. It was a good demonstration of his future fast and steady driving, because 90 laps of the Palace, with its solid walls of railway sleepers waiting barely a metre back from the road, was no mean feat. It was his best race result so far.'

'They were,' Vic Elford says, 'very wild days: live hard, play hard and not that many rules. I liked that atmosphere.' Elford prepared to drive Rindt's car at Monza – Rindt was at the Dutch Grand Prix, which, for once, did clash.

Regazzoni and Jaussaud had the two works Tecnos. Practice was over six hours and Regazzoni set an early pace with 1m 34.4s from Brambilla (1m 34.9s). Regazzoni's time survived deep into the afternoon before Bell took pole in the Ferrari (1m 33.3s). Chris Lambert didn't qualify.

The racers prepared to tackle the 45 laps (translating to 258km). Like Hockenheim the year before, Monza had not yet been clothed in chicanes and the result was a slipstreaming festival with a bewildering succession of leaders. Elford remembers Pescarolo 'because he was mixing it with Derek and me at the front.'

The slipstreaming unfolded and early on a couple of seconds covered the first 17 cars. By lap 4 Regazzoni led, but with so far to go that had no particular significance.

'There were, I guess, about seven or eight of us at the front and we slowly detached ourselves from the rest,' Elford says. 'On one particular lap [22], as we came through *Parabolica*, either something broke on Derek's car or a tyre let go. We were flat out coming through the middle of the *Parabolica* and suddenly he was facing me having done a half turn. I think I still had my foot on the gas pedal when I hit him because it was so quick. All hell was let loose. There were cars everywhere. Jaussaud's car somersaulted but fortunately in those days we still didn't have seatbelts and Jaussaud got thrown out. He broke his leg, which was a good thing because his car was burning to a cinder in the middle of the track. Everybody else got involved – whether they were overtaking or what, who knows? People were arriving and picking their way through.'

Autosport reported of the seven cars that retired the 'worst hit was poor Jean-Pierre Jaussaud: his car shot into the air, flinging the Frenchman to the ground as it turned over and then landing in a heap before bursting into flames. While Jaussaud was removed to hospital by helicopter what remained of his Tecno was burning so furiously that it started melting the tarmac and set that on fire too. It took the heavy fire fighting equipment a full eight minutes to arrive on the scene but when they did get there there was little left to put out. Indeed it smouldered on while marshals hung out yellow flags and the remaining 14 cars slipped through the narrow gap between the right of the track and the smoking metal from the Tecno.'

Regazzoni was among them and so was Pescarolo. They travelled together but in that order and at a 'furious pace'. They 'cared little' for the yellow flags and were passing backmarkers as they approached the accident.

'Some of the really hairy races were when we did Formula 2 at Monza, with Clay and his Italian friends,' Widdows says. 'No prisoners taken. None. There was the big accident and people like Regazzoni and Pescarolo drove straight through the flames at the *Parabolica* – through the bloody flames. It was big balls.'

Pescarolo was black flagged on lap 29 and Regazzoni on lap 31.

Regazzoni with Jean-Pierre Jaussaud. They both had Tecno cars for 1968. (LAT)

Leading Jochen Rindt at Crystal Palace, but it didn't end in that order. (LAT)

Kamikaze? Well …

Zandvoort was round six. To appreciate Regazzoni's subsequent career, and the reputation he'd be carrying with him, it is necessary to meet Chris Lambert. Simon Taylor 'went to most of the Formula 2 races although I wasn't actually at Zandvoort. Chris Lambert was a very good friend of mine. He was brought up in Weston super Mare. His father [John, sometimes referred to as Jack] was a schoolmaster. If you did chemistry at school there was almost certainly a battered textbook you were given to use – the standard work that every child in the 1950s and '60s had to use. It was by Holderness and Lambert. As a result, old man Lambert – who was just this little chemistry master – made a big pile of money. He had a wife from whom he was divorced and he had a son who was the apple of his eye, a little bloke with spectacles. You couldn't imagine anybody who looked less like a racing driver.

'He persuaded his father to buy him a go-kart and he was absolutely brilliant. He became the British karting champion in the top-end class. I lived in the West Country and I was karting then so I got to know him before he came into motor racing. His father then said "If you get your degree at Birmingham University I'll buy you a racing car." As a result, Chris got a Formula 3 Brabham. Everything was much cheaper in those days but he always did it on a bit of a shoestring. He got into Formula 3 and he was amazingly quick. Everybody became very excited. He won the main Grovewood Award[5] as the most promising young British driver, beating lots of people who were rather more polished and had more money than this little slightly scruffy bloke.

'When I first came to London I lived in a very disreputable flat in Kilburn. It had been a motor racing flat – various racing and rally drivers had lived there and passed the lease on to each other. I was there with Chris Lambert and Andrew Marriott.[6] Chris went on from Formula 3 to Formula 2. He towed his Formula 2 car round on a battered old trailer behind a Mark Two Jaguar. He had one engine and it desperately needed a rebuild but he was now racing against Stewart and Rindt and people like that – and he was doing a half-good job.'

Regazzoni took an immediate lead in his heat, hunted by Courage and Pescarolo for a couple of laps until Courage went by. It finished

Courage	29m 19.60s
Pescarolo	29m 19.70s
Regazzoni	29m 19.78s

The final was over 50 laps. Bell led while Regazzoni got round as far as the section behind the pits before the engine died. He got out, discussed the situation with a marshal, restarted the engine and set off a full lap down. He also set off at a furious pace and estimated he was gaining a second a lap. He was doing this because there were four corners: a left and three rights. He was taking these, as it seems, flat out. Soon enough he caught and overtook Ahrens – so that he was beginning to unlap himself. That process wouldn't be completed, of course, until he'd reached and gone past Bell in the far distance. Now Regazzoni caught Lambert, who was on his 10th lap – Regazzoni still on 9.

They went through the left behind the pits and prepared for the three rights. Lambert braked. Regazzoni didn't.

Autosport reported that Regazzoni 'came up to pass […] at the fast right-hander at West Tunnel, where a small bridge allows spectators to pass under the circuit, but which to a driver looks more like a low concrete wall. Lambert lined himself up on the left of the road to prepare to cut across to the apex of the right-hander and, as he moved across on line, he collided with Regazzoni.

'The inevitable happened: Regazzoni's left front wheel and tyre locked with Lambert's right rear, and in a flash both cars plunged off the circuit to the left. Lambert's clipped the corner of the concrete bridge and careered down the escarpment onto the road beneath.'

Lambert, not wearing seat belts, was partially thrown out.

'Poor Chris was killed instantly,' *Autosport* reported. 'Regazzoni crashed further up the road, turning over several times, but escaping with a shaking and nothing else. As news of this appalling accident filtered back, the race went on …'

Regazzoni remembered spinning nose-to-tail, turning over and landing in the sand, remembered switching the ignition off, remembered crawling from under the car and seeing two policemen standing nearby, doing nothing.

One report suggests that straw bales had been positioned where Lambert struck and they compressed as the Brabham struck them, launching it – and when it landed it killed a female spectator.

Bell remembers 'I was on pole and ahead and leading for my first win for Ferrari in my second race for Ferrari and of course Regga took Chris off. I saw Regga's car was wrecked but I didn't know Chris had gone off. In those days you found out when you got back to the hotel.' Bell 'had a problem with my gearbox but that was the least of the problems because poor old Chris died. Eventually you get done by something totally futile, something you have no control over. That is racing.

'Regga wasn't malicious. He always had that amazing, that affectionate – what's the word? – endearing smile. I loved the guy and I have a photo in front of me now of when we did some karting three or four years ago. But throughout his life the guy was surrounded by accidents and death. It was amazing to me that he was able to rise above it. I'd have shot myself – well, maybe not in that era because it was happening every day. He was certainly wild. He suited that Tecno because it was a go-kart. I never drove karts but that's what they built before they went into racing.'

Widdows didn't see the crash but he did see the wreckage as he came past it and that surely, echoing Bell, is entirely typical of incidents in that era. You pressed on. Overall, Widdows insists, Regazzoni 'was a good, tough racing driver and I had the greatest admiration for him. We knocked each other off the circuit many a time but our friendship continued. We hugged each other like brothers when we met years later.'

The Lambert accident brought an aftermath that lingered for years.

'Regazzoni had a reputation in Formula 2 for being extremely ruthless and wild,' Simon Taylor says. 'The whole of the life of Chris's father, the now retired schoolmaster, revolved around his son and when Chris was killed his father was a kind of broken man. I went to the funeral and I remember an awful thing which they used to do in those days: they had the coffin with his helmet on the top.

'His father believed that Clay Regazzoni had murdered his son and he started this single-handed and rather naive campaign to bring Regazzoni to book. All it really did, to be honest, was produce a lot of embarrassment. I remember him saying to me – because I was editing *Autosport* by then – "You've got to help me in my campaign, we've got to have *Autosport* helping to ban Regazzoni from racing" and all this sort of thing. In the end it was decided that it was merely a motor racing accident.

The Monza slip-streaming is developing nicely. (LAT)

Chris Lambert, fondly remembered – still. (LAT)

Tragic Zandvoort. The start: Regazzoni is in the middle of the front row. (LAT)

'What this whole business did was reinforce the British enthusiasts' view of Regazzoni, which for all I know might have been completely unjustified, but there *was* this general view that Regazzoni was a wild man, had had a hand in Chris's accident and was generally a scary guy.'

Regazzoni insisted he was blameless and said it was easy to prove the Brabham had struck him after Lambert had seen him too late.

John Lambert embarked on a crusade, no less (even though Louis Stanley – of him, much more later – made discreet attempt to dissuade him).

He compiled a dossier of evidence from marshals – reportedly the marshal at Post 10 beside the Tunnel felt Regazzoni was to blame – drivers and spectators. This dossier persuaded KNAC (the Netherlands *Nationale Autosport Federatie*), the club which organised the race, to set up a commission. John Corsmit, a Dutch official, read the verdict with Dean Delamont of the RAC present, and it absolved Regazzoni. John Lambert felt strongly that the RAC had been almost unpatriotic in not defending his son.

Lambert pointed out that the commission's report stated the accident happened on lap 10 when it was in fact lap 11. He described the report as a 'libellous and completely untrue account of the accident' and now raised the matter with the FIA, who (in November 1971) exonerated Regazzoni and imposed no sanctions on him. The FIA also exonerated Chris Lambert. It had been, in the time-honoured phrase Simon Taylor has already used, a racing accident.

John Lambert did not intend to let the matter rest there and pursued Regazzoni physically for years in a kind of endless haunting. We shall see.

Regazzoni was at Enna – in the middle of Sicily – at the end of August for round seven of the Formula 2 championship. He qualified on the second row, although cars had been removing their aerofoils and he was the last to do so. A driver called Samuel Brown, driving for Frank

Williams, made a mistake in one corner and the car went into a reed bed. Reportedly he came back to the pits in a dinghy, which (forgive me) sounds very fishy.

To circumvent the problem of slipstreaming the organisers tried a novel and surreal solution: they put the twin bays of the grid at intervals of 75m so that the leaders set off with a lead of almost half a mile over those at the back. It didn't work, because by the end of lap 5 Courage, Rindt and Regazzoni had all been in the lead and a ten-car bunch developed, the lead swapping constantly as in all pure slipstreaming races, of course. By lap 30 of the 50 only these ten cars were on the same lap and a great finale developed climaxing in Rindt winning from Courage, Brambilla and Regazzoni. They crossed the line so close together that all four were given the same time: 1h 02m 40.6s.

Next: Rheims and, as Robin Widdows says, 'the races at Monza and Rheims were so bloody hairy because of the slipstreaming: you were stuck together for an hour and the lead changed three times a lap.'

Rindt took pole, Regazzoni on the third row. During the early part of the race he ran third then fourth but at one point he outbraked and overtook Stewart and Rindt, which he thought entirely normal but which some witnesses thought wasn't. From this moment on, Regazzoni felt, Stewart became a persistent critic. Anyway,

Regazzoni halted after 13 laps with an exhaust pipe problem.

These days, Stewart says: 'I raced him in Formula 2 and Formula 1 but I never got to know him until Formula 1. I remember he was in close proximity at Rheims and Crystal Palace as well, I think, so I knew he was there but I didn't know much about him. I was living in Switzerland at that time, too, but the other end of Switzerland. He was absolutely Italian-Swiss and I was in the French part. Having said that, he and Jo Siffert were very highly respected in Switzerland. Marc Surer came along for a short window of time but not as deeply as Seppe or Clay.'[7]

What Rindt thought of this is not known but, during round eight at Hockenheim in October he took pole (Regazzoni ninth). In the race Regazzoni, Siffert, Rindt and assorted others tangled. Regazzoni's Tecno was bent and he cruised down the slope to retire.

At Albi, a non-Championship Formula 2 race on the purpose-built circuit not far from Toulouse, he took pole but crashed at the right-hand corner after the pits. The Tecno was so bent it couldn't be repaired in time and he didn't start the race.

It left the final championship round at Vallelunga, decided over two heats of 40 laps each with the combined time counting. The two practice sessions each stretched over two and a half hours and, in the first of them, no car

The race develops: Regazzoni, Henri Pescarolo (4), Piers Courage (32), Peter Gethin (18) and Chris Lambert (25). (LAT)

appeared for an hour. Perhaps the teams were still weighing up the organisers' ruling that the grid would be decided by a driver's three fastest laps, averaging the time (following motor racing's hallowed tradition of making anything simple as complicated as possible). Brambilla did the actual fastest lap (1m 16.7s) but Regazzoni got to within an eyeblink of it (1m 16.8s).

In heat one he had a misfire that proved so severe he pitted on lap 8 and pitted again several times after that. He finished 18th, having covered only 21 laps. He went more strongly in the second heat and came eighth.

Beltoise won the Championship with 48 points, then Pescarolo (31), Brambilla (26), Bell (15), Jackie Oliver (14) and Courage, Ahrens and Regazzoni all on 13.

The Temporada Series was run in December and, taking the Tecno, he went strongly again: fourth at Buenos Aires, fourth at Cordoba, sixth at San Juan but not classified at Buenos Aires in the last race. The points were awarded 13–8–5–3–2–1, so that de Adamich – second, first, first, fifth – emerged the victor with 36 points, Rindt 21, Courage 14. Regazzoni had 7 points to be ninth.

Gozzi sensed the time had come. 'I contacted Clay when I saw he was ready. I helped to bring him to Ferrari but nobody could do anything without Enzo. I went to Enzo and I said "I am near to doing this. Do you mind?" He said – just to put the responsibility on me – "If *you* think it is the right thing." This happened on the last day of 1968 – 31 December. Two days later, the 2nd of January, the *Autosprint* journalist arranged a meeting between Lugano and Maranello. We chose a restaurant on the *autostrada*. We met there and in half an hour we decided: OK, 500,000 lire – about £450 now – for Formula 2, and Formula 1 as soon as possible. Not immediately. We already had Ickx and Amon. All the details – tickets, passes, expenses – we didn't discuss.

'It was Clay who asked the Pederzani brothers "Do you mind if I join Ferrari?" and they said "What can we do? We can't do anything to hinder your career. They have Formula 1. We wish you all the luck in the world. You've the chance of a big career."'

He had.

Notes: 1. www.magicswitzerland.com/ascona-locarno.htm; 2. www.inside-f1.com/gpe/cir-072.html; 3. Autosport; 4. Autosport Circuit Guide 1987; 5. Extremely prestigious annual motor sports awards; 6. Marriott, long-time and versatile motor sport media person and, with the late Barrie Gill, a moving force at the PR agency CSS; 7. From 1979, Surer drove 82 Grands Prix for five teams, with a highest finish fourth. In 1986 he crashed so badly during a rally that his career ended.

Regazzoni had a reputation for being wild but here he holds off Jean-Pierre Beltoise (Matra) neatly enough. (LAT)

CHAPTER 2 ———————

IMMORTAL AT MONZA

On a wet January day in 1969 at Modena, Regazzoni eased himself into a racing Ferrari – their Formula Dino 2 car – for the first time. Mike Parkes, who Regazzoni felt was typically English in the phlegmatic way and who'd handled Ferrari Grand Prix cars in 1966 and 1967, prepared to evaluate him.

He ran into standing water and spun before he settled. He found the Ferrari completely different to the Tecno, the engine more supple, the gear changing easier, the roadholding better – but if it got away from you it took some getting back. In that sense the Tecno was more forgiving.

Gozzi remembers that when he returned to the factory Enzo, who hadn't been at the test but clearly knew all about the spin, said: 'Ah! Who is *your* young driver?'

Gozzi explains that 'sometimes Mr Ferrari was mysterious,' meaning he used mysterious ways. Gozzi gives an example of that. Nino Vaccarella, a Sicilian, had won the 1964 Le Mans 24-Hour race in a Ferrari and driven in the Italian Grand Prix the following year.

'Mr Ferrari came into my office and said "If I were *you* I'd try Vaccarella in the Formula 1 car," so I did. He was a good driver on the road: Targa Florio – good. Mille Miglia – good. Le Mans – good. But Formula 1 – no. After three laps he had a very bad crash. Fortunately there was no damage to him but the car was destroyed. When I got back to Maranello, *il capo*[1] said "Did you see *your*

RIGHT *Regazzoni was versatile in an era which encouraged that. Here he is in the Ferrari 512S at Le Mans in 1970. The Ferrari of Nino Vaccarella is behind, then the Porsche of Mike Hailwood.* (LAT)

driver? I am not sure it was a good idea of yours to put Vaccarella in the car." This was Mr Ferrari. We accepted him the way he was and we considered it an honour to work for him. I was with him for many years and nine years with Luca di Montezemolo. Somebody asked me the difference and I said "Two worlds. You cannot even compare them."[2]

This, then, was Regazzoni's new world and it's temptingly easy to caricature the internal politics which surrounded Ferrari the man and Ferrari the team as the equivalent of a medieval court. Intrigue seemed to be everywhere with *il capo* listening intently to a shifting cast of informers, spies, back-stabbers, the ambitious and – even – those who simply wanted to make the team better, no other motive involved. Each driver arriving – and as we have just seen with the example of Vaccarella, *il capo* had generation after generation of drivers arriving – needed to decide how to co-exist with this permanently unsettling atmosphere.

Regazzoni seems to have reached a most original solution to the problem.

He ignored it altogether because he wasn't interested.

Ickx and Amon were contracted to do the Formula 1 season, as we have seen, so Regazzoni was offered Formula 2. The Championship spread over seven rounds but the Ferrari proved so disappointing that he'd have no chance at it. The first race, at Thruxton in April, seemed to demonstrate that.

Rindt took pole in the Lotus (1m 13.2s) with Regazzoni 13th (1m 18.2s), just behind a young Ulsterman, John Watson (1m 18.0s).

'A friend from Northern Ireland had bought the two Lotus 48s, the sister cars to the one Jim Clark was killed in,' Watson says. 'He entered Thruxton – it was on Easter Monday. In those days the Grands Prix drivers also competed in Formula 2, which was a great proving ground because Jackie did it, Jochen Rindt did it, Jack Brabham did it. It was a pretty important Championship – the feeder race series into Formula 1 and unlike today where we don't have a feeder series which allows current Formula 1 drivers to compete against the up-and-coming drivers.

'Clay's career started late but that's how it was. The infrastructure of motor sport was nowhere near as developed then as it is presently. Karting, which is the natural route in, was barely in its infancy. There were karts and they were called go-karts and while there was a healthy racing series they didn't have the infrastructure that karting today has, which is hugely sophisticated as well as being highly competitive.

'I was in the Lotus and the thing I was aware of was that Clay had this reputation. There'd been the crash with Lambert at Zandvoort the year before. A bit like Riccardo Patrese with Ronnie,[3] Clay was in effect blamed, and in a sense that remained with him. You had this Latino guy, very Italian, smouldering you might say, passionate, almost might be called reckless because of the manner in which he drove a car. I was aware of Clay Regazzoni from that.

'I caught and passed him, and I remember thinking *bloody hell, what's that about?* These were super heroes and here's me, this youngster from Northern Ireland, overtaking and outdriving them. It was a stellar moment for me.'

Regazzoni remembered how Graham Hill was slow getting away at the start (his Lotus had a clutch problem) and, taking him on the grass, the Ferrari struck something. Rindt made a terrible start but passed seven cars on the opening lap, reaching and passing Regazzoni – seventh – on lap 4. Regazzoni pitted to have the car checked (as a consequence of whatever he hit) and finished the race tenth three laps down on the winner, Rindt.

Gareth Rees was there. 'The only time I saw him race in 1969 was in the Ferrari Formula 2 team at Thruxton when he didn't have much chance in an uncompetitive car and finished in an anonymous ninth place.'

At Hockenheim for round two he qualified on the fourth row (2m 14.4s) against Pescarolo in the Matra on pole (2m 8.9s), but the Ferrari's engine wouldn't start for the race despite all attempts. The car was disqualified after, as one source puts it, 'the usual heated Ferrari versus organisers shouting match.'

Ferrari, with Gozzi as team manager, took their three Dinos to Jarama (for Bell, Brambilla and Regazzoni) and *Autosport* felt they looked 'a trifle worn, but with a new type of camshaft fitted.' During Friday practice both Bell and Regazzoni said they hadn't enough power and Regazzoni suffered a problem with the camshaft. Next day he 'hardly got beyond the pit road before his engine went right off, sending him into the pits again' – the camshaft problem. In front of only 2,000 spectators he completed the opening lap of the race tenth and finished eleventh after a pit stop.

There was nothing to say about these races, he'd write in *Le Combat.* He did one more, non-Championship, at Monza but didn't finish because the engine failed again, this time on lap 21 of the 45.

The car 'wasn't working at all and the old man decided to stop. He freed me to go elsewhere in Formula 2 and I did a few races for Tecno.'[4]

He missed the fifth round, at Tulln-Langenlebarn – a 1.7-mile Austrian circuit with seven turns, used between 1967 and 1971 – but had the Tecno for the sixth, at Enna. This was, at last, the authentic Regazzoni. The Saturday practice session began quietly because the drivers waited for the wind to drop and it didn't. That created a rush towards the end, Italian Nanni Galli and Regazzoni in the Tecnos out immediately. So was Siffert (BMW) – and Regazzoni got a tow from both of them, crossing the line at 1m 13.5s. It looked good enough for pole but Galli took it on. In doing that he got sideways at the first bend, was rammed by Facetti in another Tecno that somersaulted over him and straddled the Armco. In missing the carnage one driver went into the rushes. Facetti, taken away in an ambulance, had only minor head cuts.

Galli had clearly been motivated by pride because, as everyone knew, Enna warmly embraced slipstreaming and that rendered grid places irrelevant.

The race was over two heats of 31 laps. Courage in a Brabham won the first after a long struggle with Beltoise (Matra), Regazzoni pressing both of them; Courage won the second, Regazzoni lost in a group of slipstreamers to be eighth. Overall he was fourth.

He didn't contest the final round, at Vallelunga.

The 1969 season was the worst of his career.

Even for a man who adored driving and, just past 30, was in the very prime of life, what Clay Regazzoni did in 1970 remains a monument of motion. He drove the full European Formula 2 season and won the Championship with Tecno, made his Grand Prix debut and won Monza, and contested Le Mans. At the same time, to use his own words, he 'was working with Ferrari. I began to test the 512' – the sports car he'd have at Le Mans – 'and the Formula 1 car.' So much in Regazzoni's story illustrates how quickly, and comprehensively, motor racing has changed but few seasons do it more accurately than this one. Years later he'd say, in an instant of great candour, 'It's not the same now in racing, it's too professional.'

The full panorama of what this amateur – in spirit and attitude – achieved is more easily understood in the form of a diary.

His season might easily have begun on 7 March at the South African Grand Prix. He'd tested the Ferrari at Vallelunga and didn't become 'hypnotised' by its aura, although, as he confessed, a Formula 1 Ferrari *did* stir emotions. He'd driven enough Formula 2 races to be able to move up without making any fundamental adjustments, although he noted it had so much power that if you applied it too quickly you had wheelspin, unlike Formula 2.

He explained that at the start of the season there were only two Ferrari 312Bs and 'Ickx wanted both for himself! The first Grands Prix [South Africa, and Spain on 19 April] he did by himself.'

In Formula 2 he'd have young Cevert as his team-mate.

30 March, Thruxton, European F2, round one

The Championship was spread over eight races from this late winter's day to Hockenheim in October and the points were the same as in Grands Prix: 9, 6, 4, 3, 2, 1. A driver's best six finishes counted. Although established Formula 1 personalities like Stewart, Hill, Rindt, Ickx and Amon continued to spice the races their points didn't count. Instead Regazzoni would wage a long struggle against Bell, with Emerson Fittipaldi never very far behind.

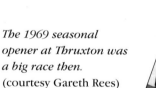

The 1969 seasonal opener at Thruxton was a big race then.
(courtesy Gareth Rees)

At Thruxton the drivers went in two 20-lap heats to qualify for the final. Regazzoni was in the first – he had an updated Tecno, not the new one – and finished sixth (26m 06.2s), Stewart winning (25m 30.8s). In the final, over 46 laps, Rindt beat Stewart with, significantly, Bell third – but of course giving him 9 points as the leading Championship runner, and therefore 'winner'. Regazzoni spun on lap 20 and had to drive hard to make up places to eighth.

Bell 9 points, Regazzoni 2, Fittipaldi 0.

5 April, Pau,
non-Championship F2

A small entry and, qualifying, Bell hit a dog hard enough to wreck his car's nosecone. Jack Brabham led the opening lap from Regazzoni, who had what one report describes as a 'moment' the next lap that left him at the rear of the field. By lap 22 he'd got back to fifth and, later, third before on lap 46 he crashed, battering the car badly. Rindt won from Pescarolo, Australian Tim Schenken third and Bell fourth.

12 April, Hockenheim,
European F2, round two

Regazzoni and Cevert had the new Tecnos. The race was decided on the aggregate time over two 20-lap heats but the qualifying, as *Autosport* naughtily suggested, was divided into grades, with the drivers the organisers wanted in the final all in one of these grades. A Japanese, Tetsu Ikuzawa, won the first heat (41m 34.9s) from Regazzoni (41m 35.0s) after a proper struggle.

Into the Stadium on the opening lap of this heat, Argentine Carlos Reutemann braked so late that Rindt hit him and that created chaos. Regazzoni got through although Bell led lap 2 – Regazzoni led lap 3. They slipstreamed and that produced a great final rush towards the Stadium, Ikuzawa leading from Bell and Regazzoni, who sliced past at the Sachs Kurve and attacked Ikuzawa, who blocked and weaved.

The second heat was quieter, and Regazzoni won (40m 26.3s) from Ikuzawa (40m 26.6s) to have overall victory by 0.3 of a second. It was the

At Thruxton in 1969 Regazzoni, driving the Ferrari Dino, leads Nanni Galli's Tecno. (LAT)

first Formula 2 victory of his career. Bell was third but less than two seconds slower.

Bell 13, Regazzoni 11, Fittipaldi 2.

The drivers felt Hockenheim dangerous and asked for two corners – presumably chicanes – to be installed before they came back, as they were due to do. Presumably, too, Regazzoni did not feel it was dangerous and did not want chicanes …

26 April, Barcelona, European F2, round three

A straightforward 45-lap race, which Bell, dominant, won from Pescarolo and Fittipaldi, Regazzoni a lap down at the end. He'd been scrapping with one of the Brambillas[5] for fifth place but, deep into the race, his engine started missing and he spent the last laps trying to lose as few places as possible.

Bell 22, Regazzoni 11, Fittipaldi 6.

Two weeks later Ickx took the two Ferrari 312Bs to Monaco but the driveshaft failed in the race after he'd been as high as fourth.

A gregarious, affable and fast-talking young driver, Nino Fiorello, first met Regazzoni 'in 1970 racing for Tecno in Montjuich, Spain. I was doing Formula 3 as an amateur, a real amateur. I met him in the pits. You are thinking about the car all the time and so you are a little bit selfish in a way –

On his way to second place at Crystal Palace in 1970 – Jackie Stewart won in a Brabham. (LAT)

not because you want to be, but because you must be. Clay was happy to talk: a fantastic man, a playboy in a way, very good looking, a very attractive man. He had a lot of women – a *lot* – and they chased him.'

25 May, Crystal Palace, European F2, round four

A big entry for what was regarded as one of the most important races of the season. The Tecnos arrived late and a special practice session was held for them (which Graham Hill joined, to work on his Lotus). Two 20-lap heats fed the fastest into the 50-lap final. Regazzoni went in the second heat and, on the opening lap at the North Tower, he and Rindt almost collided. They brought the rest of the field to a halt but Rindt got away, Regazzoni still after him and they ran steadily to the end, Regazzoni second (17m 9.6s) to Rindt (17m 2.0s).

He was combative in the final, so combative that Stewart still recalls memories of it these many years later. Rindt led from the start, then Regazzoni, then Stewart who mounted attack after attack. Regazzoni resisted them all robustly 'despite some fiery fist-waving by the World Champion' (*Autosport*), although the crowd were amazed that Regazzoni could hold Stewart back, even robustly. Whatever, on lap 22 'Stewart's fist-

waving spasm ended as he slipped by into the North Tower.' Rindt retired two laps later (a battery problem). Stewart crossed the line after 41m 56.2s and Regazzoni followed him, but some 12.6 seconds later, Fittipaldi third, Bell eighth and a lap down. *Autosport* commented that he thoroughly deserved this second place and 'what a far cry from his hairy F3 days!'

Ferrari now had enough 312Bs to send test driver Ignazio Giunti to Belgium with one, partnering Ickx, on 7 June. The idea, evidently, was that Giunti and Regazzoni would do alternate Grands Prix although, as Regazzoni would point out cryptically, 'in the end, because I was faster than Giunti, I did the rest of the season.' Ickx qualified fourth for the Belgian Grand Prix, Giunti eighth – but finished fourth. Whatever, Regazzoni would have the car for Holland in two weeks.

Bell 24, Regazzoni 20, Fittipaldi 12.

13–14 June, Le Mans

Rarely can a manufacturer have suffered such in-house decimation so quickly and so comprehensively. The race seemed to lie between seven Porsche 917s and eleven Ferrari 512s. Four of those were works cars: Ickx/Peter Schetty, Vaccarella/Giunti, Arturo Merzario/Regazzoni and Peterson/Bell. Jo Bonnier partnered Reine Wisell in a privateer entry, Mike Parkes in another.

Merzario took first stint and ran fourth while up ahead a couple of the Porsches duelled. Into the third hour rain began. Wisell, churning slowly back towards the pits with oil all over his windscreen, couldn't see where he was going but could see enough to pull to one side of the road as he churned.

Bell, Parkes and Regazzoni had been duelling down the Mulsanne Straight.

Wisell was reaching towards The White House – a noted landmark not far from the start-finish – when the duelling trio came upon him at full racing speed. Some estimates put that as travelling 100mph faster. Bell swerved and somehow missed Wisell but badly over-revved his engine doing it. Regazzoni tried to get between Bell and Wisell but struck Wisell, spun, and Parkes hit him – then Wisell hit him. Regazzoni emerged unhurt. The Parkes car caught fire. Bell continued but down the Mulsanne Straight the engine sighed that it had had enough. The Porsches finished first, second and third.

Bell reflects that Regazzoni was 'one of those guys who you knew would have to have an accident. In my opinion he didn't know where his limits were but he was outstandingly quick. We

ended up doing Le Mans for the Ferrari factory team, although not together, in 1970, which was my first Le Mans year. There was that massive bloody crash on the guardrail coming in to The White House, but I don't think that was his fault. It was a combination of chaos: everybody trying to win it in the first three hours.'

21 June, Zandvoort, Dutch Grand Prix

Regazzoni replaced Giunti and prepared to drive in what would be the first of his 132 Grands Prix. Ickx could mix it with the fast men, of course, but Regazzoni proceeded (untypically) with some circumspection. In first practice, on the Friday, Rindt went fastest (1m 19.48s), Regazzoni 12th (1m 21.71s); Ickx fastest in the opening Saturday session (1m 19.50s), Regazzoni 19th (1m 22.88s); Rindt fastest that afternoon (1m 18.50s), Regazzoni sixth (1m 19.48s). It put him on the third row of the grid.

Ickx led from the flag, Regazzoni seventh into the Tarzan horseshoe. Courage in a Williams tracked him to lap 22 but went off, rolled, and his car caught fire. He did not survive. The race continued and by the end Regazzoni had worked his way up to fourth. Ironically, because Giunti had done exactly the same thing in Belgium – his first race – they'd keep doing alternate Grands Prix. Judging by what Regazzoni subsequently wrote, he did not intend this situation to endure very long.

To score points on debut was, and remains, comparatively rare. Since 1961 only nine men had done it up to Belgium in 1970, and in the 1970s only three more would.

28 June, Rouen, non-Championship F2

Two heats of 15 laps feeding the 25-lap final. Regazzoni won the second heat (30m 53.7s) from Rindt (30m 56.5s) with Pescarolo, Reutemann, Ikuzawa and Ickx next. Regazzoni had begun to beat the big names now. More than that, he had joint pole with Peterson. In the final he finished a breath – a tenth of a second – behind Siffert, Fittipaldi third a further tenth away.

Fittipaldi would remember the finish (in his book *Flying on the Ground*). He'd pay tribute to Regazzoni as a gentleman beyond the racing, and record how, at his very first race, Regazzoni made a point of speaking to him. It was a gesture he treasured because so few other drivers did. Fittipaldi added that 'sometimes when he is

driving he just doesn't think a lot. He drives more with the foot than the head, really.' Fittipaldi thought this was over-excitement and felt Regazzoni lacked consistency, despite his sometimes awesome speed. Fittipaldi also conceded that in Formula 2 Regazzoni had a 'very bad reputation'.

To preface what happened, Fittipaldi explained that ordinarily he had hardly any problems with any drivers. In the 25-lap final Peterson (March) led from Siffert (BMW), Regazzoni and Fittipaldi (Lotus) and a great slipstreaming struggle developed. Into the last lap Peterson missed his braking point at the hairpin and plunged straight on so Siffert inherited the lead *but* Regazzoni got the hairpin wrong, too, and that allowed Fittipaldi to slice through on the inside. Fittipaldi now began to calculate that at the end of the lap, after the final right-hander, he'd be able to get past Siffert on the little straight to the chequered flag. It might be tight but it could just about be done.

Fittipaldi positioned his Lotus directly behind Siffert to get the tow and emerged from the right-hander faster: Fittipaldi to the left, Siffert to the right by the Armco. At this instant Fittipaldi realised that Siffert's BMW was simply quicker and nothing could be done about that. At this instant, too, Regazzoni created what Fittipaldi described as 'one of his special finishing line tactics'.

Regazzoni couldn't go to the right because Siffert was too close to the Armco. Regazzoni couldn't go to the left because Fittipaldi and the rim of the track were there. Regazzoni couldn't go between Siffert and Fittipaldi because they were too close together. No room, Fittipaldi concluded succinctly.

An instant later Regazzoni *was* there and 'we were going to crash! The only way to stop this was for me to drop back and leave him room. Otherwise there would have been a big shunt on the finish line.'

LEFT *Grand Prix debut in Holland, 21 June 1970, and he'd finish fourth.* (LAT)

BELOW *Regazzoni's second F1 race, the British Grand Prix at Brands Hatch. He resists pressure from Stewart's March.* (LAT)

(Fittipaldi was asked by Elizabeth Hayward, who wrote *Flying on the Ground*, whether he felt Regazzoni did this to intimidate other drivers to the point where they got out of his way, but Fittipaldi didn't. He did think Regazzoni 'imagines his car is much smaller than it really is'.)

In the rush to the line Fittipaldi got out of the way.

'I was really upset after the race, and I went to Clay, and I said: "Why did you do that?" And he said, with a big smile – we talked in Italian – "Oh, you know, it was the last lap and coming up to the finish line … that's racing!" And he was smiling at me, and I started to smile, but I said: "Clay, don't do it again, because you know what I *could* say, what I *could* do." It is very difficult to be angry with him for long.'

Hockenheim was Regazzoni's third Grand Prix. He is on the second row of the grid (15) … leading from Rindt's Lotus and the Ferrari of Ickx … in a lively battle with Rindt. (LAT)

Giunti took his turn at the French Grand Prix, at Clermont Ferrand on 5 July, qualified 11th and finished 14th three laps down. He had had a throttle pedal problem.

18 July, Brands Hatch, British Grand Prix

He settled the Giunti situation by qualifying sixth (Rindt pole 1m 24.8s against his 1m 25.8s), ran sixth early on and worked his way up to fourth after a brash attempt to take New Zealander Denny Hulme for third by outbraking him and going 'across his bows' (*Autocourse*). This happened at Druids and left Regazzoni momentarily sideways while Hulme escaped into the distance.

Mario Poltronieri, the RAI television commentator (the station covers Grand Prix racing in Italy) remembers an early quarrel. Regazzoni said 'You must pay me for being interviewed' and Poltronieri told him: 'Thanks to RAI, which puts you "on air" and gives you a presence on television, you can ask your sponsors for more money.'

In this interesting exchange, Regazzoni was being very Swiss (a nation which understands all forms of finance), and Poltronieri was being very Italian (a nation which doesn't necessarily). Whatever, a friendship was soon born and it endured, as so many Regazzoni friendships did, to the end.

26 July, Paul Ricard, non-Championship F2

Another straightforward 40-lap race, which Regazzoni won by more than half a minute from Schenken and Cevert, Hill fifth, Peterson sixth. Ickx, Pescarolo, Bell and Rindt didn't finish.

2 August, Hockenheim, German Grand Prix

He kept the drive and, in first practice, went fastest (1m 59.8s) from Ickx (2m 00.5s). He was slower on Saturday morning but improved to fifth in the afternoon. The Friday time proved good enough for the second row of the grid. By the second lap he was running third and that became second on lap 7 amid the furious slipstreaming. The lap chart looked like a battleground and on lap 22 Regazzoni led a Grand Prix for the first time in his life. On lap 31, however, the engine failed and the Ferrari spun in the Stadium Complex. He was out.

16 August, Zeltweg, Austrian Grand Prix

He dominated practice, quickest on the Thursday, second to Rindt on the Friday and fastest on the Saturday (from Ickx). Rindt's Friday time, however, was pole – with Regazzoni still on the

The might and majesty of Austria. Regazzoni will finish second, behind team-mate Ickx. (LAT)

A beautiful study of the 1971 Ferrari. (courtesy Juan Carlos Ferrigno)

front row of a Grand Prix grid for the first time in his life. No doubt because of Italy's proximity to Austria, and the expectation that hordes of Italian supporters would go to this new track to Formula 1, Giunti had a third Ferrari and qualified it on the third row.

The crowd, estimated at 100,000, filled the cramped stands and enclosures. They saw Regazzoni seize the lead from Ickx, but Cevert dropped oil and Regazzoni went sideways on it, giving Ickx the lead. Beltoise seemed poised to attack Regazzoni but eventually he'd run so short of fuel he'd have to pit for more. Ickx ran safely home with Regazzoni following him, Rolf Stommelen (Brabham) third but a long way back.

Regazzoni had 12 points from his four Grands Prix.

Gareth Rees was there. 'The Austrian is a very special memory for me – the first race that I'd ever been to outside the U.K. A great choice, as it

turned out, because the weather was glorious, the circuit and setting beautiful beyond words and it was, I believe, the race when Clay well and truly arrived at the top level. Admittedly, the Ferrari 312B was clearly the best car at the Österreichring but still he was on the front row, led the first lap and then shadowed Ickx all the way to the flag in a resounding 1–2. They even shared the race's fastest lap with an identical time set on the very same 45th lap of the race! The race has a big significance in my opinion because, apart from proving he could run at the front all race long, Clay had shown his true quality as a loyal team player, whose ego was sufficiently under control that he could follow all race long in the tracks of his established team-leader without feeling the need to make a challenge. True, it's always easier to follow than lead, especially on such a super-fast track, but I had the feeling that day, that he could have passed Ickx any time he wanted.'

23 August, Enna, European F2, round five

All very Sicilian: a burning sun, a holiday atmosphere, plenty of watermelons and a noisy, argumentative crowd. Two heats of 31 laps, the aggregate time to count, and it was tight. At the start of the first heat – and there are suggestions Regazzoni's Italian blood was responding to the atmosphere – he was so keen to do well he lost revs as he tried to get the power on. Ickx led. Regazzoni had the lead by lap 2 but it swapped to-and-fro among a tight group until Regazzoni won it, beating Jo Siffert by 0.3 of a second, Ickx third.

Ickx led at the start of the second heat but Regazzoni attacked immediately, fell back. This was a hard run for Regazzoni, and Siffert went by to take the heat from him, *but they were given the same time* (43m 55.5s) so that Regazzoni won overall by the 0.3s he carried from the first heat. *Autosport* felt he must now be regarded as the most promising driver of the year.

Regazzoni 29, Bell 27, Fittipaldi 16.

30 August, Mantorp Park, Sweden, non-Championship F2

The two-heats formula, this time over 24 laps. He had pole but was slow in the first heat – so slow that, despite setting fastest lap and winning the second heat after carving a path up through the field and passing cars as if he was back in Formula 3 again, the deficit was simply too much to make up. Compounding that, at half distance Cevert moved over to let him through. He was classified eighth.

That day Bruce McLaren was killed testing a CanAm car at Goodwood.

6 September, Monza, Italian Grand Prix

Ferrari fielded Ickx, Regazzoni and Giunti. On the Friday morning Ickx went fastest from Stewart, Regazzoni third, Giunti fourth. This is the kind of thing to put a Vesuvius eruption into its true context: Monza erupted, and would again within hours. In the afternoon Ickx went fastest from

The most emotional victory, Monza, 1970. Regazzoni leads the pack into Parabolica. (LAT)

The slip-streaming festival and Ickx is leading now. (LAT)

Regazzoni, emotionally exhausted after the race. (LAT)

Regazzoni, Stewart third and Giunti fourth, producing the second eruption.

The Saturday crowd would surely create a third when final practice produced the grid while on the morrow, race day, the thousands and thousands of Ferrari foot-soldiers tramping to the circuit would be like a lava flow. They'd make the ground tremble as they brandished their Prancing Horse flags and banners.

The Saturday was, instead, a time of silence and a time of tears.

Jochen Rindt was coming fast at the *Parabolica*. He braked, his Lotus snapped away from him into the Armco and he was struck such a blow that it killed him.

Each driver has to rationalise finality in his own way and Regazzoni did this by ruminating (in *Le Combat*) that obviously something on the Lotus had come loose and that Rindt hadn't hesitated to get into the car: in sum, Rindt was thinking about how competitive the car was, not the fact that it was being pushed to its limits.

Regazzoni built on that with a question: *Why should I let myself be intimidated by Stewart even if he is a World Champion?*

On a hot, dry day an immense crowd – voluble, preparing to go volcanic despite the Rindt catastrophe still so close – teemed. The roads to the circuit were blocked solid by 9:00 in the morning for a race that began at 3:30.

As the race neared, the crowd fashioned a theatrical atmosphere and Ferrari prepared to exploit that. The other cars emerged from the pit lane sporadically to go round their warm-up laps to the grid and they observed a kind of ritualised theatre of their own: they halted, did a dragster start – smoke, wheelspin, which of course the crowd loved (Italians do) – and went on their way. The Ferraris did not come and each moment heightened the sense of mystery and anticipation. Then, without warning, the three cars emerged from their pits in numerical order – Ickx 2, Regazzoni 4, Giunti 6 – being pushed along the pit

lane by mechanics while the drivers walked behind, saluting the crowd.

Monza did erupt.

There were no chicanes yet, and that meant the other kind of ritualised theatre, the slipstreaming, which, across the next hour and 39 minutes, would produce 27 lead changes. As the cars

waited to be unleashed, Enzo Ferrari watched impassively, a heavy man, balding and with pure white hair. He wore sunglasses, a collar and tie. He came to races rarely. He'd made an inspired decision to come to this one.

The start was messy, another Monza tradition, because not all the 20 cars necessarily waited for

But the crowd came on, emotionally supercharged. (LAT)

Two supporters and three Ferrari drivers. (LAT)

the flag as they prepared for the 68 laps. Ickx led initially from Pedro Rodriguez, Stewart third and Regazzoni fourth, although that meant nothing because the slipstreaming could alter it in an instant – but clearly Ickx was going to win if he could hold off Stewart.

This is how the race unfolded:

Lap	Leader
1	Ickx
2	Ickx
3	Ickx
4	Rodriguez
5	Stewart
6	Stewart
7	Rodriguez
8	Rodriguez
9	Stewart
10	Regazzoni
11	Stewart
12	Regazzoni
13	Oliver

On this lap Rodriguez retired when the BRM's engine let go.

| 14 | Stewart |
| 15 | Stewart |

On this lap Giunti retired when an engine problem claimed him too. The slipstreaming went on and on, of course, although Ickx got no further than lap 26, when he had a transmission failure. That left Regazzoni bearing the weight of all Italy – an easy sentence to write but not necessarily to fully understand. Ferrari had always been far more than a motor racing team: it connected with the Italian soul, it was a way in which Italy – so often wracked by all manner of crises – could confront the world and beat it. Any red-blooded Italian, gazing at the red-blooded cars, *had* to feel great and almost personal pride. On the afternoon of 6 September 1970 Monza was very, very full of red-blooded Italians, mostly working men from Milan and its industrial hinterland, and they *were* the country's soul.

Regazzoni led laps 32, 33, 34, Stewart 35, Regazzoni 36, Stewart 37, Regazzoni 38–41, Stewart 42 and 43. The leading bunch comprised five cars, however, and only one fleeting, flickering second spanned them. Regazzoni led from lap 44 to 50, Stewart 51, Regazzoni 52, Stewart 53, Regazzoni 54. Next lap Beltoise got the Matra-Simca past but Regazzoni outbraked him into a corner and led again as they crossed the line to complete the lap.

Crucially, Stewart took precious moments to get past Beltoise himself and Regazzoni realised he must create a gap. He began weaving from side to side, which had the immediate effect of breaking any tow for the cars behind. As he forced the Ferrari he glanced again and saw the menacing blue of Stewart's Matra come into view – but Regazzoni had the gap. He glanced into his mirror, the one on the right, the only one the car carried – but it had shattered. He couldn't see anything and had no way of knowing where Stewart and Beltoise were: the pit board was useless because it gave positions but no time differences down to fractions of a second. Only when he saw it say 'CLAY + 2' did he understand that he now had a gap big enough, if he could maintain it, to stop Stewart getting a tow from his slipstream. Regazzoni scoured Monza's 3.5 miles for any fractions he could find, putting as much pressure as he could on Stewart and all the ones behind Stewart:

	Regazzoni	Stewart
Lap 57	1:26.1	1:26.1
Lap 58	1:26.3	1:26.9
Lap 59	1:26.2	1:26.3
Lap 60	1:26.1	1:27.4
Lap 61	1:25.9	1:25.9

Each of these laps produced an eruption of its own as Regazzoni crossed the line and, tactically, he was putting together an intelligent finale by using wide lines to avoid any towing as well as controlling the backmarkers as he came to them. By now, however, the Ferrari pit had become a place of terrible anxiety because he'd been losing fuel, and would he make it to the end, still another seven laps away? He kept on, never knowing from one moment to the next if the engine would cough and die. On lap 65 he equalled the track record.

The engine slogged forward.

He finally knew, going into the *Parabolica* for the 68th time, that he'd make it. He beat Stewart by 5.73 seconds and on his slowing down lap he could *see* the volcano all around him, an impression strengthened when the crowd observed their annual ritual and swarmed the track. *Autocourse* noted cryptically: 'A few policemen tried to keep the spectators back, but the majority just turned and ran away.' That's *policemen* running away ...

Regazzoni was mobbed so quickly and comprehensively that he didn't even have time to take his helmet off. One account speaks of 'hysterical scenes' and points out that the slower

A star was truly born at Monza, and the Italian press let everybody know.

cars were still coming round as the crowd filled the track.

From this afternoon on, whatever happened, Clay Regazzoni would be immortal in Italy, and was, all the way to the Parma *autostrada* one winter's day in 2006.

Franco Gozzi remembers that 'Enzo was crying and me, too, because as soon as the driver showed he was good enough to be a champion he immediately became Enzo's driver, not mine. That was normal!'

After what he'd seen in Austria, Gareth Rees was not at all surprised that Regazzoni had won.

Mario Poltronieri, television commentator on Italian channel RAI, explains that Regazzoni's name was already known to people following motor sport 'through his Formula 3 and Formula 2 experiences – winning the Formula 2 category led to him convincing Ferrari to call him up for Formula 1, but the Monza victory really launched his career, almost like a snap of the fingers. In fact it launched him into great fame and into the passions of all sports lovers.'

However, brother Dodo points out that 'Clay never changed. Every time you met him he was the same person. I saw him with the Tecno in Formula 3, I saw him in Formula 2 and when he went into Formula 1 with Ferrari – and he was *always* the same person. He enjoyed being with all people. With us – the family – he was very normal. For us he wasn't a great champion of Formula 1, he was just Clay. He was a good person and his mentality never changed. My mother was very happy for him but she saw that Formula 1 was very dangerous. Every race she got agitated. And it *was* very dangerous: the accidents, the fires, the circuits.'

13 September, Tulln-Langenlebarn, Austria, European F2, round six

The two heats of 35 laps format, and Regazzoni went fastest in the first (36m 40.20s against Bell, sixth, 37m 26.90s). By lap 20 he'd been leading Cevert, nothing much else happening. He had an engine problem after four laps in the second heat. The engine went bang and a rod appeared through the side of the bodywork. Cevert won, Bell fourth.

Bell 33, Regazzoni 29, Fittipaldi 16.

20 September, St Jovite, Canadian Grand Prix

Stewart took pole from Ickx, Regazzoni on the second row, and they were running in that order

when Stewart had a mechanical problem, opening the race to the two Ferraris. Regazzoni finished 14.8 seconds behind Ickx.

27 September, Imola, European F2, round seven

Under the rules a driver could only count his six best finishes and Bell faced dropping points – the 2 from Crystal Palace – so any finish of fourth or higher became an earner. Regazzoni's no-scored in Spain and Tulln meant he kept whatever he got here and in the final round, at Hockenheim.

The two heats formula, these over 28 laps each. Fittipaldi won the first from Regazzoni (45m 31.2s against 45m 31.3s), Bell fifth. Regazzoni was strong in the second, winning it from Ickx, Bell third and Fittipaldi fifth. That gave an overall result of Regazzoni, Fittipaldi, Bell.

Regazzoni 38, Bell 35, Fittipaldi 22.

4 October, Watkins Glen, United States Grand Prix

Regazzoni thought the place looked like the set for a Western film. Ickx was strong again, taking pole, Regazzoni on the third row. Mechanical problems and a tyre stop punished his race: he finished 13th, seven laps down. Ickx was fourth and he needed to be higher to stop Rindt taking the Championship posthumously. The moment Ickx realised he couldn't be Champion he felt relief. He'd done his best, and who would want it in circumstances like that?

11 October, Hockenheim, European F2, round eight

The Championship had become a mathematical conundrum but favouring Regazzoni. Even if Bell won the race he could total no more than 41 points (9 for the win, dropping 3 from Enna, thus adding 6 to his total of 35 going in), third place for Regazzoni (worth 4 to add to his 38 going in) gave him 44, which Bell could not equal. Fittipaldi was out of it by now, of course.

A crowd of 100,000 watched a rolling start and they knew that the order crossing the line to complete lap 1 – Regazzoni, Cevert, Peterson, Dieter Quester, Fittipaldi – meant nothing when the slipstreaming developed. In fact by lap 4 the first three had drawn clear and broken the tow so all that remained was to slipstream each other. They did.

On the final lap Quester led Regazzoni into the right-hander before the Stadium and there they came upon Vittorio Brambilla, a lap down but on the racing line. Quester and Regazzoni both went to the same side to overtake. One of Regazzoni's wheels went between the front and rear wheels on Quester's BRM, launching it. It landed and spun – but Quester caught that. Regazzoni's Tecno embarked on an enormous slide and almost stalled. As Quester stole off towards the line Regazzoni limped to second place, 1.7 seconds behind.

Quester	1h 16m 34.4s
Regazzoni	1h 16m 36.1s

Bell was a distant sixth.

23 October, Mexico City, Mexican Grand Prix

Regazzoni took pole from Stewart by an eyeblink: 1m 41.86s against Stewart's 1m 41.88s. Ickx was strong here, too, leading from lap 2 to the end while Regazzoni moved in behind him on lap 16 when Stewart suffered suspension problems. They finished like that, although he was 24.74 seconds adrift because his engine was some 500rpm down on practice: it emitted a little smoke throughout the race but otherwise pulled surprisingly strongly.

His consistency and pace gave the Championship table a slightly startling look bearing in mind he'd missed the first four races and would miss France, representing more than a third of the season: Rindt 45 points, Ickx 40, Regazzoni 33.

There are a couple of postscripts and they illustrate two widely different approaches to motor sport.

Robin Widdows retired at the end of 1970, 'walked away from motor racing completely to break the drug. A lot of my mates were being killed, of course. That year Piers was killed, Bruce McLaren was killed and Jochen was killed in a matter of weeks. I thought *hang on, I must have made the right decision here to walk away* so I got married at the end of the year, which I wouldn't do before.'

Regazzoni, moving upwards from Tecno, said he took with him happy memories, particularly of the atmosphere in the team. 'It's not the same now [1977!] in racing, it's too professional. I liked it when I first started in Formula 2. There were none of the safety problems we have now.'

After Monza, Enzo Ferrari invited Regazzoni home for a meal. He was a Ferrari driver now, all right, and in *his* soul always would be.

Pole position and a second place finish to Ickx in Mexico. (LAT)

Victory in the 1971 Race of Champions at Brands Hatch from Jackie Stewart and John Surtees. (LAT)

Unfortunately he'd joined at the wrong time, which he'd find out in 1971.

Alan Henry has written: 'As the season progressed, Ferrari fortunes waned. The problem was that the B2 wasn't a very predictable and progressive machine to drive close to the limit and [Technical Director Mauro] Forghieri's efforts to sort out its handling were not helped by continual complaints from the drivers in addition to enormous and increasing problems with Firestone's tyres.'[6]

In fact, Ferrari would probably have been better advised simply to run the 1970 car. As it was, they took the B2 to Kyalami for pre-season testing and Regazzoni crashed it into an earth bank. He, Ickx and Mario Andretti ran the B1s in the Grand Prix there. Andretti won, Regazzoni third – after briefly leading at the start – and Ickx eighth after a puncture and pit stop.

Regazzoni took the B2 to the Race of Champions at Brands Hatch but found it bounding all over the place and couldn't risk getting his foot full down on the accelerator even in a straight line. The race began wet but he'd heard the weather forecast and it said the rain would soon stop so he risked dry tyres while Stewart chose wets for his Tyrrell. The weather forecast was right and Regazzoni won, but only because of the tyre choice. Luck, as he said himself. The victory, however, encouraged Forghieri – who'd been in the background when Regazzoni posed for a picture at his first Monza Grand Prix – even more in his belief that the B2 represented the future.

(Mario Poltronieri remembers Forghieri saying to Regazzoni during some testing – it must have brought the house down: 'Are you only here to make me angry? You could have stayed at home.')

In fact, Ferrari would run the B2 through 1971 and to the end of 1972. It was, as Regazzoni described it, a 'fatal' decision. In 1971 he'd have two more third places after South Africa – Holland and Germany – and a sixth at Watkins Glen. Stewart romped the Championship with 62 points, Ickx fourth (19), Regazzoni seventh (13) and Andretti eighth (12). This was Regazzoni's season, qualifying position in brackets:

South Africa	(3)	3
Spain	(2)	did not finish, engine
Monaco	(11)	did not finish, accident
Holland	(4)	3
France	(2)	did not finish, accident
Britain	(P)	did not finish, oil pressure
Germany	(4)	3
Austria	(4)	did not finish, engine
Italy	(8)	did not finish, engine
Canada	(18)	did not finish, accident
USA	(4)	6

Gareth Rees saw Regazzoni race three times in 1971. 'The first two were at Brands Hatch and both added to his reputation as a top driver. In the non-Championship Formula 1 Race of Champions, held on a typically cold day in March, he led from the front and won convincingly in the new Ferrari 312B2, this time beating the world's best driver, Jackie Stewart. A month later in the BOAC 1,000

A stunning start as Regazzoni moves towards the lead in South Africa – but he'd finish third. (LAT)

Kilometres, sharing with Ickx, their nimble new Ferrari 312P took the challenge to the Porsche 917s and led convincingly, but finally finished second after Ickx tripped over a backmarker.

'In addition I saw Regga race at the wet Dutch Grand Prix in 1971 when he finished third, driving with his nose cone pointing skywards for much of the race.' (It was very wet and drivers crashed all over the place. Regazzoni even got into, and out of, catch fencing on the approach to Tarzan near the end.)

Before we leave it, Regazzoni qualified – as we have just seen – eighth at Monza for the Italian Grand Prix but, as Nigel Roebuck explains, 'in those days "jumped starts" were commonplace, and anyway a Ferrari driver at Monza could get away with anything. Clay, I'm sure, was in at least second gear by the time the flag dropped, and led by about 50 yards as the pack headed off towards the Curva Grande…'

The engine failed after 18 laps.

There was the consolation of a more competitive car in the 1,000 Kilometres sports car races, where he partnered Ickx. They took second place in the BOAC despite a stone smashing Regazzoni's visor. He kept going at full speed, was struck in the eye by another stone but completed his stint. They qualified second fastest at Monza but in the race Ickx ran full into somebody else's accident and that was that.

They were fifth fastest in practice at Spa, a circuit Regazzoni had never driven before. Unusually he was off the pace and they were classified eighth in the race. They took pole at the Nürburgring and Ickx led, breaking the lap record, but he had to pit because the car was losing water. Evidently Forghieri tried to coax other teams to lend him sealant for the radiator but they weren't having that, thank you. Ickx was instructed to ignore the rev counter and watch the temperature gauge instead. On lap 15 Regazzoni took over but retired six laps later with cracked cylinder heads.

In Austria they qualified second quickest and led for whole tracts of the race but on lap 149 of the 170 Regazzoni said he felt a vibration. The Ferrari snapped away from him in a right-hander and he hammered the Armco.

There remained a Formula 2 race that he did in a March at Vallelunga in October but the car broke down and, a month later, the 9 Hours of Kyalami, where he was partnered by Brian Redman.

'I'd first met him in 1968 in European Formula 2,' Redman says. 'He had a reputation for being slightly wild – well, he was like that all his life. Following the November 1971 race at Kyalami we became much more familiar and of course we both drove for Ferrari in 1972–73 so I saw a lot of him in those days. He was incredible, a bon-viveur of the highest order. He wouldn't have lasted long in today's Grand Prix world.

'How did he approach Kyalami? I have no idea! As drivers or as co-drivers, whoever I drove with we never really discussed how we were going to approach the race. Occasionally Jacky Ickx would say "Let's just sit back a little bit and see what's happening," but with Clay we didn't talk about it. Even in the nine-hour race you went as fast as possible. That suited him very well, but if you happened to be in a good position – in a good lead – then of course you would be a little easier on the car.'

Regazzoni and Redman won from Ickx and Andretti in the other Ferrari.

'At Kyalami after we'd won we were celebrating and it went on into the night,' Redman says. 'After we'd thrown all the dining room chairs into the swimming pool Mario went to bed. This would be midnight or one o'clock. Clay said "Let's give Mario some excitement." The roofs at the Kyalami Ranch Hotel were straw and each room was separate, so Clay lit a newspaper and he threw it into Mario's room. Unfortunately he got the wrong room – a guest who was nothing to do with the race. The Police came and we had to smuggle Clay out of Johannesburg the next day. It was an era of eat, drink and be merry because tomorrow we die – very much so.'

The 1972 season began with the Buenos Aires 1,000 Kilometres in January, Redman the partner again. The irony of 1972 was that while the Ferrari B2, modified but still experiencing chassis problems, struggled, the 312P was poised to dominate the World Championship of Makes. Peterson/Schenken won Buenos Aires from Ickx/Regazzoni. That was 9 January. On the 23rd, at the same circuit, Regazzoni put the B2 on the third row of the grid for the Argentine Grand Prix, Ickx on the fourth and Andretti on the fifth. Regazzoni made a strong start and ran fifth but during the race a newspaper blew against his radiator, forcing him to slow or risk overheating. He finished fourth but 1m 06s behind the winner, Stewart.

At the Daytona 6 Hours Ferrari sent three new cars and they qualified at the front of the grid: Ickx/Andretti (1m 44.22s), Regazzoni/Redman (1m 44.96s), Peterson/Schenken (1m 46.04s). In the race Regazzoni was struggling for the lead against a Lola when a front tyre burst on the banking at an estimated 185mph and the front of the body was not only plucked off but cast towards the Lola. Regazzoni was just getting into his stride,

Glimpses of 1971: third in Germany behind Stewart and Cevert, duelling with Stewart at Monza, celebrating pole at Silverstone. (LAT)

however: the car suffered a further puncture, it lost a brake pad, Redman spun at an estimated 150mph, knocking the rear bodywork off, and the clutch began to fail. In what was little more than a carcass they finished fourth …

'Ferrari was not authoritarian,' Regazzoni explained. 'We followed the programme, of course, but in the races we were free from the start. I remember at Sebring there were three jump starts: each of us tried to get into the lead but the course director hadn't lowered the green flag. Afterwards, whoever was capable of taking the lead took it, and those who were capable of overtaking overtook. It was the pit stops which made the difference. Certainly towards the end of a race if we were 1–2–3 we stayed in our positions.'[7]

After Daytona, Ferrari tested at Le Mans because they had entered four cars for the 24-hour race. Ickx went quickest – from Regazzoni.

At Kyalami he qualified an eyeblink from pole with 1m 17.3s against Stewart's 1m 17.0s but had an unhappy race, because in an effort to reduce the fuel load Ferrari had weakened the mixture – and lost power. A pit stop after a puncture didn't help and he came a very distant 12th.

At Sebring for the 12 Hours, again with Redman, he led but the driveshaft failed, cutting the cable to the main battery. The car caught fire and by the time he'd stopped and hopped out it had become a blaze, not helped by the fact that the fire crew took long minutes to get there.

At Brands Hatch for the BOAC 1,000 the Regazzoni/Redman car took pole but had ignition problems in the race and fell back to fifth.

At Monza for the 1,000 Kilometres he partnered Ickx but race day was very wet and on the warm-up lap Ickx spun in the *Parabolica*. Peterson unwisely signalled what he thought of Ickx doing that by hoisting a very rude gesture. Unwisely? Peterson promptly spun off into mud. The race was delayed until these two Ferraris had reached the grid and been cleaned up. You didn't start races at Monza minus Ferraris and, anyway, this was a particularly weak field – Alfa Romeo and Mirage weren't there. In the race the Ferrari had mechanical problems and spent 12 minutes in the pits but still won it from a Porsche.

He qualified eighth for the Spanish Grand Prix at Jarama and produced one of his enormous starts to run third but fell back. Particularly heavy attrition – 14 cars retired – brought him up to third. He had not been on a Grand Prix podium since Germany the year before.

At Spa for the 1,000 Kilometres Ickx/Regazzoni put the Ferrari on pole. Redman remembers what happened next. 'I was very impressed. We had agreed to go out to dinner so I went and knocked on his hotel door. He said "Ciao, come in!" I opened the door and there he was in between the landlady and her daughter. He was quite happy for me to go in. He wouldn't think twice about it – and he *didn't* think twice about it …'

Of all this, Franco Gozzi says: 'In my mind Clay was not a good man with his family and if his life

had been more tranquil this could have been helpful for him to become like Niki Lauda. Just to give you an example, in Belgium we were not in a hotel, we were in a private house run by a nice lady who had three daughters. It was, you know, a nice place for everybody. Clay *knew* them all, including the youngest. So there was an argument and Arturo Merzario said that *it* was impossible because that afternoon Clay was with him playing golf – but he was with the young girl.'

Whether this was the same establishment Redman refers to, or whether Regazzoni specialised in inter-generational seduction all round Spa, is not clear.

(Gozzi, warming to his theme, adds: 'Another time we flew to Johannesburg, South Africa, and during the night there was a young girl who ran right down the plane naked with Clay's helmet on – for a bet. The bet was with a *Playboy* photographer. Clay said "Give me a couple of hours and I will make that girl do it." And he did. And she did. Unbelievable.

'We were at the Kyalami Ranch Hotel. Another girl was there but this was only an amusement. That was Clay. A man. There's an Italian expression for this: forever young like a student. But he didn't do bad things – it wasn't like robbing banks, he was making people happy. I am sure that you can judge the man positively. Clay was a man who fascinated women. He had sex appeal.'

Something about South Africa, and the Kyalami Ranch Hotel, clearly stimulated Regazzoni in much the same way as Spa's landladies did.)

At Spa, the 1,000 Kilometres was a typical tumult of a race: Regazzoni led from the other two Ferraris but had a dramatic puncture that affected the bodywork and oil tank. This took some time to repair in the pits but he and Ickx still finished second.

At Monaco for the Grand Prix he qualified on the second row but, in a filthy wet race, spun on oil when Stewart was pushing him hard for third place. He hammered the Armco at Gasometer Hairpin (now known as *Rascasse*) and set off on foot to go back to the pits. Evidently he went into a prohibited area, a policeman got prickly, Regazzoni got prickly and took a swing at him. This is not the sort of act to endear you to the police in Monaco, or anywhere else. One report suggests he was taken away to the police station with his arm behind his back. Further details are obscure (and certainly Regazzoni does not mention the episode in his autobiography) but clearly he was released because he took part in the 1,000 Kilometres at the Nürburgring two weeks later.

There the Ferraris circled in their familiar positions, 1–2–3, but stayed on wet tyres as the track dried. Bell was on dries. 'Regga became brilliant in the 3-litre Ferrari when I was in the Mirage. I'll never forget he was leading at the Nürburgring and all the flags were waving. I came round a corner called *Wippermann* [far out in the country and 16km from the start] and there was Regga sitting in the middle of his own wreckage.' He'd spun and crashed heavily. The two other

Monaco in the wet – and he'd crash on lap 52. (LAT)

Ferraris finished 1–2, so that the company won the World Championship of Makes with three rounds to spare. They withdrew their entries for the Le Mans 24-hour race, which was next.

The Belgian Grand Prix was at Nivelles and he qualified second fastest (1m 11.58s) to Emerson Fittipaldi's Lotus (1m 11.43s). He led to lap 9 when Fittipaldi went by. Ickx attacked and the two Ferraris *raced* until Ickx had a mechanical problem. Towards mid-distance Cevert (Tyrrell) went by too, and on lap 58 he was lapping Galli's Martini Tecno at the hairpin. They collided. Regazzoni defended himself by explaining that Galli wouldn't let him through and spun, leaving him nowhere to go.

Galli wasn't happy about Regazzoni's driving and said so.

He missed the French and British Grands Prix because he broke his arm playing football but he came back for Germany and qualified seventh, although that had little meaning on the Nürburgring's 14.18 miles. The race might be pivotal for the World Championship because Fittipaldi had 43 points and Stewart ('it was the year I had my ulcer and I came back') 27. With four races after the Nürburgring, Stewart could still win it.

Stewart's position improved significantly when Fittipaldi's gearbox casing cracked after 10 laps. Ickx led, as he was to lead throughout, Regazzoni second and Stewart attacking to get that second place from him, 'the Championship still within my grasp'. Regazzoni knew that the Tyrrell was quicker through the corners but the Ferrari quicker in straight lines.

Stewart describes what followed as a run-in. 'He was the first driver I had ever raced against who weaved going down the straight to keep me behind. That didn't happen at all in those times – really hadn't happened before. That sort of behaviour did not exist.

'The other thing was I only had braking in two wheels and I kept trying to get inside him but, of course, two-wheel braking is not quite as good as four-wheel braking and it was always a struggle.'

They moved into the last lap and at a sharp left-hand loop – *Hatzenbach* – Regazzoni's Ferrari went wide. It slowed, too. That brought Stewart up as they approached a sequence of corners towards *Flugplatz*. Stewart went left, the next corner was a right after a short straight. Regazzoni sensed that Stewart would have to outbrake him and, as a matter of personal creed, nobody outbraked Clay Regazzoni. They went into the right-hander side by side.

'Then in the end he had me off,' Stewart says. 'I was making a fairly bold move on the outside and he drove in such a way that I couldn't get past. I went into the barrier and got a ride back on a motorbike.'

Stewart was angry and when the Press gathered round him he gave full vent to his feelings.

'I was pretty upset with him, and I went to the Stewards but of course you have to keep in mind that they didn't have cameras round the track in those days so they couldn't see it. I didn't bother to face him in the end because he was still running when I went to the Stewards [he finished second to Ickx]. It didn't change our friendship or anything, it was just a behavioural trait that I didn't like. The cars and circuits were dangerous. By that time they'd been made slightly safer but it certainly was still the Nürburgring, which was to be closed a few years later.'

He didn't finish in Austria (fuel vaporisation) and by Monza heavy rumours circulated that his Ferrari contract would not be renewed. They were true. Enzo Ferrari explained that the plans for 1973 were uncertain and Regazzoni could wait until December to see what might develop or perhaps search for another team.

Ferrari sometimes fielded three cars if Andretti was available, and he was for Monza. At the team lunch before Saturday qualifying he was amazed to see Regazzoni having a glass of red wine with his pasta. 'That was Clay, and [Vittorio] Brambilla was the same – and they were inevitably quicker right afterwards! Jeez, imagine that now ... you'd be excommunicated.'[8]

The splendour of the Nürburgring and a second place finish, although Jackie Stewart would have something to say about Regazzoni's conduct there. (courtesy Gareth Rees)

Regazzoni qualified on the second row, and he and Ickx both led before – approaching one of the new chicanes – he saw to his horror that marshals were push-starting the March of Carlos Pace. As Regazzoni approached, the March fired up and set off, but it was too late. His wheel struck Pace's wheel and the Ferrari careered helplessly down the track on fire. Regazzoni got out of it very, very quickly.

He finished fifth in Canada and eighth at Watkins Glen.

In the 9 Hours at Kyalami, partnered by Merzario, he won. In the background two young men – an Austrian by the name of Lauda and an Englisman by the name of Hunt – were showing great promise, Lauda already in Grand Prix racing, Hunt about to reach it.

A new generation was coming but it can't have troubled Regazzoni. He intended to go on for years and if young men wanted to take him on, isn't that what young men want to do? The truth is that, although 33, he could still drive like a teenager in a go-kart.

Perhaps to counterbalance that he grew a moustache at Watkins Glen. It suited him, and from this moment on always would.

At Interlagos, Brazil, he drove a March in a Formula 2 race and finished third.

His love affair with South America had truly begun and would continue. Juan Carlos Ferrigno, an Argentine and leading motor sport artist with a rare gift for communicating speed (see pages 48 and 84), captures that. 'The series we had was called *Temporada Internacional* and it gave me one of the best memories of my childhood. When I was just 10 or 11 years old I remember the best cars and drivers coming to Buenos Aires to race Formula 1 and also the Sport Prototypes series. The circuit was almost overcrowded and it provided the highest excitement for Argentinean petrol heads! It was the time that I fell in love with motor racing and started to draw those fantastic cars, due of the strong impression they made on me. I waited anxious for January …

'Clay Regazzoni was one of the heroes who would come every year with those beautiful Ferraris and the Swiss cross on his helmet. His name will be linked forever in my mind with the excitement of looking at, hearing and being so near the fantastic cars: Porsche, Matra, Lola, Alfa Romeo and so many others.

'On the personal side Regga, as people called him, was maybe the most charismatic and friendly driver at the *Temporada*, because being Swiss-Italian he could speak a mix of Italian-Spanish. It was funny to listen to it. In some ways his smiling presence, his moustache and open attitude to people made you feel he was your famous Italian uncle who, once a year, come to Buenos Aires to visit his family. I remember him being so easy-going and accessible to autograph hunters. He'd chat and have his picture taken with everybody who asked him.

'At that time I liked the Sport Prototypes much more than the Formula 1 cars. I was captivated by the shapes of their rounded and brightly-coloured bodywork, and in the case of Ferrari I *still* love the golden wheels they had. I always felt those racing cars were real works of art. That's why I like painting them so much, trying to capture their beauty and reflect their power and speed. Regga is part of the time I remember as the happiest in my life, and he will be my "racing uncle" forever.'

Notes: 1. Il capo means quite simply The Boss; 2. Enzo Ferrari the typical feudal tyrant, di Montezemolo the typical modern, international businessman, at home running Italy's World Cup soccer finals in 1990 or Fiat; 3. Riccardo Patrese was heavily implicated in the crash that killed Ronnie Peterson at Monza in 1978. It happened in the jostling just after the start and Patrese, young, impetuous, was easy to blame. He wasn't exonerated for a full ten years; 4. Autopassion; 5. There were two Brambillas, elder brother Ernesto – Tino – (born 1934) and younger Brother Vittorio (1937–2001), known as The Monza Gorilla. Both were hard racers; 6. Ferrari: The Grand Prix Cars; 7. Autopassion; 8. Roebuck interview with Mario Andretti after Regazzoni's death

Brothers in arms: Ickx, Regazzoni and Mario Andretti. (LAT)

CHAPTER 3

ADVERSE CAMBER

If Clay Regazzoni comes to us from a different era, so do Louis Stanley and the BRM (British Racing Motors) team he ran. Stanley always wore a jacket and tie, wrote on subjects as diverse as religion and tennis, and had a permanent suite at the Dorchester Hotel in London, where he had once been manager. He carried many great strengths and many great weaknesses, including the world of the technical. Everybody called him Big Lou and when Continentals, beguiled by his presence, called him 'My Lord' he smiled – like a lord.

He married the sister of Sir Alfred Owen, who was chairman of the Owen Group, which owned BRM, and that helped.

His organisational skill seems to have been suspect, too. During the 1972 season, BRM contested the 12 Grands Prix with 47 cars – and sometimes three different versions, designated the P153, P160 and P180, were competing simultaneously. This has been aptly described as chaos, compounded by Stanley's attempt to run a six-car team and – when that was reduced to three – the quixotic tactic of dropping drivers at the last moment. Stanley compounded it further by making enquiries about where all the *other* drivers in the paddock would or would not be the following season. Perhaps he heard that Enzo Ferrari couldn't guarantee Regazzoni a drive and Enzo said if he could find a drive elsewhere, fine. Enzo added that the Ferrari door remained open to him if future events permitted that.

RIGHT *Unhappy 1973. This is Sweden and Denny Hulme in the McLaren is about to lap Regazzoni's BRM and win the race.* (LAT)

Team manager Tim Parnell outlines the background, itself an example of the change in Grand Prix racing. 'Regazzoni came to us through Marlboro. We were the first people to bring Marlboro in, mainly because of Jo Siffert being Swiss.'

Siffert's involvement with BRM went back to 1962, using their engines in Lotuses and Brabhams until, in 1971, he drove for the team. That year they fielded several drivers, including Pedro Rodriguez, Gethin and Elford. Tragedy was to decimate this: Rodriguez killed in a sports car race in Germany between the French and British Grands Prix. Siffert, however, won in Austria, and Gethin heroically at Monza in a desperate,

Louis Stanley, emperor of all he surveyed. (LAT)

desperate slipstreaming finish (the three cars behind him at 0.01, 0.09 and 0.18 of a second).

'The team was looking ever so good and ever so strong. After we lost Rodriguez we concentrated on Jo. We were very successful – BRM was right up at the top,' Parnell says.

Then Siffert was killed in a non-Championship race at Brands Hatch that October.

'Marlboro were based in Lausanne and they used to help Siffert with personal sponsorship. That was the connection that brought Marlboro in. We were with Yardley as sponsors at the time. When we went to Jo's funeral in Switzerland the Marlboro people came to us and said "We had an agreement we were going to sponsor you with Jo and, because we have done so much in regard to that, we want to continue".'

It led to a three-year contract. 'We started off with Marlboro and Beltoise, who had come to us, in 1972. He won the Monaco Grand Prix, which was then one of the most televised Grands Prix, and Marlboro said that was "Fantastic, it's the greatest reward we could ever have expected and we are right behind you. We will do everything we can." Afterwards they said "We really ought to get a top driver and we would like to bring Regazzoni" – again a Swiss – "to the team." This is what they did. They paid Regazzoni quite a fee to come to us at BRM and in fact Marlboro moved into personal contracts with several racers. They wanted to get big in the sport and they did a terrific amount of advertising. Their hospitality at the circuits was colossal. They had great big motorhomes and more or less fed all the Grand Prix world. It was quite amazing.'

For 1973 Stanley restricted BRM to a modified P160 and would field three drivers in them, Beltoise and young Lauda partnering Regazzoni.

Patrick Head, who'd work with Regazzoni at Williams in 1979, recounts the folklore. 'There was a wonderful story about the first time he drove the BRM, up at Silverstone. They had, I think, three cars there and Clay had two monumental accidents. Each time, he'd walk back to the pits and say "Where's my next car?"'

Emerson Fittipaldi, writing in his book *Flying on the Ground,* said: 'I think Clay is a very good driver, though he drives a lot over the limit. I think he loses his concentration. He changes his line very often. Sometimes he brakes too late, and sometimes too early, and then he comes too much on the inside of the normal line. He changes a lot. He doesn't always have the right balance. But he has a lot of natural ability, and I think with more experience he can improve a lot. If he just concentrates more he can be a much better driver.

It may help that he is no longer with Ferrari, and I think he will be very good in the BRM.'

Regazzoni did not, in his own words, know Stanley very well and discovered that he 'just talks and talks and talks. I don't believe he knows anything at all about racing.'[1]

Aleardo Buzzi, then President of Philip Morris, confirms that Regazzoni 'started with us with BRM. I hired also Niki Lauda. The big problem at BRM was mainly the tyres. They did well when it was raining and badly when it was dry, and it should be the other way round. And that season there was no rain.' The deal was that Marlboro and BRM would share the payments to Regazzoni.

Regazzoni found that the BRM astonished him, because it handled so easily he lost the impression of speed. 'There weren't too many problems setting it up. The engines weren't fantastic but they were good enough, and we did some good times round Silverstone and Ricard. As a result, I felt confident for the start of the season.'[2]

His first Grand Prix in the car, the Argentine, ought to have produced a great triumph. 'Clay was a hell of a forceful driver,' Parnell says. 'He led the race and I'm damn sure he would have won it but the Firestone tyres let him down. He led the race for quite a while.

'We went from there to Brazil and he did quite well [sixth, albeit a lap down] and then we went to South Africa and he had the accident and the bloody car caught fire. That great hero Mike

Hailwood stopped and pulled him out. He was pretty badly burnt on his arms and was in hospital in South Africa for a bit.'

He qualified on the second row but ran at the back of the field after a confused start: some drivers had been given a signal *4 minutes to go* and then found the starting flag waving at them. On the third lap, at Crowthorne corner, a Lotus snapped sideways and tapped Hailwood's Surtees.

The moustache had become a trademark, and the smile never varied. (LAT)

Everything normal in South Africa but in a moment it won't be. (LAT)

Hailwood kept his car in the middle of the track so that those behind could pass him on either side. At least five did but Ickx in the Ferrari struck the rear of it, punting it to the inside and into Regazzoni. The BRM burst into flames and Hailwood, who'd parked, ran across and saw Regazzoni unconscious in the cockpit. He undid Regazzoni's seatbelts, seized one of Regazzoni's arms – the only one he could get at – and tried to haul him out.

This was almost impossible and Hailwood's overalls caught fire. Frantically he tried to put this out, couldn't and sprinted across the track to a sandy-grassy area where he rolled over and over to smother the overalls. One report says Ickx leapt on Hailwood to help.

The BRM burst into flames again and Hailwood went back across to help marshals finally haul Regazzoni, still unconscious, out.

Typically, Hailwood subsequently made light of this bravery and did so at the time, too. When he returned to the pits he signalled his wife Pauline that they were leaving the circuit for the house where they were staying. He didn't mention it and

He'd be third in the 1973 Daily Express International Trophy, behind Stewart and Ronnie Peterson. (LAT)

she only learned what had happened when she saw the newspapers the following morning.

Regazzoni spent three days in hospital in Johannesburg and then a week in hospital in Lugano. Fortunately the South African Grand Prix had been on 3 March and the non-Championship *Daily Express* Trophy at Silverstone wasn't until 8 April. It gave him time to recover and he drove at Silverstone with a hand bandaged. It was bleeding by the end but he still finished third.

The races in Britain brought a particular kind of problem for Regazzoni: Chris Lambert, or rather John Lambert. Parnell describes the whole thing as a 'black spot. I know that at several race meetings people came to Regazzoni and were really very officious. Lambert's father got very upset about it all and I had to calm the situation down. I know it was five years after the accident but he was still pursuing it. One of Clay's close friends used to warn me about what was going on and I had to step in on several occasions. At meetings Lambert's father would come up and start bloody rowing and carrying on and all that. I personally told Lambert he'd better back off or he'd be in serious trouble, not only legally but he risked getting a thump from somebody. Regga was a bit concerned but he was a pretty tough character and he could stand up to it. As he said to me "It was a racing incident and in racing these things happen. It didn't bother me. I just got on with the job."'

Capturing another mood altogether, a follower called Colin Ward and a friend took time off to go to Silverstone. Ward points out that in those innocent, unbuttoned days people could go into the paddock and talk to drivers. Regazzoni was there and Ward chatted to him. He still remembers how pleasurable that was, how charming Regazzoni was and how Regazzoni autographed the programme he still has.[3]

By now Regazzoni was nursing doubts about the car. It 'started out well. I was in the pole position in Argentina, and the car also go well in Brazil and South Africa. And we also drive on Firestone tyre, which was better in practice but not good in the race because after 20, 30 laps they started to go off. When I spoke to Big Lou he say we have only two cars, you and Beltoise. You are the first driver. Then they take Niki. We have one, two, three cars and only five engines! We make all season with only five engines … was not good.'[4]

For the next race, the Spanish, all cars had to be modified to protect the fuel tanks.

As Parnell says, 'the BRM 160 was a very quick, good car. Our weakness was in the engines, which never really performed anything like satisfactorily.

We had to alter the chassis, putting on a deformable structure to assist with the new impact regulations, and what we did with the BRM then wasn't successful at all. The car had been developed very highly in wind tunnels and we had been close to the Imperial College in London who had helped with that. We were one of the first teams to be big into wind tunnels. Having changed during the season, the streamlining was very much affected.'

Regazzoni finished ninth in Spain but tyres hobbled Lauda. In fact Lauda started the season quietly: oil pressure stopped him in Argentina, eighth in Brazil, an engine failure in South Africa.

'Regazzoni was very good with Niki Lauda, no doubt about that,' Parnell says. 'They formed a companionship. Lauda was coming on in leaps and bounds and he would test all day and all bloody night. Unbelievable – and so was the physical effort he put into his racing.' Lauda would describe this most delicate of relationships – two men, same team, same car, both wanting to win – like this: 'We were never real friends, but I valued him.'[5] Lauda once explained why he didn't race in sports cars by saying that 'the era of specialists had already begun. There were more and more private tests and a Formula 1 driver was obliged to concentrate on them.'

Lauda, like Regazzoni, doubted the car and doubted Stanley as the man to move into a new era. Stanley, Lauda concluded, belonged to the 1960s and was intent on staying there.

After Spain, Regazzoni – the antithesis of the specialist – competed in the Targa Florio with Facetti in an Alfa Romeo but they crashed during practice. This was, incidentally, the last year that the race was a round of the Sports Car World Championship.

Lauda finished fifth in Belgium – Zolder – where Regazzoni crashed at the hairpin when the brakes failed. Neither finished at Monaco, although Lauda outqualified Ickx in the Ferrari and kept him behind him to lap 25, when the BRM's gearbox failed. Enzo Ferrari noted that and in due course contact was made.

The BRMs were far off the pace in Sweden (Regazzoni ninth, Lauda thirteenth), far off it in France (Lauda ninth, Regazzoni twelfth). That

If you like a drink, there is an obvious solution: just open your own pub. (LAT)

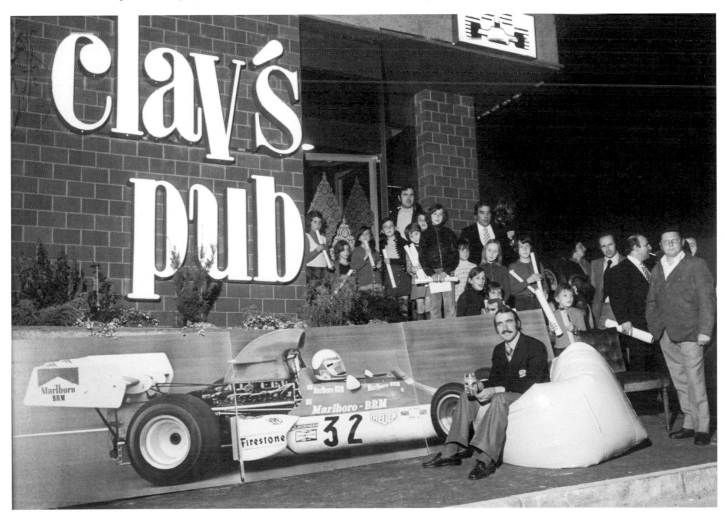

brought them to Silverstone. No doubt John Lambert lay in wait for him there …

He finished seventh, Lauda twelfth – and so it went in Holland and in Germany, where Lauda crashed after a puncture and broke his arm.

That August a Ferrari employee whose name Lauda didn't at first catch rang saying he'd like a meeting but in heaviest secrecy. It was Luca di Montezemolo, and Lauda met him in London. Di Montezemolo made an immediate impression, a man on the move within Fiat, and upwards. 'How would you, Lauda, like to drive for Ferrari?' How much money would he want? They talked it through and agreed to talk again.

Regazzoni did haul the car into the points (sixth) in Austria despite frustration with the rev

Glimpses of 1973: in the middle of the pack in tragic Holland … engine failure in Germany … Targa Floria practice. (LAT)

A lot to discuss in Canada. (LAT)

At Fiorano, 'because of my experience with English cars – easy to drive, giving little impression of going fast – I suddenly realised it was an important change,' Regazzoni said. 'The B2 demanded a lot of concentration. With the chassis on the B3, Forghieri had followed the English technology.'[6]

Understandably, news of this test enraged BRM, although Regazzoni claimed that Stanley never spoke to him about it and Regazzoni 'never said anything either'.

Ferrari pulled what Parnell describes as 'a dirty trick'. They took a driver who 'was under contract to BRM and got him testing at Ferrari on the promise that they would sign him up for Ferrari the following year. That was one of the dirtiest tricks ever served. I was a member of FOCA and I said to Bernie Ecclestone "This is absolutely disgraceful – that somebody can take a driver, dress him up in a different uniform, different crash helmet and carry out bloody testing for the team." Bernie thought it was pretty bad and so did the rest of the teams, Ken Tyrrell especially. He said it was absolutely appalling. I think Regga was a Ferrari fan. Well, of course he wanted to get to Ferrari and quite frankly he was quite sheepish about it. He really was. Because of this incident Big Lou wouldn't let him drive in Canada. It was very unusual in that era to suspend a driver and Regazzoni took it pretty badly.'

There was talk of lawyer's letters and so on, and no doubt Regazzoni's mood wasn't improved by being told *after* he reached Canada. (It must be said at this point that Regazzoni claimed BRM hadn't been paying him what they owed and got his lawyer to write to Stanley saying that if he wasn't paid in Canada he'd have to decide whether he'd be in the race or not.) Gethin deputised.

Marlboro, most unusually, issued a highly undiplomatic statement. 'We share responsibility for Regazzoni's retainer with BRM and we feel that the team's management has ignored one of the fundamental courtesies implicit in the relationship between a sponsor and a team.'

At Mosport, Beltoise finished fourth but an oil pump belt failure halted Gethin and a transmission failure halted Lauda.

Regazzoni gave a version of all this. 'After the first two races,' he claimed, 'Stanley didn't pay. I say *if you don't pay I don't make race*. So Tim Parnell called me one day, tell me no race for Regazzoni in Canada. I ask Tim why, and he say Big Lou say I am like a football team, because I want to be paid!'

Whatever, a week later Regazzoni was due to drive in the final Formula 5000 race of the season

limiter. This was ordinarily set at 10,000 but with an on/off switch so the driver could stop it working while he tried to overtake the car in front, then switch it on again. He was following Merzario and switched it off but nothing happened.

Lauda practised but the broken arm would not permit him racing. After the Grand Prix, however, he agreed to join Ferrari. Regazzoni had kept in touch, too, and in Austria he was asked how he'd like to test their car, the B2, for 1974.

Yes, he thought, *I would.*

'They called me to do some tests, of course in secrecy, at Fiorano.'

Neither he nor Lauda finished at Monza. Beltoise, meanwhile, had had three fifth places.

By Monza, Regazzoni had agreed to rejoin Ferrari.

in Seattle in a Lola owned by Californian millionaire Chuck Jones. He was third until someone ran him off the track, although other reports suggest he had a mechanical problem. Or both.

That autumn Parnell 'said to Big Lou "I think you've made the point and he ought to finish off with us in Watkins Glen"' – the United States Grand Prix which habitually closed the season.

There, in practice, Regazzoni tried the rev limiter switch on the straight and again it didn't work. He raised this with the team but was told the engine needed protecting. He finished the race eighth, Beltoise ninth and Lauda didn't finish again. 'And that was the end of it,' Parnell says. 'He went away and joined Ferrari. Clay and Niki both went to Ferrari from us and took, I think, a lot of our ideas with them.'

Aleardo Buzzi adds to that. 'Then Enzo Ferrari wanted him back and he went. Then Enzo Ferrari asked him who he wanted to have as a team-mate and he said "Niki Lauda". So that is how Niki Lauda came to Ferrari. He'd come to us because we had an Austrian driver who lost one eye so we took another Austrian – him – and funnily enough he was good.' (The first driver was Helmut Marko, who during the 1972 French Grand Prix at Clermont-Ferrand was hit by a stone thrown back by a car ahead – the circuit lacked curbs, and cars cut the corners. He was partially blinded, his racing career over.)

Actually, after Watkins Glen the Lola from Seattle was flown over for Regazzoni to drive in the final race of the European F5000 championship. Evidently the choice of driver lay between Regazzoni and Mario Andretti, and Regazzoni got it because of his popularity with the British crowd. He said he liked the car and savoured racing it at Brands.

It wouldn't be that happy. Naturally the main interest in the paddock centred on the Lola, but a broken pushrod in practice limited his laps and he was trying to sort the handling out too. Belgian driver Teddy Pilette (Chevron) took pole with 1m 34.2s, Regazzoni on the eighth row with 1m 42.0s. Nor was the race much better in front of 10,000 on a fine autumnal day. On lap 11 he pitted with a fuel pressure problem and that cost him six places. He stopped again on lap 24 to try and improve the handling (and the fuel pressure problem persisted). He slogged to 12th at the end.

Gareth Rees remembers: 'There was a race I could easily have forgotten. I'm sure Clay would like to have forgotten it too, but it said a lot about him and his pure enthusiasm for racing. Exactly six years after that Formula 3 race in October 1967 he

was back at Brands Hatch, this time for the last Formula 5000 race of the season. He was entered in a pretty scruffy orange Lola T330 run by a little-known American team with no experience of running in the UK series, called Jones Eisert Racing.

'I suppose Regga was just curious and between jobs, and wanted to try a Formula 5000 car. It was exciting to see his name adding a bit of Continental colour and quality to the field but even for me as a 17-year-old it was a bit embarrassing, to be honest. In the damp qualifying he was 15th of 26 cars, and 8 (eight!) seconds slower than pole-man. In the race he grimly soldiered round to the finish in a car that must have handled like the proverbial supermarket trolley, and came home 12th, three *laps* behind the winner, Guy Edwards.

'Remember Regga was already an established Formula 1 driver and had just been through the low of a fruitless year with BRM. Remember he already knew he was headed back to Ferrari and better times. Why did he do it? Could be that he was well-paid – I hope so! – because it was certainly not a career-enhancing move, but maybe he just thought whatever the Italian is for "Sod it, I've got a Ferrari contract for next year so I'll just do a Formula 5000 race while I can. Even if nobody's heard of the team, it'll be fun." A less modest guy with his standing in the world would never have risked his reputation in such a car.

Niki Lauda, the team-mate – and it would become controversial. (LAT)

The rain in Spain in 1974 didn't trouble Lauda, who won, or Regazzoni, who finished second. (LAT)

driver was hurt he got him the best medical treatment. He was very good at getting people like Yardley and Marlboro on board. He kidded them along but after a few months they realised what a load of rubbish he'd told them and I had to try and pacify the situation …'

Ferrari had strength: engineer Mauro Forghieri – and di Montezemolo, who reported directly to Enzo and, uniquely in the Ferrari fiefdom, did not embellish or distort in his reports. Ferrari withdrew from the World Sports Cars to concentrate on Grand Prix racing. In fact Ferrari had so much strength – when Lauda first visited the factory and saw the resources, he did what generations of drivers had done and wondered how it was possible they did not win every race – that Regazzoni might have had the Championship, and Lauda might have had it too.

Franco Gozzi insists that Regazzoni 'was a good guy, a true friend. I will never forget that he suggested to the factory and to Enzo: "Call Lauda." Honestly, he said "I am happy to come here but if you want another good driver let me give you the name Lauda." Enzo was very grateful to Clay for this because when Lauda came immediately he showed his qualities and he and Clay were at the same level.'

Lauda would remember: 'The public image of a dynamic, forward-looking and totally integrated squad was marvellously rounded off by the presence of Clay Regazzoni. For me, he was the ideal team partner. Our relative positions in the Ferrari stable were to develop as time went on.'

In fact, their relationship would become more problematical but this first season together at Ferrari masked that because Regazzoni, the senior man by age and experience, almost won the Championship while Lauda the apprentice finished fourth. The natural order had been observed.

Leo de Graffenried was one of those close to Regazzoni. 'He was like my brother, if you want. We were both Swiss. The language was French when I worked with Alain Prost, never anything but English with Niki but with Clay always Italian, always, always. Never in French. We were always laughing and joking in Italian.

'I first met him in 1973 when he rejoined Ferrari and I was working for Philip Morris. I'd been with them since 1972. My first job, because of speaking Italian, was with Lancia – we did a contract with them. Then afterwards I was told to go to Formula 1. "We have two drivers joining Ferrari, and Marlboro will do personal contracts with them – Niki and Clay." I'd known about him

That weekend I stood around that orange Lola for a long time in the paddock when Clay was getting fitted in and warming the car up. I had a cheap roll of Russian colour film and used it all taking photos of him in the car. Afterwards, I never got the pictures developed because I felt the quality was probably poor and all the pictures pretty much the same. How I regret it now, when I think back to the little money I saved …'

The last word ought to go to Tim Parnell. 'Regazzoni was a man's man. I found him in that vein. One of his downfalls was perhaps women, but there we are. Clay looked like a real man, didn't he? A tough character. He had a charm which captivated women and there was also the way he spoke. He could speak Italian, French and English, couldn't he? We never had any problem talking. As a race driver he was terrific, absolutely terrific. He wasn't bothered who he was racing with or against, he'd give it his lot.

'The amazing thing was he was always ever so pleased to see me in the years after he'd left and we'd always talk about certain things. A lot of the drivers later on only pass a casual word to you but Clay would talk for ages. I always felt he really *was* so pleased to see me. We'd laugh and joke, especially about Big Lou. He'd *always* do that.

'What was his relationship with Big Lou? Well, one day it was good and one day it was bad. Big Lou was a strange character, he really was. His commercial side was absolutely nil, although if a since when he was in Formula 2, let's say. I was always following motor sport, and he knew my father.[7] They were very close friends. I was only a young boy at that time.

'For me he was a talented driver like Siffert, if you want. He was, as my father always said, a gentleman driver.'

That was, of course, in the sense of the pre-war amateur motivated by the ethos of racing and risk and danger and adventure. In those days only gentlemen did it, with rare exceptions (like the Mercedes driver Hermann Lang, who'd been a mechanic, about which autocratic team-mate Manfred von Brauchitsch mocked him).

Surveying the 1974 season, Peter Lyons wrote in *Autocourse* that Regazzoni was 'demonstrably *not* the best driver in Formula 1; he got himself into too many difficulties to claim that, but he was consistent.'

This is a nice and subtle point because the gentleman amateur would always get himself into too many difficulties but only hard professionals would achieve consistency. The endearing aspect is that Regazzoni managed to do both simultaneously.

In those days English was not as dominant or as all-pervasive as it is now, and that lead to a certain isolation of groups. John Watson was in his first full season, with Brabham. 'I never really knew Clay. We'd say hello. When I did get to know him a bit through Formula 1 he was a Ferrari driver, primarily Italian-speaking with a little bit of English. The people that he was close to and the people he mixed with were people like Jacques Laffite. Maybe Clay spoke French. I don't know. I was more the Anglo-Saxon who'd mix with the Swedes and the Brits as they were, the Germans – the Latin group of drivers stuck more to their own kind.

'For example, there's a place called Bareloche, which is over in the west of Argentina in the Andes and apparently it's like going to Bavaria. The mountains are wonderful, they've got a great lake, wonderful fishing. When we went to South

Moving to third place in France and only four points behind Lauda, leading the 1974 Championship. (LAT)

America, Laffite would frequently go there with some of his mates and Clay would go along as well.'

In fact, one of the Germans – Jochen Mass – did go with the Regazzoni group, if that's what it can be called. 'I've got some very nice pictures of him because in those days I liked him a lot. Laffite, Regazzoni, Depailler – we chartered boats occasionally, once in the Caribbean and once in Hawaii. So we sailed around in small boats and we knew each other quite well. He was a great, great, great character, a great man and a delight to be with. If ever there was a gentleman and a very wonderful person – a wonderful human being – that was Regga. I remember him on the deck and Laffite and Depailler having a gun and shooting at something in the air in Hawaii when we sailed the boat. I remember picnics and things like that. It was great.'

Simon Taylor, journalist and broadcaster, felt that 'in Regazzoni's day as a Ferrari Formula 1 driver, certainly to the English journalists he always seemed to be slightly aloof. I'm sure he got on very well with the Italian and Swiss journalists. It might have been language – I don't even know what his English was like. In those days things were very different. We didn't have endless press conferences. Nowadays it is not possible for a driver to be self-effacing or aloof because he is constantly put into a situation where he has to talk at press conferences, and he has to learn English.'

A strong beginning: Peterson (Lotus) pole from Regazzoni in Argentina, Hulme (McLaren) winning from Lauda, Regazzoni third. Fittipaldi (Texaco) took pole in Brazil, Lauda on the second row, Regazzoni the fourth. In the race Lauda retired early (broken wing) but Regazzoni worked his way up to second behind Fittipaldi. In South Africa, Lauda took the first Grand Prix pole of his life (Regazzoni third row) and 'dominated' – his word – part of a Grand Prix for the first time in his life. Eventually the ignition failed and Regazzoni didn't finish either, oil pressure. Reutemann (Brabham) won.

It gave an intriguing Championship leader board: Regazzoni 10 points, Hulme, Fittipaldi and Reutemann 9, Lauda 6. It would become more intriguing still.

Lauda took pole in Spain and won – from Regazzoni. Regazzoni took pole in Belgium from Jody Scheckter (Tyrrell), Lauda on the second row. This was – astonishingly – only the fourth pole of Regazzoni's career. He led to lap 39 when, lapping backmarkers, he went wide. He'd finish fourth, Lauda second.

Fittipaldi 22, Lauda 21, Regazzoni 19, Hulme 11.

Lauda took pole at Monaco (1m 26.3s) from Regazzoni (1m 26.6s), who led until he spun at *Rascasse* after 20 laps. That let Lauda through and he ought to have won but the ignition failed. Neither Ferrari finished in Sweden but they dominated Holland from the front row, Lauda winning from Regazzoni.

Fittipaldi 31, Lauda 30, Regazzoni 28, Scheckter 23. Lauda took pole at Dijon for the French Grand Prix but Peterson won it, Lauda second, Regazzoni third. Lauda 36, Regazzoni 32, Fittipaldi 31, Scheckter 26.

Lauda took pole at Brands Hatch, Regazzoni on the fourth row but he made one of his starts, Peterson attacking and attacking. Punctures sorted that out, making Regazzoni fourth at the end, Lauda – who'd led from the start to six laps from the end before his puncture – fifth.

Lauda took pole at the Nürburgring from Regazzoni, but now a sequence of mistakes punished him. A wet day, and the mechanics pushed his car from the garage to the pits on his race tyres rather than a set of wets. One tyre was damaged and had to be changed. It would require care until it was scrubbed in. On the parade lap drizzle fell, forcing Lauda to go so slowly that he couldn't scrub it in. He confessed[8] that impatience consumed him because, if Regazzoni made one of those starts and got away, Lauda wouldn't see him again. That led to Lauda making a bad start, Scheckter ahead and Regazzoni leading. Lauda challenged Scheckter, drew up, but under braking swerved into him.

Scheckter was able to continue but not hold Regazzoni, who beat him by 52.2 seconds.

Gareth Rees was there and 'lucky to be there for, surely, one of his greatest performances when he led every lap after Lauda went off. Yes, the Ferrari 312B3 was a great car in 1974, but only a special driver could win so convincingly at the 'Ring. For me, one of the hallmarks of Regazzoni's career was a fast and steady style with only few mistakes.'

Regazzoni 44 points, Scheckter 41, Lauda 38, Fittipaldi 37, four races left.

Reutemann seized the Austrian Grand Prix from the front row (Lauda pole, Regazzoni the fourth row) and led every lap with, at moments, Lauda second and then Regazzoni who finally drifted back with a rear wheel problem that forced him into the pits. He finished fifth.

In Italy Maria Pia, Alessia and Gian Maria made what was described as a 'rare appearance.'[9] They saw him move into second place behind Lauda by lap 5, the lead by lap 30 and then have an engine problem. Neither Ferrari finished.

LEFT *Faces of the race: Regazzoni will be fourth at Brands Hatch but the Championship was tightening.* (courtesy Gareth Rees)

A pleasant Italian, Giacomo Tansini, was in the crowd. After the race he managed to get to the pits and noticed Regazzoni, at the door of the Ferrari hospitality area, discussing with di Montezemolo what had gone wrong. Then Regazzoni walked by and Tansini asked him for an autograph. Regazzoni signed a cap and gave it to him – which impressed Tansini, who thought he might still be irritable (and irritated) because he hadn't finished the race. Nobody knows what the future brings, but Tansini would be one of the last people Regazzoni ever spoke to.

Regazzoni 46, Scheckter 45, Fittipaldi 43, Lauda 38, two races left.

Of the 15 races drivers could count their 13 best finishes, but none of the contenders would be affected by that. It meant they all went to Mosport for the Canadian Grand Prix with a chance.

One spectator, Craig Burkett, remembered the Friday – a sunny day – like this: 'Standing on the outside of turn 10, across from pit-in, my friend and I were watching the afternoon F1 practice, this being our first exposure to Formula 1.

'Clay Regazzoni in the Ferrari 312B3 came through the Mosport esses and into the short chute to 10 when his brakes locked up and the Ferrari ploughed through two rows of catch fence and hit the embankment head-on, the nose buried into the dirt and the rear of the car launched into the air at about a 50-degree angle headed right for our position. We're getting a birds-eye view of the 312B3 heading right for us when it suddenly lost momentum and slammed back down on the rear wheels. Regazzoni's head/helmet slammed with such force into the Ferrari's airbox that it cracked the fibreglass of the airbox … without hesitation Regazzoni was unharnessed and out of the car and headed back across the track and into the pit area … one hell of a sight to behold on our first day … welcome to F1!'[10]

Fittipaldi took pole from Lauda, Regazzoni on the third row. Lauda led to lap 68, when he came upon earth and stones strewn across the track by a car that had ploughed off when its suspension failed. Now Lauda went off, so that Fittipaldi took the win, Regazzoni second after repulsing a sustained attack from Peterson. The Championship was at last clear. Going to Watkins Glen, Fittipaldi and Regazzoni both had 52 points and Scheckter 45. Lauda could no longer win it.

The tremendous win in Germany from Sheckter and Reutemann, which burst the Championship open. Now he was leading. (LAT)

Reutemann took pole from Hunt's Hesketh, Fittipaldi on the fourth row alongside Watson, Regazzoni immediately behind Watson.

'Luca di Montezemolo came over to me,' Watson remembers. 'He recognised that I had a pretty damned quick car that weekend and potentially it had the pace to beat Regazzoni. He leant over the cockpit. "John, John, can we rely on you to help Clay *blah blah blah*?" and I said we'd see what happened. Really, Luca was just doing his job. He could say "Clay, don't worry about Watson, he's sorted out." Clay's car looked undriveable on the opening lap – I don't know why – and it didn't become an event. He didn't challenge Fittipaldi at all and Emerson won the Championship.'

Regazzoni had a problem with the front suspension and one report describes the Ferrari as wallowing. He completed the opening lap seventh and drifted helplessly back, despite Lauda trying to protect him. Scheckter retired on lap 45 with a fuel pipe failure and Fittipaldi moved majestically to fourth place. It was more than enough.

Lauda, who ought to have won the Championship, would correct that within a calendar year and do it twice more after that.

Regazzoni would never be so close again.

There is an interplay between team-mates which can be, and usually is, fascinating, especially if the established man finds himself co-existing with the coming man. Regazzoni, born in 1939, had now driven 44 Grands Prix for Ferrari spread over four seasons. That offered no protection, especially at Ferrari, against the coming man – Lauda, born 1949, who felt that increasingly Regazzoni found himself 'a little in the shadow of the Lauda/Montezemolo pairing.'[11]

Unsurprisingly, Regazzoni didn't see it like that, if only because proud, competitive men rarely do. Across 1975 Lauda asserted himself in a methodical, logical way which some compared to a computer – an analogy he sometimes used himself. All *Autocourse* could summon when the season ended was a cryptic 'it is still too early to write off Clay Regazzoni as a has-been.'

It is, however, time to examine the Regazzoni-Lauda relationship.

Franco Gozzi says this: 'Clay was a good driver but unlucky because Lauda came. So many times I told Clay "Stop going round and round – you can learn from the *piccolo* [little] Austrian," but Clay would not accept that.'

Watkins Glen, the crown so near and so far away. (LAT)

Years later Gozzi would do the same thing with two very different Ferrari drivers. 'I can hardly tell you how many times I said to Jean Alesi "Don't try and race with Alain Prost all the time, you stay with Prost, see what he is doing." Impossible for Alesi to do it! Sometimes you can have the opposite to this: a man like Barrichello. He was happy to be there driving a Ferrari, happy to take the money, happy to win sometimes.

'I remember something Enzo said. "It is not very difficult to become World Champion, it is very difficult to remain World Champion." Clay could have been a champion but to do that he should have accepted Niki Lauda in the development of the car and then beat Lauda during the races: he couldn't do that. Today is the age of the computers but then *Lauda* was a computer. He knew you could go slowly and still win. And another thing about Clay: people like Lauda and Schumacher, if something is not good they say *OK, I can't win this race so I'll win the next one.* For some people – like Clay, like Alesi – it's always now and there is no next week. If you lose that possibility of accepting good days and bad days it is very difficult to be champion.

How an artist remembers the 1975 Ferrari, travelling fast. (courtesy Juan Carlos Ferrigno)

'In Italy there are some people who say Lauda did not help Clay and Clay did not help Lauda. It all began when they touched in the German Grand Prix on the first lap. After that there was a big respect by Lauda for Regazzoni. In my opinion it was not the same for Clay with Lauda. Don't forget that Clay was comparatively old alongside Lauda and that's why he had the pressure to win, to do something now – because it would become much more difficult as time went on. Lauda was more sure because he *did* know how to wait from race to race. Once in Sweden, he told me "I saw Vittorio Brambilla. He was really mad. I will win another day. I don't take the risk of going near him." This is intelligence: to understand who is prepared to do anything on the track and who is not.[12]

'One thing more. I heard Clay on the Swiss television saying that probably it was the factory that was more for Lauda. Not true. I told him. I said "A team has two possibilities to win and you do whatever is possible for both".'

Subsequently Lauda said: 'He taught me to love life. He was a friend, a brother. I learnt about the art of witty remarks but also about the risks of going to the gaming table or having a taste in beautiful women. We went out often when we were driving together for Ferrari but I was shy. It was teaching me what to do. I learnt the taste of life from Clay and after my accident at the Nürburgring [in 1976] what he taught me became even more important, because if there was a talent in him superior to other men it was thinking positively.

'At Ferrari we had also some problems but he was straight. We also had some quarrels, but I have always seen this as a loyalty thing [Regazzoni instinctively loyal to Ferrari].'

In 1977, in his book *For The Record*, Lauda wrote: 'We were never real friends, but I valued him. He is so perfectly the type of racing driver: women; small, rough and stocky; moustache. He is a typical cinema champion, such as people sometimes think of as being the real thing. He is still one of the old guard drivers. Nonsense, of course; Clay just happens to look like that by chance.'

Regazzoni did not read this until January 1981 but when he did he felt his heart beating abnormally fast. He wrote 'I suddenly understood the man and his character. Having driven alongside him for four years, I had divined certain things but without looking at them profoundly. I read and re-read certain chapters without believing my eyes, without understanding how he who believed himself so intelligent and superior

Luca di Montezemolo, one of the driving forces at Ferrari. (LAT)

can attach such presumption, such an insult to one close to him.'

What drove Regazzoni crazy was Lauda claiming that, without him, Ferrari wouldn't have been able to win the championship in 1975.

What drove him equally crazy was being reduced to the cliché of 'women; small, rough and stocky; moustache'. He pointed out that twice he had opened doors for Lauda, at BRM and Ferrari, and never sought to make Lauda feel grateful or even spoken about it at all.

In 1986 Lauda returned to his theme: 'Off duty, I always got on incredibly well with Regazzoni. We led a pretty hectic life. To the Italian public he was the original macho man, a no-holds-barred womaniser, and I must say that it was anything but dull being in his company. I have never since had a team-mate whom I hung around with so much after hours. He was honest and direct. You could tell what was going through his mind by the

Treasured moment in 1975: Regazzoni wins Monza by 16.6 seconds from Emerson Fittipaldi (McLaren) with Lauda third. (LAT)

expression on his face: when something didn't suit him, he let you know at once.'[13]

'My father wasn't a calculator,' Gian Maria says. 'If he had been he'd have won more but he wouldn't have been Clay Regazzoni. He said Lauda was the first political driver. The others, they did what they had to do at the track and then they went to the hotel, had fun. Lauda would stay at the circuit choosing his tyres because in those days the tyres weren't exactly the same.'

Shorthand covers the 1975 season – until the final race, which developed into a wonderful, improbable and enraging Regazzoni panorama – and demonstrates how Lauda *was* taking control.

John Watson says: 'When Regazzoni and Lauda were both at Ferrari they did a fair bit of "sheet time" [looking at the performance sheets] but because Niki had a very analytical mind he'd go in, do the job, have a quick *douche* [shower] and was standing outside Clay's door saying "Come on Clay, it's time to go." Clay was still going through the sheets. That was a typical Latin male.'

Here is the shorthand, building on what Watson has just said. Qualifying is in brackets, then where they finished:

Argentina	Lauda	(4)	6
	Regazzoni	(8)	4
Brazil	Lauda	(4)	5
	Regazzoni	(5)	4
South Africa	Lauda	(4)	5
	Regazzoni	(9)	did not finish, throttle
Spain	Lauda	(P)	did not finish, accident
	Regazzoni	(2)	running not classified
Monaco	Lauda	(P)	1
	Regazzoni	(6)	did not finish, crash
Belgium	Lauda	(P)	1
	Regazzoni	(4)	5
Sweden	Lauda	(5)	1
	Regazzoni	(12)	3
Holland	Lauda	(P)	2
	Regazzoni	(2)	3
France	Lauda	(P)	1
	Regazzoni	(9)	did not finish, engine
Britain	Lauda	(3)	8
	Regazzoni	(4)	13
Germany	Lauda	(P)	3
	Regazzoni	(5)	did not finish, engine
Austria	Lauda	(P)	6
	Regazzoni	(5)	7

Breaking the sequence here, 16 drivers went to Dijon to contest the non-Championship Swiss Grand Prix. Lauda didn't but Regazzoni did, putting the Ferrari on the second row and winning.

'We were always joking during the Grands Prix and we were together when he did things away from Formula 1 in the nights,' de Graffenried says. 'He did a lot of things during the night. We did funny things together. I always remember the Grand Prix in Dijon. Aleardo Buzzi and Jacques Deschenaux [compiler of the *Marlborough Grand Prix Guide* and TV presenter] and a Swiss journalist for *Le Matin* in Lausanne created the "Cardinal Paf". You have a dinner and you have to do many things in the correct way. When you do them wrong you have to drink a full glass of wine.'

You get the idea: a sequence of minor infringements and you've the equivalent of several bottles inside you.

'So we went to the "Cardinal Paf" party and we played. That night Clay was completely pissed and he was due to test at Modena. Next morning I left in my car and he passed me with his Ferrari – I couldn't believe it, the way he had been and the way he was driving. At that time the speed limits were not so important and, anyway, if you have the name Clay Regazzoni it would be easier for him than me should you get caught. I called him in Modena and said "Did you get there safely? Because you were driving *quite* fast." He said "I had a little problem with my head".'

| Italy | Lauda | (P) | 3 |
| | Regazzoni | (2) | 1 |

Regazzoni's father was at Monza and evidently celebrated the victory by hugging everybody he could reach.

| USA | Lauda | (P) | 1 |
| | Regazzoni | (11) | withdrawn |

Lauda won the Championship at Monza and led at Watkins Glen, Fittipaldi tracking him. Regazzoni ran eleventh, rose to tenth but on lap 5 ran into the McLaren of Jochen Mass. He had to pit for a new nose cone and resumed a lap down.

Lauda and Fittipaldi, clear of everyone else, came upon Fittipaldi's brother Wilson (Copersucar), who briefly held Lauda back so Emerson could draw up. By lap 18 Lauda had reached Regazzoni, who let him through a lap later and then blatantly blocked Fittipaldi by weaving.

That meant the gap from Fittipaldi to Lauda went out to 4.4 seconds on lap 20, 5.6 on lap 21 and 10.4 on lap 23. During these laps Fittipaldi was brandishing his fist and blue flags were being waved, signalling Regazzoni to get out of the way. At lap 23 the Clerk of the Course, Berdie Martin,

held out a rolled up black flag to Regazzoni. On lap 24 Regazzoni finally let Fittipaldi through but did not pit, so next lap Martin held out the black flag unfurled.

Don Nichols (of him more later) remembers that Martin 'black-flagged Clay and Clay continued,

James Hunt has arrived, winning the Dutch Grand Prix. Lauda looks pleased and Regazzoni looks thirsty. (LAT)

A star, everywhere he went. (courtesy Gareth Rees)

and Berdie – who's a kind of direct person – walked out on the circuit and virtually hit Clay on his helmet. Well, it looked like he tried to, in order to stop him racing and come in for a lecture. That made Clay what he was. He was to racing what Ilie Nastase was to tennis.'[14]

Regazzoni came in to where a group of officials stood. Di Montezemolo was there, enraged that anyone outside Ferrari had dared signal the Ferrari in. He began shaking the officials but didn't know which one he wanted. A McLaren team member helpfully pointed out Martin and di Montezemolo took a swing at him. Then he was pulled off.

What Martin wanted to do was lecture Regazzoni about ignoring the blue flags and caution him about doing it again before allowing him to rejoin.

One report suggests that once Regazzoni was out of the car and walking to the garage someone from the crowd took a swing at *him* and he took a swing back – or maybe even threw his helmet at him. The people at Ferrari applauded him warmly (presumably for his driving rather than his swinging, although probably both).

Regazzoni went back out but four laps later di Montezemolo signalled him in again and withdrew him from the race as a protest at what had happened. Di Montezemolo was saying *I am running this team and I am the only person who brings a Ferrari in.* Later, and perhaps having had time to cool down, he offered his reasoning: 'The whole episode must have upset Regazzoni and it wasn't a good idea to have a driver going round in that frame of mind.'

Gareth Rees likes 'to recall Watkins Glen when Regga's out-of-form Ferrari was being lapped by Fittipaldi', and the fist-waving. 'When he was asked for his reaction after the race, Clay explained that the McLaren could have passed at any time, but whenever Fittipaldi waved his fist, he stretched his body and that caused his right foot to lift off the accelerator …'

Into 1976, the power shift within Ferrari towards Lauda had become evident to Regazzoni, who complained about all sorts of insinuations within the team. If he was uninterested in the politics of the medieval court, the politics were not uninterested in him.

Writing about 1976 always means two intertwined factors: Lauda's crash at the Nürburgring and James Hunt's championship. Everything else seems curiously irrelevant and difficult to remember. I am afraid that includes Regazzoni. Here it is set out as the previous season, with qualifying in brackets, then where they finished:

Brazil	Lauda	(2)	1
	Regazzoni	(4)	7
South Africa	Lauda	(2)	1
	Regazzoni	(10)	did not finish, engine
USA West	Lauda	(4)	2
	Regazzoni	(P)	1

Long Beach was a commanding victory in a weekend that belonged entirely to Regazzoni. The grid: Regazzoni (1m 23.099s), Patrick Depailler (Tyrrell, 1m 23.292s), Hunt (McLaren, 1m 23.420s), Lauda (1m 23.647s) – although, because the drivers had not been to Long Beach before, they were about to make an interesting discovery as they ventured out to practise. Ronnie Peterson took the Theodore March out immediately, Regazzoni clinging to him. Completing their first lap they worked up big speed along the pit-lane straight and found that the 90° turn at the end of it really *was* 90°. Peterson went straight on down the escape road, Regazzoni *still* clinging to him, and they were soon joined by an assortment of others.

No such mistakes in the race: Regazzoni led every lap and Lauda needed five laps before he reached second place, but he'd flat-spotted[15] his tyres, making the Ferrari vibrate. Regazzoni pushed the gap out to 12 seconds and circled very comfortably to the end. It was his fourth win for Ferrari, and his last.

This did not disturb the advance of Lauda, who left Long Beach with 24 points, Depailler 10, Regazzoni 9. Hunt only had 6.

Spain	Lauda	(2)	2
	Regazzoni	(5)	11
Belgium	Lauda	(P)	1
	Regazzoni	(2)	2
Monaco	Lauda	(P)	1
	Regazzoni	(2)	did not finish, accident
Sweden	Lauda	(5)	3
	Regazzoni	(11)	6
France	Lauda	(2)	did not finish, crankshaft
	Regazzoni	(4)	did not finish, crankshaft
Britain	Lauda	(P)	2
	Regazzoni	(4)	disqualified

his right and behind because of the grid's stagger. This was Lauda's choice because, in the surge and lunge to Paddock Hill Bend – the adverse-camber dipping right-hander – Lauda calculated that, since the track was slightly banked from left to right, being on the left and therefore higher might give him an advantage into Paddock. Lauda had Andretti in the Lotus directly behind him, Regazzoni directly behind Hunt.

Hunt made 'my usual lousy start' while Lauda accelerated away quite normally, but Regazzoni – typically, as we have seen – could make a car into a rocket from any grid. He went to mid-track and 'sliced' back so that now Hunt had the Ferrari in front of him. It gave him the inside line into Paddock but to claim the corner he had to get there before Lauda.

He didn't.

These are perilous milliseconds and men high on adrenalin are trying to ride them. These are perilous millimetres: the unleashing of almost unimaginable power, the brutal acceleration, the cars a sudden mosaic of movement towards Paddock Hill which is so close and falling away like a cliff face.

Hunt felt Regazzoni's attempt on the inside was 'ridiculous' because Lauda was *already* turning in to Paddock Hill.

Lauda felt that Regazzoni trying to pass on the inside was 'simply not possible'. Because of the adverse camber, if Lauda had been able to corkscrew away from Regazzoni he'd have gone off the track and, as he'd say, into the fields.

Regazzoni felt that if Lauda had *not* come across, the two Ferraris could have passed through Paddock Hill quite normally and then enjoyed themselves. Instead, he claimed Lauda squeezed him.

Subsequently, Lauda and Regazzoni exchanged fire over centimetres rather than the millimetres. Lauda said if a car is even 10cm behind, it is *behind*. Regazzoni said he searched and searched for a photograph that would show he was those 10cm in front. He couldn't find one.

Regazzoni's car touched Lauda's. Lauda went sideways, Regazzoni slewed round and Hunt sailed helplessly into him. Hunt was launched and landed in the middle of great mayhem. The race was stopped and Regazzoni went to the re-start in the spare. For a while it seemed Hunt had been excluded: hence the threatened riot.

He won the race and was then excluded.

So was Regazzoni.

In simple terms, the rules had been interpreted and reinterpreted since the crash at Paddock Hill, there were grey areas, and everybody who could

Pole at Long Beach, 1976, and he'd lead every lap. (LAT)

He was never on the pace in Spain, finishing three laps down. (LAT)

This British Grand Prix was so riven with controversy that at one stage the police feared a riot after a crash at the start – which widened the growing distance between Lauda and Regazzoni.

The geography of the grid, and the topography of Brands Hatch, were central. Lauda's pole position was on the left, Hunt on the front row to

played politics. The crash, however, did carry consequences, because Regazzoni came to believe it was instrumental in ending his Ferrari career.

Lauda recorded[16] how *il capo* became enraged by what Regazzoni had done at Brands Hatch and even more enraged because, while driving to Modena, he had seen some girls wearing Clay Regazzoni jeans with the famous Ferrari prancing horse on their bottoms.

Lauda also recorded that *il capo*, Piero Lardi (his illegitimate son), Forghieri and senior team member Daniel Audetto met and *il capo* didn't even want Regazzoni in the next Grand Prix, Germany. Regazzoni was permitted to drive, however, provided he was on his best behaviour.

He did not discover any of this until he read Lauda's book some five years later.

| Germany | Lauda | (2) | did not finish, crash |
| | Regazzoni | (5) | 9 |

The Lauda mythology began at the Nürburgring, and it's a story often told: the fire, the hospital, the Last Rites, the recovery. Ferrari did not go to Austria, the next race. Regazzoni played tennis and played such a violent shot, bending, that the spare ball he had in his pocket broke a rib. Cortisone took care of that. Ferrari did send one car to Holland and Regazzoni put it on the third row. He finished second to Hunt but started to complain that the team – literally – were not occupying themselves with him.

Lauda returned for the Italian Grand Prix, immediately deepening the mythology and increasing it further when he finished fourth. Who remembers Regazzoni second to Ronnie Peterson?

Canada	Lauda	(6)	8
	Regazzoni	(12)	6
USA	Lauda	(5)	3
	Regazzoni	(14)	7
Japan	Lauda	(3)	withdrew
	Regazzoni	(7)	5

More Lauda mythology, because in stormy weather he did withdraw, although Hunt still needed to be third. He got there but had to overtake Regazzoni to do it. One journalist said provocatively to Franco Gozzi that if Regazzoni had kept Hunt behind, Lauda would have been champion. That is dubious, to put it mildly, first because the Grand Prix descended into very great chaos with few drivers or teams (especially Hunt) having the remotest idea of the positions – their own and everybody else's – and whatever Clay

Regazzoni did or did not feel about *il capo* and Ferrari, whatever he did or did not feel about Niki Lauda, he didn't let anybody through if he could help it: not in Formula 3, not in Formula 2, not in Grands Prix, not in sports cars, not on every *autostrada* in Italy and not, as we shall see, trucks in the Sahara.

Lauda, playful at Zolder. He could afford to be. He'd won. (LAT)

Regazzoni, concentrating at Monaco but it didn't help. He crashed. (LAT)

Either at Watkins Glen or Fuji – Regazzoni couldn't remember which – Forghieri had led him to understand that he would not be with the team in 1977. Carlos Reutemann was coming. Lauda claims he made a determined effort to change *il capo*'s mind but it couldn't be done.

By now Giacomo Tansini had become a friend and he illustrates the difference between Regazzoni and Lauda. 'I started to go to Maranello and we'd have dinner in the evening. You couldn't do this with Niki Lauda. He was different. He'd test and go to his hotel. Clay would be in the bar having an aperitif and chatting with people. He loved champagne! We became very close but then Clay left Ferrari and we lost contact. He was a very human man. When somebody said to him "Look at these little children in hospital, they'd like to meet you," he'd go there even if he had an official engagement.'

Evidently (according to Lauda) when Ferrari fired Regazzoni they gave a wonderful, theatrical performance – *we don't want to stand in your way, Clay* – so convincing that even some of the actors in it didn't know what was really happening.

Gareth Rees, watching the racing so intently, gives a neat summing-up. 'Apart from the lost year in the Marlboro-BRM team, which started so promisingly with pole and leading in Argentina, and then headed steadily downhill from that time on, Regga seemed the ideal Ferrari driver in the period from 1971 to 1976 – it was the perfect match.

'First with Ickx, and later with Lauda, he appeared to be the best second driver a team could wish for. Always near the front, he kept popping up to win the odd race, and even went to the last race of 1974 with a chance of taking the championship. How different history's perception of Clay would have been if the cards had fallen his way at Watkins Glen. For the purity of Formula 1, maybe it was right and proper that Fittipaldi took the title, because Clay wasn't quite *that* good, and Emerson was. Perhaps it's also equally true that he never wanted the title *that* badly, either.

'Occasionally there were some embarrassing moments, like the first lap collisions with team-mate Lauda in Barcelona '75 and at Brands '76. I can't say for sure, but I always felt that Regga was the one who should have avoided the collisions, although Lauda never bad-mouthed him publicly. I like to think it was because he, in common with others, liked Clay too much and forgave him easily.'

Aleardo Buzzi, so influential through Marlboro, gives another summing-up. 'Clay was a very happy man, very natural. He was not like the drivers of today – he enjoyed life, also. He was good looking

and [*chuckle*] … yes! He was a wonderful driver. As a matter of fact, after he left Ferrari he was driving better and better. He was mature. It's a pity I couldn't have had him at McLaren but it was not possible. I had wanted him to come to McLaren from Ferrari to replace Ronnie Peterson, but Teddy Mayer didn't want him and of course the final decision was the one taken by the head of the team. Teddy Mayer didn't like Clay at all.'

Ah, the magic roundabout.

John Watson anticipated driving the 1977 season with the Penske team. 'Four o'clock in the morning the phone rings. I didn't know where I was. I picked up the phone. Roger Penske told me in these early hours of the morning that with great regret he had decided to pull his Formula 1 team. He was going to wrap it up. The reasons are irrelevant now.

'Talk about being winded. I'm lying in bed trying to put it into focus. I went back to sleep again and first thing in the morning I went down to Penske's in Poole. Heinz Hofer was the team manager at that time. We sat down and said "What the hell is going on? What has Roger done? Is this recoverable?" Heinz might have taken over the

team himself but he probably didn't have the funding to do it. There was a drive available at Shadow, still a drive at Brabham with the Alfa Romeo engine – Reutemann had buggered off [to Ferrari, of course].'

Watson's plight was put to Bernie Ecclestone, who initially refused to believe Penske had pulled out and thought the people telling him that were taking the mickey. Ecclestone said to Watson "I've got Martini[17] on my back. They want me to take Clay. Come up and see me." So I went to Nick Brittan who helped me with my management stuff, then he and I bowled up to see Bernie at his flat overlooking the Thames. Bernie said "I've got Clay coming over" – but he made a decision: *I'll have Watson now*. He got me for buttons because I didn't have any negotiating position. So in 24 hours I went from being a Penske contracted driver to signing a deal with Bernie, but because the deal wasn't concluded until nine or ten o'clock at night it was too late to contact Clay to tell him not to come.

'So Bernie rang Herbie Blash [of Brabham and a confidant] and asked him to get to Heathrow, meet Clay, apologise, and say "Terribly sorry but

Bernie's signed up John Watson. That's the way it is." So Clay turned up at Heathrow and was met by Herbie. Poor Clay – but I was looking after myself, not Clay. Clay had to get on the next plane back. I don't think he held that against me.'

Watson concludes that 'it just gives you an indication of how Grand Prix racing was – and frankly still is.'

Ah, the magic roundabout.

Regazzoni's Grand Prix career had four more seasons to run, and before each one of them the roundabout would turn again.

Notes: 1. Autosport; 2. Ibid; 3. www.autoblog.com/2006/12/16/rip-clay-regazzoni-1939-2006/; 4. Autosport; 5. For The Record; 6. Autopassion; 7. Emmanuel de Graffenried, known as Toulo, a Swiss who raced before and after the Second World War; 8. For The Record; 9. Autocourse; 10. www.northamericanmotoring.com/forums/showthread.php?p=1288997; 11. To Hell And Back; 12. The implication being that you didn't ever mess around with either of the Brambillas; 13. To Hell And Back; 14. Ilie Nastase, the Rumanian tennis player, became a 'character' as his career declined, no doubt in order to compensate for the decline; 15. Flat-spotted means that if you hit the brakes hard the wheels lock and that skims rubber off the tyres where they've locked. These flat spots can make the car difficult to drive afterwards; 16. For The Record; 17. Martini were then a leading sponsor.

The crash which almost led to a riot at Brands Hatch. You can't miss Regazzoni – he's the one moving against oncoming traffic. The drivers couldn't miss him either. (LAT)

CHAPTER 4 ————————

SHADOW LANDS

'The first time I met Clay was in a hotel in London where we made a deal,' Mo Nunn says. 'It was October or November of 1976. The guy who introduced me to him was named Chuck Jones, a Californian who had a Formula 5000 race. Brian Redman used to do it. Clay drove for him in, I think, Riverside. Chuck said "He's the guy we should get," and he made the arrangement.'

Jones, who moved from dragsters in the 1950s to involvement in many facets of motor sport, joined the Ensign team in 1975 to handle what has been described as driver development.

We have met Nunn before, of course, as a racer, but his subsequent career is much more interesting. He began to make Formula 3 cars and in 1973 Rikki von Opel, an heir to the car company of that name, commissioned him to do a Formula 1 car. Von Opel soon departed but Nunn secured sponsorship from a Dutch company and ran Gijs van Lennep. In Germany he finished sixth – Ensign's first Grand Prix points. In 1976 Nunn ran Amon.

Regazzoni had 'lost the Ferrari drive at this stage. We told Clay we had Castrol sponsorship, which we'd agreed with Castrol, and they either wanted Jacky Ickx or Regazzoni in that order. If we could get one of those two drivers the sponsorship was ours. I met Clay and we were negotiating. He'd been driving for Ferrari and now here was our little team – it was our first introduction to someone who we thought was a

RIGHT *The most extraordinary weekend, 1978, the split between Monaco and Indianapolis – and he didn't qualify for the Grand Prix. Here he is trying to.* (LAT)

racer. What I remember is that Clay didn't think we had Castrol sponsorship because Jackie Oliver [of the Shadow team] was trying to sign him up and Oliver told him they had Castrol. So what I did was, I got Castrol on the phone and passed it to Clay and then we made the deal.

'When I shook hands with him on the deal I looked into his eyes. This is the first time it ever happened to me: it was like I could see straight through him. I said to Chuck afterwards "I had the strangest feeling when I shook hands with Clay and looked in his eyes." It was something I've

Mo Nunn, who knew he had a racer on his hands. This is Austria, 1977. (LAT)

never had with anyone else. I don't know. Something happened that I can't explain. His eyes were very deep.

'Then started a very enjoyable time in my racing career, where we had a driver who we knew *was* a racer.

'We had the same four engines. When Rikki von Opel left and took the sponsors with him, we had Chris Amon's money. He sold his shares in a garage in Australia and gave me the £20,000 and we bought four engines off Bernie for £5,000 each. They are the ones we ran while we were in Formula 1. We ran the same four engines time after time. I was certainly still running them in 1980.

'Clay was a very easy-going guy, wanted to do everything for the team, never took any money. He said "Put the money in the team." He signed a two-year deal and we never paid him a dollar. All the money we earned went into the team. He didn't even take any prize money or contract money! We had Tissot as a sponsor, wasn't a big sponsor. I'm pretty sure it was around £60,000. What was Clay living on? I saw his place in Switzerland, in Lugano, and they owned a whole street and they lived on top of it in a beautiful penthouse. I don't know what he'd earned in the past but he seemed to be financially OK. However, it is absolutely unique for any driver to say "Look, put my money back into the team".'

Nigel Roebuck remembers 'it was January or February 1977 and absolutely freezing. *Autosport* wanted me to do an interview with him and, as you did in those days, I just rang him. No PRs or anything like that. He said "I'm going to be in London in ten days." Etienne Aigner was one of his personal sponsors and he was doing something with them in Bond Street. I was just round the corner. He said "OK, we'll do it there."

'That was what happened. I left the office on this freezing morning with my tape recorder, walked the couple of hundred yards to Bond Street, and got there when he'd just arrived. It was quite a fashionable shop – they were primarily very expensive leather goods – and full of the sort of girls who work in those shops. They were just eating out of the palm of his hand. As far as I can remember I think we finished up in the stock room. I do remember all these girls were desperate: "Is there anything, *anything*, we can do for you?" He'd say "I'd like a coffee," and they'd bring one then they'd be back five minutes later. "Like another coffee?" He really did have that attraction in spades, had tremendous charm – the sort women adored but men liked too. That was the thing. It wasn't the sort of greasy charm that would make most men go *ugh!* He was just a lovely bloke.'

The headline to the interview captured everything: FOR ME, THE THING IS TO RACE. Regazzoni reviewed his career and with some candour. Here is a sample, verbatim. 'Whenever I crash another car, Regazzoni crash another car. What about Peterson, Brambilla …? All drivers crash, you know, but always if I am involved in a crash with someone they say it is my fault. It's like everyone say Niki is a computer, Niki is a computer. Niki is *not* a computer, no? But when people start to say Niki is a computer, now he is a computer in all the life! I am a crazy man, so now a crazy man all the life, no?'

At this Regazzoni exploded in laughter.

He finished sixth in Argentina and they went to Brazil. 'We got a sponsor – well, he got it,' says Nunn. 'This was a wine drink. They gave Clay a car that was all painted up in their colours for him to drive to the track. He wrote it off. Coming back from the track he reached a roundabout, went straight across, hit the kerb and took the suspension off. The car just dropped to the floor on the far side. First they were angry, then they got a lot of advertising out of it so they were OK.

'On the first day he was fourth or fifth quickest and on the second day we dropped back to ninth. It was a 40 minute drive from the circuit to the Hilton in Sao Paulo. Clay came up to me, he'd got his bags and there were a couple of friends with him. He said "OK, boys, see you back at the hotel." I said "Clay, where are you going?" and he said "I go back to the hotel now." I said "I need to talk to you about the car. " He said "No, no, Morris, the car is OK, it's good." I said "Yes, Clay, but we were fourth or fifth yesterday and now we're ninth." This was only the second race we'd done with him. He came up and he put his arm around me. He said "Morris, you worry too much. I'll be fourth at the end of the first lap."

'From the grid I think he was fifth into the first corner. His starts were exciting. He was a man's racer, that's what I can say about Clay. Some guys are all nervous at the start. I remember Chris Amon was – a bit – and would lose places. Clay would always gain them.'

He was running fifth when Mass lost control of his McLaren and slewed into catch fencing, spreading some of it onto the track. Regazzoni helplessly ran into this and retired.

Nunn remembers that in South Africa Regazzoni 'turned up with two rear wings! A couple of Ferrari fabricators had started their own business and made these wings. He'd purchased a couple of them and carried them as hand baggage.

He arrived with a huge grin on his face and he said "Morris, look at these!" They were beautifully made compared to what we used to make by riveting the wings together. On these you couldn't see a rivet – so we fitted them.'

Nunn also remembers 'we went to a place called *Rogantino's* in Johannesburg. There was a little group in there with a drum. Clay and Mario Andretti took the instruments off them and started making just one hell of a noise. They had a banjo and Clay had that but he couldn't play! He was just making a big noise. We had a lot of fun.'

Nunn guards other memories, like 'going to a famous lobster restaurant they always went to but it was my first time. Brambilla's in one car, Clay's in another – me in that – and another with Laffite in. We were on the freeway and a local was in front of us, wouldn't get out of the way. They got one car on either side and one on the rear bumper. This guy couldn't move anywhere and the car behind – I think it was Laffite – started pushing him. It scared the guy to death.'

Nunn also remembers the team stayed at the Kyalami Ranch Hotel, a favourite for the Grand Prix drivers and international air crews flying into Johannesburg – the very same place where Regazzoni had tried to liven up Andretti but set fire to the wrong room. 'One breakfast the waiter comes round. We were just about to leave and the waiter said "Air crew?" Clay said "Yes, Alitalia!" We never paid …'

He was ninth in the race and a gearbox failure stopped him in Long Beach. In Spain he collided with Vittorio Brambilla. Regazzoni was running sixth, Brambilla seventh and a consensus developed among those watching that combative Regazzoni versus combative Brambilla, known as The Monza Gorilla, would culminate in a short, sharp shock. On lap 10 Brambilla tried a 'suicide' (*Autocourse*) move down the inside as they went through the double-apex right-hander at the end of the pit lane straight. There was another consensus at that instant: not enough room.

When, literally, the dust began to settle the watchers saw Brambilla stride over to where Regazzoni sat in the Ensign. As he strode, Brambilla began to undo the strap of his crash helmet but when he saw Regazzoni, enraged, waving his arms and shouting, he decided to keep the crash helmet on …

Regazzoni now embarked on something typically audacious. He'd drive in the Monaco Grand Prix and the following week the Indy 500 at Indianapolis in a McLaren-Offenhauser for Theodore Racing, meaning he was sponsored by Teddy Yip.[1] (Alan Jones ought to have driven the

McLaren but during testing wasn't happy and withdrew.)

The qualifying system at Indianapolis permitted this. There were four *progressive* sessions, two the weekend before Monaco and two on the Monaco weekend. If you were fast enough you could qualify in the first or second sessions and not have to go near the remaining two.

Regazzoni, of course, had no experience of an oval with its different demands and skills. He had a problem with the tyres, which, on such a circuit, he found disconcerting – average speeds were in the high 180 miles an hour. He didn't make it, and here was the audacity.

Thursday: first qualifying – Monaco.
Saturday: third qualifying – Indianapolis.
Sunday: Grand Prix – Monaco.

On the Thursday he took the Ensign round Monaco, complaining of understeer. He was 21st. Rain wrecked the second session that afternoon and only 20 cars were allowed into the race. Regazzoni hadn't made it. It meant he'd have to stay and try to qualify in the Saturday session – Friday then, as now, kept clear for promotional activities, pleasure and business.

On Saturday morning, he and Nunn gazed up at a leaden sky and of course more rain would

prevent him getting anywhere near the top 20. 'Indianapolis!' he said and headed for Nice airport and a New York flight.

Ickx deputised at Monaco, it didn't rain and he put the Ensign onto the second last row of the grid.

Regazzoni flew from New York to Indianapolis in a private plane and a police car took him to the circuit. He qualified 29th of the 33 starters (and in the race went as far as lap 25 of the 200 when he had a fuel problem).

The engine failed in Belgium and he was seventh in Sweden and France.

The British Grand Prix at Silverstone remains an immense event, and for several reasons. *Fourteen* drivers had to pre-qualify to join the other 26 in qualifying proper. Gilles Villeneuve in the McLaren and Patrick Tambay in an Ensign were among the 14.

Regazzoni, Tambay explains, 'was an official Ensign driver with Mo Nunn, and Mo Nunn put a second car up for Teddy Yip, from the British Grand Prix on, and although I was not an official driver I was the second guy in the team. That was my first Formula 1 ride – Silverstone '77, when the historical story will be that Gilles Villeneuve did his first race with McLaren, and Renault started

In Spain, before he crashed with Brambilla. (LAT)

with the yellow teapot' – turbo power had come to Formula 1.[2] 'I had not met Regazzoni before. He was – how can I say? – a very, very cheerful, open, sympathetic sort of human being. Very, very glamorous in the way that the image of the old-fashioned racing driver was. Lot of fun, lot of play, always joking, a womaniser – always chasing – and obviously a very fast, very good driver.'

Nunn has another of his precious memories. 'Regazzoni was a charmer. For the British Grand Prix we had a babysitter who came to look after the kids. My wife introduced him to the babysitter, a girl of about 19 or 20. He comes up with this big grin, puts his arms around her and hugs her. Then he strokes the back of her body with his hands, and they go down over her backside. Imagine that for a British girl. *Oh! Oh!* She was in a state of shock but he was charismatic and he could get away with that. We'd get arrested if we tried it.'

By now he was thoroughly at home at Ensign, who were very English. Nigel Roebuck remembers popping round to see them in the paddock. Regazzoni sat there and 'normally he'd have said "Coffee?" but no, he said "Tea?" I said "Yes." He said to Mo's wife "Sylvia, please put off the kettle" – he almost had it right ...'

To which Nunn says 'We were known for tea: *if you want a good cuppa go to Mo's team.*' In direct contrast, 'Clay introduced me to Italian food, which I have loved ever since.'

If the culinary treats and beverages were sweet, the racing could be hard. For the first time Regazzoni did not qualify for a Grand Prix. The car, he said, simply wasn't fast enough while Tambay in the other one was 'sensationally quick on Thursday morning' (*Autocourse*) and put it on the eighth row of the grid.

The German Grand Prix had left the old Nürburgring forever and found a new home at Hockenheim, where the teams went to test. 'We were there for two days to improve the car,' Nunn says. 'The first day when we'd finished we'd done a 1m 58.2s, and I remember that like it was yesterday. We were disappointed because the quickest cars were in the 1m 55s. So we ran the second day and our best was still a 1m 58.2s. It's about 4:30 in the afternoon and Clay pulls in and goes to get out of the car. I said "Clay, what are you doing?" He said "Mo, that's it, that's all the car's got." I said "Well, I just want to try one more thing." He said "No, it's not going to make any difference." I wanted to move the front and rear roll bars, which weren't adjustable from the cockpit. You had to adjust them in the pits. He repeated "That's going to make no difference,"

Plenty to contemplate in Holland: he qualified in mid-grid and didn't finish the race because of a throttle cable problem. (LAT)

and I said "Well, just try it for me, Clay. Give me a couple of laps."

'His first flying lap was 1m 56.8s and his second was 1m 56.2s, so I was really overjoyed because we were getting on the right path here. So as he comes up the pit road instead of pulling into the pits he went through the gate and parked the car by the transporter. The track hadn't closed and there was still running time left. I go round to the transporter and he was pulling his overalls off. I said "How's the car?" and he said "Just the same. No difference." I said "But Clay, you went two seconds quicker." He said it again: "No, it's just the same, Morris." I asked "Well, where did the two seconds come from?" He said "I didn't try as hard!" I said "Clay, the object of racing is to do the fastest time with the least effort." He looked at me and said "Morris, I can't drive like that. That's not racing." Chris Amon used to do the best time with the least effort but if Clay wasn't fighting the car he didn't think he was doing the job.'

He qualified on the second last row of the grid: lack of engine power again. As the cars threaded through the Stadium astonishing things were to happen, even by his standards. Sometime in the morning, a breakdown truck damaged the starting lights and a flag was to be used instead *but not all the drivers knew this,* Depailler (Tyrrell) on the eighth row among them. The leaders settled on their bays and Depailler, stationary, craned to see the green light. Further back Regazzoni came round *very* slowly and a consensus developed among those watching: *he's not going to stop at all, he's going to do a rolling start* – something familiar at, say, the Le Mans 24 Hours but completely unprecedented in modern Grand Prix racing except chaotic Monza!

The flag fell, Scheckter (Wolf) fast away from Watson in the Brabham. Depailler, still waiting for the green light, did not move. Regazzoni came like a missile into the pack as they began to accelerate. Because Depailler was stationary, three cars in the column behind him pulled to mid-track to avoid him – and into the trajectory of the missile. Regazzoni emerged from the multiple crash with three wheels on his Ensign and drivers condemnation ringing in his ears.

Austria – the Österreichring – was being used for the first time. It was damnably wet and, from the sixth row of the grid, he spun off on the opening lap. The Ensign crossed a grassy meadow, went through a fence and plopped into a ditch.

Holland was different. He ran strongly until the throttle cable broke and Tambay was actually third with a couple of laps to go when he ran out of fuel, so, Nunn says, 'we lost some of our best positions there.'

Regazzoni was by now immensely experienced, of course, and Tambay still exploring it. Did

Regazzoni help? 'No, he didn't help me at all. In fact if you look at the time sheets and so on I think I was a little bit in front. I had a fuel pick-up problem in the first race at Silverstone. In the second race I battled with Ronnie Peterson for sixth place at Hockenheim and I finished sixth in front of Ronnie. In Austria I battled with the Ferraris. It was a situation where a young guy, like all young guys, comes in and they are a little bit insolent. They have no complexes and they have no hang-ups: they just get in the car and drive as fast as possible. Relationships come later.'

Regazzoni was fifth in the Italian Grand Prix at Monza and fifth again at Watkins Glen. He crashed on the first lap in Canada, but not perhaps for technical or racing reasons. Let Patrick Tambay tell it.

The start at Mosport, Andretti leading and Regazzoni (22) a long way back. He didn't have far to go, either, for personal reasons. (LAT)

'I have some extraordinary memories of Mosport before the Canadian Grand Prix. It's something very private that I can't talk about. He was a woman-man. [Translation: he liked women.]

'Half an hour before the race … didn't scare him at all doing it. She had a fabulous fur coat and a garter belt.'

We need men like that.

[*Roaring laughter*] 'I don't know if *we* need men like that, but women need men like that! Then he spun off in the second corner of the race: no strength left or he may have lost a little bit of his focus! It was perfect for me. My first coach in these matters was Regazzoni and my second was James Hunt when I got to McLaren. No wonder it was tough for me in 1977 and 1978! You need to be wild. Some come through that and some don't. You have to be able to control this energy, this gladiatorial attitude and it takes a little time. When I came back to Grand Prix racing in 1982 I behaved.'

By Japan – Fuji – Regazzoni had regained all his strength. 'He was in second place chasing Hunt, who was leading in the McLaren, and he had an oil line break. I thought if we'd given that car to a top team which had the resources to give it reliability it could have won races,' Nunn says.

'We had a two-year deal and at the end of the season in November somebody called me and said Clay was testing for Shadow. So I called him up and I said "Clay, what's going on?" He said "Why?" and I said "Well, I heard you were going to test a Shadow at Silverstone." He said "Well, Morris, I can't drive another year for nothing. I'd love to drive for you but you don't have anything at the moment and I do need to earn some money." That was the first time he'd said that. I said "But Clay, you have a two-year contract." He said "No, it was just one year." I said "Don't you ever read your contracts?" He never did read them!

'He went and checked and called me back. "Morris, I have to earn some money. This is an opportunity that's there." I said "OK, I understand. The world won't stop, and have a great Christmas." That's how we ended it: honourably, absolutely honourably.'

Shadow, run by an American, Don Nichols, was a small team, moving from CanAm to Grands Prix in 1973. It had a factory in England and ran such drivers as Georges Follmer, Oliver, Revson, Jarier and Welshman Tom Pryce – killed in South Africa. In 1977 Alan Jones won the Austrian Grand Prix for them. The team, however, fragmented and several members left to create Arrows.

Nichols says 'We knew Clay well before we signed him.' Nichols was soon to get to know him better. He'd partner Hans Stuck.

'I was putting the pedal to the metal, no problem,' Stuck says, 'but he had more experience in Formula 1 than I had and when it came to the qualifying I think I didn't beat him very often. As a team-mate he was super. Absolutely. I had two or three team-mates I'll always remember. Number 1 of course was Derek Bell, long-distance world champion, then Ronnie Peterson – I admired him and his driving style – and number 3 was Clay.'

In Argentina he qualified on the eighth row of the grid and Nichols remembers 'we were coming out of the circuit after one of the practice sessions. As we neared the perimeter road of the circuit we paused because there was a military column of troops walking, and tanks and other vehicles blocking the way. As we got closer we saw Clay trying to dart between two of the tanks and

Team boss Don Nichols, who decided discretion was the better part of valour when the Argentine army seized Regazzoni. (LAT)

he was stopped immediately because that's absolutely taboo in every army in the world. The next thing we saw was Clay out of his vehicle and he was spread-eagled against a tank. They were frisking him. We were under direction by the traffic controllers and they waved us on. We decided the best choice was to disappear and let Clay sort this out himself. He came into the hotel and it was a big joke with him – they hadn't done much to him. It was a Clay Regazzoni thing: he did everything on impulse.'

He finished the race 15th, a lap down.

In Brazil, however, he worked a passage up from the eighth row of the grid and overtook Tambay – who felt dizzy in the heat – for fifth place. That was deceptive. In South Africa he didn't qualify.

Meanwhile, Stuck had settled down to life with Regazzoni.[3] 'This was not only my funniest year, we also had a great year together because we'd known each other for a long time and of course I admired him as a driver. So when I had the chance to become his team-mate we had lots of fun and we got along very, very well. There are many funny stories, as you can believe.'

Tell me one funny story.

'You cannot print those! Well … in those days let's say that we had a lot of time for doing other stuff than motor racing.'

A sponsor had a caravan that was taken to the circuits for his use, and Regazzoni's use too. The sponsor, as Stuck says, 'wasn't there very often and Clay said "Hey *Hanslie* [his nickname for Stuck], let's go and chase some girls and bring them back to the caravan." This was always his first thing when he arrived at the racetrack. So … he was kind of a cool guy, you know?'

Yes, by now we know.

In those days the *Daily Express* Trophy, run at Silverstone, was an important part of the calendar and it attracted a lively entry of 15 drivers, including Andretti and Peterson in the Lotuses, Hunt and Ickx – though (not yet) Regazzoni.

The fragmentation of the team (resulting in legal action against Arrows for plagiarism) weakened Shadow or, as Nichols puts it, 'we were in a bit of financial distress at that time.' Nichols's solution was to run an American driver, Danny Ongais, who had the backing of a 'multi-*zillionaire*' called Ted Hughes.

In the first three races, Regazzoni had been driving the Shadow designated DN8 but the new car was imminent.

'Clay came to the race at Silverstone,' Nichols remembers, 'and said "That's a nice new DN9 there painted black." I said "Well, that's Danny Ongais's car." He said "Is Danny going to drive?" I

LEFT *Even Regazzoni didn't challenge the Argentine army – but they did challenge him.* (Julian Kirk)

Typical of a disappointing 1978 season: he only did four laps in France before the electrics failed. (LAT)

He tried two versions of the Shadow at the 1978 Swedish Grand Prix and preferred the red and white one. He took it to fifth place. (LAT)

said "No, Danny's due in on Monday and the car is being readied for him." Clay then gave us some sort of a story about Danny would really appreciate him shaking the car down because no driver likes to drive the car the first time. There's all the debris from filing and bits of metal flying around getting in the driver's eyes. It was quite a convincing story so – unfortunately – we agreed.'

Regazzoni qualified it towards the rear of the grid for a race which would be very wet. Nichols 'cautioned him just to break the car in'. The cars set off into the spray to cover the race's 40 laps and to his consternation Nichols heard the voice on the Public Address system saying *Regazzoni is challenging Hunt for the lead!* Nichols remembers the 'lull' after that and 'Clay didn't come round. Finally he did arrive – walking. He said the engine died and he'd pulled off but he assured us that he had left the car well off of the circuit. Then a couple of laps later Mario Andretti came in and said "Don, I'm really sorry. I thought I was on ice, it seemed like the car would never stop." I said "Yes, I know what you're going to tell me …"

'There was this beautiful car. It had no livery on it, just a number and a little lettering – four letters: C L A Y in a tiny typeface.' Mario had T-boned it right in the midships.

'On Monday morning Clay's car was just coming down the production line when Danny arrived and we were busy painting it black …'

Ongais tried and failed to qualify for Long Beach, so did Stuck, and Regazzoni finished tenth. It was frustrating, or, as he'd describe the season, 'catastrophic'. He didn't qualify for Monaco, didn't finish in Belgium after running sixth, didn't finish in Spain after running far down the field but he came fifth in Sweden. There would be no more points: the electrics failed in France after four laps, the gearbox failed at Brands Hatch, he didn't qualify in Germany, finished seven laps behind the winner in Austria, didn't qualify in Holland and finished seven laps behind the winner at Monza.

That brought them to the American Grand Prix and one of Stuck's favourite stories. 'The day before, we all went to play golf at the Watkins Glen Golf Course, a famous local course. We had these golf carts, he was in one and I was in another. All of a sudden instead of playing golf Clay started to race me. We went through the bunkers and everything. Clay came out from a bunker on my right side so I couldn't see him. We touched and his cart went over. I just managed to hold mine on four wheels. We got a lifetime ban from the course.'

Tragic Monza, Peterson dead, and nobody would remember Regazzoni's lowly finish. (LAT)

RIGHT How to make a golf course into a race course, and who cares about the bunker? The club at Watkins Glen did ... (LAT)

In the race he finished three laps behind the winner and didn't qualify for the final race, the Canadian at Montréal.

Nichols nurses happy memories. 'Clay was always telling us he really hadn't intended to be a racing driver, he wanted to be a professional tennis player. My wife was an amateur but she was very good. She was essentially a club player and that's all she did full-time every day. That was one reason we lived in Pebble Beach – she was every day out in Carmel Valley which had its 320 days of sunshine a year. She was tanned and I was pale. So she and Clay played and I never heard the score but he came up to me and said "Wow!" My wife related the story, too, and she said he was terribly embarrassed, he was crushed but a good sport about it. He said "I didn't realise before but it's a damn good thing I did decide to be a racing driver."

'He was a good squash player. James Hunt and I always like to go to South Africa. Squash is a big thing there, as it is in England, and it's rare that you can find squash courts elsewhere. James and I played all the time whenever we could. Clay was an all-round athlete.'

Nichols nurses one particular memory. It is of an advertisement. 'Clay is standing behind this

beautiful lady and he has his arms under her arms and he is grasping her by the breasts with a lascivious look on his face. It was in such poor taste that I don't know what country it might have been done in. I don't know whether it was ever published or even used. I can't even remember what product it was about. It was just Clay Regazzoni: I don't think anyone else would have done that. He could get away with it because he had a knack. He was ever so charming in a very gentle sort of way. And the man could really drive. Yes, yes, indeed.'

Whatever the miseries of 1977 and 1978, and however much he contemplated retirement, the magic roundabout rotated again. From nowhere came an offer to drive a car which could win Grands Prix from the front, and he was only ever going to give one reply to an offer like that.

Yes.

Notes: 1. Teddy Yip, born in the Dutch colony of Sumatra, was a successful businessman in property and finance who became a figure in Formula 1, as sponsor and team owner; 2. Renault introduced the turbo engine to Grand Prix racing at Silverstone in 1977, amid much scepticism. Within five years turbos dominated; 3. Hans-Joachim Stuck, son of Hans Stuck (who raced before the Second World War), a charming man and gifted all-round driver who'd win Le Mans.

CHAPTER 5

STROLL IN THE COUNTRY

'In 1979 we were gradually and slowly expanding,' Sir Frank Williams says. 'We didn't have any real money – the Saudi money from the airline[1] was just starting to come through. They said "Here's all the money you need now. There'll be more at the end of the season."

'Bernie Ecclestone was very clear, and so were we, that we should all have two-car teams. In 1978 we had been a one-car team with Alan Jones and I bought John Surtees's FOCA rights because he was selling.[2] He was in the big London hospital right next to Shell on the south bank and I went to see him several times. He couldn't raise the money, he was sponsored by Durex and all that sort of thing,[3] and he was finding it hard going financially. I paid him a certain amount of money. So we bought Clay that space, if you like.

'We wanted an experienced driver and when the Ferrari was quick he had been very competitive. I'd seen him in the Tecno in Formula 2 in 1964 and he was absolutely fantastic in that. He'd had a reputation as a crasher early in his career but they mature. He was a charming person.'

You once said that Jonesey spoilt you because he didn't whinge and moan, he'd get in the car in all circumstances and wring the balls off it.

'Yes, and Clay was a bit like that. In many ways they were similar although Clay was more Latin. They were both men's men. Jones, despite his bulk, was actually a very, very remarkably

RIGHT *The sweet moment for Regazzoni when he wins the 1979 British Grand Prix at Silverstone, but bittersweet for the Williams team. Their prodigal son, Alan Jones, didn't finish.* (LAT)

disciplined kind of driver. We had competing team-mates for the first time but I don't remember it being any problem. They made a strong team and they were both adults.'

Patrick Head, the other pillar of the team, gives the perspective of the expansion Williams has just spoken about. 'We started in 1977 with a March car, we ran one car of our own design and manufacture in 1978 with Alan Jones, we ran two cars in 1979 and we won the World Championship in 1980 so it was a steady progression and it happened quite quickly.'

Neil Oatley joined Williams in 1977 as a young engineer. 'Obviously I was a fresh-faced student when I turned up and Patrick was a very, very good engineer. I was fortunate because he was a tremendous person to learn from and I was green. I think 1978 was a very simple non-ground-effect car. We had a couple of races where we looked fairly promising and that proved Patrick's credentials as an engineer. We drew a lot of inspiration from the Lotus 79 for the design of the FW07 [the 1979 car, and using ground effects] but Patrick's pragmatism and his understanding of structures was very good. That's where Lotus let themselves down in that they had a good idea but were poor at exploiting it. I was on Jones's car some of the time in 1978 – four or five races in the middle of the year – so Patrick would have been running it for the rest of the period. Then at the beginning of 1979 Williams went to a two-car team.'

Frank Dernie, engineer and aerodynamics expert, 'joined at the end of 1978, when things like moving into the area near the team to live were not thought about. Nobody really knew at that time whether a Grand Prix team was going to survive or not, and I was advised early on in my Formula 1 career that the first thing you do when you get your air ticket to go to a Grand Prix is check there is a return stub – because some of the team owners didn't have enough money to buy both directions, and they bought the return ticket out of the start money.

'There were only 23 people at Williams. I was number 23. [Oatley says 'There were only 13 when I joined a little over a year earlier']. The way it worked was that we had four people in the engineering office, Patrick, who did everything mechanical, me who did everything suspension geometry and aero, Neil who had just left university and was doing detail design, and a draughtsman. That was the lot. Going in to 1979 nobody knew that Williams were going to make it.'

Like the Lauda mythology, the trials and

torments of the Williams team in its infant years have been exhaustively chronicled. A thumbnail sketch will suffice here. The man himself fell for cars and motor racing early, realised that his talents were not as a driver and started a team that by 1969 was in Grands Prix. There followed a long, impoverished slog to 1977 when, in an inspired move, Williams attracted sponsorship from Saudia, the Saudi Arabian airline. Then Jones came, then Regazzoni.

Approaching 1979 the team had yet to claim a pole position or win a race.

Head and Dernie were 'running Alan, and Neil Oatley was running Clay. Although this was our first year with two cars, it was fine,' Head says. 'Clay was very well regarded when he was with us, a lovely bloke. He got on very well with Alan Jones and he got on very well within the team.'

Oatley 'hadn't met Regga before he came and the first time I came across him would have been at a test in January. He was a really nice guy and, also, he'd been around. In fact he was a bit of a schoolboy hero of mine when he was at Ferrari nearly ten years before. It didn't make it difficult, to be honest. Quite often when you meet a hero they don't turn out to be what you expect but he really was a super guy: very laid back and never

got particularly excited. He wasn't as Italian as you might expect, wasn't one for throwing histrionics or whatever. He was reasonably placid.'

The test was at Paul Ricard and after 20 laps Regazzoni judged the car easy to drive and with much more power than he'd had at Ensign or Shadow. He realised, too, that the team was well organised and functioned *as* a team.

By coincidence Dernie found himself in exactly the same position as Oatley. 'I didn't know Regga before and when I'd joined Williams I was in my 20s and Regga was *my* hero. Of course, as you get older you find that the drivers are younger than you are. When Keke Rosberg retired he was the last of the drivers older than me. People laugh nowadays that you could actually have a designer who was younger than the driver he was designing the car for, but it wasn't that uncommon then.'

Oatley explains that Regazzoni 'was pretty good with the feedback. In absolute terms I'd say Alan was a bit better. Alan was very much a non-technical person but he was very precise in being able to relay what the car was doing and where its shortcomings were. He could tell you what the problem was and where it was a problem. Then it was "OK, now it's *your* problem. Go and fix it," and he'd be off doing something else. He was very

LEFT *Facing up to 1979.* (LAT)

Mutual admiration society: team-mates Alan Jones and Regazzoni, no friction at all. (LAT)

good at giving you the information to solve a problem but not willing to get involved himself in finding the solution. Regga wasn't a lot worse than that but I'd say Alan was a bit more critical.'

We need to explore this a little further because it is central to what would happen.

Head 'got on pretty well with him although I don't remember ever building a relationship. With Alan one almost got used to building a telepathic relationship in knowing what he needed on the car. He didn't have to say very much and it was easy to convert. With Clay I'm not sure. You almost felt with Clay that whether he was on it or not – or whether he wanted to do a quick lap or not – was much more significant than whether you changed the set-up of the car. With Alan, if he was on the track he was on it 100 per cent. With Clay most of the time he was out there doing 90 per cent and it was rare occasions when he would switch in to 100 per cent – but it was there. If he needed to do a quick lap he had the skill to do it but he'd got to a stage in his career when he was going to be measured by *when* he did it [namely how often] rather than whether he could. I don't remember him being particularly good at testing, and one of the things was that the engineer running the test never knew what percentage of the exploitation of the car Clay was giving, or whether after lunch he was putting more effort or less effort in than before lunch. He really was a man who only responded to a race.

'The problem for us was that he would nearly always qualify three-quarters or a second behind Jones. The race would start and by 15 laps he'd be 30 seconds behind. From then on he'd go like a dingbat and often actually be quicker than Alan. I really don't know why that was. He never seemed to be able to be quick out of the box although once he got into it, particularly if there was a race going on – you know, somebody he could race – then he drove some storming races, but usually from too far back.'

Oatley confirms this. 'Most times, Regga raced better than he qualified. Quite often he would race very, very strongly even if he hadn't qualified particularly well. I guess, to him the sport was just about the racing and not the grid position. I don't think he ever really hung it out in qualifying like some of the other drivers would. He was getting on a bit and perhaps he didn't need to do that. He'd been there before and he knew that in a race he could turn it on as he needed. If he got in a battle with somebody during the race he was very good. In qualifying he was not really in that situation.'

The season began at Buenos Aires in January and Dernie underlines how compact and direct a team's personnel were then. 'When we came to a Grand Prix, Patrick and I used to split running the No 1 car 50–50 – I did half the races and he did half – while Neil Oatley ran Clay in all the races and also looked after the racing paperwork, updates and all that sort of thing. And the draughtsman stayed at home drawing the bits. That's the way you operated in those days. Frank, Patrick, Neil Oatley and myself – that was about it in terms of the people who interacted with the drivers.'

Here is the season unfolding, with qualifying in brackets then the race:

Argentina	Jones	(15)	9
	Regazzoni	(17)	10
Brazil	Jones	(13)	did not finish, fuel pressure
	Regazzoni	(17)	15
South Africa	Jones	(19)	did not finish, suspension
	Regazzoni	(22)	9
USA West	Jones	(10)	3
	Regazzoni	(15)	did not finish, engine

The team ran the 1978 car, the FW06, to these races. 'The first race we took the 07 to was Long Beach, but we didn't race it,' Head says. 'We never intended to race it, although Frank wanted to [and, according to Oatley, Jones was quite upset not to]. I said no. We went testing with it to what was called the Ontario Motor Speedway, which is now a housing estate, just after the Long Beach Grand Prix.'

The car had been briefly tested at Donington beforehand. 'It seems odd now, looking back, why we then took the car to the USA rather than continue in Europe, other than that the race drivers were already there. I cannot remember the reason,' Oatley says.

Jones handled that test at Ontario and told Regazzoni afterwards the car was exceptional.

Oatley echoes this. 'It was a strong season, particularly if you consider the first races we did with the old car, which at that time was totally outclassed and almost a waste of time. It wasn't until we got the new car in Europe that we began to show our strength.'

Not immediately, however.

Spain	Jones	(13)	did not finish, gear selection
	Regazzoni	(14)	did not finish, engine

For once Gareth Rees was not there, but he did watch from afar. 'The FW06 was, as expected, steady but very much mid-field. With the 07 things suddenly got a lot better. The first time the potential of the car struck me was when I watched the Spanish Grand Prix at Jarama on TV. Jones was part of a battle up front but as the leaders reached the end of the long start-finish straight I kept noticing that Regazzoni was coming into view at the back of the picture and it seemed like he was appearing earlier each lap. In other words he, too, was lapping at least as quickly as the leaders, and often quicker. The commentator, Murray Walker, didn't seem to spot it and soon Regga broke down, but clearly this new Williams was good.'

Belgium	Jones	(4)	did not finish, electrics
	Regazzoni	(8)	did not finish, accident
Monaco	Jones	(9)	did not finish, accident
	Regazzoni	(16)	2

He was fourth fastest in first qualifying but could not subsequently improve on that – one of only two drivers who didn't. Hence 16th, a prison sentence rather than a grid position at Monaco, where overtaking is so tightly rationed. Scheckter led in the Ferrari from Lauda (now Brabham) and Villeneuve in the other Ferrari.

Regazzoni covered the first three laps in … *fifteenth*. By then Villeneuve was past Lauda and a Ferrari exhibition stretched all down this warm, dry afternoon.

Patrese (Arrows) had a suspension problem … *fourteenth*.

Hunt (Wolf) had a mechanical problem next lap … *thirteenth*.

Regazzoni remained there until lap 16, when Laffite (Ligier) pitted with a loose wheel … *twelfth*.

Regazzoni ran there for three laps, when Depailler (in the other Ligier) crashed with Pironi (Tyrrell), Depailler hobbled … *eleventh*.

One lap later Regazzoni overtook Stuck (ATS) by outbraking him into *Mirabeau* … *tenth*. Stuck was the first car he had actually overtaken. *No problem*, Regazzoni thought.

Stuck is quite candid. 'He was the better guy into the corner and at Monte Carlo when a guy puts his hand on the corner you shouldn't play any tricks because there isn't much room. I would say from the driving standpoint he was always a little bit better than I was.'

Shadows in Spain – the engine failed. (LAT)

The epic drive at Monaco when he almost gave the Williams team its first Grand Prix victory. (LAT)

Two laps later Lauda and Pironi crashed, and Andretti (Lotus) retired when his rear suspension failed … *seventh.*

Reutemann (Lotus) lay ahead and he stayed ahead to lap 33, when he lost a little power through a cracked exhaust and Regazzoni surged by … *sixth.* If he finished there it would be his first point for Williams.

Jarier (Tyrrell) halted at *Ste Devote* with a rear suspension failure on lap 35 … *fifth.*

Ahead now, in the order Regazzoni would reach them, were Mass (Arrows), Jones, Villeneuve and Scheckter.

On lap 44 Jones clipped the barrier at *Tabac* and damaged the steering … *fourth.*

Regazzoni cut into Mass's lead and on lap 49 Mass stayed on the racing line during the descent to *Mirabeau* but, at *Ste Devote,* Regazzoni rammed the Williams down the inside, a muscular and psychological moment.

'Cars breaking down was the usual thing in Monaco,' Mass says, by way of explaining how Regazzoni reached him. 'I never really deliberately held somebody up but I also fought because I was in the points so I didn't really give way easily. He got by me one way or the other. Difficult to overtake at Monaco? Sure. He would never have been unfair. He would try hard, of course, but I knew where he could try – so you were aware of it then.

'Nobody would have given me any credit had I just let him slip by. I had done it once in 1974 when I drove the Surtees at Brands Hatch. It was quite quick on the straights but slow round the corners – not enough downforce – and a lot of people got stuck behind me. Occasionally I left the door open. They passed me quickly and then they were gone. John Surtees gave me one heck of a *lip* afterwards and said "Are you crazy!?"'

Mass would never forget that. Here at Monaco he did what he was fully entitled to do, and Regazzoni countered with what *he* was fully entitled to do.

If Regazzoni stayed where he was that would put him on the podium, of course, but he wasn't in that mood. He wanted everything, the whole race. Immediately he pulled away from Mass and began a long thrust towards the Ferrari.

Regazzoni the racer was loose.

At lap 50 the Ferraris were 18 seconds away, Regazzoni coming. One contemporary source suggests a rising level of anxiety reaching towards consternation at Ferrari – amplified on lap 55 when Villeneuve eased his car into the pits. The transmission had failed … *second*. And still Regazzoni came with such pace that, on lap 58, Scheckter was a mere eight seconds away and 18 laps remained.

Then – potential disaster. On lap 59 he surged into *Tabac* and changed from fifth gear to third and couldn't get it. *Third's gone*, he thought. He was in neutral, desperate to find any gear, and realised he'd made a mistake. It was second gear that had gone, and it never did come back. *Damn*, he thought.

For a moment that calmed the Ferrari pit, Scheckter's lead out to 13 seconds, but Regazzoni adjusted, going straight up and down through the gears without using second.

His response was entirely typical of the man. He went racing again, but he wasn't wild, he was compact, controlled, neat. Still he came, the white Williams taut, but flowing not bounding. The gap:[4]

Lap 65	12.2
Lap 66	10.6
Lap 67	8.4
Lap 68	8.1
Lap 69	7.7
Lap 70	7.0
Lap 71	6.8
Lap 72	5.8
Lap 73	5.0
Lap 74	3.5
Lap 75	1.6

They moved into the final lap together, Scheckter trying to maintain control of the race, Regazzoni trying to prise a gap. In the surge down to *Mirabeau* he flicked the Williams to the inside and got it alongside but not level and Scheckter cut across, keeping the lead. It was decisive because from *Mirabeau* to the end overtaking was almost impossible.

He could do no more than apply pressure, and he did. Scheckter resisted it and crossed the line 0.44 of a second ahead. Regazzoni estimated that as 20m. It was a fraction and a lifetime because, as he himself knew only too well, only one man wins the race. What he didn't know was that, although he'd driven Monaco six times before, he never would again.

'I had a picture of Clay on my shelf for years,' Patrick Head says. 'He's coming out of Casino Square and he's absolutely sliding with the front wheels right out. Wonderful! Early on in the race Alan Jones and Villeneuve were going at each other then Alan hit a barrier and bent his steering arm and Gilles had a problem. It left Jody Scheckter in the lead and Clay behind him. Clay closed right up on him and finished just behind. If Clay had not been asleep for the first sort of 20 laps of the race that could have been our first win.'

France	Jones	(7)	4
	Regazzoni	(9)	6
Britain	Jones	(P)	did not finish, water pump
	Regazzoni	(4)	1

'We should probably have won a couple of races prior to Silverstone,' Oatley says. 'We were certainly in a position to fight for a win with Alan if not Clay. If the cars held together the thinking was that Alan would always be in front of Regga, although their race paces weren't all that different. Alan would start higher up the grid and be more aggressive early on in the race so he'd always be in a position where he was further down the road than Clay.'

The Monaco result would always be misleading because Jones had qualified three rows in front of Regazzoni and by lap 22 caught the Ferraris at the front – Regazzoni seventh at that point. His rise, as we have just seen, was largely inherited from the misfortune of others. This is not to diminish his performance, but Jones was a *long* way up the road: exactly what Oatley and the others anticipated all the time.

Listen to Dernie. 'Generally speaking, people were disappointed in Regga because he didn't have the pace of Jones and that wasn't what was expected. I think that probably was the first reaction people had at Williams, although obviously I can't put words in their mouths. Everyone thought that Regga was going to blow Jones away and he clearly didn't. He was never as fast under any of the conditions we met. He was great fun and he was a great gentleman but I think that the team in general were slightly disappointed by his pace.

'It wasn't lack of determination, he just wasn't as fast. He was, of course, no longer young. Silverstone [which we'll come to in just a minute]? What we did there had been coming. We were going to be 1–2 everywhere that the car finished. We were so much faster than everyone else at that stage with the ground-effect car but it was always going to be Regga second.

'One of the things it's very easy to forget is that in the career of a driver there is a drift up to a peak – they obviously have to show well enough to get in – then it's a question of at what point they peak, then how their pace declines after that. It is not the same from one driver to another. I don't think we have ever really had a period of two of the greats peaking at the same time. I look to the mid-1980s when we had Prost, Piquet, Senna and Mansell racing each other: Piquet was actually not past his peak but near it whereas Senna was on his way up. Prost and Mansell were in between, so making a clear comparison was difficult.'

Williams took part in the official testing at Silverstone immediately before the British Grand Prix and all are agreed that what Oatley describes as 'a couple of aero modifications' transformed the car, the race, the history of the team – and confirmed that, truly, there was life in the old dog yet.

Jones did two laps and then, on the third, 1:13.4.

To appreciate the overall impact of this, pole in 1975 (Tom Pryce in the Shadow) had been 1:19.36; the 1976 race was at Brands Hatch; pole in 1977 (Hunt in the McLaren) had been 1:18.49; the 1978 race was at Brands.

Of course the cars were getting quicker and quicker and, as if to emphasise that, during a tyre testing session at Silverstone a month before the official testing, Lauda took the Brabham round in 1:13.6 (143mph). *Autosport*, breathless and in awe, spoke of how he 'annihilated' the opposition who 'could only laugh at mention of his lap times'.

Now Jonesey had *already* covered Silverstone's broad acres faster in his first three laps. Another way of appreciating the impact is that Frank Williams consulted a second stopwatch to make sure his own hadn't malfunctioned and Jones *really had* done the 1:13.4.

Jones was barely into his stride, however. He came out again and in sequence achieved

1:13.5
1:13.3
1:13.1
1:13.1
1:12.9
1:12.7

The aero modifications 'really did transform it – and we had a good car anyway,' Oatley says. 'Now we had a leap in performance. It's not often you get something like that out of the box, so there was a fair bit of optimism from the test that we were strong. Silverstone is a high-speed circuit and we were racing against some turbo cars, which should have had an advantage on the straights if not the corners.'

Dernie confesses that 'effectively I was trying to be a cunning bugger. I'd realised quite early on that aero was the thing that gave the performance. Harvey Postlethwaite[5] said to me "D'you know, the only thing we ever do that makes any difference to the car is improve the aero."'

Yes, but what was it?

Head explains that 'all in all, by the time we arrived at Silverstone for the pre-British Grand Prix test, we were a bit frustrated. We hadn't won a Grand Prix yet but we'd got close. We made a big improvement with the car: a very, very small bit of aluminium on the underside of the car which filled in a leakage gap. Literally those pieces were knocked up overnight and put on for the first time at Silverstone. We were running in the mid-1m 13s without our new panels – and then, with them, on the same tyres Alan upped and did the 1:12.77. It was a massive improvement and we knew we were in pretty good shape.'[6]

To which Dernie concludes: 'We were all thrilled to bits. To be honest it was a euphoric time because we knew we were fast then. The new mod to the underbody fixed a problem that the car had had from the beginning. We were fairly quick before but after we'd fixed that we were miles quicker than anyone else.'

The Jones lap had been set on what they called control tyres. What might he do with qualifiers? Nobody knew, including Frank Williams, but one word kept coming back and back: *anything*.

'Interestingly,' Oatley says, 'the really dramatic lap time improvement came when we increased the wing level on top of the aero change – not something we had previously considered at the nominally high-speed Silverstone circuit, but with the high efficiency of the wing car the circumstances were a little changed and the combination worked a treat.'

Different Williams men would react in different ways to Silverstone and what was already happening there.

'I'm the other end of the spectrum to volcanic,' Neil Oatley insists. 'I'd say I'm a very different sort of character to Patrick. Phlegmatic? That's one way of putting it. I went to Silverstone for the Grand Prix in a phlegmatic mood.'

It was about to be sorely tested.

The British Grand Prix doesn't have charisma (and doesn't pretend it has) but the ghosts of yesteryear linger. The World Championship began in 1950 and three of the circuits used then were still being used in 1979 (as indeed they are today): Monaco, of course, Monza and Silverstone. It meant several generations of drivers had explored the broad acres, including all of the greats. *That* meant several generations of British spectators had witnessed them and cumulatively the Grand Prix became a great annual gathering. It could never be Monaco, could never offer the animal passions of Monza but it did have something else: the sense of a great, committed community – sometimes 100,000 strong – who seemed to know each other, knew what they were watching and appreciated it enough to keep coming back.

To this, primed with their own anticipation, came the homespun Williams team and their Aussie driver who'd pass for a full-blooded Anglo-Saxon any day of the week, mate. In this context, Regazzoni would be there to support him. He wasn't in any sense an outsider because, after all these years, he was an insider everywhere in Grand Prix racing, but Jones was the prodigal son.

'Jonesey in qualifying used to do his lap time on a Friday afternoon and generally speaking it was so much quicker than everyone else that, in order to demoralise the opposition, he used to change into his civvies and wander up and down the pit road in full view of all the other drivers who were sweating blood to try and get anywhere near the time he had set the day before. That is the performance benefit we had over everyone else, and I've never had it since,' Dernie says.

'It must have had a psychological effect on Regga. With most drivers, if their team-mate goes quicker than them, the first thing they believe – certainly nowadays – is that the team is favouring the other guy. That's what they go on about but, of course, why would a team ever do that? It is always an absurd comment – although part of your self-protection method, a way to convince yourself that you're good enough to keep going. Whether in the old days people felt that I don't know, but Regga was a very quiet man. Patrick and I ran Jones and he probably felt a little bit isolated in that respect. The person who talked to him most would be Neil.'[7]

In the Thursday untimed session – the Grand Prix then on a Saturday at Silverstone – Jones had what he described as 'brain fade' and went off at Copse. The car needed minor repairs. 'He spun and damaged the rear wing,' Head says. 'He came in to the pits and we replaced the rear wing.'

A career reborn, and even René Arnoux – who was second – seems delighted for the old master. This is Silverstone. (LAT)

('In that era,' Oatley points out, 'both first-day sessions and the second second-day session counted for grid times. Only the morning session on the second day was "untimed" and was generally used for full-tanks running.')

First qualifying, on a hot, dry afternoon, was in no sense a struggle for provisional pole. It was domination, breeding devastation, on a scale rarely seen. The breathless awe reached Nigel Roebuck, who wrote in *Autosport*: 'You had no need of a stopwatch to identify the pole man. Five minutes of watching at the entry to Copse or Stowe – or anywhere else on the circuit where the road turned – told the story far more graphically. The Williams was measurably, demonstrably, *visibly* quicker into, through and out of the turns than anything else in the place, its particular strength its turn-in ability. The sheer adhesion of the car was breathtaking.'

Jones did *1:11.88* and Williams had their first pole.

He could, if he had wished, have come straight in, changed into his civvies and strolled the pit lane in his pomp.

Head remembers this as 'an extraordinary moment. The whole pit lane just stopped and stared. There was almost a stony silence up and down it, and even we at Williams looked at each other. Jabouille next did 1:13.27. It was a second and a half! People had been waiting for a driver to get into the 1:12s [testing times have no status so Jones's 1:12.77 there didn't count. What Head means is a driver getting into the 1:12s at a Grand Prix meeting.] He went straight into the 1:11s. Now everybody thought *that's it, there's no way we're going to get that.*'

Regazzoni, running without the new panels, finished seventh on 1:14.32.

That evening Jones re-signed for Williams and, if Regazzoni hoped to stay, he needed to qualify well and finish the race well.

Next day, when the new panels had been fitted to his car, he found it transformed. 'It goes into the corners so quickly that you consciously have to lift off later and brake a little harder. Each time you think *hell, I'm going to go off …*' He explained that you turned the steering wheel quite normally but, travelling this fast, 'logically' you should finish up on one of the grandstand roofs. Instead the car went round. More than that, the adhesion was so good that when you positioned the car into the corner you could accelerate flat out and the corner became a straight. He estimated the increase in cornering speed at 15mph.

Jones was quickest again (1:12.13) while Jabouille and Piquet went down to the 1:12s too. Regazzoni qualified fourth.

Joy to the world. Hey, amigo, you won it! (LAT)

	Jones
Jabouille	1:11.88
1:12.48	
	Piquet
Regazzoni	1:12.65
1:13.11	

A warm, dry afternoon, and when the great throng had cleared from the grid Jones prepared to win the British Grand Prix from pole. He had a new engine – the latest Cosworth – which his mechanics had fitted at 11:30 the previous evening and then found a defective fuel pump. The engine would have to come out. They finished at dawn – but the engine was fast. With it Jones intended to paralyse the race from the start, win the second Grand Prix of his career and become a dominant force. Head expressed it more cautiously: 'I wouldn't say we expected to win but we knew we ought to.'[8]

Alan Jones's wife Beverley was 'terribly nervous before the start'. She and Williams's wife Ginny positioned themselves 'out of everyone's way on some Goodyear tyres at the back of the pits and prepared to close our eyes for the first lap.'[9]

Regazzoni lined his Williams up behind Jabouille and concentrated hard. At the green light he moved instantaneously and got off the line without too much wheelspin: the perfect start. He glanced and saw Jabouille alongside, was past him by the end of the pits and travelling into Copse so urgently that he reached it half a car's length before Jones. Regazzoni felt a moment of deep satisfaction. 'Everything had gone just as I planned it.'[10] Jabouille followed him through Copse, then Jones. They stretched into the broad acres and accelerated hard-hard-hard down Hangar Straight. It went wrong for Regazzoni there because Hangar Straight adored speed and Jabouille and Jones were simply faster. Jabouille was intent on overtaking into Stowe corner and drew up on Regazzoni's left, Jones coming strongly on Regazzoni's right. He lifted a fraction because, he judged, halfway round the first lap of 68 was no time or place to indulge in 'stupid' jousting.

Jones took Stowe with the move of a man harnessing the Williams's speed and imposing his own wish for dominance. Jabouille harried him but concluded that the Cosworth in Jones's car had as much power as any he'd met before. They dropped Regazzoni, who ran alone, musing that maybe he ought to have jousted, although the fact that Jones and Jabouille pulled away so easily confirmed his initial decision. He made a second decision, to run at his own pace for the initial 20 laps to conserve tyres and fuel.

Jabouille clung to Jones for six or seven laps but all at once his soft tyres began to go off. At lap 10 Jones led him by five seconds with Regazzoni a further seven seconds behind the Frenchman. The outcome of the race seemed decided.

As if to confirm that, Jabouille pitted for new tyres on lap 17 and the stop went horribly wrong. He accelerated before an air hammer had been fully withdrawn and that tore part of the bodywork off. He pitted again for repairs and the engine failed.

At some point Ginny Williams glanced across to Frank on the pit lane wall and noticed his 'eyes were riveted grimly to the lap charts in front of him as if his life depended on it' – in these days, before TV monitors, Frank was the team's lap chart man. Neither Ginny nor Beverley moved or spoke 'in case we broke the spell'.[11]

Regazzoni ran stately, in second place to Jones, and was still content to maintain his own pace. He could, he knew, have gone faster, but felt that it would be pointless because he couldn't match Jones and, anyway, harboured concerns about making the tyres last to the end, despite protecting them so far. There was a broader aspect: Jones 'was in the same team as me so I was very happy to be second.'

He had Rene Arnoux some four seconds behind but, as the Williams fuel load went down, shed this Frenchman and 'from lap 20 I used only fourth and fifth gears, and never broke 1m 20s. Apart from a few minor vibrations at the start of the race everything went just fine. For the first time in my life I drove about 80 per cent of what the car was capable of. It was too easy … just a stroll. I had time to watch the countryside go by. I recognised some of the journalists and photographers around the circuit. I scarcely even sweated into my overalls.'[12]

Oatley remembers 'Jones was quite comfortable and I did have a feeling that this was going to be it. Being an engineer, all the things that could go wrong are constantly running through your head and of course we'd had those couple of races we could have won before we had a mechanical problem. As the race goes on that starts gnawing away at you. Alan was cruising.'

Then …

Frank Williams waited for Jones to come round a 37th time, ticking off another lap towards the inevitable. Instead Williams glimpsed a whiff of whitening smoke from the back of the car. *He won't cover more than two more laps*, Williams murmured.

On lap 39 Jones angled the Williams into the pit lane and as he travelled along it Regazzoni went

| Williams Grand Prix Engineering Limited |
| TESTING/PRACTICE LOG |

DATE 14th July	EVENT British GP	CHASSIS FW07/02	WEATHER	F. CAM STD
DRIVER C. Regazzoni	CIRCUIT Silverstone	ENGINE 2.9 (226)	AMBIENT	LAP. DIST. 2.932

TOE	F.	0° IN/OUT	CASTOR	F.	0°		RIDE	F.	28"
OVERALL R.		30' IN		R.	0°		HT.	R.	39"

CAMBER	F.	1/8° NEG L 1/8° NEG R	ROLL	F.	TYPE 3/4° φ × 16 SWG	SPRINGS	F.	800
	R.	1/2° NEG L 0° NEG R	BARS	R.	TYPE 3/4° φ × 16 SWG		R.	950

| DAMPERS | F. | TYPE 8 to R .2 | ROLL | F. | SETTING Full Soft | BUMP | F. | 1 3/4" + 1 3/4" PACKER |
| | R. | TYPE 8 B R 10 | BARS | R. | SETTING Full Stiff | STOPS | R. | 1 1/2" + 3/4" PACKER |

| RIMS | F. | 11" | TYRES | F. | CODE Dia L R | TYRE | F. | HOT   COLD |
| | R. | 15" | & DIAS | R. | CODE Dia L R | PRESS | R. | HOT   COLD |

| GEARS | 1 | 2 | 3 | 4 | 5 | 6 | CWP 8:31 | WINGS | F. | 2° + C' FLAP |
| | 13.85 | 16.8 | 17.51 | 19.29 | 20.27 | | DIFF Salisbury | | R. | HOLE 6 + 1/2 FLAP |

FUEL IN 57 1/2 GALS | FRONT SUSP' | REAR SUSP'

LAP	TIME	COMMENTS				CHANGES	
1	—	P3		67	5	15.91	17
2	18.29			66	52	15.69	16
3	17.61			65	68	15.86	16
4	17.28			64	54	16.62	14
5	16.81			63	55	5.92	13
6	16.84			62	56	16.09	12
7	16.54			61	57	15.13	11
8	16.37			60	58	17.32	10
9	16.05			59	59	15.18	9
10	16.48			58	60	15.19	8
11	16.15			57	61	16.49	7
12	15.87			56	62	15.82	6
13	15.92			55	63	15.88	5
14	16.17			54	64	16.24	4
15	16.09			53	65	15.43	3
16	15.55			52	66	15.37	2
17	16.04	P2		51	67	15.05	1
18	16.29			50	68		
19	15.95			49			
20	15.67			48			
21	15.95			47	FUEL OUT - 2 GNS		
22	15.44			46	CONSUMPTION - 5.86 MPG		
23	15.50			45	(PRACTICE 6.2 MPG)		
24	15.47			44	WEIGHT - 1298 LBS (on hers 5/8)		
25	16.14			43	OIL CONSUMPTION - 8 pints		
26	17.78			42	TELLTALE - 11,050		
27	16.09			41	PADS -		
28	15.65			40	WEIGHT - 606 KG (SILVERSTONE)		
29	15.20			39	(1383 LBS)		
30	15.31			38			
31	15.96			37			
32	16.09			36			
33	15.90			35			
34	17.37			34			
35	16.12			33			
36	15.00			32			
37	14.71			31			
38	16.53			30			
39	14.37			29			
40	15.08			28			
41	16.52			27			
42	15.13			26			
43	14.94			25			
44	15.61			24			
45	14.62			23			
46	15.65			22			
47	15.40			21			

Neil Oatley's time sheets, recording in numbers what really happened. (courtesy Neil Oatley)

by, the cars almost parallel – but Regazzoni out there on the track, in the lead.

Dernie explains that 'we had modified the water pumps on the engine by cutting off the existing mount for the water pipe and welding on a new one so it got out of the way of the underfloor. Most people had done a similar thing so we weren't unusual. It turned out that, on the one on Jones's car, the weld had been polished off to make it look nicer and whoever had done it had polished far too much off. It was very, very thin. It cracked and the water leaked out. Jones was much quicker than Regga but his car had an engine failure due to that water leak.'

Oatley 'was on the pit wall. Frank and Patrick and everyone was. I remember when Jones came back to the pits he looked like thunder – sheer anger on his face.'

Beverley wept and Ginny steered her towards the team's motorhome.

Regazzoni had 29 more laps to negotiate and no other car threatened him. He could proceed in tranquillity – his own word. All he needed to apply was common sense. He did, however, allow himself a gesture because on this lap 39 he set fastest of the race …

Ginny consoled Beverley, who sensed how important the next moments would be because *Williams* could win their first Grand Prix after a struggle stretching back these many, many years. 'Go back,' Beverley said and Ginny went. Beverley found Jones, who said goodbye to Frank on the pit wall. Then he and Beverley left the circuit.

On lap 57 Regazzoni came upon Scheckter's Ferrari and was 'surprised' to see it a whole lap down. He overtook on the exit of Copse and momentarily his thoughts were of Enzo 'down there in Maranello in front of his TV'. Once he owed Enzo a great deal but now he didn't owe anybody anything. He felt a simple satisfaction at having been able to demonstrate that in a good car he was still the man he had always been.

As the team counted down the laps the media began to gather round the Williams pit. That had never happened before. A specific tension began to rise: Frank Williams and his team were very British. They'd been bulldogs down all these years, never letting go whatever adversity struck them with and now here they were on a summer's afternoon about to win the British Grand Prix. The crowd *willed* the Williams forward just as it willed Regazzoni forward over the last couple of laps – the Regazzoni who, as a racer, had won their admiration down all these same years. As he crossed the line 24.28 seconds ahead of Arnoux many in the Williams team were in tears. They were not alone.

Oatley remembers 'those last 30 laps were agony. Clay was a long way ahead and you're thinking "Please God, don't let the thing go wrong." It was the sheer relief of him crossing the line at the end of that last lap. I think I was still phlegmatic. I think I'm a bit like Frank in that respect. I'm not particularly emotional. Clay was over the moon. It had been a long time since he'd won a Grand Prix and probably a long time since he'd won a race of any description. It could easily have been in his mind that he never would win another one again, if he was being honest with himself.'

Gareth Rees was there. 'The weekend was too good to be true. Watching with friends, all of us mates of Neil Oatley's, I had a lump in my throat and tears in my eyes as car number 28 came through Woodcote that last time. Partly it was for the joy of seeing Regga win again in what had to be the twilight of his career, but it was also the double-thrill of it being in the car that Neil was engineering – and so also Neil's and Williams's first wins. It still seems unreal even today, nearly 30 years later.'

Through the emotion, Frank Williams saw the overall picture. Because Williams were sponsored by Saudia Airlines, some of the Saudi princes were at Silverstone and the Koran forbade alcohol – which in a few moments Regazzoni would be getting in Champagne magnums on the podium, to gorge and spray Arnoux and Jarier (third) with. Williams sent one of Regazzoni's mechanics, a Japanese called Yui, to remind Regazzoni. Yui wrote out in pencil a note *Don't forget, no Champain* [sic] and gave it to him.

Regazzoni went onto the podium. He was handed a magnum which he passed to Arnoux, was handed a second magnum which he passed to Jarier, but when he was handed a third – for himself – he put it gently on the ground. This did not prevent Arnoux and Jarier from shaking their magnums and giving Regazzoni full volleys. In the midst of the foam and froth he raised both arms – not surrender but saying *I'm not drinking, I'm empty-handed.* Eventually he settled for a can of pineapple juice. It must have tasted sweet enough.

He did the traditional lap of honour standing on the rear of an open lorry. Whole sections of the crowd came onto the grass at the side of the track and saluted him. Then he did the traditional press conference and said he didn't deserve anything: the credit should 'not go to me' but Head for designing the car and Frank Williams for running the team.

Ginny was walking back to the motorhome. 'I had just reached the back of the garages when I saw Clay heading in the same direction. He'd collected his prize and now, for some reason, he was alone, a small figure looking rather sad and lonely, walking across the grass. He'd obviously sneaked away from the interviews and attention. I went up and congratulated him. I felt I knew exactly how he must feel. He'd just driven his heart out and given Williams their first ever success and yet there was no escaping the knowledge that most people in Williams were slightly disappointed that it wasn't Alan who won. He gave me a hug and a smile and we walked together the last few yards to the motorhome.'[13]

A picture which sums up the re-birth of the career, Regazzoni hammering past Jabouille in the Renault. (courtesy Gareth Rees)

Others would hug him, Jackie Stewart and Bernie Ecclestone among them.

The feeling of ambivalence is expressed by the team members.

'Jonesey should have won it,' Sir Frank Williams says. 'I was very disappointed for Alan. He deserved it. He'd grown with the team and become a core member. At another level we were naturally happy to have our first win because that confirmed everything that had been coming.'

Head: 'Many of us were a little disappointed for Jones at Silverstone. Ultimately it was sad that Alan didn't win but, as it was, he went on to win four races. Everybody liked Clay so it wasn't as if people were upset. There was the expectation that Alan would be the man. Like a lot of things in this world, not everything pans out perfectly but I have to say that we were very happy that Clay won. He was a very popular person in the team.'

Dernie: 'The first win? It should have gone to Jones.'

Oatley: 'The team had really grown up with Alan. In 1978 he was almost at a loose end in his career and we were just a fledgling team. Perhaps it was a gamble for any driver to come to us. Alan was really a good journeyman driver at that time although he won one race [Austria 1977] for Shadow. Through 1978 the relationship between Alan and Frank and Patrick gelled. They were very much of a like mind.'

Charlie Crichton-Stuart, now a senior member of the Williams team, said: 'We were all delighted for Clay's win … but it wasn't the same thing. We didn't feel fulfilled after that British Grand Prix: not until the next race when AJ won at Hockenheim. That's because our ambitions were on his back.'[14]

In the motorhome, the Saudi notables waited to greet Regazzoni and one of them gave him a box that was heavy – heavy as gold. When they'd gone, and he'd done a lot more interviewing, he reached for a bottle of Scotch.

He'd earned a drink, one with a little more to it than pineapple.

Gareth Rees says that 'Neil is not known as being an overly emotional guy but I really expected to see him reveal his joy on this occasion. That evening, when Neil's motorbike arrived at our tent on the Silverstone infield, he amazed even those of us who had known him from being kids by taking it in his stride: nothing more than a grunt and the faintest trace of satisfaction. Regga never won again, but for the rest of the season he continued, ego fully under control, to do what he always did best, being a content and reliable number two who kept on

picking up points for Williams, while Jones ran away up front and headed for stardom.'

Regga wouldn't have seen it that way, but never mind.

Here is the rest of the season:

Germany	Jones	(2)	1
	Regazzoni	(6)	2
Austria	Jones	(2)	1
	Regazzoni	(6)	5
Holland	Jones	(2)	1
	Regazzoni	(3)	did not finish, accident
Italy	Jones	(4)	9
	Regazzoni	(6)	3

Italy was a tumult of a race. On lap 2 in the *Curva Grande* Regazzoni and Piquet touched, and Piquet speared into the Armco, bouncing across the track to the Armco at the other side and back again. The engine, wrenched off, caught fire at one side, while Piquet sat in what remained of the Brabham at the other. Subsequently he lodged a complaint about the way Regazzoni had been driving but this was dismissed.

By lap 42 of the 50 Regazzoni had caught the Ferraris, running first and second, and drew up to within two seconds, provoking a crisis of hysteria in the crowd – they loved Ferrari and they loved Regazzoni – while the Ferrari pit betrayed consternation. Alas, he was conserving his fuel and the engine began to cut out. Into the last lap the Ferraris led by 4.0 seconds, the race decided.

'Monza?' Neil Oatley muses. 'That whole place oozes history. Even if you're wandering round a deserted track by yourself you can *feel* what has happened there before. It *is* a special place. We were willing him on because he wasn't that far behind the Ferraris.'

He'd driven the Italian Grand Prix nine times before and the 1970 victory was safely into eternal mythology, the 1975 win hardly less so.

He'd never drive it again.

| Canada | Jones | (P) | 1 |
| | Regazzoni | (3) | 3 |

Since 21 June 1970, when he'd finished fourth in the Dutch Grand Prix, Regazzoni had scored a total of 208 points. Now, on 30 September 1979, he had 212. He would never score another.

| USA East | Jones | (P) | did not finish, rear wheel lost |
| | Regazzoni | (5) | did not finish, accident |

He was not retained by Williams. Patrick Head 'said to Frank "The problem is, we have got a major car advantage this year with the 07. We ain't going to have that next year because everybody will close up and the problem will be, instead of Clay being one or two rows behind Alan, it's going to be six or seven rows." I think at the same time Carlos Reutemann came along to us and said "I want to get out of Lotus. Any chance of a drive?"'

As Head points out, they didn't fire Regazzoni: they had him on a one-year contract and did not renew it, which is not quite the same thing. He'd fulfilled his part, they'd fulfilled their part.

Williams were now in a position to choose who they wanted in their second car (as against Ye Bad Olde Days not long before when they were forced to take rent-a-car drivers). It fell to Frank Williams to tell Regazzoni, something of a novel experience in 1979, however much it would be repeated in the years to come. Before he answered my question about what that had been like he paused for a long time. 'It's never easy when you have to disappoint somebody – when they lose their job – and a racing driver doesn't have very many options. Let's say his career span is up to the age of 30, whereas an engineer has another 30 years after that, so it's not easy, no, but it has to be done and you have to take a decision. We decided on

Carlos and he won Monaco. Jonesey won the World Championship and we won the Constructors' Championship, but Clay will always be known as the man who won the first Grand Prix for Williams. He will always have a place in our hearts.'

Before we leave it …

'After those great seasons at Ferrari which ended in rejection,' Gareth Rees says, 'Regga proved to us all how much he must have loved racing, feeling no apparent shame in going straight from the front to the back of the grid when he joined Mo Nunn's struggling team in 1977. In fact, sometimes like in the Ensign at Silverstone he suffered the humiliation of not even qualifying for the back of the grid. It was the first of two difficult seasons, one with under-financed Ensign and then with the under-financed and disorganised Shadow in '78. When he joined Williams in 1979, it seemed like a good move compared to Shadow or Ensign but hardly likely to lead to reviving past glories at the sharp end of the field. However, it was a big thrill for me because he was moving to the team where Neil was. We'd been following and watching racing since we were 9- and 11-year-olds.'

Oatley feels that Regazzoni 'arrived with us at a good time and was a very good, competent No 2

Happy birthday to you. Icky clearly fancies a piece of the cake, and no doubt Lauda will in a moment too. (LAT)

driver. That was icing on the cake. I think Frank didn't want a young blood in to learn about Formula 1 at our expense. He wanted someone who was going to put mileage on the car and not get involved in crashing it. Ultimately that gap in pace between himself and Alan – once we were established as a leading team – was crucial. We needed someone who could regularly get into a position to win races, and then win them.'

Frank Dernie is delightfully irreverent. 'The cars had three times the grip of the cars that Regga'd been winning in previously. I'm sure all great drivers adapt to any sort of car but I think it was probably quite a big step between that and the Williams. Physical fitness would be an issue. Guys in those days partied a lot. The only time you ever needed to drive flat out in Formula 1 was qualifying. The race was generally a race of attrition and the drivers were all big, fat, old and really knackered by lap 10 – but they were all like that! With three times the grip he would have been even more knackered. I suspect most of the drivers of that era who suddenly got in a ground-effect car were struggling. They found out they were pulling 4G round corners instead of 1.5. They probably couldn't drive near the limit of the car for that many laps.'

It makes what Regazzoni did at Monaco and Monza all the more remarkable.

I wondered if Patrick Head missed the buccaneering days that Regazzoni & Co inhabited in glorious Technicolor.

Suddenly Williams were an overwhelming force. Jones won Germany – from Regazzoni. (LAT)

'The thing is, Formula 1 is very intense, very hard work. Every hundredth of a second is fought for technically and I don't think we'd be very happy if we had a driver who was on it one day and not on it the next because he didn't feel like it. We'd be looking for somebody who was a real professional, more of a Stirling Moss: if he's there he's working 100 per cent. I mention Stirling Moss only because he was probably the first of the really professional drivers. But no, I don't regret it, no. I'm very pleased that I was involved at the time that I was, but, bearing in mind all the work that gets put into it now, I'd be very impatient with a driver who wasn't really on it all the time or had been, say, at the Tip Top Club in the early hours.'[15]

And we all know were Clay Regazzoni would have been.

Notes: 1. Frank Williams attracted title sponsorship from Saudia Airlines *from 1977; 2. John Surtees, the only man – in the hallowed phrase – to win world championships on two wheels and four. He formed his own team in 1970; 3. Durex were a sponsor but, by the nature of the product, that gave the BBC problems covering Grands Prix; 4.* Autocourse; *5. Postlethwaite, known as The Doc, had a long and distinguished career as a car designer, including time at Ferrari; 6.* F1 Racing *magazine; 7. Dernie adds that whenever a driver says he's not getting equal treatment 'he goes down in my estimation. There's no gain for the team to ever do it. I personally don't believe it has ever happened in the history of racing. Prost was convinced that Senna had a better Honda engine than he did. Bollocks! Johnny Herbert was convinced that Michael Schumacher had special bits on his car. Bollocks! It just wasn't true. It's actually more difficult for a team to produce two different cars than it is to produce two the same. In addition to which the first time you show favouritism to one driver and the other car's not as quick is the time your favoured car breaks down or crashes and you then don't finish as well as you could, so to the team it makes no sense. That's why I don't believe any team's ever done it and certainly drivers who believe their team is doing it are just deceiving themselves. I suppose you could argue that perhaps in those days there may have been the odd occasion, with such limited resources, that when they came up with a new bit it may well go on the No 1 car because you hadn't got enough to put it on the No 2 car. But frankly the updates that we did in those days were very limited. We didn't have the time or the money to do much of that, so the likelihood of there being an update in the middle of the season – a performance update which only went on one car – was minimal. Most updates were to stop overheating or resolve an oversteer problem or one of the other things. We didn't have the massive R & D resources a team has now'; 8.* F1 Racing; *9.* A Different Life, *Virginia Williams; 10. Neil Oatley says: 'As an aside, a couple of months ago [in 2008] that race was shown on one of the satellite TV channels and I had never actually seen it before. I didn't realise that Clay led halfway round the first lap – he did that from the first corner – because in the pits you never had TV monitors (or video cameras at home) and by the end of the lap he was in fourth place. It was a bit of an eye-opener because he never mentioned it at the time and I'd not seen it before'; 11.* A Different Life; *12.* Grand Prix International *magazine; 13.* A Different Life; *14.* Driving Ambition, Jones; *15. A celebrated Monte Carlo watering hole once regularly frequented by drivers.*

LIFE CHANGE

I am a fatalist. I believe that everything is decided for us.
– *Clay Regazzoni*

The escape road was on my right with the racetrack coming from the left so this thing unfolded from my left to my right. Gene Hackman and I had been standing there not longer than a minute. I was aware that this was an enormous amount of energy in front of me. I don't know if you say a prayer – you don't really have time – and as it took place it was almost more than you could absorb.
– *Dan Gurney*

I could tell from the way he was sitting and the way the car was bent that he had a lower spinal fracture. It was almost as if he had a new waist. His legs were trapped to his knees.
– *Dr David Rasumoff*

There were no communications so you didn't know anything. All the PA said was that there had been a crash down at the hairpin. I thought *Oh, no*. Once Regazzoni didn't come round I wandered off there because people used to vandalise the cars after the races if the they hadn't been moved.
– *Gary Anderson*

I took with me a neurologist who had perfected a technique which I employed on other patients of putting electrodes on the nerves to the bladder, and the bowel, and the penis so that you could – with external electrical stimulation – control the bladder, and the bowel, and get an erection. I told Clay about that just in case he didn't recover: that there was some hope of controlling all these functions. He didn't seem to be particularly moved by that. He was clearly very depressed then.
– *Professor Sid Watkins*

CHAPTER 6 ────────────

THE WALL

─────────────────────────

'We'd got Unipart as a sponsor and they wanted Clay,' Mo Nunn says. 'They thought it'd be great so we went after him again and this time we did pay him. I can't remember how much and although Unipart seemed a big sponsorship it wasn't. Williams were running on about £3 million and we had $200,000. Even then it wasn't anything really.'

So Regazzoni went back to Ensign. 'I prefer to be the only driver in a team that is perhaps less prestigious, less complicated and poorer in terms of money, but one where I feel that everyone around me is counting on me, has confidence in me and is working for me,' he said.[1]

Ensign now prepared to use their trusted and (very) tried Cosworth DFV engines for the fourth season. 'Bernie Ecclestone had had the use out of them so we kept rebuilding and rebuilding them. John Judd at Northampton used to build them for us,' Nunn says.

Ensign may have been small but it resonated with talent. 'We had Nigel Bennett, Ralph Bellamy and Gary Anderson,' Nunn reflects now. At the time he expressed the firm opinion that 'we have everything we need to take on the best and even win,' adding that the era of excuses was over.

'From the first stroke of the pen we built the new car [the N180] in 70 days and had it on the track at Snetterton. Clay did a few laps breaking it in and so on. Having come from the Williams he said it had a lot of downforce, turned well, no

RIGHT *The old master still wanted to race in 1980, still delighted in it all.* (LAT)

understeer at all. There were all the signs that it was a good car.'

Gary Anderson nurses reservations about aspects of that. 'We knocked the car together – it was a bit thrown together, to be honest with you. Seventy days? The ambitions were a bit higher than the abilities in the company. I worked flat out to get the thing together and it was quite a quick little car but a lot of bits fell off it. Regga was really good. Coming from the big team status to a small team – working in a tin hut! – was a fairly different deal for him, you know. He kept his head up and he really did a good job. I didn't know him until he came along.'

Meanwhile, Regazzoni insisted that Nunn had 'never been in a position to prove his worth.'

By now, beginning the season in Argentina in January – with Brazil following two weeks later – had become almost traditional. At Buenos Aires, Regazzoni did a very respectable 1m 47.18s in first qualifying (Piquet provisional pole 1m 46.04s) but had teething problems in second qualifying and couldn't improve. The 1m 47.18s put him on the eighth row of the grid.

That Saturday night before the race, Nunn says, 'we all went to dinner – about 15 of us – on the River Plate, a little place outside Buenos Aires. Clay's father was there. There was a girl sitting either side of Clay and when it got to about 11:00 I looked at him. I pointed at my watch and said

"You ought to go to bed." He stood up, grabbed a girl's hand either side of him and said "Come on, Morris says we have to go to bed." And he was gone. I don't know what happened after that …

'He was a man's man. He was charismatic. Of all the drivers I thought would make good World Champions, Graham Hill made a great champion. He looked the part. Then you take Denny Hulme. Never looked like a champion. I think Regazzoni would have been a great champion. He had charisma, like Emerson.'

In the race Regazzoni suffered from a sticking throttle, made three pit stops and, although he was running at the end – he'd covered 44 laps against the 53 of winner Jones – he wasn't classified.

'What happened was the chassis was pretty weak and was popping rivets,' Nunn says. 'The panels were bowing and it was an aluminium construction. In fact I remember during those first few races we added 60lb of weight into the chassis by reinforcing things to gain something like a second and a half a lap. It started to understeer, too.'

In Brazil, as *Autocourse* reported, 'the Unipart Ensign's lack of testing and teething problems continued to interrupt practice. The side pod supports had been strengthened but continued fuel feed problems meant that the car had to carry a handicap of 17 gallons of petrol. With that in

mind, a place on the sixth row of the grid was a fine effort on everyone's part.'

In the race Regazzoni had a handling problem and retired after 13 laps.

By South Africa in March the car had been revised and the fuel feed problem cured. Regazzoni qualified, however, on the third last row – he had understeer – but took the car to ninth, a lap behind the winner, Arnoux's Renault.

Before the United States West Grand Prix, Ensign tested at the Riverside circuit with their new titanium brake that they'd be using for the first time in the race. There were no problems.

However traditional, Argentina was a long, long way away from Grand Prix racing's epicentres and Brazil had been in doubt because Interlagos needed drastic improvements. The race had been switched to Jacarepagua at Rio. The track there started to *sink* into soft ground and the race went back to unimproved Interlagos, the drivers initially threatening a boycott. South Africa was an isolated place under apartheid and, equally, a long, long way away from the epicentres.

Long Beach and California weren't any closer but they *felt* they were. Maybe that was to do with the pervasive presence of Hollywood, and America itself, everywhere; maybe to do with the imagery of California, sunshine and peachy girls and the good life. Argentina, Brazil and South Africa were extreme outposts of Grand Prix's imperial reach, Long Beach was a gathering point.

Richard Burton would be there, spectating.

Jackie Stewart would take his family and George Harrison of the Beatles, there on holiday.

Patrick Tambay, out of Grand Prix racing and now in CanAm, would be there, spectating. He'd been skiing and during the race would catch a flight to Hawaii, joining his parents-in-law on holiday. The time of the flight meant leaving the circuit early but at least he'd see some of the race.

Gene Hackman would be there, spectating, with Dan Gurney – in Grand Prix racing from 1959 to 1970 – standing alongside him.

Patrick Segal, a Frenchman who had been a talented sportsman – athletics, skiing, rugby, martial arts to the level of a black belt – would be there in his wheelchair. Eight years before, he'd been involved in a shooting accident but spent two years going round the world in the wheelchair. He'd written a book about that, *The Man Who Walked in His Head.* He'd sailed the Atlantic and worked as a photographer during the 1976 Montreal Olympic Games. He'd not seen a Grand Prix before.

James Hunt, legs in plaster after a skiing accident, would be there in a temporary wheelchair working for the BBC.

Leo de Graffenried would be there, working for Marlboro, who sponsored two teams, McLaren and Alfa Romeo. He'd be having a busy weekend.

Professor Sid Watkins, by now Formula 1's resident doctor, would be there in a fast car, to be driven by former World Champion Phil Hill,

The preparations for the 1980 United States West Grand Prix at Long Beach were quite normal. (LAT)

poised to reach any accident in the minimum time. Watkins barely knew Regazzoni, which was nothing sinister but just sometimes how it goes in Grand Prix racing. 'In the 1970s he spun at Brands at the start and caused a big accident. That was the first time he came to my notice. I was a spectator in those days. I wasn't close to him in any way. I knew him in a distant way, really. He was a very, very polite and extremely fit guy. He had a sprightly walk and a great shine in his eye. He really looked fantastic, I always thought: fantastic health and spirits.'

Martyn Pass had never been to the United States before. From the Midlands he followed Grand Prix racing with something approaching passion. He'd take a holiday and fly to Long Beach to spectate – and see the peachy Californian girls, all right. At Long Beach 'the fans were a breed unto themselves. You'd have the motorhomes and girls standing on top of the motorhomes in bikinis, dropping their tops and all that sort of thing. It was a total and utter education, nothing like I had ever witnessed before. I could not believe it.'

In Friday qualifying Regazzoni did a 1m 21.477s, 19th (Didier Pironi provisional pole in the Ligier, 1m 19.305s) and on Saturday 1m 20.984s, 22nd (Piquet in the Brabham pole, 1m 17.694s). That put Regazzoni on the last row of the grid, next to Fittipaldi. The Ensign wasn't turning in properly for the slow corners and the team couldn't find the answer, while Fittipaldi described the car which bore his name as 'bad in everything'.

	PIQUET (Brabham)
ARNOUX (Renault)	
	DEPAILLER (Alfa Romeo)
LAMMERS (ATS)	
	JONES (Williams)
GIACOMELLI (Alfa Romeo)	
	REUTEMANN (Williams)
PATRESE (Arrows)	
	PIRONI (Ligier)
VILLENEUVE (Ferrari)	
	JABOUILLE (Renault)
JARIER (Tyrrell)	
	LAFFITE (Ligier)
DALY (Tyrrell)	

	ANDRETTI (Lotus)
SCHECKTER (Ferrari)	
	MASS (Arrows)
ZUNINO (Brabham)	
	CHEEVER (Osella)
DE ANGELIS (Lotus)	
	WATSON (McLaren)
ROSBERG (Fittipaldi)	
	REGAZZONI (Ensign)
FITTIPALDI (Fittipaldi)	

So the old masters – Regazzoni (born 1939) and Fittipaldi (born 1946), giving a combined age of 75 – were lost at the back. The presence of Dutchman Jan Lammers on the second row merely emphasised that. He'd been eight when Regazzoni and Fittipaldi began their competitive careers. What might the old masters do within the constrictions and hazards of a street circuit across 80 laps of 2.0 miles, giving a race of 162 miles? Fittipaldi, World Champion in 1972 and 1974, hadn't missed a Grand Prix there and knew how those hazards could take their toll. He estimated that if he 'kept out of trouble' he might get into the top six by the end. What Regazzoni thought is not recorded but he knew what the hazards could do, too.

Long Beach was hard on brakes and Ensign had that new, specially designed titanium brake which might give Regazzoni an unexpected advantage across the 162 miles.

It was a typical Californian day, sunshine and blue sky, as the 25-minute morning warm-up session began, the stands already full. Piquet and Derek Daly did their own warming up by crashing into each other at the hairpin at the end of Shoreline Drive. Regazzoni's CV joint failed and he had to be towed back to the pits.

The weather was nicely hot as the clocks ticked towards 2:00 and the start.

In Lugano, the Regazzoni family prepared to watch the race on television.

Dodo Regazzoni prepared to watch it with his family.

They'd be hearing Mario Poltronieri, preparing to commentate with Sergio Noseda, a Swiss-Italian TV colleague and lifelong Regazzoni friend. Poltronieri would give the overview as the race developed; Noseda would work the pit lane for news.

Pass positioned himself a couple of corners beyond the hairpin.

Professor Watkins, driver Hill and an anaesthetist, Peter Byles, sat in the fast car at the medical centre on the bay side of the circuit.

Gurney prepared to walk the circuit with Hackman, sampling proximity to the cars from different vantage points.

Piquet seized the lead but the hazards began to bite immediately. On the opening lap a crash, a mechanical failure and a puncture claimed four cars.

'At Long Beach you had the start and then in what seemed like only a few metres you reached the turn, a very, very tight turn,' Ricardo Zunino says. 'We all arrived in a group, everybody together. Everything was so quick, you know: *so* fast. Jochen Mass pushed me against the wall but it was not intentional. I touched the wall and I broke the suspension.'

As the cars emerged from the hairpin, Depailler stole past Arnoux. Piquet led the crocodile as it worked its way through the rights and lefts towards the back straight, and as he did that Zunino found the Brabham undriveable.

'When I crashed, the car was impossible to drive. The people – the assistants – they pushed the car until the escape road and they pushed it to the end of the escape road. I got out and walked to the pits, which were not very far away. The system then was not so efficient as it is now and they didn't remove the car: it stayed in the escape road. Today it would have been no problem at all because there has been a big advance. They have cranes to lift the cars away and they have the Safety Car.'

The escape road was at the end of Shoreline Drive and if you couldn't take the hairpin it was where you went.

Meanwhile, hardly noticed, the old masters overtook Elio de Angelis (Lotus) and circled 18th and 19th.

They ran in that order to lap 3, when de Angelis re-took Fittipaldi. On lap 4, Bruno Giacomelli's Alfa Romeo spun into the hairpin beyond the pits and a multiple crash followed. 'It was amazing,' Fittipaldi said. 'I arrived and the track was completely blocked. I stopped. I was blocked in, completely at a standstill. I looked to the right, I looked to the left and I just couldn't see how I was going to get round them. Then I saw a gap and off I went again'[2] By then Regazzoni had stolen through too. Giacomelli recovered.

The old masters circled: Regazzoni 12, Fittipaldi 14.

All eyes were on Piquet, controlling the race beautifully from urbane Depailler in the other Alfa Romeo. As Jabouille brought the Renault into the pits to have his brakes bled, who noticed Regazzoni was up a place, and Fittipaldi too? They ran there to lap 14, when Regazzoni got past Rosberg in the other Fittipaldi and, a lap later, Fittipaldi got past Rosberg, too.

The old masters circled : Regazzoni 10, Fittipaldi 11.

On lap 17 Regazzoni came up towards Daly, whose brakes were fading. 'For two laps I didn't use them at all and they got better,' Daly said, 'but when I ran hard they disappeared altogether.' Within two laps Fittipaldi was on him and Daly couldn't resist any more than he had been able to resist Regazzoni.

The old masters circled in tandem to lap 27, when Pironi, immediately ahead, pitted with a puncture; circled in tandem again to lap 33, when Piquet burst past to put them a lap down. More than that, Giacomelli – on the same lap as they – burst past too, but poor Laffite had a puncture which was so sudden and severe that he had to abandon the Ligier.

The old masters circled: Regazzoni 8, Fittipaldi 9.

Somewhere around now, Patrick Tambay left the circuit for the airport, listening to race commentary on the car radio.

On lap 40 Depailler retired with a broken suspension, his Alfa Romeo parked in the escape road. On lap 41 Villeneuve pitted after clouting Daly. The hazards were striking hard.

The old masters circled 6 and 7 and continued in tandem to lap 47, when Jones was clouted by Giacomelli. Perhaps now, as Jones got a ride back to the pits on a marshal's motorbike and Giacomelli prepared to retire, the big crowd were noticing.

The old masters circled 4 and 5 this lap, 49, Piquet still leading from Patrese, Arnoux third. Mo Nunn thought *Geez, we're going to be on the podium.*

Regazzoni took the Ensign along Shoreline Drive to begin lap 50, forcing it up to between 165 and 175mph. Some 150 yards from the hairpin, he passed two white lines on the road which he used as his marker to come off the power and hit the brake pedal for the hairpin, which was, by general agreement among the drivers, the hardest braking point anywhere on the calendar. He twisted the Ensign through the hairpin into what someone[3] described as a 'series of squirt-and-point left-right turns that follow each other in a blur of crossed arms and dancing feet, leaving no room for thought.'

Gurney and Hackman reached the area beside the escape road and would spectate for a moment or two from there.

Regazzoni took the Ensign through the geometrical right from Pine Avenue to Ocean Boulevard, a straight where paradoxically the pits and the finishing line were – paradoxically because the starting line was on Shoreline on the other side of the circuit. Ocean was straight with, at the end, a geometrical right and a crest that dropped down Linden Avenue to a sharp-left sharp-right. The track curved to the left and fed Regazzoni onto the 'up' lane of the Shoreline triple carriageway, the Ensign bounding because the circuit here was through a car park, coated in dark asphalt.

He was hard onto the brakes for the 20mph hairpin that fed him out onto the 'down' lane. This was the majestic white-concreted sweep of Shoreline, in everyday life limited to 50mph. From the hairpin at this end to the hairpin at the other end – where the escape road was, with the Brabham and Alfa Romeo parked there – Shoreline represented almost half of the whole circuit. By definition it was the fastest part: a driver got onto the power as soon as he could, the cars slewing towards the outside retaining wall, the power kicking the cars forward.

The clocks ticked to 3:16.

Regazzoni forced the Ensign's speed up and up towards what he estimated as 175mph, as he had done quite safely 50 times before. He reached the two white lines – the braking point – and hit the brake pedal because he needed to haul his speed down by about 150mph in the 150 yards to the hairpin.

The titanium brake should have felt hard as he applied so much pressure to it and within a handful of yards the brakes would begin to bite. Nothing happened. He thought the brake oil might have boiled and hit the brake pedal a second time. Nothing happened.

The escape road was screaming towards him very, very fast but he knew his reactions were normal and, although everything happened in what he'd remember as the space of a breath, fantastically he drew comfort from knowing his reactions were normal. He changed down from fifth to third gear to slow the car, just as he had done 50 times before, then switched the engine off.

Fittipaldi, behind and watching horrified, thought Regazzoni was trying to spin the car to scrub off speed as it screamed towards the escape road but Regazzoni wasn't. He had no room for that with the Alfa Romeo and Brabham parked there. He weaved the Ensign from side to side: it was all he could do.

The escape road was approximately 50 yards long (see next chapter) with, at the end, a tyre wall, a three-ton concrete wall behind that and a debris fence mounted on it. He'd remember these screaming towards him. He saw the Alfa Romeo on the right of the escape road beside a low side

The old master putting together his final Grand Prix masterpiece as he comes up through the field. (LAT)

wall – the one Gurney and Hackman stood behind – and if the car hadn't been there he might have been able to thrust the Ensign against that wall, ram the speed off as the concrete clawed the flank of the Ensign.

No chance with the Alfa there.

The Brabham lay further up and on the left.

'The escape road, which was perhaps a little more than 50 yards, was on my right with the racetrack coming from the left so this thing unfolded from my left to my right,' Gurney says. 'Gene Hackman and I had been standing there not longer than a minute. We were as close as we could get to the action. I was aware that this was an enormous amount of energy in front of me. I don't know if you say a prayer – you don't really have time – and as it took place it was almost more than you could absorb. I'd say if you made a conservative estimate he was probably going at 150 when he went by and he wasn't really slowing. It could have been more than 150 but I don't think it was less. It's a good estimate. If he had the presence of mind to change down, well, that's amazing. Things were happening very, very rapidly – because of this enormous amount of energy – and so rapidly that I don't know the span of time covering it.'

Regazzoni missed the Alfa Romeo but the Ensign's left front struck the Brabham's right rear tyre. That might have saved his life because the impact reduced his speed, although nobody can ever know by how much. The Brabham was launched so sharply that it cleared the tyre wall.

It hammered the concrete blocks hard enough to move them backwards and almost went through the debris fence before what remained of the car bounded back into the tyre wall, destroying that.

Fittipaldi remembered that 'when I turned into the hairpin I lost sight of him but I heard an enormous crash.' Others remembered 'an explosion of debris, dust, wheels, metal, accompanied by a dull thud.'[4]

Gurney remembers Regazzoni 'not careening off or collecting the Brabham but hitting it. I don't think that slowed him much at all. He just sort of flicked it. Then there was this enormous hit into the tyre barriers – a substantial number of piled-up tyres. The pieces of the car – a wheel and tyre, other pieces of suspension – went very, very high in the air, maybe 35ft. The speed and the energy had had nowhere to go. He'd been hard on the gas all the way down that straight, he'd been building up energy in the car and you're obliged to take that energy out with the brakes. If the brake pedal snaps off you can't take it out. You're just along for the ride.

'I knew this was a big one and I elected to try and make my way to see whether he was alive or if I could be of any help or find out what had taken place. I wasn't sure what it was, but something made me go there. I don't know if I said goodbye to Gene Hackman or didn't say anything and just left. I probably got there as soon as anyone did, although I don't know if I was the first one to get there.'

No-one would ever see this again. (LAT)

At the instant of the crash Poltronieri 'understood immediately' that it was bad, very bad. Noseda set off to try and get to the scene but a policeman would turn him back.

In Lugano, Gian Maria – only 12 – was trying to be a man and calm everything down in the Regazzoni house. 'I was so used to seeing my father coming out of the accidents he had had. I thought he was already out of the car, but it was a marshal [or more probably Gurney]. I remember saying "Don't worry, he doesn't have anything serious" because my mother was very agitated.'

Dodo had the opposite reaction. 'When I saw the accident I said to my wife "This is very dangerous." I could see it was bad. I remember when he'd had an accident at Indianapolis – bad – but I saw him get out of the car. In Long Beach he was still in the car.'

Gurney imagined Regazzoni must be dead and thought it would have been incredible if anyone survived an impact like that. 'It was a horrendous accident … incredible that anyone could survive. I didn't expect him to be alive.'[5]

A cloud of smoke shrouded the end of the escape road, already beginning to drift.

Fittipaldi felt his own legs begin to tremble. 'I couldn't drive and I don't think John Watson, who was behind me, could either. He slowed down as well.'

Watson 'saw the incident. I didn't see it occur but I did see there had been a crash at the end of the straight. I wasn't really aware of who or what it was.'

The monocoque was so distorted that Regazzoni's knees touched his helmet *but* the little white cross emblem on his helmet was moving from right to left. It meant he was alive. In fact he was not only alive but fully conscious. His sides hurt.

'You could see within the tyres of the barrier a car, and sure enough there was someone sitting in it. That was Clay,' Gurney says. 'He was still facing in the direction he had been travelling but he was scrunched down almost in the foetal position, his knees practically in his face. He seemed to be up almost where my eyes were. I was standing and he was pinned in the car somehow and up at my eye level. I could look him right in the face. He appeared to be conscious or semi-conscious.

'I wasn't real sure whether Clay was fully conversant in English or not. I tried to ask him if he was in pain or was there anything I might do or should know about. I tried, I think unsuccessfully, to get some conversation going. I could touch his legs but I had been around first aid situations long enough to realise that you don't want to start

moving people until you know more about it or the professionals get there. If he'd been screaming, however, you try and do something about that. He wasn't, although I was assuming that he was in plenty of pain.'

He was. He immediately recognised Gurney, a Ferrari veteran. He asked for his helmet to be taken off, and carefully. The *Los Angeles Times* reported that Gurney did that although 'it was awkward, like a turtle with his neck pulled in.' Then, as Gurney leant forward, Regazzoni 'said he felt he was being strangled by his seatbelt.' Again carefully, Gurney released it and Regazzoni realised it wasn't the seatbelt but the twisted monocoque causing the pain. (Speaking today, Gurney insists that he doesn't remember taking the helmet off, and a precise reconstruction is impossible anyway, by the nature of the rescue, never mind the passage of time. The real point is that clearly somebody took it off.)

'By then,' Gurney says, 'the other crash people were starting to arrive.'

A rescue truck, with three men standing on a platform at its rear, came through the drifting smoke, almost surreal. In the background a slip road running alongside Shoreline Drive rose, and normal, everyday traffic went up it observing the speed limit.

Dr David Rasumoff, the Sports Car Club of America's chief track physician, arrived in an emergency vehicle in some 20 seconds. The SCCA was responsible for any incidents on the circuit but paramedics were responsible for anything off circuit. When they arrived there was some initial confusion about roles, not helped by the fact that the paramedics didn't recognise Rasumoff (in the sense of knowing who he was).

Professor Watkins, however, remained in the fast car. 'It was very strange we were not released to go to the scene. Race control was very twitchy about Phil [Hill] taking me on the circuit and so they wouldn't let us go, and anyway the radio communication between where we were and race control was in and out, as it were – but they were very peculiar, race control that day. A lot of people were upset that I didn't go, particularly as it turned out that he was paralysed. I'm sure he was paralysed from the outset and that it wasn't anything to do with his extrication, because he had a profound fracture in the thoracic spine.'

Pass hadn't been able to see anything from his vantage point two corners on and 'the PA commentary was absolutely diabolical. They'd got no idea of what Formula 1 was all about and they had no one to give any kind of information to Europeans in the crowd who did know what it was about. All I can remember them saying was "There's been an accident," and that was it. They never said any more. Half the people watching didn't know what they were watching. It could have been anything to them, just another sporting afternoon out.'

Oatley, in the Williams pits, points out that there was no closed circuit television and as a consequence you 'weren't really aware' of the crash during the race.

Whatever the limitations of communications in 1980, there was one sure way for commentators, teams and spectators to know which driver had been involved, and that was to check off the cars as they passed on the following lap and see which one was missing.

Piquet came round, Patrese, Arnoux … Fittipaldi, Watson, Scheckter, Rosberg, Pironi, Mass, Daly and Jabouille.

Then they knew.

'There were no communications so you didn't know anything,' Gary Anderson remembers. (Mo Nunn still can't remember when or how he heard.) 'All the PA said was that there had been a crash down at the hairpin. I thought *Oh, no.* Once

Regazzoni didn't come round I wandered off there because people used to vandalise the cars after the races if they hadn't been moved. My thinking was to keep an eye on the car, stop people taking bits off it.'

De Graffenried was in the Alfa Romeo pit and when he heard 'I felt cold, I felt like Hell freezing over.'

Regazzoni was lucky in one sense at least. One description of Rasumoff was that he was 'larger than life. He was expert at bringing specialities together in the realm of emergency services. He had fire-fighters talking to nurses, paramedics talking to doctors. His goal was to make sure the medical professionals appreciated and understood what was going on in the field.'[6]

He applied that skill now. The paramedics asked Rasumoff's firemen if they could help but the firemen said it was their job, not the paramedics'. However, Rasumoff stressed that the paramedics were not 'rebuffed' and in fact they helped get Regazzoni out.

Rasumoff made an initial judgement. 'I could tell from the way he was sitting and the way the car was bent that he had a lower spinal fracture. It

The crash. (DPPI)

was almost as if he had a new waist. His legs were trapped to his knees. We had to be careful how we took it all apart so as not to injure his back further. The main thing to do was see if his condition would dictate whether we had the luxury of time. Was he bleeding massively? Was he having trouble breathing? That did not seem to be the case.'

The race proceeded quite normally, no suggestion it should be stopped and no change in the order: Piquet, Patrese, Arnoux, Fittipaldi, Watson, Scheckter, Rosberg, Pironi, Mass, Daly, Jabouille. Each forced their cars to big speed along Shoreline, each braked and went round the hairpin into another lap.

When Anderson reached the hairpin 'there was all this commotion going on so I went over to that and saw the car sitting on top of the concrete wall. The front of the car was up on top and it was bent double. He was still trapped and they really didn't know what to do.'

Anderson remembers himself and Gurney – both, of course, knowledgeable about racing cars and their construction – helping in the 'operations to cut the car in two and get him out of it.' As I say, there is an understandable confusion about details and Gurney again insists he did *not* do anything about the car's structural problems.

Anderson can't remember if at that stage Regazzoni was 'conscious or unconscious. His knees were behind his shoulders. My recollection was that the medical group were treating him and I was just helping cut the car apart, so for me to judge whether he was conscious or unconscious would be very, very difficult. And it was a panic – you know what I mean? – so I wasn't paying attention to that sort of thing at all. I discovered inside the front of the car that the brake pedal was broken …'

Rasumoff estimated it took eight or nine minutes just to get the remnants of the tyre wall cleared away.

Watson and Fittipaldi engaged in a lively duel, Fittipaldi overtaking him on lap 60 at just about the moment the tyre wall was cleared.

The firemen began work with a Hurst Tool, more commonly known as The Jaws of Life, a hydraulic device invented only eight years before specifically to cut drivers out of crashed racing cars (and so successful that its uses became widespread); because it reduced the time to extricate a driver it snatched them from the jaws of death – hence The Jaws of Life. Gurney explains that 'it's like a hydraulically-powered tool that can split debris or metal, or prise something out of the way without necessarily hurting whoever was in there. In certain applications it's a big help. My

recollection is that Regazzoni was confused as to what was going on with his legs, probably because he couldn't feel anything there and they were kind of trapped. You were hoping that the thing that might have happened to him hadn't, and maybe there *was* a way to prise something out of the way, extricate him from the wreckage. He was crammed into this thing and a lot of it was broken and bent, and he was a big, strong man as well.

'The crash team people took over and soon they were trying to insert a back support. Eventually you have to move someone and they have like a flat board they try to strap someone to in order to move them without bending anything and risking causing further injury. I was just trying to stay out of the way while at the same time not just turning around and leaving him. I was there as a presence.'

Rasumoff said 'it was almost as if you could peel the car from around him like an artichoke.'

While the Jaws worked a fireman arched over Regazzoni to prevent any bits of flying metal from hitting him. The fireman held a hosepipe, ready to extinguish any flash fire – but it dripped.

Regazzoni craned his head to the right and murmured 'I'm getting wet.'

Tambay, driving to the airport, 'was listening to the race on the radio when I heard that he had a big shunt. I knew it was him because the report on the radio said it was.'

Gurney 'did not try to get involved. These people, some semi-volunteers, are dedicated to help out and they have been trained to a lesser or greater extent. I think sometimes they are worried that someone without the training might get involved and do more harm than good. So they start yelling and that kind of stuff. I watched them get him out and once they got him onto the board then I couldn't maintain any eye contact with him.'

On lap 68 Arnoux pitted with a puncture, and who in the crowd realised that that would have put Regazzoni onto the podium? As it was, it did put Fittipaldi there. Among so many bitter ironies here was one more: Arnoux pitted at about the same time Regazzoni was cut free – after 22 minutes – and taken directly north to St Mary's Hospital, a few blocks away.

Gary Anderson 'went back and said to Mo and Nigel Bennett and Ralph Bellamy "Big shunt blah blah blah and the brake pedal broke." They all turned round to me and said "Ah, no, no, no, couldn't break." I said "The pedal *has* broken off." Morris didn't disbelieve me but the others did and, to be honest, that was the reason I left the team. At that point in time there was a lot of fragility in the car. I wasn't a designer at the time. I was coming from the mechanical side saying "Look, this won't stay on the car, this'll break, this'll fall off," and they said "No, no, no, it's fine, no problem." Next practice session the thing falls off. I was fighting a losing battle and when the brake pedal went I thought *OK, that's enough.* You have to live by your convictions and when people take note it's OK, but when you're fighting a battle it's not OK.'

Piquet won the USA West Grand Prix, the first of his career. He covered the 162 miles in 1h 50m 18.55s, Patrese easing back to finish 49.28 seconds behind him, Fittipaldi – who'd unlapped himself with ten laps to go – at 1m 18.56s. By then, Regazzoni was at St Mary's. One old master made his way to the podium. The other never would again.

Piquet would win 22 more Grands Prix and take two World Championships. Patrese wouldn't ever get near a championship but his career stretched to 1993. Fittipaldi would win one more point, at Monaco two weeks later, and retire at the end of the season.

From 21 June 1970 to 3:16 on the hot Californian afternoon of 30 March 1980, that had been Regazzoni's world.

It wasn't now.

A brief retrospective of the career:

Alan Jones, writing in 1981, said[7] that Regazzoni 'had a very good, natural, easy balance. He was a dispassionate driver in his last years; all of us become that way as we look on the racing world with a colder eye and recover from our early enthusiasm.'

Nigel Roebuck says that 'on his day he was as quick as anybody. It was strange in that he'd have days when he looked … not cack-handed, exactly, but you'd think *How many mistakes can a bloke make?* He'd drive a bad race, he'd be spinning, he'd hit somebody trying to pass them and all the rest of it. Other days … well, I remember the British Grand Prix in 1975. Carlos Pace led initially in the Brabham with Clay second, and Clay passed him into Woodcote. It was one of the best passing moves I have ever seen: perfectly judged, perfectly pulled off and there was nothing Pace could do. Clay left him no way to resist.

'I remember Long Beach in 1976. He just completely dominated. It was the first time they'd had a Formula 1 race there so it was new to everybody. He was in a class of his own the whole three days. At that time Niki was winning everything. Clay was on pole, took the lead at the start and he was gone. The German Grand Prix in 1974 at the Nürburgring – again he was just gone,

Nelson Piquet won the first Grand Prix of his career and could afford to smile. Only later did the extent of Regazzoni's injuries weigh down on Grand Prix racing. (courtesy Camel)

and if you could do that at the old Nürburgring you *had* to be able to drive.

'Some of his drives for Frank were tremendous. He won the British Grand Prix, of course, but he was second at Monaco to Scheckter's Ferrari and he was only about a second behind him. At Monza, where the Ferraris – Jody and Gilles – were unstoppable, there at the finish was Clay only a couple of seconds behind.

'The other thing about Clay was that his first few races in Formula 1 were absolutely stonking. He arrived with the reputation of a wild man, although he'd won the Formula 2 championship with Tecno. A lot of people were very chary indeed when they heard *Regazzoni's coming to Formula 1 and he's going to be driving a Ferrari.* From the start he looked terrific, and for his fifth race, the Italian at Monza, he had all the pressure in the world: Jochen Rindt killed in qualifying and Ickx and Giunti in the other Ferraris were both out very soon, so the whole of Italy was depending on him. He responded by driving a perfect race.

'I can't explain the good days and bad days. I once asked him about it and he couldn't either. He burst out laughing. "*I* don't know! I know it's true but *I* don't know why!"'

Notes: *1.* Grand Prix International; *2. Ibid; 3. Jeff Hutchinson writing in* Autosport; *4.* Grand Prix International; *5.* Los Angeles Times; *6.* Daily News, *Los Angeles; 7.* Driving Ambition.

CHAPTER 7

LONG JOURNEY HOME

Professor Watkins waited out the end of the race in the medical car, until Piquet won and the other nine finishers came home.

'I think it was timorousness on the part of race control. They were nervous. I mean, it was pretty stupid really in the sense that it was 1980. I'd been following the first lap and going out on the circuit for two years by then and I always had a respectable driver after an incident at Watkins Glen when I didn't have one. I'd got Phil Hill and he was great. He'd make such a good start we were often in amongst the back two or three rows and Phil was saying "What's with this Formula 1 racing?!?"

'At the end of the race, with the helicopter standing by, they wouldn't let me use it to go to the hospital – Jackie Stewart complained to [Jean-Marie] Balestre [President of the FISA] that I hadn't been allowed to go. So for the second time in my life, and the last time, I went on a motorbike.'[1]

This was a police motorbike and it took him to the main road, where he picked up a 'prowl car' – a patrol car. 'I got to the hospital and there was nothing I could do except to take the pressure off his spinal chord. I called an old colleague from Los Angeles, a very great neurosurgeon, Gene Stern. It was apparent that Clay was paralysed when I first saw him in the hospital. As soon as I saw him I knew. That's when he was very brave. [In his book *Life At The Limit*, Watkins writes: 'When I told Clay

RIGHT *Jackie Stewart, who complained after the race that F1's medical supremo Prof Watkins hadn't been allowed to go to the crash.* (LAT)

the score he very calmly and bravely said "OK Doc," and that was that.'] He'd got a compound fracture of, I think, his right leg and it wasn't painful at all – which showed that he had lost his sensation. You don't know whether he will ever get it back.'

Leo de Graffenried 'went directly to the hospital. Aleardo Buzzi was there.' A spinal operation was required and 'I gave the authorisation after a phone call to his wife. I rang her to get the authorisation. She had seen the accident on the TV. I said "Listen, he's had an accident and he has to have an operation. Is that OK for you, because I have to tell the doctors?" I made the call from a phone box at the hospital. It was around seven o'clock in the evening.'

Gene Stern came down and he and Professor Watkins 'did Regazzoni together,' with a local neurosurgeon who happened to be one of Stern's protégés. Regazzoni had cuts to his forehead, a compound fracture of his right leg and, far more seriously, the 12th vertebra in his spine was injured. The operation lasted until 12:30am, when he was transferred to intensive care, his leg in plaster.

He regained consciousness and was evidently 'lucid and alert.'[2] He remembered that the first person who spoke to him was Watkins.

A spokesman said that his spine had been 'realigned and stabilised, and the pressure on the nerves in the spine has been relieved. However, there was no movement in the legs when he was brought to surgery, and there has been none since. At this point, it is too soon to know whether or not he will regain movement in his legs. His vital signs remain stable but he will have to stay in intensive care for at least 14 days.'

He woke at dawn, in a room painted yellow. His friends Paolo and Ugo Piccirillo were there and he asked who'd won. They told him Piquet.

De Graffenried 'spent from the previous evening until six in the morning at the hospital. I didn't see him, by the way, I never saw him – I didn't go in. I left Long Beach at seven o'clock that morning. The next time I saw him was in Washington some time afterwards.'

Regazzoni phoned home because he wanted to hear his children's voices and, anyway, he was concerned about what the newspapers there were saying about his condition – which family and friends would be reading. When he got through Maria Pia had already left for Long Beach.

This Monday doctors began testing to see if there was any reaction in his lower back. A spokesman said: 'There was no movement of the legs when he was brought here and no change in that condition when he left the operating room.

There were no complications from surgery but it will take several months before we can tell the extent of the damage. There is a possibility of permanent paralysis.'

Meanwhile, the FISA issued a statement: 'As a result of the accident which took place during the US West Grand Prix on Sunday, March 30, and the conditions in which they took place, the FISA is opening an investigation to establish whether or not safety rules were respected. As well as this the FISA considers that the accident and injuries of which Marc Surer and Alain Prost at Kyalami, and Clay Regazzoni at Long Beach have been the victims, requires the agreement of an accelerated calendar to reinforce the strength of the cockpit plus the car as a whole, as it has been sacrificed by certain constructors for the benefit of speed.

'As a result, The Safety Commission, the Technical Commission and the Formula 1 Commission of FISA are convened in extraordinary session to study all the necessary matters which must be presented for decision of FISA Executive Committee meeting on April 15 at Rio.'

This clumsily-worded statement would provoke a backlash.

Oatley subconsciously reveals how remote those days were from the mass coverage of today. 'To be honest, it wasn't until we got home to England that the enormity of what happened became clear to us. Obviously later on race day we knew he'd had a big accident but the full seriousness didn't really become apparent for perhaps a couple of days.'

On the Tuesday a spokesman for Ensign said: 'There are no thoughts that Clay will be paralysed.'

The wreckage of the Ensign was flown back to England but most of the team remained at Long Beach and Nunn visited Regazzoni. So did Alan Jones, Mario Andretti and Jacques Laffite.

Gian Maria and Alessia flew out and Gian Maria still thought their father looked 'indestructible. I didn't really realise what had happened to him because I said to myself *that's just my father* when I saw him in hospital. In the beginning it was the shock for him and I remember him with a sad eye or – or maybe he didn't have. To me – and I don't know how to explain it to you properly – it was *not* a shock because I thought that someday he was going to stand up again, and he thought that too.'

He'd spend hard days and nights at the hospital because he needed to be turned over every two hours and the staff did that by putting him on what resembled, he thought, a long straight plank. It was a lengthy and delicate procedure, and he didn't get much respite between these rotations.

He hadn't lost his sense of humour. The first time they did it he asked if they were trying to make him into a sandwich.

Someone wondered if he'd race again. He replied: 'What other reason is there to walk? Tell Mo Nunn not to sign a full-time replacement.'

Journalist Malcolm Folley, newly married, had 'never, ever been to America. I'd been on the *Daily Express* for five years, as a football man. Rachel [his new wife] had been, as a student. I was 28 and I was thinking *I'm never going to get there unless I take a holiday*. So off we set for California – a young bride, a great adventure – and we arrived just after the Long Beach Grand Prix. Of course he'd had the big accident. I said to Rachel "I've got to go and interview him." She looked at me and I said "I know we're on holiday, it'll be fine, but I must try. I can't *not* do this."

'He was still in the hospital where he'd been taken. I rang and got through to his room. I didn't know him from Adam. I'd covered one Grand Prix abroad, 1979 Spain, where Alan Jones led and that was one of the signposts that Williams were really going to become a force.

'Regazzoni took my phone call and I asked if I could come and see him. The *Express* was a big title then, especially in motor racing, and he'd driven in the *Daily Express* Trophy. He said "Look, I'm in no state to see anybody but go ahead and ask your questions. I'll speak to you now." So I

interviewed him on the telephone. Nowadays, with the way motor racing has grown, you'd have got 1,200 words – I got about ten paragraphs [300 words], but those were the times we lived in.

'I introduced myself to him many years later when he was in a wheelchair coming back to the races. The great thing was – and I always think the same about Frank Williams – they hadn't been embittered by their experiences. They knew the risks that they took. Clay knew it on the racetrack and Frank knew that he drove far too fast on the roads. They seem to have accepted that it was a probability more than a possibility.'

Naturally Ensign wanted to be sure of the cause of the accident and there is slight confusion about who did what next. Nunn says: 'For that car we had titanium brake pedals. We'd had three of these manufactured and we sent the other two to be tested because we didn't know if Clay's had been broken *during* the accident. They put up a hydraulic rig and we even went into how many times the brake pedal had been pressed on the car. They put the other two through the same cycles and they both broke in the same place. It was the same structural fault in all three.'

Gary Anderson says: 'So we went back home and the test to destruction was actually me sitting in the car pushing the brake pedal. This happened in the workshop back in the factory. You didn't have any equipment at that time so it was just me

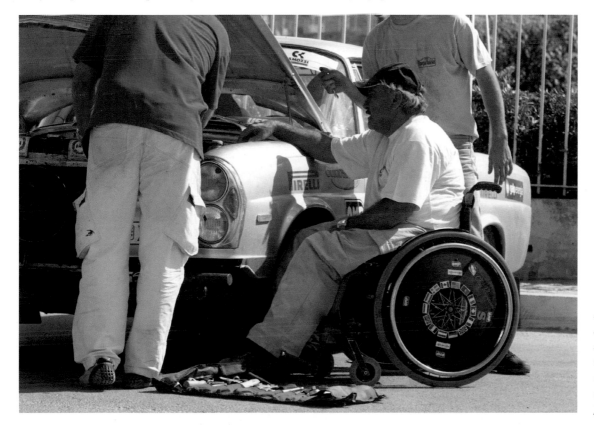

From the evening of 30 March 1980, Clay Regazzoni would have to accept that he'd grow old disgracefully in a wheelchair. (Michael Johnson)

sitting in there seeing what pressure I could put on this thing and then bang! Another one went.

'Williams had 23 people and that was a big team. McLaren in the late 1970s was no bigger than that. I remember Brabham being 16 people: eight travelled, and that was it. You had three cars, and I used to drive the truck as well. Things have changed dramatically, but you did what you did. So me sitting in the car testing the brake pedal was fine. I was a strong bloke, I did it and that was the way life was. The analysis that can be done nowadays is a different deal. That's why a team consists of 800 people now instead of, as Frank Dernie says, 23.

'We lost something in that accident and I always blame myself for these things – I suppose I blame myself because I should have found that the brake pedal would break before it did. Well, I shouldn't have done but you always think that.'

The first week after the accident, the *Los Angeles Times* reported that on the door of his suite somebody had put a sticker: I'D RATHER BE RACING. In the suite Maria Pia was watering flowers while the phone rang. A nurse murmured 'Grand Central Station' – the phone must have been ringing the whole time, mail coming thick and fast. Regazzoni was wheeled onto the roof to do a little sunbathing, although he wasn't sitting up.

On the Thursday, the FISA Safety Commission met in London, and Balestre, as was his style, created a groundswell of controversy (see next chapter). Regazzoni, however inadvertently, was at the centre of it because the crash – as we have seen, the third of the season, and this in only four races – demanded an inquiry with, if appropriate or possible, action to follow.

In Long Beach, Regazzoni claimed (in *Le Combat*) that the doctors decided to send him back to Europe because, they explained, there was a special clinic in Basle – the Schweizer Paraplegiker-Zentrum at Nottwil – which had treated the Swiss downhill ski racer Roland Collombin. He'd fallen badly in a race at Val d'Isere, France, in December 1974 and injured his 12th vertebra. The clinic got him back on his feet, although he never skied competitively again. Regazzoni thought his own injuries were comparable and convinced himself that staying in America would serve no further purpose.

Reflecting later, he thought he might have done better if he'd concentrated on his own state and, in particular, prepared himself for the worst, because he still had no real feeling in his legs. Publicly he wouldn't say anything like that.

On Thursday 17 April he left St Mary's on a stretcher specially moulded to his body. He flew from Long Beach via Los Angeles and San Francisco to Frankfurt, where a Swiss medical plane met him and took him to Basle. A helicopter completed the 16-hour journey by taking him to the clinic. He was immediately examined by a specialist, Dr Guido Zäch, who pronounced his general condition satisfactory.

On the Monday Zäch decided his legs needed a further operation and it was carried out. Zäch explained that nobody would know for two months if his injuries would be permanent and estimated he'd have to stay in hospital for five months.

At least publicly he remained in good spirits. He gave an interview to Swiss television, saying confidently that he'd brought his shoes with him and intended to leave the hospital wearing them.

Leo de Graffenried 'saw him in Basle in the clinic. We gave him a huge toy St Bernard dog – like you buy for the kids – and I said "With that you will never be alone." He laughed.'

Professor Watkins muses about whether Regazzoni was blocking the world out. 'He was a bit like that when I went to see him in Switzerland. I took with me a neurologist who had perfected a technique, which I employed on other patients, of putting electrodes on the nerves to the bladder, and the bowel, and the penis so that you could – with external electrical stimulation – control the bladder, and the bowel, and get an erection. I told Clay about that just in case he didn't recover: that there was some hope of controlling all these functions. He didn't seem to be particularly moved by that. He was clearly very depressed then. Normally, if somebody is offering you that kind of hope you'd jump at it, absolutely. I said to him "You may not need it but if you do it's there for you."'

(Charmingly, Regazzoni compared a hospital to a motor racing team, the beds replacing pits, doctors instead of mechanics, instruments instead of tools.)

'I suffered terribly,' he would write.[3]

What the accident did do was give him an insight into the 'hidden pain' of other people. They did not see his. The very people who had created his myth didn't want to see its demolition, He found himself having to pretend to be optimistic and, even, in high spirits behind that familiar big moustache.

Tansini chose not to go to Basle because Regazzoni 'didn't want to see anybody. He wasn't in the mood.'

Dodo Regazzoni did go and perhaps unconsciously his words reflect the confusion of the situation. 'His morale was good although he didn't *look* well – but he said "After three months I will come back to Formula 1!" I said "Very good."'

There was no Grand Prix in April, in fact none until the Belgian at Zolder on 4 May. There, after negotiations with Mike Thackwell and Brian Henton, Ensign gave the drive to Tiff Needell, a young Englishman. He qualified on the last row of the grid and the engine failed after 12 laps. Needell kept the drive for Monaco on 18 May, and didn't qualify.

On May 31 Regazzoni took his first bath at the clinic.

On 1 June Patrick Gaillard, a Frenchman who'd driven Grands Prix in 1979, replaced Needell for Spain and put the Ensign on the last row of the grid, but the power struggle between the FISA and FOCA – the constructors' organisation – reached

an early climax when the race was declared non-Championship (Gaillard finished sixth, albeit five laps behind the winner, Jones, but because of the status of the race his single point – the only one he got – does not appear in the records).

Next day Regazzoni was taken into the fresh air at the clinic for the first time.

Soon enough there would be other operations in other places.

Aleardo Buzzi reiterates that 'after Long Beach he had long operations, one after the other. Finally we got him back to Europe, then he went to Basle and then the last operation he had was in Paris. I live in Monte Carlo, he lived in Monte Carlo too, so we were very close. We'd play cards. I saw him every month if not every second week, depending on where I was and where he was. He was depressed, of course, but very courageous at the

This is how the local and Swiss press covered the crash.

same time. He was always hoping for something.

'After the crash we didn't sponsor him, no, but we were helpful, yes. That's true. That was the Paris-Dakar [which we'll reach in a moment]. Then we did little things from time to time. Financially he was in very good shape. Clay was very careful with money, very, very careful. He had some businesses of his own. There is a Clay Regazzoni watch and he went into perfume, although that was not so successful. He was licensing his name.'

Nunn remembers how he 'loved racing. He was just a racer. After the accident I met him many times at the hospital and then in Monte Carlo. He had all those operations, he had all these people telling him about this surgeon and that. He seemed to be making some gains and then it went the wrong way. You've got to remember Clay used to play tennis, he'd been on bobsleighs. He did so many sports so it hit him pretty hard. I think he was depressed for quite a time, although I didn't actually meet him when he was depressed. Unlike Alex [Zanardi].[4] I've never spoken to Alex when he was down. I've never seen or heard him be down.'

Regazzoni's recovery is very difficult to discuss with any precision because there seems to have been no precision about it but, rather, a process of realisation, desperation, resignation, acceptance, rejuvenation and, as a constant theme which would keep on surfacing in the years to come, recrimination. He firmly believed, to put it bluntly, that he was the victim of medical mistakes and, if they had not been made, he would have been able to walk again. It's easy to write out the sequence from realisation through to rejuvenation as if he was on a train journey, moving between rails in one direction only, with desperation, resignation and acceptance merely stations along the way.

To show you how imprecise this all was, he described himself how a question was always on his mind: *How at the end of Shoreline Drive were there no brakes?* Someone wrote to him and said he had a friend who was a spiritualist and who could talk to the dead. This friend said the brake pedal had not snapped but was 'desired' by some power who made the pedal dematerialise. Regazzoni requested a horoscope to see where the stars had been on 30 March.

You don't have to be a psychologist to see the turmoil and when you try and relate the material word – titanium brake, Anderson testing it to destruction – with strangers talking to the dead and horoscopes, you're on a very strange journey indeed with no visible stops.

Rainer Küschall, a Swiss like Regazzoni but, as you can tell by the name, from the German north –

Basle – 'was diving one day when I was 16. I hit my head on the bottom and broke my neck. I was paralysed and now [2008] I am 60, so that is 44 years ago – the last time I stood up. I'm a quadriplegic, which means from the neck down I have no muscle control. It's possible to compensate with certain techniques, but Clay, for us, had an advantage. This is because you have 12 chest cervicals[5], you have six or seven neck cervicals and that's already 19, plus four or five down there – that's 25 cervicals. If you're paralysed from the top four or five down, you can hardly move an arm. You just can't do it. And it descends on a sort of scale, what you can't do depending on the number of cervicals. He broke his at the very, very bottom of the scale, so we say he *only* can't move his legs.

'That's nothing to us. For us he's a luxury paraplegic. He can move his trunk, he can lean forwards – and he even can stand, which is another dimension and one I haven't experienced for 44 years. If you can stand and put your wheelchair away, that, for us, is nearly like walking. Zanardi got huge publicity but he's not even paralysed. He's only got two artificial lower legs. If he trained he could run the hundred metres in 11 seconds.

'But you have to be strong enough. I went to Stoke Mandeville with the world's fastest barefoot marathon runner – Adebe [Bikila – he had a car crash in 1969]. He was an endurance athlete, in the way that the marathon is the toughest thing to do, and in bare feet – but he wasn't strong enough to cope with what happened. You'd have thought the situation would be no problem for him but he died because he was *not* strong enough to deal with it. Then I see quadriplegics who were book-keepers, office people – ordinary people, no passion – and they became so strong and had such fantastic personalities, and they got more out of their lives afterwards than before. You know, I've met so many people who have had a sudden crisis in their lives. I have seen heroes who, when it comes to basics, are weaker than a little schoolboy who's got more balls and more guts and more willpower than the best sportsman in the world. So I'm looking at it from a different viewpoint.

'At the time of my accident there was hardly any treatment at all, so I was two years in bed and 14 years in hospital. Only when I was 30 did I meet a girl and she took me out to see life. Then I started to explore a little bit. Then I started to produce the wheelchairs and that's a long story.

'I did not know Clay before Long Beach. I only met him when he was brought to the clinic in

'Autosport' magazine faithfully recorded how big a story it was, deeply touching many thousands of motor sport followers in Britain.

...problems in practice, Clay had worked the Ensign up to fourth place at Long Beach. The accident came on lap 51.

Pit & Paddock

Clay makes progress

After sending nearly two weeks in the Intensive Care Unit at Long Beach's St Mary's Hospital, Clay Regazzoni will shortly be flown to a hospital in Basle, in his native Switzerland. The latest reports of his condition are cause for a certain degree of optimism, although the doctors in California are understandably unwilling to make any firm prognostications.

Although Regazzoni is still unable to move his legs, there is now some feeling in them. While saying that this is an encouraging sign, hospital staff stress that there is no guarantee that Clay will regain the use of his legs. Spinal injuries are unpredictable in their mending. Dr Marvin Schneider, of St Mary's, confirmed this when we spoke to him last week: "The reaction in his legs is very positive, and a good sign, but nothing more than that at the moment. Sometimes you have to wait ... before you know whether ... is going to return to the ... am co... best ... Euro...

mains very cheerful and optimistic, and has had a tremendous number of visitors over the last 10 days. Many Grand Prix drivers, including Alan Jones, Mario Andretti and Jacques Laffite, have spent a lot of time with him. Pia, his wife, did not attend the race, but flew out to California within hours of the accident, together with Clay's brother, Mauro. Most of the Ensign team personnel remained at Long Beach last week.

No formal statement has yet been made as to the cause of the accident, but the most widely held theory is that the titanium brake pedal sheared at a weld point. As we reported last week, one of the Formula Atlantic drivers told our American Editor that the Ensign definitely decelerated momentarily before hurtling down the escape road, and his observations would appear to tally with the brake pedal theory. The pedal assembly was recovered from the wreckage, and was broken; it has not yet been established whether this was the cause of ... or merely an effect ... Ensign ... mains

barrier, was Ricardo Zunino's abandoned Brabham, which the Ensign hit. On the face of it, the Brabham was dangerously sited, and it is difficult to understand why it had been put there, rather than round the hairpin and out of the way, like Alan Jones's Williams.

The fact that Regazzoni hit a moveable object — the Brabham — certainly reduced his speed for the final impact with the wall. Conversely, the Brabham also served to launch the Ensign over the huge tyre barrier and into the wall direct. If Clay had hit the tyres first, the consequences of the accident would assuredly have been less, for the effectiveness of the Long Beach tyre barriers has, indeed, been proved many times — we cannot understand why the idea has not been more widely adopted.

The Brabham was also completely destroyed in the accident, and Regazzoni thinks he was extremely fortunate that no fire ensued, for Zunino's car completed only a few hundred yards and was absolutely full of gasoline. He is very anxious that it be known that he attaches no blame for the accident to Morris Nunn and the Ensign ... and he considers the fact ... lived to be ample ... was a very ... days

Regazzoni's accident

...wing all the joy in Nelson ...Grand Prix victory at Long ...onday was the news of Clay ...appalling accident towards ...ace. The Swiss's Ensign ...end of Shoreline Drive, ...ually released from the ...St Mary's Hospital in

...ng Regazzoni under...of surgery. In the ...leg suffered com...here were severe ...ad, but by far the ...s to his spine. ...is spine.

...al on Monday, ...s: "Mr Regaz...2.30am, and ...Care Unit, ...l leg have ...rest. The ...ry. The ...s spine, ...bilised, ...there ...n he ...has ...o ...ill

regain movement in his legs. His vital signs remain stable, but he will have to remain in the Intensive Care Unit for at least 14 days."

No official reason for the accident has yet been given, and the wreckage of the Ensign was so devastating that the precise cause may never be known. It seems certain, however, that some form of brake failure took place. At the end of 180mph before braking very hard for the first gear Queens Hairpin. It is, the F1 drivers agree, the hardest braking point on any circuit they visit.

One of the Formula Atlantic drivers spectating at this point, says that Regazzoni definitely came off the power as he approach to the hairpin, which rules out any question of a stuck throttle. He says that the car then appeared to decelerate momentarily before plunging down the escape road, which is the continuation of Shoreline Drive. This escape road is approximately 50yds long, after which there are the tyre barriers (used extensively at Long Beach), and then a concrete wall with a debris fence mounted above it.

As the Ensign shot down the escape road at virtually undiminished speed,

there was no opportunity for its unfortunate driver to take evasive action. Parked near the tyres was Zunino's abandoned Brabham. Regazzoni's car hit the Brabham a glancing blow at an estimated 160mph, flew into the air, cleared the tyre barrier completely and hit the debris fence, almost going through it. The Ensign then rebounded back.

The task of releasing Regazzoni from the wreckage was the more difficult because of the tyre barrier on which the car lay, but the marshals worked away with great diligence and care. Clay was conscious throughout the rescue, and able to talk quite coherently to the marshals. After 20 minutes or so, he was removed and transferred to St Mary's Hospital, where he was attended by Dr Stern, a top UCLA neuro-surgeon.

The hospital spokesman told us that, following six hours of surgery, Regazzoni recovered consciousness, and was lucid and alert. We asked if there was any danger to his life, and were told. "As things stand, it seems not. It looks like he's going to make it." This was wonderful news, and we know that all Autosport readers will join us in wishing the enormously popular Gianclaudio a swift and total recovery.

Regazzoni: condition 'stable'

Clay Regazzoni was very seriously injured in the late stages of last Sunday's Long Beach Grand Prix when his apparently brakeless Ensign went off the track and hit a wall at 160mph.

After being trapped in the wreckage for more than 20 minutes, Regazzoni was rushed to hospital where he underwent lengthy surgery to severe injuries to his spine and right leg. On Monday the hospital bulletin reported that the 40-year old Swiss veteran appeared to be out of danger, but that his spinal injuries, even after surgery, had left his legs paralysed. It would be some time, the statement concluded, before the doctors would know if this condition was temporary or not.
More details — *Pit & Paddock*.

Basle. My shop was just beside the clinic and that was very convenient for patients. They'd come over and talk with me, drink a coffee and see how I made the wheelchairs. It was a meeting place, and Clay was a client I had to make a wheelchair for.

'My job in making the wheelchairs is to understand everything that's required – I have now made 100,000, custom-built. Every one is built with the owner's level of disability in mind, and that's why I know the problems better. When you understand those problems you can choose the right version of chair. That's how I met Frank Williams. He asked for me in Stoke Mandeville. Frank can move his arms but he preferred to develop his brain and take on the responsibility of running his team again, which he did and does very successfully. He could push my chair himself.

'Clay's crash was not so bad. He had no damage to the liver and the chest, he had just a compression problem. Every country had a different method of dealing with this, and Americans, they like very much to operate. I am very lucky: in my day they did not operate. They put weights on and things like that, and in that way I had the maximum chance for my body to make a slight recovery.

'Clay realised he had to have a wheelchair. He could not walk. The muscle function in his legs was too little. You know, you have 365 basic muscle components which are co-ordinated. I have three left. If a component of five or six muscles is missing, it doesn't help to move the legs in the right way, but you're much more manoeuvrable in a wheelchair. That's why it doesn't make sense *not* to accept a wheelchair. There are some people who have a mental problem in taking a wheelchair and being a hundred times faster. At least when Clay loaded the chair into his car he was standing up, and he could fold the chair and put it in sideways – I saw it. This was luxury for a handicapped person.

'The first thing is that he had the *capability* to enjoy life. Actually, he did that in the past too. He lived both lives – which means being a sportsman, racing and wanting to win on the one hand, and the girls, the women, the scenery, the travelling on the other.

'You cannot believe it: the chicks came! Just after the operations, just out of intensive care, and women were lining up to visit him in the hospital. They said "We just want to see him doing well" – but they were doing stripteases and everything. The clinic had never seen anything like it before. It was Casino Royale! It was two in the morning sometimes. Amazing. So it had already started

there. That enjoying life was very important.

'How was he then? Clay was not so strong. Actually he was in a very comfortable situation because, as I have said, he could get up onto his legs and stand. He couldn't walk, but with stimulation he could stretch his legs, and he could get very comfortable in a car as well. But he already had a lot of problems, because his character was quite difficult to deal with. He was very strong-minded and if things didn't go as he wanted them to he got extremely angry. He was always swimming against the tide before, when he was with Ferrari, when he was with Williams, in his marriage, when he was living in his home Canton, which he left because of tax problems. People loved him, they hated him. In Italy he was much more famous and loved than in Switzerland.'

When he decided to make a new life in the wheelchair he became very strong again?

'No, I don't think so. He'd got one big plus which most people don't have – that is, he had a fantastic social environment in Italy. For some people he was a hero, and what was very strange was that right to the end he still had a lot of people who stuck to him. He did not lose these contacts because he now had a different life, and so he had the luck to be able to continue doing things he liked. Always he had a friend at his side. He'd say "I've been invited to a go-kart race" and they'd say "I'll come with you."

'The most anger he had wasn't about being paralysed – that absolutely was *not* the problem. In my opinion the problem was two things: first of all he was very angry because he believed that he had been treated wrongly in the operations and so on: if they had handled it better then the damage wouldn't have been so bad. That is understandable, as part of his character. The second thing he was angry about was that he could not be the playboy any more.

'The amazing thing was that he was a person with strong willpower, very strong, but that doesn't mean he was always a strong man in life. He had weaknesses – but everything has two sides, and the strength side compensated. That's why he went just a little bit crazy, looking for difficulties, looking for an argument, acting almost like a provocateur. It's like saying "I have a problem on this side so I must over-accelerate on the other side."'

Küschall is not being unkind, but entirely objective. To him, Regazzoni's disability was comparatively slight but, of course, it was something quite different to Regazzoni. He had been hyperactive for 41 years and now, in the context of that, had become a prisoner: the *reason* for his life – the racing – seemed to be over. There may have been another factor at play, too. He had seemed indestructible – death had beckoned at Monaco in the Formula 3 race, had claimed the life of Chris Lambert, but not his, in the crash at Zandvoort, had beckoned again at Kyalami when his car caught fire, never mind all those other accidents, and he'd survived. His body did not bear the scars of his career.

Once, Johnny Herbert explained that before his crash at Brands Hatch in Formula 3000 in 1988 he felt invincible. The crash was so bad that he almost lost one of his feet. He never felt invincible again.

Suddenly Regazzoni, too, had to confront the one physical thing he had defied these many years: frailty.

On 29 June 1980, Jan Lammers, neat and enthusiastic Dutchman, replaced Gaillard in the Ensign but didn't qualify it for the French Grand Prix. Regazzoni was invited to the British Grand Prix two weeks later (Lammers didn't qualify again) but declined for reasons of loyalty. If he was to attend a Grand Prix again it would have to be the Italian. As a consequence he declined an invitation to the German Grand Prix too, where Lammers put the Ensign on the last row of the grid but didn't qualify it for Austria nor Holland on 31 August.

A day after the Dutch Grand Prix, Essex Motorsport[6] invited 15 Grand Prix drivers – Regazzoni among them – to come to Monaco to eat, drink and be merry. One report[7] said the others 'were delighted to find that they were joined by good old Clay Regazzoni, ever the iron man of Lugano, still smiling in spite of that awful Long Beach accident. Guests in the Hotel de Paris were lost in admiration for his wheelchair antics …'

They all went to a leading restaurant, the *Moulins de Mougins*, to celebrate Regazzoni's 41st birthday (on 5 September), with a great big cake and French musical celebrity Eddie Barclay on the piano, accompanied by a violinist, rendering *Happy Birthday, Clay*.

Leo de Graffenried 'had said to Aleardo Buzzi "I think we have to pull out all the stops to help Clay. He has to come back to Formula 1 to see his friends even if he's in a wheelchair. I will take care of him."'

The Italian Grand Prix was at Imola two weeks after Holland, the only time it went anywhere but Monza. (From 1981 the San Marino Grand Prix inhabited Imola, which was such a useful way to give Italy a second race that it endured for

generations.) Regazzoni was taken to Forli, near Imola, in a private plane and de Graffenried 'went to collect him in a private helicopter'. De Graffenried would 'take care of him the whole day'.

The helicopter reached Imola and Regazzoni, gazing down, saw the circuit covered in light mist. The pilot said they were at an altitude of a hundred metres and as they descended through the mist Regazzoni saw before him the world he had been torn from eight months before: the paddock, the trucks and the motorhomes, the grandstands, the circuit itself. The steps to the Marlboro hospitality room in the main stand over the pits were steep and it took four men to lift the wheelchair up them. A great many people fussed over him there, and more when he was carried down and toured the pit lane. People joked – perhaps understandably they were unsure what to say or how to say it. Others – Frank Williams, Bernie Ecclestone – wanted to shake his hand. Regazzoni remembered sharing a joke with Laffite about tennis and whether the game still made his – Regazzoni's – arms hurt.

There's a precious photograph of this, Laffite bare to the waist seated and leaning forward, Regazzoni, arms across his chest and fingers interlocking, with his broadest smile.

He watched Piquet win from Jones and Reutemann – Reutemann in *his* Williams – and that evening returned to Basle and the clinic. He recorded (*Le Combat*) how, there, everything seemed to close in on him and he wrote a significant sentence. '*Tout était fini.*' The words mean *everything was finished* but can be interpreted two ways: *the long day to and from Imola was finally over*, or, because he'd been to Imola and then the room closed in on him again, *my life was finished*.

The next day however, animated, he discussed the race with the staff and was clearly enthused by the memories.

He could not know, or even simply suspect, that far from everything being over everything would begin again, and in a way which was much more profound than anything that had gone before; but, before that, he had to go on another long journey – part surgical hope and anguish, part growing from his wheelchair into a giant.

In October he left the clinic for the last time, although he returned for check-ups, starting in early December.

At home at the end of October he felt at the end of his strength and his mental resources but others still regarded him as strong and he'd

The 1982 Monaco programme, and Regazzoni's heartfelt tribute to Gilles Villeneuve.

remember how they came to him – one in tears – saying *Give me some of your strength.* Somehow, as it seems, it helped him to forget his own weakness.

Professor Watkins remembers that Regazzoni 'made something of a recovery at one stage and I recall him riding a stationary bicycle. They showed him on BBC television. He was on one of those walkways you use in physiotherapy, where you hold onto the sides and the walkway moves under you.'

De Graffenried remembers that he and Regazzoni 'spent two or three weeks in the States to see an IndyCar race. We also went to Brazil. If he wanted to go back to the hotel I'd always help him into a taxi and one night in Rio I said "You can do it by yourself." In the morning he came to me and said "Listen, Leo, I appreciate the way you are with me – treating me as a normal person." That, for him, was a very important moment.'

In December he took a phone call from a friend in New York, saying that a surgeon who'd done wonderful things with paralysed people would be in Bologna in the New Year. Regazzoni went there and met him. It would lead to an operation, or, as Professor Watkins puts it, 'he went to Washington and had another operation

and he was paralysed again. I'd advised Clay not to do it.'

Is that a difficult thing to do, because he could legitimately say to you 'Look, Prof, I've got nothing to lose any more'?

'No, he was recovering. He'd got some sensation back and he was walking a little bit, riding his bicycle a little bit. I can't remember what date that was, but it looked to me as if he was going to make a reasonable recovery. He'd never be the same as he was before but he might have been able to walk around a bit with a stick.'

Regazzoni described the operation on the 12th vertebra, and how the surgeon couldn't gain entry from the back but had to cut out a rib. Afterwards he caught a fever and even the touch of the bedsheets was painful. It was a 'terrible month'.[8]

De Graffenried can't remember how many operations Regazzoni did have but does remember how he began blocking everything out again. 'Always I tried to call him and he never replied, never answered my calls. He did a sort of block-out of everybody. He was depressed. He'd seen so many people, in Paris, a Chinese guy, he'd had operations – so many guys – and his morale was low. That was why he did the block-out, and I was more a friend than a business associate.'[9]

The chronology of these operations, and the details of them, scarcely need detain us because, whenever they were and whatever they were, the man who went into them in his wheelchair emerged from them in his wheelchair. Regazzoni, as I've said, felt strongly that much of the medical treatment he'd received was simply wrong and it was that which had put him in the wheelchair. He'd give an example of what he considered ill-advised treatment. At one point he was told to try and touch his toes to get the muscles working and 'you could not do a thing like this'.

He recorded how in total he went through five operations and was under anaesthetic for 60 hours.[10]

Roebuck, for many years *Autosport*'s Grand Prix reporter, remembers that Regazzoni didn't come back to the races – apart from Imola – 'for quite a long time. He did have all sorts of surgery. There was one particular operation he had, I think in Washington. The man doing the operation was setting himself up as some sort of miracle worker for people in Clay's position.'

Watkins told Roebuck 'he "couldn't blame Regazzoni because if you're in that predicament you'll do anything." If someone says *I can put you right* you absolutely want to believe this. He said to Sid that he was going to Washington and Sid said "Don't" – but Clay wanted to believe and, even if it's one in a million, I'll take that chance. I remember what Sid said to me: "There was a chance that Clay might have recovered, certainly to some degree, and this surgery he had in Washington just ended it."

'He did have quite a lot of surgery and a fairly lengthy period of rehab. Also there was this dread of going back into a familiar scenario – the place you belong – where everybody knew you, and now you're in a wheelchair. Clay said it is very hard to be in a situation where you know everybody is glad to see you and everybody is thinking *poor man*. He said it's hard *because* you know every single person is feeling sorry for you.

'The thing I remember more than anything – and I think it might have been that year at Monaco when he wrote the tribute to Gilles in the programme [see left], or might have been the year after – I was up at Casino Square watching one of the practice sessions. In those days you could literally be just the other side of the Armco. I suddenly realised that there was Clay, and he was standing leaning against the Armco – his elbows on the Armco – watching the session. There was a moment of silence and then I said "You're standing!" He said "Yes, I can stand all day." He'd got strength back in his legs somehow. "The problem," he said, "is that I can't tell them to move."'

Gilles Villeneuve had been killed at Zolder qualifying his Ferrari for the Belgian Grand Prix two weeks before. In the Monaco programme, Regazzoni wrote:

Hello, Gilles,
I learnt of the tragedy from my bed in Washington where I was undergoing a new operation. It shattered me.
You [tu[11]] were young, loyal, ardent, straightforward, and you loved to express yourself in our sport in a way nobody else could these last few years. You had just reached the summit of glory and, like a clap of thunder, destiny cruelly took your life away.
I remember the last time I met you at Lugano during my racing car show. We spoke about our common love: the Ferrari. For a while you enabled me to rediscover some lovely memories and I was proud to think that this year you would have passed my record of fidelity to the Prancing Horse. I was proud and you were joyous at the same moment. You have left, leaving an immense void. Your virtues were exhibitions of tightrope walking which will be sorely missed by sports lovers who held you in such affection and to whom you gave the maximum. They will never forget what you have done, and you leave memories to all the people who are passionate about motor sport which will never fade.
Joann, Melanie and Jacques, [Villeneuve's widow and children] *like us, will always be proud of you.*

Goodbye Gilles.
Clay Regazzoni

I repeat: whether Roebuck's encounter with Regazzoni at Casino was 1982 or 1983 is as irrelevant to our story as the chronology of the incessant operations. The point is a starkly different one. Motor racing was dangerous in the early 1980s, although Regazzoni remained very much alive. Despite the strength of the Ensign, that was purest chance, however.

Villeneuve, travelling fast, came upon a car going much more slowly and, as it tried to get out his way, guessed wrong. He committed to the side of the circuit now filled by the slower car and was, in that instant, as helpless as Regazzoni had been. Villeneuve struck the car, and the rest, as someone noted, was more like an aeroplane crash. In every important sense Villeneuve died there, although he was not officially pronounced dead until later that evening. Chance had worked itself out in the other way to Long Beach.

Whatever, Regazzoni was alive, and somewhere back there – perhaps in a sequence of private moments – he decided that if you're alive you might as well *live*.

He fully intended to.

He'd said, albeit in the aftermath of the crash and before the extent of his injuries was known: 'It was an accident, nothing else. I don't stop my life because of an accident.'

In that sense, nothing would change.

Notes: 1. Professor Watkins: 'The first time I ran out of gas in my car. This chap came along with a motorbike and I got on the back. I was in charge of the trauma at Ratcliffe Infirmary. I had no crash helmet and I hoped to hell I didn't fall off and find myself in my own emergency room …'; 2. Autosport; 3. E la Corsa Continua; 4. Alessandro Zanardi drove in Grand Prix racing then went to America, where he won two CART titles. He returned, unsuccessfully, to Williams and went back to CART with Mo Nunn. He crashed in a race in Germany in 2001 and his legs were amputated. This did not stop him competing in touring cars; 5. Cervical – relating to the neck, or the neck of any organ; 6. Essex Motorsport, run by David Thieme, a successful businessman who set up the Essex Overseas Petroleum Corporation. That allowed him the funds to indulge his passion for motor sport; 7. Grand Prix International; 8. E la Corsa Continua; 9. Bike rider Wayne Rainey crashed at Misano and was permanently paralysed; 10. E la Corsa Continua; 11. Tu, the familiar address in French, is used only among families, close friends, and adults talking to children (all the rest are vous, so be careful). By using tu in what he wrote Regazzoni indicated closeness.

CHAPTER 8

PIECES

Two drivers had already been lucky in this season of 1980, as we have seen. Prost, a young Frenchman making his way into Formula 1, went into a wall in South Africa during unofficial testing. Something, as it seemed, broke on his McLaren. Next day the rear suspension failed in the spare car, pitching him into a second heavy crash. Surer, Regazzoni's fellow countryman driving an ATS, crashed too. Evidently his foot slipped off the brakes and he hit a concrete wall hard enough to be trapped for 30 minutes. He was flown back to Switzerland with both ankles broken.

After what happened at 3:16 at Long Beach so soon afterwards, Regazzoni was more unlucky than Prost or Surer, but, repeating Gurney, was mighty lucky to be alive.

Words and fractions capture his plight when he pressed the brake pedal and got no response. The words come from John Watson, who drove Long Beach every year from 1976 to 1983, when he won it. He estimates that Regazzoni's speed was probably '160, perhaps 165 miles an hour. I don't know about 175 but certainly you were galloping on.' He also estimates you'd be taking the hairpin at less than 50–60 miles an hour. 'It was very slow. At the apex, if you'd been doing 40–45 miles an hour you'd have been doing well.'

As we have seen, Regazzoni said his braking point was 150 yards from the hairpin. Taking Watson's estimate of 165mph, Regazzoni would have covered those 150 yards in 1.86 seconds – or

RIGHT *The lost world. Never again could Regazzoni clamber up onto a roof and have a look.* (LAT)

fractionally less, because, once his foot came off the accelerator, the car would naturally begin to slow, however slightly.

Zunino's Brabham was parked towards the end of the escape road.

Understandably, reports differ on the exact length of the escape road. Some talk of 100 yards, others 50 (Gurney says it definitely wasn't 100 but maybe a little more than 50). Working on the round figure of 50, and with the Brabham some 10 yards from the end, at 165mph Regazzoni would have covered the distance from his braking point to the Brabham (190 yards) in 2.36 seconds, plus the natural slowing.

If Regazzoni had indeed been doing 175mph he'd have covered it in 2.22 seconds, plus the natural slowing.

That slowing can't have been much because one estimate suggests he was doing 125mph *after* he hit the Brabham, and Gurney, with it happening in front of him, suggests Regazzoni hardly slowed at all.

Zunino himself says 'maybe hitting the Brabham helped because it could move [absorbing some of the impact] and so when he hit the fence his speed was reduced, but it's very difficult to know. The people who understand say he did it on purpose – hitting the Brabham – to try to slow his car down. I can imagine at that speed, at the end of the long straight at Long Beach, it was very difficult because his brake had broken. I was talking with Bernie [Ecclestone] after the race. We analysed what had happened and we concluded that it slowed the speed. It was very sad. I am sure I had nothing to do with it although it was my car there.'

Regazzoni claimed to have tried to brake, tried again, braked again, changed gear from fifth to third and switched the engine off: each a logical move for a driver (and a sequence of moves he may subsequently have convinced himself he made), but each required time. Did he have time?

'Normally when you're braking you're braking at what you consider to be your limit,' Watson says. 'To pump the brake is basically about all the time you have and then there's not an awful lot left you can do to recover – or mitigate – the situation. He may well have snatched third gear but it would have meant pushing the gearlever forward, across and back because it was a five-speed gate.'

Then he says he turned the ignition off …

'Frankly I don't know whether the driver has the presence of mind in those circumstances to do all those things in the rational way that he appears to have done them because, when you're

in a situation where the brake pedal goes to the floor, all you can try and do is avoid a head-on collision – even though the braking zones were much longer than they are now. The only time I had something similar was in Zandvoort, 1980, and frankly all I could do was get quite a long way round the corner before I hit the tyre barrier on the run-off area. Really, as I've said, you just try your best to avoid a head-on collision – but in his case he didn't have that option.

'When I was braking for a corner I would hit the brakes hard initially, then come off the pedal and balance the speed – the amount of slowing down – with the amount of pressure I had put on the pedal. So you have a very hard hit initially and then you modulate the pedal. If you flick it to the floor and nothing's there, suddenly you have to

re-programme everything in your mind.'

Maybe he changed down because he did that every time to take the hairpin.

'My style of driving was to use the brakes exclusively to slow the car down and at the point where I'd got the speed to the level I judged appropriate then I would take the gear for the corner. Other drivers would brake and use the gearbox in conjunction. That was very typical of the time. You'd go fourth–third–second, say. That's what most people did.

'To switch the engine off may have been an intuitive thing. He may have thought that the throttle was jammed – he might have thought lots of things, like if *I do hit this barrier there may be a fire.* Again, I don't think you think those things through that rationally in such a situation.

John Watson, here in conversation with Regazzoni. (LAT)

LEFT Alain Prost, who throughout his career exercised prudence and self-preservation, especially after South Africa.

The lost world: missing the straw bales ... contemplating Miss Switzerland. Telling journalists about the race ... crashing in Formula 2 ... and being at the centre of everything. (LAT)

'If you look at some of the circuits in North America – including Canada – even today there isn't a huge amount of run-off. What they do is put in tyre-bales or something like that to create a little chicane.

'There's another aspect. Where today differs is that they take into account the approach speed to any given corner, so if we were still running in Long Beach, for example, there would be a wholly different kind of run-off area available. To put it in its modern context, coming in to the hairpin at the far end of the circuit in Canada, they have had to take the hairpin nearer to the previous corner at Turn 9 because that was the only way to get the room for this bigger area of run-off, principally to kill the speed, not kill the driver.

'The escape road's length in 1980 was a function of that particular racetrack. They had to block off the road at some point and that was the choice made, but there was enough road for them to have gone on for another couple of hundred yards. That's the way they did it, though. In the context of what we were doing it was perfectly adequate and perfectly safe but the difficulty Clay had to deal with was those two cars in the run-off area which hadn't been removed. Today they would have been, and you may well have had the Safety Car out while it was being done.

'It meant Clay was left with a bad situation compromised by other cars being where he needed to be.'

Conversely, Zunino's car may have saved his life, because it was a movable object and it must have decreased his speed before he hit the concrete.

'A direct hit in my opinion would have been fatal.'

The first thing to say is that Regazzoni himself did not blame either the car, the circuit or the time it took to cut him free. He pointed out that the crash might even help safety because everything improved all the time and the crash could lead to specific improvements on Grand Prix cars. If he did have a regret it was that the brake hadn't broken during testing at Riverside where, by definition, he would not have faced the nightmare sequence.

The second thing to say is that the Long Beach organisers believed their circuit was safe. In the five runnings of the race, nobody before Regazzoni had been taken to hospital, and Gurney said[1] that 'at the time we planned it [the escape road] it seemed fairly long but for that kind of accident you want it a darn sight longer. I know

we can make it longer. We will make it longer – and yes, we will figure out a way to get wrecked cars out of the way.' Gurney added that consideration would be given to making the tyre wall deeper.

Sir Jackie Stewart says that 'the cars in the run-off area, and its length, were the problem. Sid and I worked very closely at that time because he was the man that was involved in that and obviously I knew Sid very well. We were good friends apart from knowing each other and they *had* to listen to him because they had appointed him.'

Understandably, a whole chorus of views rose round the crash, fuelled by the FISA statement (read Balestre) immediately afterwards about the strength of the cars and cockpits 'being sacrificed by certain constructors for the benefit of speed'. Interestingly, Jody Scheckter of the Grand Prix Drivers' Association was saying the same thing.

Chuck Jones, who owned part of the Ensign team, explained in direct response that weight did not necessarily equate to safety and 'in some cases' might even work the other way. 'You could build one heavy enough to avoid being damaged, but I'm not sure I'd want to be inside of it when it hit.'[2]

Mayer of McLaren reacted vehemently, calling Balestre's statement 'typically ill-considered and possibly libellous' to imply that Prost's problem in South Africa 'was the result of unsafe cockpit design' or construction sacrifices in the quest for more speed. Mayer ended: 'Your lack of technical knowledge or qualifications in no way excuses your making such sweeping statements to score cheap political points. Even you must be aware that it is impossible to build a car to protect a driver from injury in a 150mph crash like the one from which Regazzoni was fortunate to escape alive.'[3]

The FISA Safety Commission met at the RAC Competition headquarters in London. Balestre was there and so was Ecclestone. Reportedly strong words were spoken and the subsequent statement reflected a calmer approach by the FISA. It spoke of discussing the three accidents at length 'and it was confirmed that the two circuits concerned had complied with the safety requirements' for a Grand Prix.

The statement added: 'It must be emphasised that the three accidents specifically studied were not related to each other. All three drivers received very different types of injury for different reasons. Prost suffered a wrist injury from a steering kick-back, Surer a foot injury from his foot being caught between the brake and the accelerator, and Regazzoni had a head on crash

Alex Zanardi, who also suffered terrible leg injuries and kept on smiling.

3. *Building in of a reinforced deformable structure in front of the pedal box (to be defined before May 31) to improve the protection of drivers' legs.*

4. *Building in of a protective cockpit cell to reinforce resistance to frontal impacts, by means of longitudinal panels and transversal hoops with new internal dimensions for the cockpit (to be defined before May 30 with the constructors).*

It is necessary to say that the struggle between Balestre's FISA (*Fédération Internationale du Sport Automobile*) and Ecclestone's FOCA (Formula One Constructors' Association) was a bitter thing, and you could argue that some of the posturing, and positions adopted, were a product of that – including Balestre's provocative remarks after Long Beach. You can equally argue that this is what Balestre *should* have been doing, albeit in more temperate ways. Never mind. The tentacles of the political struggle threatened to choke Grand Prix racing and, within a couple of years, almost did, but they are not part of our story.

In theoretical terms every accident is preventable except the racing accident, involving human error that you can't ever eradicate and/or a random set of physical circumstances that can't be predicted. That held true for Long Beach. If the parked cars had not been in the escape road, if the escape road had been half a mile long – both things entirely possible – Regazzoni's Ensign would have coasted gently to rest and he'd have strolled back, watched the race go by.

To speak of consolations in such matters is very delicate, but every accident – the racing accidents aside – should lead directly to examination, and improvement. Cumulatively, you end up with a whole store of situations that should never happen again.

Regazzoni's consolation, as he watched and commentated on races in the years to come, was the alacrity with which cranes and trucks hoisted stationary cars from anywhere on the circuit and took them away if they posed any risk. You'd hear commentators talk, with a tremor in their voice, about *cars in a dangerous position*.

Nobody, you see, can ever forget Long Beach, 3:16 on 30 March 1980.

Three years before, discussing safety, Regazzoni had said: 'I am a fatalist. I believe that everything is decided for us.' He even worked out that he'd known 17 drivers who'd been killed.

Perhaps he found consolation in that.

into a concrete barrier and suffered various injuries to his legs and back.

'It was not felt that any of the three cars involved in the accidents were unsafe. However, it is accepted that regulations should be drawn up to give greater protection to the drivers' legs in modern Formula 1 cars. Regulations drawn up in respect of protecting fuel tanks have been successful. It therefore follows that additional regulations can be drawn up to help protect the drivers' legs. It does say a great deal for the design of current Formula 1 cars that the Ensign driven by Regazzoni in his accident withstood a head-on collision at a speed of around 170mph.'

A few days after London, the FISA Executive Conference met in Rio and Balestre announced a wide range of changes covering circuit safety, race organisation and the 1981 calendar as well as changes to the safety and technical regulations. These had been 'decided for safety reasons and will come into force according to the calendar laid out below.' Seven measures were specified, with 3 and 4 directly related to the accidents:

Notes: 1. Los Angeles Times; 2. Ibid; 3. Autosport.

THE SECOND LIFE: WHEELCHAIR WARRIOR

He was extremely intelligent. He understood people. He understood everything. It was why I stayed all those years with him, because he had had a lot of women in his life. Why me and not somebody else? Once he told me *someone has put you on my route.* That was at the beginning. That was clear. It was not necessary to ask why.
— *Maddalena Mantegazzi*

In Italy it was not possible for disabled people to drive. He put up a very strong fight for the disabled to have the opportunity to drive every type of car. I think he was a great man.
— *Andrea Stella*

He was more active than a normal person. Paralysed people should take him and what he did during his life as an example. Nothing is impossible. He was a kid in his head. He never accepted his age. He did more after he was paralysed than when he was not paralysed.
— *Leo de Graffenried*

I wasn't sleeping really because I could hear animals – *peep, peep, peep, cuuk, cuuk, cuuk, took, took, took* – and you could feel them coming closer and closer. Clay started snoring very hard. Then he woke up. 'Clay, I can hear a lot of animals.' 'No animals here!' 'Clay, to me all the animals *are* here. We're in the *jungle*.' 'Bullshit! There's nothing. Don't worry.' Then he goes back to sleep.
— *Massimo del Prete*

He was very personable, he made people feel very comfortable and especially women. When I met him I think he was in his late 50s and he could still make women feel as if they were the most interesting and beautiful person in the room.
— *Carol Hollfelder*

CHAPTER 9

DESERT STORM

The first part of this book – the first life – follows a certain orthodoxy because it charts, season by season, a competitive motor racing career. Each of those seasons was structured by the racing calendar and, primarily, the Grand Prix schedule, which in his case involved 132 races over a decade. Even before, the Formula 3 and Formula 2 races imposed their own structure.

That changed absolutely now.

The daily currency, so constant and familiar that it becomes subliminal – qualifying sessions, grid positions, fastest laps, laps led, team politics, team-mates, inter-driver feuding, the magic roundabout – ended, too. He'd been accustomed to measuring his life in seconds, but in hospital time expanded and slowed. He had to measure it in days, months, even years.

This second part – the second life – follows a different orthodoxy because it charts year by year an unstructured motor racing career governed not by calendars of races but, instead, a variety of events he chose to take part in. These involved the Paris-Dakar rally, arguably the most brutal test of man and machinery in the world; the London to Sydney marathon, by definition the longest event in the world; and others roaming through South America, Central America, North America, North Africa, South Africa, the Middle East and China. That a man in a wheelchair did this was, is and will always remain genuinely astonishing. That he did it at racing speed – and resurrected his

RIGHT *And now for something completely different: rallying his big Mercedes once he'd banished depression.* (Michael Johnson)

reputation for crashing – remains more astonishing still.

After Long Beach he said he felt two strong emotions about cars: hatred because they'd brought destruction, love because they offered a means of resurrection.

This chapter and the next three are not an attempt to recreate the story event by event as you would championships, one race building to the next and at the end of it a winner. Rather it explores those events – some briefly, some at considerable length – because they are wonderfully improbable in themselves and, cumulatively, they portray a man increasing in stature all the time. Here the real man is expressing himself without the constrictions of the calendar.

Franco Gozzi says that 'the first two years after the crash were for Clay a big fight. Two times he told me "Sometimes I think I will buy a gun and shoot myself." Then there was the argument with Maria Pia. I have to say that after one year more I met her and she said "Life is not so fluent, but it's OK." Talking with him, he said "Now it's OK. This is life. In this condition I have to do something." He *had* to find something to do. So I suggested to him that he thought about journalism, TV, radio, and he did in fact commentate on TV.'

This was on Italian television with Mario Poltronieri. They wanted him to comment on all the Grand Prix races but initially he felt he'd been away from it too long and wasn't necessarily well informed about the contemporary scene. He thought that would make for confusion, which in

turn made him reluctant to attempt it. Gradually he became accustomed to it, however, and tried to make himself into a professional.

He discovered early on that television commentary boxes left a lot to be desired – especially, no doubt, for someone trying to get in to them in a wheelchair. Monte Carlo, as we shall see in a moment, became a battleground.

'We'd lived through a dramatic moment when he crashed, we'd lived through the first optimistic news from doctors during the following days,' Poltronieri says. 'We'd lived through the long pilgrimage to doctors, surgeries, specialists and perhaps also some illusionists who made us hope for a "recovery". Then we'd had the verdict: paraplegic. That brought him to think of suicide, but his temperament and his body and his *unbreakable* love for life won. Little by little he understood his situation and his physical state, and he understood that his bodily limitations need not stop him having an active life.

'Among all Clay's activities after the accident there was a long period of collaboration with me. We were friends and it makes the job not only easier but funnier. Clay was extrovert, an optimist, likeable, modest, happy to collaborate – and always available despite his numerous engagements all over the world. Also, he was loquacious – an easy, fluent speaker – and that permitted me the time to give the race deep attention. *That* permitted me to give the audience a better explanation of what was going on!

'Among all the nice memories, I remember an annual battle. It happened at the Monte Carlo Grand Prix. After a long period commentating from the grandstands we prefabricated boxes two floors high at the exit from the pits. Obviously Clay preferred to remain at ground level. I'd say *Yes, but there's always the possibility of a tyre or something else coming in – better to be on the second floor.* He was such an independent man but he had to rely totally on others to get to that second floor. During those years I tried to explain that he was being given help not only because of his physical limitations but as a tangible expression of the affection everybody had for him.

'I always saw him happy when, alone, he got out of his car, opened the wheelchair in record time with his strong muscles – using only the power of his arms – and, moving quickly, was ready to face every obstacle.'

The marriage with Maria Pia did not survive. The reasons for that are entirely private but it is reasonable to say that she was Swiss and he, really, a citizen of the world, constantly here, there and everywhere – and frankly a lot of the time living as

A new world found: Regazzoni would compete in all manner of rallies – and attack them like Grands Prix. (Michael Johnson)

if he was a single man. Mario Poltronieri says Regazzoni had 'fame as a big lover and "with every woman it is sufficient that she was still breathing".' This is not necessarily the avenue to a happy marriage.

When they separated he went to Monte Carlo and began again.

Rainer Küschall dismisses the talk of suicide as a 'minor thing' because, far from trying to carry it out, Regazzoni 'chose the other way: an active life. Everyone who is a hero at the top of a mountain and falls to the ground has some things they have to deal with first, and work on them mentally. I think everybody asks one question: what will life be like for me and does it make sense to continue? You don't know what value to put on things like this. If somebody sleeps badly for one night he feels terrible but other people have 20 years of pain and that's another world of emotions. It is something each person has got to work out for himself.'

Clearly Regazzoni had.

Sir Frank Williams explains that wheelchair users 'are all members of the same family. You don't say it, you just recognise it. If you see someone else in a wheelchair you'd always speak to them.'[1]

Like motor racing, it was a family of people bonding because, however different they were in other aspects, this they had in common. Regazzoni would complain about something they all must experience: confronted with someone handicapped, people are either too condescending or ignore you altogether. He'd complain about something else they all must experience. At airports, railway stations and in public places, ticket clerks and assorted officials would speak to the person you were with rather than you, as if being in a wheelchair meant you couldn't understand what was being said. This openly enraged him, as we shall see.

He asked why there should be prejudice against the handicapped, why this discrimination? Man has reached the moon, he thundered, and didn't walk there! Electronics – and he specified computers – can be used by anyone. Voice-activated devices opened up all manner of possibilities, from making phone calls to driving cars.

From the tenor of this, you can gather that Regazzoni had – in Küschall's phrase – over-accelerated to the other side. From all the negatives he was about to become very, very positive, for himself and the wheelchair family.

Son Gian Maria says: 'From time to time he'd get mad with someone because he wanted to be able to do everything by himself. I am sure that occasionally in the morning he did, because he couldn't just get out of bed and stand. When you see other people in wheelchairs you might see they are suffering but when you saw my father sitting around the table you wouldn't even have thought he was in a wheelchair. It wasn't that he was Clay Regazzoni, it was that he gave the impression he was normal.

'In Italy it was really bad: handicapped people couldn't drive and he got mad about that. "Who said you drive a car with your feet? You drive a car with your brains!" So he had to find a way to make it possible – and that was the school …'

Inspired by a girl in Modena who had artificial arms but who could drive a specially-adapted car easily, he began speaking to Stefano Venturini of a specialist company called Guidosimplex, which means 'driving made simple'. They've spent four decades finding 'technical solutions designed to allow handicapped people with disabled or missing limbs to drive in complete tranquillity.'

Venturini says that, like everyone who has had a similar trauma, 'Clay did not accept it lightly and it must be harder when you fall from such a height. Because of his passion for engines, cars and speed we created the *Scuola di Pilotaggio per Persone Disabili* [Driving School for the Handicapped].' This was at the Vallelunga circuit because, Regazzoni reasoned, Monza and Imola might be unusable in the winter, but that much further south the weather was invariably mild, allowing the school to function all the year round. He was what Venturini described as a promoter of the School as well as adviser.

'Later,' Venturini says, 'we created the FISAPS [*Federazione Italiana Sportiva Automobilismo Patenti Speciali*]'. This was a federation to encourage and promote the development of car and kart driving for the disabled. 'Clay was Honorary President. He could not have a management position because he was Swiss and the positions went only to Italians. He brought his sporting experience into this Federation, and it was of great value for the general organisation, racing participation, rules, sponsors, driver contacts, organisations and corporations …'

Regazzoni had extensive contacts and used them because he wanted to make the three-day courses – theory and practical – free, with participants only having to find the money to get there. Alfa Romeo came in as a sponsor, the Italian Association for Sport made a contribution, and others came in too: Pirelli, AGIP, Marlboro, Parmalat, Simod (a shoe company sponsoring the Formula 1 team Minardi), Jeb's (helmets), MOMO

The driving school at Vallelunga, proving to disabled people that they can drive – and fast. (courtesy Guidosimplex)

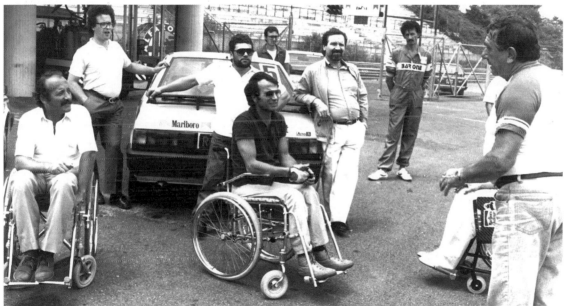

(steering wheels), Sparco (overalls) and Fiuggi (mineral water).

He recognised that he was not an instructor but, as Venturini says, 'he made other contributions. He spread the message to all the people who came, and to all the people who were handicapped like him, that if you have the courage you can, through the cars, make dreams come true.

'Clay was more active than able-bodied people. During parties and at dinner he was always joking and funny, but he became Swiss when he spoke about engines and cars, always precise – and controversial. He was stubborn in all things, not least because frequently he was right. He always fought all restrictions on handicapped people in Italy and the birth of the driving school made him well known in the handicapped community. He didn't use the wheelchair as propaganda or personal justification for what he was doing but as a means of protesting against institutions which pretended to be listening, and a means of solving handicapped people's problems travelling in cars, trains, boats and planes.'

Gian Maria sums up. 'What my father used to say was that he had had a beautiful life and he was lucky, even after the accident. "I had the luck to be Clay Regazzoni and that enabled me to do whatever I wanted. I couldn't have helped people if I wasn't Clay Regazzoni." The reason he felt sorry for other people in wheelchairs, especially in Italy, was because he saw they couldn't be anything. They were stuck in the house.'

He insists his father was strong-willed. 'Especially when he was playing cards he couldn't stand losing. Always it was the other guy's fault! There were a few of them who knew him and with them it was OK, but others didn't. If you had an argument he yelled at you and ten minutes later it was finished. He'd slam his fist on the table but everybody respected him and they used to love him. At times he didn't have a very nice character but you had to know him. Possibly it was a bit worse after the accident, but it's the Regazzoni family. We are very nice people but … we get mad. It's a family thing.'

By 1985 the driving school was open.

The friendship with Tansini the ultimate fan began again at a reunion party at Maranello. 'It was a time of remembering all the adventures. Then every time Clay passed through Milan he called to see me, which was frequently – there was a guy in Milan who provided Clay with spare parts for the wheelchair. He was very active. Driving back to Lugano at one o'clock, two o'clock, three o'clock in the morning was not a problem.'

Roebuck remembers Regazzoni saying 'for a long time I felt very sorry for myself but when something like this happens, you move into a different world, a world you never thought about. You see little children with cancer and you feel ashamed. You've had years of good life which they will never have. I can't walk but I can drive my Ferrari, I have my driving school for handicapped people, I can still go to races. I don't feel desperate any more.'

De Graffenried remembers staying in a hotel with Regazzoni 'and the son of Hugo Boss was there. He had a crash when skiing as a little boy – 14 years old, but more paralysed than Clay – and he said to me at breakfast "That kid, he didn't think he was risking being paralysed, he was just skiing. Me? I went to the maximum, 300 kilometres an hour, and had a crash. Normally I should be dead and I chose that line of work. It was my job. So when I see people paralysed, and they didn't have a chance to start enjoying their life, when I see a kid like that, it hurts me a lot."'

A month after Monaco he took Alessia and Gian Maria to Detroit for the USA East Grand Prix. He found that the facilities at the airport there – no stairs, no barriers – made collecting his luggage and passing through easy. He rented a car with hand controls. He wondered if this was a legacy of the Vietnam War and, more distantly, that in Korea, when so many disabled soldiers had come back.

He contrasted that with the situation in Italy, where *Ironside* – the American TV show about a detective in a wheelchair – was popular on television *but* you still found obstacles everywhere, couldn't get into toilets, and the service stations on the *autostrada* were not handicap-friendly. In another great thunder of noise he exclaimed that taxi drivers didn't want to take you. Once a taxi arrived for him and the driver complained 'Why didn't you tell me you were in a wheelchair?' before recognising him. This enraged him, not least because once he was recognised the taxi driver was happy enough to accept the fare – his fame was an advantage unavailable to the rest of the wheelchair family.

However, one of Küschall's stories directly contradicts the spirit of this. 'Clay was surrounded by friends and that made it very easy because he was a hero and in his Formula 1 time the main "rebel" of all of them. That is what the women loved and why afterwards he had so many friends. In Italy at every petrol station they knew it was Clay – he was a national hero. He had a very recognisable face, so everybody knew him. Well, one person didn't and he became very angry. We had a problem with parking and he couldn't park where he wanted to. He shouted at the attendant and then said "I'm Clay Regazzoni, I am now in a wheelchair and I need to park there to go in for a conference," but the attendant didn't know who he was. When Clay realised he was not known he became angry again. "Regazzoni – the Formula 1 racer." The attendant still didn't know him! So Clay used to bring his reputation into the game.'

I propose to give a variety of views from those people who saw him in the wheelchair.

John Watson is strikingly candid. 'Being a racing driver, or working in the media, there was something of the *here but for the grace of God go I, I could have been in that situation* when you saw him. It was as if you never felt entirely at ease. It's a very awkward feeling to be in the company of somebody who is paralysed because you're always conscious of the fact that these people have suffered horrendous injury. I find I was awkward trying to be perfectly normal and natural, in part because I didn't know Clay in the way others of his colleagues and team-mates would have known him. I didn't want to sense that I was having to be nice or risk seeming patronising. We'd see each other at races and you'd have your "Hello" and "How are you, how you getting on?" but it wasn't as if you were going to go out for supper with him or anything like that. In truth, that was partly language as much as anything else but also the slight awkwardness of dealing with someone who … well, I've come out of it unscathed in relative terms, and he came out of it traumatically.

'Niki Lauda has got fairly unpleasant facial scarring, but Niki's character and personality and his ability and language and many other things made it not a problem. You didn't look at his face, you looked at the man. All it was was a purely cosmetic thing. It was a mechanical thing with Regazzoni – you had to look down at it, and I'm not particularly capable of dealing with it.'

Gary Anderson gives a different view. 'I didn't meet him after the crash – well, I did at Monaco one year in his wheelchair, but I didn't *really* meet him. I was in Germany when Zanardi crashed and lost his legs, and I had to do a sort of police thing with the chassis because I was working with Reynard at the time. My memories of Alex before losing his legs and afterwards are in a different world to Regga, because Alex had that ability to overcome and walk and do his thing, whereas Regga was trapped in his wheelchair and I suppose to some extent I wanted to remember him more the way he was when he drove the car. I was a nobody at the time, just a junior mechanic to Regga and it wasn't long enough to get to know

him. We never got to be bosom buddies, going out for meals, because it was just too early.'

Professor Watkins captures how, although the world of Formula 1 is relatively compact, it remains still large enough for people to exist within it and not be rubbing shoulders the whole time. 'He never had much to do with me after Long Beach. He used to say "Hello" and that was about it. Mind you, I thought what he did in the wheelchair was brilliant.'

It was time to move to the next stage: from 1 January to 22 January 1986 and the Paris-Dakar.[2] Regazzoni had been speaking to Aleardo Buzzi of Marlboro, you see.

This is how it happened. Mario Poltronieri knew the Paris-Dakar and in 1983 had even organised a Press expedition to it. 'I made a proposal to Mr Buzzi – Philip Morris president and Clay's big friend – for the Dakar. Buzzi was the third man, after Bernie Ecclestone and Enzo Ferrari, to understand the potential exponential growth of Formula 1 (so he knew the subject, all right). Buzzi spoke to me about his doubts. "And if he does it, and he hurts himself again?" I was able to convince him that Clay's big heart would truly benefit from this new adventure, and I turned out to be a prophet because since that moment Clay became a rally specialist!'

Franco Gozzi remembers that Regazzoni 'came to Maranello – he was allowed to go anywhere in the factory – saying "*Ciao*" to everybody. [Regazzoni maintained excellent relations with Forghieri, who was also a leading figure in the world of historic cars, and had taken to visiting Maranello once a month.] When he came into my

The first foray on the Paris-Dakar Rally and it ended in disappointment. (courtesy Claudio Bonicco)

office he said "I think I will have not have a problem for the future because I have decided to race again. I came here from Lugano driving my car. I have a couple of proposals for a truck in the Paris-Dakar and I am arranging something in South America. I feel like a kid now. I feel alive again." I said "This is fantastic." That was six years from the accident and his mind was perfect once more. No problem. He accepted his situation and he said to himself *OK, if things are this way, things are this way.*'

Graham Bogle was Director of Event Marketing at Philip Morris, who, of course, had such intimate connections with motor sport through their Marlboro brand. 'We were invited to help him do the Paris-Dakar. We co-sponsored his entry and his team but the whole exercise was more like a personal challenge and his desire to compete was better than the quality of the team, the equipment, the organisation and everything else. The team really didn't set out to do anything other than get to Dakar. It said so much about him that he was wanting to do the Dakar in those circumstances.

'Paris-Dakar! This is the last place you'd expect somebody paralysed to be going. I've got friends that do it even today and they've shown me pictures of their journeys. The physical discomfort for healthy athletes is extreme so therefore if you're in his condition it tells you an awful lot about the person. Nobody will say a bad word about him and his courage – that's what you'd call it really, wouldn't you? – and his competitive spirit.

'Everybody was very worried about whether this was a challenge that he shouldn't have taken but he was persuaded that he was able to do it, and he had enough back-up to do it. I suppose the other thing was that the organisers had asked themselves the same questions: have we got the right back-up to look after him in those circumstances to accept his entry? They must have felt they did because he was allowed to compete.

'I think these challenges were just part of keeping himself focused on projects and staying involved in motor sport in some way, and in part to communicate to a wider audience that you can overcome your disabilities. It sounds a very simple statement but he was for me a typical racing driver [*chuckle*]. Do you know what I mean by that? We have a certain category of racing drivers where they're everything that you'd expect them to be. He was cavalier, he had an admirable personality, you felt you were in the company of somebody special. He was fast. From a racing point of view I'm not sure that he was necessarily a team leader, a No 1 – it was Ickx–Regazzoni, wasn't it? And you did feel that Ickx was the main man. In some other teams you could have said the same, but he was probably the strongest No 2. He had a certain charisma which was superior to a lot of his contemporaries. Regazzoni: the name itself says a lot about the image of the sport and the excitement of the sport. He had an international fan base, which not a lot of those drivers had at that time. Maybe I'm inflating it, but I sense that if the Internet had existed then and you'd done a ranking you'd find him as a very, very internationally popular driver.

'If you look at all the photographic files of Regazzoni, he *looked* like a racing driver, and he behaved like one on the track and off the track.'

Now, though, it was going to be Africa.

De Graffenried remembers 'we did the announcement. We said "Clay, how can you do the Paris-Dakar?" He wanted to touch so many things because he didn't want just to stay at home. For example, in the States he went in the swimming pool and I said "You have to be careful." He couldn't move his legs, of course, but he swam using only his arms. The guy was so strong. Sometime he went to see races and I'd pull him out of the chair. He'd grab something and stand because he could hold himself up.'

By now he considered himself privileged in what he was doing and even more motivated than he had been before the accident. He also considered himself a symbol and wrote this resounding sentence in *E la Corsa Continua:* 'I want handicapped people to be able to leave their houses, I want to meet them in everyday life, I want them to drive, I want one day the bravest of them to be able to take part in racing.' He didn't want to be given favoured treatment, didn't want to be 'president of something,' didn't want a title, and ultimately wanted just to be regarded as Clay Regazzoni who happened to be sitting in a wheelchair.

He said that when he went to the Italian Ministry of Transport to speak, he explained that driving brought technical not physical problems to anyone who was handicapped, although each handicapped person faced different issues, reacted in different ways, and had to build their life in a way that suited them.

It was precisely what he was doing.

He approached Küschall to get a special wheelchair made that would negotiate sand (he was, after all, going across the Sahara Desert). 'He came and said "Rainer, I'm going to do the Paris-Dakar. How do I survive in the desert?" So I brought my knowledge and my expertise to bear. I said "OK, I'm going to do it for you." I made a wheelchair that would be as good as possible on sand and, in addition, could be folded small to fit in the truck.'

Küschall is not at all surprised Regazzoni returned to competition. 'Motor racing was a part of his education. It motivates you to do something. Sport in a wheelchair forces you to strengthen your willpower, it forces you to get more disciplined because you need to train in order to be good, it forces you to be much more mobile and active because when you go out into the world you're moving away from the security of your home.

'He could continue his life's passion. Like Frank Williams, he could actually do this, even though in a different way. Both had something from the past that could be continued. Clay couldn't have done that if he'd been a rider or a swimmer, for example – no way. If he'd been a rider it would only have been possible for him to create a horse-riding team. He couldn't have ridden himself.'

That Regazzoni was doing this, Küschall thinks, is a sign of strength. 'Only strong people can continue. Clay had a little bit of hot blood, which was mostly uncontrolled passion. In those days [in motor sport] you could drive fast by having more guts and taking more risks, and gain an edge over your competitors by doing that. He was one of those guys. He was brutal! You know how when you get into a fever some people do things and are so controlled, based on a level of knowledge that it is fundamental to them? Clay was one of those people who went into a rage, into hunter mode or fighter mode. He challenged things. That's why he didn't finish the rallies – the Dakar, for example.

Rainer Küschall, proving what can be done, in a car and a wheelchair.

Rainer Küschall
Winner of 21 Paralympic medals

Rainer Küschall

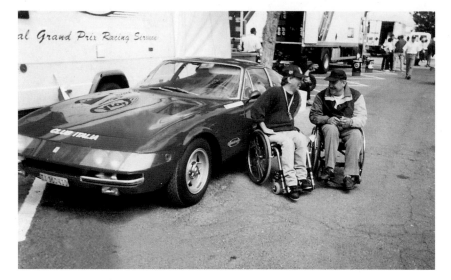

Different wheels: Küschall, Regazzoni and feline Ferrari. (courtesy Rainer Küschall)

'I chose a wheelchair for him with a footrest that could be adjusted, because he was still in the hard process of trying to regenerate some leg muscles, and I had to think about practical considerations – like him going to the exercise walking bar. When he got there he could have his legs at a 90° angle to the ground. That would enable him to get up more easily.

'It was quite a compact design, a concave formation of the chassis so it was very manoeuvrable, to go to the toilet, stand up and turn around. For the Paris-Dakar I put on different wheels: super balloon air tyres on the front and the widest tyres I could find on the back. The chair was very small, because in Africa some of the hotels have no facilities for the handicapped. He wouldn't be sleeping in tents all the time.'

Franco Pipino lives in the pleasant town of Cuneo, deep in the heart of the Piedmont region and roughly halfway between Turin and the Mediterranean. 'There was a club of people passionate about motor sport and the club's chief was called Geraldo,' Pipino says. 'He was a good friend and Clay was looking to build up a team to go on the Paris-Dakar in 1986. The team was called *Paris-Dakar Regazzoni*. There was a truck for Clay and a back-up truck. Geraldo needed someone to be the navigator. I had some experience in rallying and some experience of Africa so he thought I might be the right person. I'd done local rallies. I didn't have as much experience as a proper competitor but I'd also had a lot of experience on bikes.

'I was a little bit embarrassed by this offer from Geraldo because everybody knew Clay Regazzoni very well – *everybody* – so I decided to meet him in Milan and the occasion was the presentation of the team. This presentation was very important because it was the first time Clay had returned to

competition. He'd had a big depression after the accident – as he describes in his book – but then he had to decide what to do. Sometimes he told me in confidence that he had considered suicide but in general he was very positive in life.'

The team, incidentally, comprised six vehicles, of which two were trucks, and a total of 14 people.

Pipino, a mild-mannered man, was the first of Regazzoni's many co-drivers (who in rallying are really navigators), and therefore the first to confront a most sensitive problem: if there was a crash, they might well have to help Regazzoni – itself a problem with a big, heavy, immobile man – and what if *they* were hurt, and unable to help him?

Küschall rationalises that and explores the whole subject from, shall we say, *Regazzoni's* point of view. 'I'm a racing driver and there is always the discussion "Can he get out of this car?" [Regazzoni once gave a demonstration of this in the tunnel at Monaco and onlookers were astonished at how fast he did it].[3] That's not a factor any more these days. If you want a competition licence you go to a little circuit racecourse, and the first thing you learn there is, after an accident, to ask *Can I see? Can I lift my arms? Can I breathe? Can I lift myself? Can I move my feet?* That enables me to give the information to the first aid people who are coming. So it would be stupid to unfasten your seatbelt and jump out: you may have a fracture and shouldn't move. It makes sense to do the opposite. Nobody thinks like that and that's why I need to explain it, because it is all-important.

'In truth 99.999 per cent of people are somehow disabled. *Why doesn't he react?* – because he can't hear what's happening. *Why does he walk bow-legged?* – he could have been a sprinter, but because of his bow-legs he can't run. Those are disabilities. Why do you say someone's a cripple or handicapped or a disabled person just because he's in a wheelchair? If he plays sport people say "It's disabled sport," but I say "No, it's sport in a wheelchair, like ice skating is a sport where you need skates and skiing is a sport where you need skis." They have to have technical equipment to move. In Clay's case he had cars, so he was lucky; but when you speak about disability you need all the contexts.

'I come back to the question *If something happens to me, what can the co-driver do?* What he can do is limited, although you never talk like that about an accident because – even if you're in a single-seater and crash, and you're unhurt but the chassis is damaged – you need help. You can't help yourself. If two people – one of them Clay –

are in a truck in a rally and they have an accident, and Clay had been able-bodied but had got a broken leg, he wouldn't be able to help then either.

'It's all relative. For me, 20–30cm is already an obstacle like a wall. For you an obstacle would have to be two and a half metres before it became a wall. That's when you have the same limitations as me. Only the proportion is different. Everybody has these limits. So it's the same thing with the co-drivers: it's relative.'[4]

In Pipino's case, however, there might be a third man in the truck: an experienced mechanic called Virginio Mana, whom Regazzoni was counting on. There was a seat for him but whether he'd always be riding with Regazzoni or in another of the team's vehicles is a moot point.

Mind you, Pipino was not going to get the shock of his life because that implies a singularity, and the shocks would keep coming at racing speed.

The chosen vehicle was an Iveco truck.

Stefano Venturini remembers that during the Lugano fair there was an exhibition of a manually-adapted car and 'we decided to go the day after to Turin, where the truck was being prepared, to check on progress. We met in the morning and set off but soon it began to snow. We stopped for fuel and Clay said that in view of the weather we wouldn't be able to get to Turin in time. I replied that he was right and sat expecting him to say "Let's call it off." Instead he set off like a rocket. The way was blocked and the snow was falling hard but we got through. I convinced myself that the man – the pirate of the *autostrada* – knew what he was doing, and that that wasn't because he didn't appreciate the situation but because he was using all his experience. A certain security flowed from that. I convinced myself that *the only way* to travel with Clay was to convince yourself. We reached Turin on time.'

The Paris-Dakar rally was founded by a French motorcycle racer called Thierry Sabine. In 1977, competing in a race which passed through Libya, he got lost in the desert and thought it might be a good place to have a rally. That December the first of them was run, starting at Versailles just outside Paris and snaking down to Dakar in Senegal. It was long, it was an endurance test, a test of organisation, very, very dangerous and sometimes lethal. Apart from the harshness of the topography – people died of dehydration – it would have to contend with wars, civil wars and terrorist threats.

It would also have to contend with criticism that it was a plaything for the rich and brought little benefit to the places it passed through. Rather, it brought a lot of dust plus collisions with people and livestock. (In my experience, the rich and their playthings tend to avoid deserts and war-zones, but never mind.) It crossed the Western Sahara, which led to political disputes. And the Greens voiced their disapproval, although in terms of fuel used and pollution created such a rally barely registered when measured against the average daily consumption of the world.

What the Greens were doing was no doubt symbolic, and in one sense that was entirely appropriate because the rally was itself symbolic: an ultimate examination across 15,000km of what men, a few women and machines could tolerate. Now you know precisely why, at the age of 47, Gianclaudio Giuseppe Regazzoni entered, wheelchair and all. He'd call it the last great sporting adventure left. He didn't know Africa and it fascinated him. More than that, he'd be covering the equivalent of fifty Grands Prix. The Paris-Dakar might just be the most important thing he'd done in his career.[5]

The 1986 event attracted 500 competitors, 133 on motorbikes, 320 in cars (Jacky Ickx among them) and 70 trucks, some as competitors, some as service vehicles. Very few of these were professionals with well-funded factory teams, but they were the only ones with any realistic hope of winning. The rest were adventurers, and that struck a deep chord with Regazzoni.

To give you the flavour of the event, Sabine described the competitors as 'real explorers' who at one point would face a 'wall of sand' and 'we discovered there is no longer a defined track from Mali to Guinea so they will have to drive through thick bush, sometimes in grass two metres high which can hide enormous potholes.'[6] During the reconnaissance, Sabine added, they'd come across a place so remote that they'd had to 'follow camel tracks to find water holes.' Add a couple of mountain ranges for spice, and you have it.

Fred Gallagher, a leading British co-driver and veteran of the Dakar, reinforces what Sabine has just said: 'If you did the Dakar you'd find it bloody difficult because once you get out of Morocco into the proper Sahara you're camping for maybe five, six days at a time and, certainly in the days when Clay began, there were no showers, there were no loos whatever. You would pitch your tent – which would be tricky to begin with, and I guess he needed someone to do that for him – and then if you wanted to go to the loo you just went off into the night with a torch over a sand dune. It was basic stuff like that. I just have no idea how he did it.

'The 1986 route would be pretty horrendous, a particularly difficult one. These were the days before GPS[7] when the navigating was by compass, just an electronic compass. It wasn't at all easy, as you can imagine.

'The trouble in the desert is that the first guy makes tracks and what happens is that unless someone is desperately confident they tend to follow the tracks ahead. I've seen situations in the Paris-Cape Town rally where the entire field – the first 200 cars – all went wrong at one point because they were following each other.'

Nor did the problems cease as the competitors finally emerged from the Sahara because, as Gallagher says, 'when you come out of the desert you faced maybe the last six days when there were lots of little tracks going everywhere. You think about Africa: if people are walking or herding animals, it makes sense that nobody bypasses a town or a village, so all the tracks go into the village and out again. Consequently when you're leaving a village the first thing you might see is a hundred tracks. If your compass tells you "Heading 265" it's quite difficult to know the difference between 260, 265 and 270, so navigation was a problem.

'The terrain beyond the desert tends to be thorny bushes and what they call camel grass, tufts of it – like speed bumps. Quite difficult. The whole thing is difficult.

'At times, I remember, you'd finish a 500–600km stage and you were weary. You'd get out of the car and it could be an effort to walk to where the dinner was. To try and get round in a wheelchair is almost beyond belief. You'd find people like [rally greats] Ari Vatanen, Björn Waldegaard and Timo Salonen getting to the end of a Dakar stage and *they'd* be knackered. Quite what it's like for a bloke who's handicapped I can't imagine.'

The immense cavalcade would leave Versailles and move south to Sète, a working Mediterranean port in the Languedoc region when they embarked for Algiers. There they'd head south to a place called Ghardaia, the Sahara beckoning. They'd keep going south to Ramanrasset, and already they'd have done 1,000 miles as the crow flies. They'd turn south-east to Agadez, the largest town in northern Niger and, on the trans-Sahara trading route, a place which still saw salt caravans. They'd turn east to Dirkou, then work a contorting route to Niamey, the capital of Niger. They'd travel west to Bamako, the capital of Mali, cross into Guinea, corkscrew north to Chinguetti, a medieval trading centre in northern Mauritania, corkscrew south and head for Dakar. Down this route the locals prepared to multiply prices by, in some places, a factor of ten.

The rally began with a prologue at Pointoise-Cergy near Paris, run over 7.6km of gravel at an off-road driving school. An ice-clad day, snow falling, but some 100,000 spectators came to watch, which made a strong impression on Pipino. And on Regazzoni. 'He was good,' Pipino says. 'Everyone was impressed and they applauded.'

Regazzoni met Sabine and described him as the 'genius' of the event, tall and blond. He also described the prologue as like something from a Fellini film.[8] Perhaps it was.

The next day some 300,000 came to watch the start from Versailles to Sète, a 'boring haul down the N20'[9] with its 90kmh speed limit. It was, Regazzoni estimated, 900km with a couple of refuelling stops and a couple of check points. By now he understood that the truck was not what he expected and not what he wanted: it couldn't reach maximum speed in top gear (sixth) because the gears were too long. That would make him slow, although, as the cavalcade moved south towards Sète, he had plenty of time to ponder what to do. The decision was simplicity itself: he would compensate for whatever the truck lacked by driving it like a Grand Prix car.

It was not good news for Pipino's nervous system.

A Japanese competitor on a motorbike had a crash on the road not far from Sète and became the first fatality on the event in 1986.

Autosport described Regazzoni as 'a favourite with the fans' when the competitors loaded their vehicles onto the overnight ferry. On disembarking they headed south although the 'real action'[10] didn't begin until they were leaving Ghardia, a white-walled town shimmering in the brilliant Sahara sun beside an oasis, the sweet smell of dates sometimes on the wind. The cavalcade moved into a 397km special stage, an authentic taste of what was to come.

Poor Pipino: he saw, minute by minute, a rush of impressions coming towards him. 'Clay was not a truck driver, he was a Formula 1 driver, so he had some problems in handling this world, which was not his world … it was very tough being his co-driver … I discovered that he was the kind of person who was ready to take risks … he wanted to do his best, he was competitive, but he also he wanted to prove he was still a good driver even without legs, so he was pushing *very* hard … I said to him "Pay attention, because if we hit problems I can get you out of the truck, but if something happens to me you couldn't do anything like that to help."

'I'd done some rallies but I'd never seen anyone driving like Clay did … I was particularly afraid about the way that he drove, because he drove in a very crazy way … I thought *Is it in his mind that he wants to commit suicide?* Then I thought *Can that really be true?* Then I thought *I don't want to die in Africa with him* … It was a bad moment for me … Clay was obviously frustrated … He said "If we go at less than 200 kilometres per hour you can't do anything like kill yourself …" I was really afraid because he drove at 300 – for him, 200 was nothing.

'When he came to an obstacle he didn't stop … We reached a bridge which was not in very good condition, but that didn't pose a problem – we went straight over it, so he really didn't see the obstacles for what they were … I was very nervous about the situation, and to try and solve this I started to give him false pace notes, hoping he'd slow down … I told him we missed going down a ravine by 20 centimetres.'

Regazzoni saw, minute by minute, a rush of impressions coming towards him: on sand you can go *faster* into vastness and the emptiness, travelling at speed for long hours and not seeing another human being … then the women bearing loads on their heads, who waved and smiled so simply … and the Sahara, so silent and mysterious … and the nomads, who could negotiate it even in total darkness by sniffing the wind, reading whatever grass there was.

The truck, already uncompetitive, suffered mechanical problems, especially with the rear shock absorbers. Over the hostile terrain, often with all four wheels off the ground, Regazzoni found his legs being battered against the steering column and the gearbox. The wind from the east skimmed dust through the windows.

Because it was uncompetitive they were getting to the overnight halts late, sometimes too late for meals. Fellow competitors, who'd eaten long before, were now asleep.

'When we arrived at a service station everyone was gone, including the cooking and food,' Pipino says. 'The others arrived there at eight o'clock and we'd get there at one o'clock in the morning – and Clay couldn't understand why the truck was not at the level of his driving. Anyway, instead of 24 hours' driving we'd have to do 30. I was constantly telling him "We have to accept the fact that we don't have a good truck, so let's put this Paris-Dakar down to experience," but for Clay it was a race.'

The rear shock absorbers were now gone and at one halt, while they attempted repairs, there were other trucks waiting in a queue for fuel.

Regazzoni beside the Mercedes which needed to be as strong as a battleship. (courtesy Rainer Küschall)

Regazzoni paid the drivers in the trucks in front so he could get the fuel sooner – he got it in 15 minutes – to save a little more precious time.

Regazzoni and Pipino would be cold and tired. Apart from trying to find something to eat the truck sometimes needed work done on it. They were only getting a few hours' sleep and Regazzoni found these nights particularly hard. The team's organisation seems to have been lacking, because he complained that while other teams relaxed he was hunting for hotel rooms.

At least they carried plenty of mineral water and plenty of sausages from the Italian Citterio company.

He railed that, although they'd been promised a good truck by Fiat before the start, promises were not kept, they had to improvise too much and there were too many delays.

He was demolishing the truck, day by day. Pipino, visibly anxious, solemnly informed him that, to avoid disqualification – you have to arrive at certain points by certain times – he was over-driving to a truly terrible degree. Pipino ticked off the damage: those rear shock absorbers, a bumper torn off, the air-filters not working, two of the doors wouldn't close properly, the springs were damaged. Regazzoni had asked for spare shock absorbers to be sent but they never arrived – and with them, he felt, he'd have been in the race.

It could not go on, and by the time they'd reached Tamanrasset they'd lost so much time they were disqualified. At Tamanrasset there wasn't a hotel room for them or the possibility of a shower even, and Regazzoni felt very badly about this.

He was determined, in the race or out of it, to make Dakar, and Pipino says it was only this determination which literally drove them on. Regazzoni expressed it in a phrase *I must reach Dakar*. Pipino had essentially given up hope of getting there and it may well be he had had enough. He stayed.

Then, during the second week, a helicopter carrying Thierry Sabine, a singer-songwriter, a journalist and a radio engineer crashed into a sand dune in Mali killing them all and the pilot. It was a terrible blow to the rally and a terrible blow to Regazzoni, who appreciated that Sabine could originally have created a soft event where everyone could play but instead created something very hard indeed.

Now as he set off again Regazzoni had a different rush of impressions: a truck on fire and the driver beside it crying ... the naughty magazines that they'd bought in Paris and now gave to some natives, who laughed at the pictures ... reaching deep into real Africa, mud and straw dwellings, teenage mothers holding babies, women selling necklaces ... hiring a man to guard the truck overnight for a packet of biscuits ... and how the prices really were up tenfold along the way ... how a girl tried to sell Pipino half a drum of fuel for a big price and, when he walked away, was visibly upset ... and on reaching Senegal a feeling of nostalgia for asphalt, because he hadn't seen any for so long.

Then, one evening, the dust-caked, sand-blasted truck came into Dakar.

De Graffenried really had thought Regazzoni mad to try the rally, so mad that a bet was struck: a case of champagne that he wouldn't reach Dakar. It must have tasted sweet, whenever Regazzoni claimed it.

There'd be memories, of course. One of Regazzoni's sponsors had been Fresh and Clean handkerchief wipes, and clearly the truck had had a goodly supply of them. He'd always remember giving some to African women, and the almost magical way they reacted.

At the end of the rally there'd be wondrous tales to tell ... a ferocious sandstorm in Mauritania ... Prince Albert of Monaco's car *sinking* somewhere ... a man who ate a whole sheep ...

There'd be wonderful memories of taking himself, equally dust-caked and sand-blasted, down to the Senegal river and somehow bathing with the locals, under the moonlight. The timelessness, the purity and the peace of Africa cleansed him at the same time as the waters of the river did.

A journalist asked him whether he considered he'd be going home a winner or a loser. 'A winner,' he said, 'because Dakar was my target.' He had

proved that a man without the use of his legs could do it, and that was the victory.

More than that, he'd be back.

This was not a sentiment shared by Pipino. 'Now I've seen how you drive in a truck and I'll never come with you in one again.'

Pipino was wrong, although he'd have to wait a decade and more to find that out.

Nor was Regazzoni finished with this first expedition without firing a broadside. As television man Poltronieri puts it, 'that first Dakar was not without quarrels and strong comments.' Regazzoni's Iveco had been specially prepared for sandy surfaces but in his fury Regazzoni gave an interview to *Autosprint* where he said it was so slow 'I was overtaken by a milk float!'

Iveco were not pleased, but then neither was he.

In May, four months after the rally, he fulfilled the ambition of a lifetime by taking part in the historic Mille Miglia. The race – actually a time trial, cars going at intervals – ran from 1927 to 1957, starting in the northern Italian city of Brescia and looping down one side of Italy to Rome and back up the other side to finish in Brescia. The distance was 1,000 Roman miles, equivalent to approximately 932 Imperial miles or 1,600km.

It quickly became more than a national, and international, institution. Here down the years some of the greatest drivers in some of the greatest cars competed on the public roads, shrieking and hammering through villages and towns, and everywhere huge crowds lined the route in a high state of intoxication. Imagine that, rather than going to the cinema and witnessing an epic film it was really happening directly in front of you, and so near that you could almost reach out and touch it.

Because the crowds were close, and because speeds were intense, the Mille Miglia was hungry for victims and before the War so many were killed that the dictator Mussolini called a halt. It resumed in 1940 and continued after the War. In 1955, driving a Mercedes, Stirling Moss won by covering the distance in 10h 7m 48s, an average of 97.90mph (157.65kmh).

Such speeds were genuinely awesome, especially if anything went wrong. In 1957 a driver called Alfonso de Portago, driving a Ferrari, had what had always been believed to be a tyre blowout. The car snapped from his control, and he, his co-driver and 11 spectators were killed. That was only two years after more than 80 spectators were killed at Le Mans when a Mercedes vaulted into the crowd. It meant that the Mille Miglia itself was dead.

Regazzoni had clearly been intoxicated by the idea of the race as, growing up, he followed it from afar. The intoxication increased with a kind of proximity because drivers from Lugano took part. He regretted that he'd been too young and had dreamed of doing it with Moser as his co-driver. Now, in his Lancia Aurelia B-20 – it had *Driving School Clay Regazzoni* on the side – he was finally there, albeit for the much more genteel historic version, first run in 1977.

There would be a rush of impressions: the crowd not quite knowing what the *Driving School* meant but going wild when they saw him in the Marlboro cap he'd worn for so long (he wasn't wearing a crash helmet) … the crowd beating their approval on the Lancia's roof and slapping its sides as it went to the start … then out on the route the roads and the unprotected trees as they had always been … his co-driver taking headache pills … his co-driver shouting 'Clay, please, I have three children!' … a great crowd at the end forming a tunnel for him to drive through, people waving their arms, people crying … his co-driver shouting 'They're crazy,' taking the last of the pills and then lighting a cigarette.

Regazzoni got out of the car, leant against the door and his legs were bleeding.

Evidently a doctor said 'It's just too much.'

Regazzoni replied 'After the Paris-Dakar this is a picnic in the countryside.'

He was, to turn a phrase, back into his stride, whether he could use his legs or not, and the career was back into its stride, too.

Nigel Roebuck remembers the morning of the Spanish Grand Prix, at Jerez three months after the Paris-Dakar, and a poignant moment. 'Regga was alone in the courtyard of the hotel. I thought he would have transport arranged to get him to the circuit and he had, but it was outside and there was a ramp which was too steep for the wheelchair to go down. I stopped, we chatted and I suddenly realised how helpless he was. I thought *Only seven years ago I was watching you going round Silverstone in the Williams.*'

The Mille Miglia, the event Regazzoni had dreamed about – and was about to compete in. (LAT)

In 1987 he met Maddalena Mantegazzi at the Expo Auto Show in Bologna. 'I was working for Lancia. His eyes! The look – I cannot forget the look. So I fell in love and he fell in love,' she says. 'Immediately he asked me to come to Menton [where he had a house] and I said OK. At the beginning I was afraid because I told him "I don't know, in a week, a month maybe you'll want somebody else." He said "I wouldn't ask you to come and live with me if I didn't really want that." I asked him three times "Are you sure?" He was in the process of leaving for Tunisia [and a rally there]. It was the last time I asked. I decided. He told me "I travel all over the world but I had to come home to find true love." We had lived two kilometres apart in Switzerland.'

Did you not think you were taking on a difficult life because, for instance, you couldn't say 'Let's go to the shops'?

'Do you mean because he was in a wheelchair? I never thought that I'd have a hard life. Very rarely did he ask me for something, because he was able to do everything but, of course, he was in a wheelchair, so sometimes I had to push him and fold the wheelchair away. But he was so independent that even the first time we went to a restaurant – or on a trip together, anyway – I left the wheelchair at home because I didn't think like that. I never saw him like a man in a wheelchair. I forgot the wheelchair! We reached Cannes and he said "Where is it?" I said "I've left it in the house!"'

That is a great compliment to him.

'Yes, I think it is.'

Did he see himself like that?

'No. He got angry with people, even with me, but it was not through nastiness, because he was not a nasty man. No, it was his character and I think he always had that character – fiery – and perhaps in the wheelchair it became a little more *passionate*.

'He was very strong and not easy to live with. That wasn't because of the wheelchair – no, no, no – but because of him. The wheelchair didn't matter in that sense. He was Virgo. Like all Virgos he was very precise, *very*, and he took so much out of himself. He was *very* hard with himself. That's why he did a lot of things: because he *was* very hard with himself, and he was hard with other people. That's why it was not easy to live with him.

'For me it was a lesson, a big lesson, of life, because to live with a man like Clay and not to become crazy you have to work on yourself to understand him. It's up to me to change because

He met Maddalena in Bologna and he'd found the rest of his life. She wrote her own caption: 'Can you see that I was in love?' (courtesy Maddalena Mantegazzi)

he will never change. It's me who must do it to understand him. That was not easy but it made me bigger because it was a lesson in living. Thank you, Clay, for the great lesson!

'I was very jealous but with him it was not possible to sustain that. Even when we were together women wanted him, and I'd leave. He'd say *Maddalena, Maddalena!* and at that moment the game was finished, because for him it was a game. I accepted that he attracted women and you cannot change a person like this. It was part of his character. I mean, once in Sicily we did the Targa Florio. The secretary of the organiser fell in love with Clay. She was married and her husband was there. We were at the Pergusa circuit, some people came to see Clay and there were two women there. "'Clay, how are you?" The secretary came to me and said "What are you going to do?" There was nothing you could do. You had to accept it. In the beginning it was difficult but jealousy is not good. If you stay with a man like Clay – a *man* – it is not good to be jealous. Change him? No way, absolutely no way.'

Was your house arranged for somebody with a wheelchair?

'No. The only thing was the lift, which enabled you to go from the garage to the bedroom. In this area [Menton] it is very rare to find a garden at the same level. He went up and down with his lawnmower. Guidosimplex gave him an electric bike to go up and down the garden. He loved it. He did a lot of crazy things with this.

'Once he had a driving accident in the mountains and I went to get him. He waited patiently for me. When I got there he put his hand out of the window and told me to drag him out. It was dangerous to try that but he wanted me to. He did things like that every day. He did not fear danger.'

He adored danger?

'Yes. It was not a problem for him.

'It was not easy for a disabled person to go around the town in Monaco. At home in Menton he had his garden. He loved flowers, trees, and when he didn't have work and he was at home, in the morning he invented things to do. He couldn't live without working. I love work, I love gardens and we worked together. I was 19 years with him.

'We never spoke about his Formula 1 career. With friends or other people, yes, they did. He was still thinking about the two World Championships he just missed with Ferrari and he was sad about that. He didn't speak to me about it because it wasn't the driver who interested me. When I met him I asked myself how a man can go on who'd seen everything in life and then seen his life change completely. I was very curious to know Clay in order to understand that. He loved life, loved life fully – at 360 degrees – and he loved *being* alive. If you don't, you can't live.

'He had goals, in the sense that he did things for handicapped people in Italy like the driving school and he drove himself for such goals. He did the same about the "architectural" barriers – he'd get to somewhere and then he couldn't get in, those sorts of barriers. I remember once in a hotel in Asia, to go from the bedroom to the bathroom there were two steps. Even if you make a room for normal people you have to step out of the shower, so the architecture can affect even them. It got on his nerves when he saw things like that because it isn't necessary.

'By contrast I have seen him in countries like Peru, Chile and Colombia when we were in little hotels and several times he couldn't get into the bathroom in the wheelchair but he never complained, because in those countries they didn't have the money or expertise, so it wasn't possible to design things any other way – but in places where they did have the money and expertise he didn't accept it. Sometimes he was demanding, and when it wasn't necessary he wasn't. So I think in the beginning he had this will to do things and to do his best.'

Did he understand how important he was to lots of other people?

'Perhaps. I don't know if he was fully conscious of this. He did the Paris-Dakar because he had the patience, and to prove to people that even if you have problems you can do something like that.'

Far, far away in California a lady called Carol Hollfelder crashed on a motorbike on 3 May 1987 and 'was run over by two cars. I ended up breaking my back so that from about the middle of my chest down I'm paralysed. It was a similar level of injury to Regazzoni.

'I was 18 years old when it happened and most of my life at that point was wrapped around horses. I was a competitive equestrian. I'd been riding since three and competing since ten. That was the focus of my life. I had loved cars since I was young, I was a huge Ferrari fan even at 18, but horses were my life. I can still technically ride a horse but my ambition was to go to the Olympics. I rode hunters and jumpers and that's not something that I can do at the level that I'd planned to do.

'My dad is one of those fix-it sort of men and since he already knew that I loved cars he encouraged me in that direction. He was kind enough to buy me a new car to drive on the street. This was hand controls. Driving was actually one of the very first things I thought about when I

woke up in the hospital and they told me what was going on. I was concerned I wouldn't be able to drive again.

'We were as clueless as most people when it comes to this sort of injury and disability in general, and the way that Clay came into our lives is that my dad – again being one of those fix-it guys – had heard of Clay Regazzoni. I believe it was while I was still in the hospital in rehabilitation he wrote a letter to Clay telling him about me and asking if he knew of where to get hand controls for manual transmission, because at that time in this country the only hand controls available were for automatic transmission. In the four members of my family we had six or seven cars and all of them with manual transmission, not a single automatic, so I didn't have a car to drive when I was first hurt.

'Dad wrote this letter to Clay asking if he could help us find controls for manual transmission. We didn't hear back from Clay for years. There was just no response.'

There would be.

Notes: 1. Sir Frank 'met Rainer when I went to Stoke Mandeville for a check up after I came out of hospital. I heard the nurses talking and they were saying "We've heard of him, he's quite a special guy. What he can do is get himself out of his wheelchair by himself." When he did it they couldn't believe it. He's my hero.'; 2. Fred Gallagher says. 'Let's call it the Dakar Rally. It originally always went from Paris to Dakar so that's what it was called, then at various times through France, Spain, whoever got interested in hosting it, and clearly the organisers got keen on the money – so it became known as the Dakar. I've done it when it started in Marseilles, I've done it when it started in Granada in Spain. The last few years it started in Lisbon. There were years when it didn't even go to Dakar. For example when it went to Cape Town it didn't go anywhere near Senegal. Three or four years ago it went to Egypt. So it's gone all over the place.'; 3. Gian Maria remembers a Porsche race at Monza, Pescarolo in the same team, and Regazzoni fast, all right, in practice but they wouldn't let him race. 'There was a rule that you had to be able to get out in case of an accident within a certain time. He said "If somebody has a big accident they can't get out anyway."'; 4. Carol Hollfelder had a fire driving at Road America. 'I've had a couple of heavy hits in a race car. The fire is the only thing that gave me a twinge after the fact. I could have got out except that I had a quick-release steering wheel that wouldn't release, so in order to get my legs out of the car easily I have to take the steering wheel off. Because I couldn't do that we think I was in the car for a good three to five minutes, which is a long time. The line to the fuel cell actually melted. The one thing I screwed up in first is that for some reason I didn't hit the kill-switch to get the engine off – because the car came to a standstill. I didn't switch the fuel pump off, which meant that it was constantly dumping raw fuel into this fireball behind my head.' Clay says he switched the engine off at Long Beach. 'That's the bright thing to do.'; 5. E la Corsa Continua; 6. Quoted in Autosport; 7. Global Positioning System using satellites that transmit very precise signals, enabling someone to know where they are; 8. Federico Fellini, an Italian film director who specialised in fantastic images; 9. Autosport; 10. Ibid.

Regazzoni retained his love of karting – hard, competitive karting of course. (courtesy Rainer Küschall)

CHAPTER 10 ————————

JUNGLE NOISES

The desert called again in 1988 and this time he put together an effort that was better thought-out and better equipped. He'd have a truck prepared by a company called Kempf in Alsace, a 600hp Tatra[1] with a right-hand brake and an automatic clutch.

'It was sponsored by Marlboro,' Daniel Kempf says. 'I don't know what top speed was. We adapted it so it could be driven manually. Therefore it had an accelerator worked by hand and the brakes by hand too.

'I met him at the Philip Morris headquarters at Lausanne. He was in his wheelchair. We had to overcome problems in that the truck couldn't go through Switzerland with Marlboro on it because of the law about tobacco publicity. We got it to Lausanne and he got in. I'm not sure he had a licence for driving one! I was in the passenger seat – the first to go in the passenger seat with him in the Tatra. Anyway, off he went: Regazzoni was like that. He was very fast and very precise – overtaking with 200cm to spare. All I thought was *I hope he doesn't crash this truck*. As a man he was very *sympa*, polite, charming – absolutely – but a typical Formula 1 driver, without self-doubts about anything even at 100kmh in the truck.

'A Swiss-Italian company – Guidosimplex [of the driving school] – was involved in cars for handicapped people and they took Regazzoni as a symbol for their cars. Guidosimplex is a big company based in Rome which transforms cars,

RIGHT *An illegal short cut through 400km of forest in the Congo ended like this – and wild animals were watching.* (Julian Kirk)

Always look on the bright side of life: a Regazzoni birthday, with (left to right) Aleardo Buzzi, Maddalena, Laffite, Brigitte Nielsen and husband. (courtesy Maddalena Mantegazzi)

and he'd already had cars prepared by them, not by us, but it seems Guidosimplex didn't want to do the truck so he came here. It was the only thing we did for him.'

After 1986, Regazzoni clearly knew what awaited him. That he went back for more is remarkable enough, and even more remarkable when you set out the route: 8,000 miles (12,874km), of which 4104 miles (6,605km) were

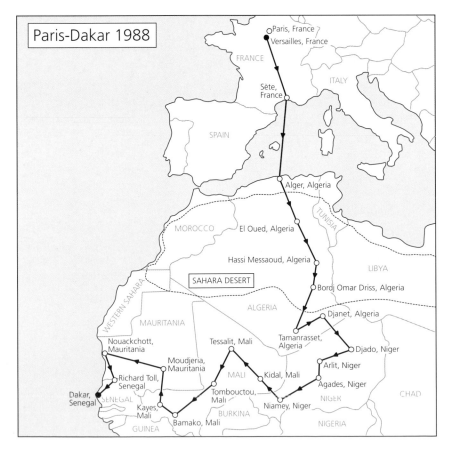

Paris-Dakar 1988

special stages, through France, Algeria, Niger, Mali, Mauritania and Senegal. Some 2,500 people would take part – 311 cars, 183 motorbikes and 109 trucks – and fewer than half would get anywhere near Dakar, including Regazzoni.

One of the assistance lorries came across the Tatra stuck in a sandy rut between El-Oued and Hassi Massaoud in Algeria. The lorry tried to tow him out – this involved shovelling a lot of sand as well – but in the end the differential broke and he had to abandon it.

As Kempf says, 'he didn't finish but he gave all his friends on the rally great pleasure.'

Patrick Tambay came third in a Range Rover. 'Being in a wheelchair was a difficult situation to adapt to but Clay did it with a lot of courage – like most of the people who're facing these types of situations – and it didn't stop him from being hyperactive, didn't stop him from being very interested in the female species and trying to drive as fast as possible with only his hands. He did stuff that he couldn't do before, such as the Paris-Dakar, and being involved in the school for handicapped people – teaching them how to behave and react and be capable of coming out of their handicap by finding independence in their driving.

'He was the same personality. I've seen him many, many times on different occasions – motor shows, on the Paris-Dakar – and he was always his old, cheerful self, always cheering people up. He wasn't sulking about himself, he was very, very positive about life and everything, in spite of his condition and in spite of what he'd been before.

'The Paris-Dakar was rough and tough for fully fit people. Can you imagine what it was like for someone handicapped? For hygienic conditions it's difficult, resting is difficult, recovering at the end of a hard day is difficult. He took all that with great spirit. My admiration for him increased 100 per cent, 200 per cent. My affection towards him did too. Mind you, I had a lot when he was racing.'

His toughness was demonstrated by the fact that three competitors died, while a camera crew went into spectators in Mauritania, killing a mother and child. A ten-year-old girl in Mali was hit and killed by one of the cars.[2]

That year Regazzoni also did the Pharaoh's Rally, where he finished first in his category – six-wheel drive – and third of all the trucks. To achieve it he survived this:

'For 11 hellish days each year, the Rally winds across trackless miles of Egypt's wild and multicoloured deserts in the most prestigious – and punishing – motor rally in the Arab world.

'In a ritual driven by prestige, profit and plenty of sheer personal challenge, several hundred cars and motorcycles mass noisily each October outside Cairo, on the dusty plain at the foot of the Giza pyramids. They are there for the Pharaoh's Rally. They are off-road drivers and motorcyclists, professionals and amateurs, mostly from Europe, but also from Japan, Australia and Egypt. In 1985, top racer Said El-Hajry of Qatar was one of the few non-Egyptian Arab drivers ever to enter, but he made a very good showing. He won.

'Among off-road rallies, the Pharaoh's Rally ranks second in guts and glory only to the devastating 21-day, 12,000-kilometre (7,500-mile) Paris-Dakar. Veteran rally motorcyclist Herbert Schek of West Germany describes Paris-Dakar as "much crazier," but in the Pharaoh's Rally, he says, the terrain is "really just as hard, maybe harder."

'According to organisers and participants alike, however, the Pharaoh's Rally is the most fun of any rally going. Elaborate buffet dinners await weary participants at the end of every day, earning the race the affectionate title, "le rallye chic." "This is a rally people can really enjoy," said Rami Siag, Egyptian representative of Pharaoh bv SARL, the Lebanese-registered, French-based company that organises the rally.

'Six of the 11 rally nights are spent in the desert camps, two of which, at Bahariya and Farafra, feature natural hot springs. Another, at Abu Simbel, lets early-rising ralliers watch the sun rise over Lake Nasser and illuminate the ancient temple. The other five nights are spent at top hotels in Aswan and Hurghada where pools, showers, air conditioning and – in Hurghada – the waters of the Red Sea soothe and refresh the weary.'[3]

However intimidating this sounds, especially when combined with the Paris-Dakar, it

The Tatra, looking like a fortress. It would need to be strong. (courtesy Claudio Bonicco)

Comrades in the desert: Ari Vatanen, Pipino and Laffite. (courtesy Claudio Bonicco)

Massimo del Prete, who proved he was strong enough – and lived. (courtesy Emily Davenport, xpb.cc limited)

represented Regazzoni's new world, his second life, and you know the story by now. In 1989 he'd challenge the Paris-Dakar again.

'When he was in Formula 1 I knew him from the newspapers,' Massimo del Prete says. 'I did the Paris-Dakar with a woman called Chantal in a small truck. I was the co-driver but I drove because she was not able to cope with the difficult parts. She was very friendly with Clay. A few months later she phoned me and said "Are you interested in doing the Paris-Dakar with Clay Regazzoni?" He wanted to do it but he had to find someone who could take care of the mechanical side, who could navigate and, if necessary, could drive – and was strong [to lift him out], because he'd had some problems before. I said "For me it's not a problem, in fact it's a very interesting idea."'

Del Prete was an enthusiast, a skilled mechanic and a very strong man. It didn't trouble him at all that Regazzoni was in a wheelchair. 'I'd be co-driver for a very famous driver, one of the most popular drivers of his time: everybody knew Clay Regazzoni. So I said "OK. How can I meet him?" She said "He'll phone you very soon."

'A few hours later Clay rang and the first thing he said was "*Ciao* Massimo, how are you?"' – a very familiar greeting, as between friends. 'I'd never met him! He said "I got your telephone number from Chantal," and explained that he needed someone who could fix problems with the vehicle. He had a truck.'

Regazzoni: 'You're strong enough?'
Del Prete: 'Yes, I hope!'
Regazzoni: 'And you have a strong mind?'
Del Prete: 'Yes, I hope!'
Regazzoni: 'Are you worried about anything?'
Del Prete: 'No, I hope!'
Regazzoni: 'I want to do the Paris-Dakar but I don't just want to go there, I want to win. I'll never do something just to finish second.'
Del Prete: 'I'm happy with that.'
Regazzoni: 'OK, we start with the Tunisian Rally with the truck.'

The Tunisian Rally was well known in these circles, but del Prete said 'Sorry, Clay, but I already have a job on that with Mitsubishi Italia.' He added, however, that since they'd both be in Tunisia they could meet and 'talk about the future, if you want'.

Regazzoni responded: 'I'm unhappy about that, because I want to start immediately.'

Although del Prete had the Mitsubishi commitment he also sensed that they'd established a rapport, 'a good feeling between us'.

During the Tunisian Rally, del Prete remembers, Regazzoni 'was working on his truck with some tools – something to do with the engine – and he was standing up. I said "Hey, Clay, how are you?" He said "Ah, Massimo!" He recognised my voice without looking round. "Help me, please. I have low oil pressure in the engine because of this [expletive] turbo. What do you think?" I said to put something behind the spring to increase the pressure. He said that could be an idea, so we opened the valve and started to work. I took the spring out and put a few Tunisian coins behind it – something like 2mm width of them – to increase the pressure. We closed the engine and the pressure went up. "It's better!" we said, then we started to talk about the project.'

And the project would grow. Klaus Seppi raced with his Mercedes 'as a private driver. I hadn't much money and no sponsors. It wasn't easy. I always had to ask my co-driver for money. I liked desert races.' He got in touch with Marlboro and 'they said it could be a nice idea if Clay and you make a team under the brand name Chesterfield – they didn't want Marlboro on the Paris-Dakar.

'The first event we did together was the Pharaoh's Rally. It was catastrophic because the cars – Mercedes – were not as Clay wanted them. He wanted the cars perfect.'

Afterwards Regazzoni wrote to Seppi, and this is the gist of the letter: 'If we'd been on a plane we'd all have been dead, killed by the lack of preparation. The windscreen wipers didn't work. The shock absorbers broke and after 30km my car

Perpetual motion, especially in deserts. (courtesy Martin Taylor)

had no more oil. It's not permissible to start with a car like this. We had one and a half mechanics but I only got the half. Even the back-up lorry had problems. I'm not able to ask the sponsors for money if it's organised like this. The mechanic: even if I gave him 12 months he won't be able to get any better. Personally, I don't feel today that I can let the sponsor spend more money for gastronomic tours.'

Next: the Paris-Dakar, Regazzoni and Seppi in Mercedes G-wagons. 'For me, joining Clay was the only way to race on a higher level. I worked at Mercedes and I had the contact with AMG[4] – they prepare engines and racing cars for Mercedes – and I got the car from them. Clay got a car from AMG too, but he paid a lot of money. The cars were the same.'

Before they set off, Regazzoni and del Prete went to northern Italy and a riverbed to test it. That completed, they embarked on – this year – the 10,831km (6,730 miles) with 6,605km of special stages (4,104 miles), visiting Tunisia and Libya rather than Algeria. If the place names in Africa are unfamiliar, no matter. They would have been to the competitors as well …

Depart:	25 December, Paris
First stage:	Paris to Barcelona (1,120km)
Prologue:	Barcelona (6.3km)
Second stage:	Tunis to Tozeur (647km)

Once they reached Africa 'we rolled over immediately,' del Prete says. 'The first thing that we had the first day was a problem with the front axle. It was in the dark. I was talking to Clay and he said "We must lighten the car because it's heavy." One time we'd done a really big jump and we landed on the nose of the car. We broke the steering and the wheel was immediately like *that*. We stopped. At the same time the other Mercedes arrived with Seppi in it. We started repairs: five minutes to take the broken steering off and put a new one on. I did that and then when we started I made a navigational mistake – no GPS, just the notebook and your eyes. It wasn't easy. I said "Clay, there must be a passage control. It's round here but I can't find it." So we probably lost half an hour before we met our team-mates again. I asked Seppi "Where's the control?" He said "Ten kilometres from here." So we went ten kilometres back and it was 200 kilometres to the end of it. We finished it together with the other car. Clay said "OK, today you made a mistake so tomorrow I can make a mistake." I said "No, why?" "Because it's my turn!"'

| Third stage: | Tozeur to Ghadames (724km, 308 special) |

'A day later,' del Prete says, 'we started off again and we had an accident after two kilometres, a big accident. We broke everything, including the rear axle. It took us five, six hours to change that. Then we started again and Clay went a little bit crazy, because he wanted to regain his position. We were now more than ten hours behind.'

| Fourth stage: | Ghadames to Sabha (819km, 469 special) |

'He was fast, I can tell you. I did a lot of rallies as a co-driver, with good drivers and not-so-good drivers, and for me Clay was the one who was the fastest, but he was – how can I say it? – calm in the car, even in dangerous situations. He always controlled the steering wheel using two fingers, even when you were in a situation where you knew something was going to happen, when you can see the condition of the track and that your line is wrong for a corner. I used to think *We're in the wrong place at the wrong speed …*'

| Fifth stage: | Sabha to Tumu (620km special) |

In *Autosport,* Joe Saward was following the exploits of a camera crew from Videovision, including Rob Hurdman. 'The convoy reached the bivouac at 5:30am and there was time for two hours' sleep,' he wrote. 'And then it was off through the stony desert towards Dirkou.'

Regazzoni, del Prete says, 'was very quiet. I can give you an example that's easy for everybody to understand. You look at in-car cameras on championship rallies. When they have an accident you can see that the people in the car behave as if they're in a trance, just waiting for the end of the accident. When we were in some accidents Clay simply put the car into neutral and stopped the fuel pump. I was impressed. I'd never seen anything like that. He was talking to me quite normally – completely calm – when we were rolling over! It was unbelievable. He was doing everything – neutral, engine off – not just sitting waiting for the end of the accident. When you roll over, if you can do things when the tyres touch the ground maybe you can stop it rolling again and he was talking with me about that at probably 160kmh an hour doing ten roll-overs. Talking! Yes, incrediblc. Hc was cold-bloodcd in that sense, and I'd never met anyone quite like that before in my life.'

The letter Regazzoni wrote to Klaus Seppi.
(courtesy Klaus Seppi)

Saward wrote that Hurdman & Co 'had two punctures in ten minutes, leaving them with no spare tyres. It was then that they bumped into Clay Regazzoni, who had rolled his Mercedes and was sitting beside the road in his wheelchair, changing a tyre. In the middle of nowhere – in a sandstorm. "That's what real courage is," says Rob.'

Hurdman stopped to interview him and see if they could help, finally setting off to reach Dirkou in the middle of the night. He remembers that 'there was a Mercedes G-wagon on its side and a guy that was, I thought, unconscious. Regazzoni was in his wheelchair trying to winch the vehicle back onto its wheels while tending to this guy who had been knocked out in the accident. It was absolutely amazing. He'd hit some rocks that had launched the vehicle on its side and the co-driver had been knocked out. Regazzoni managed to get himself out of the vehicle into his wheelchair. We stopped and helped him for 20 minutes.

'Regazzoni being Regazzoni, to help him seemed almost like a sign of weakness. We met him that night and it was a bit awkward for that reason.'

This may be the incident that has entered folklore, because Mo Nunn heard it. 'On one of those rallies he turned the car over and they were in shock when they realised he couldn't use his legs.'

Sixth stage:	Tumu to Dirkou (577km special)
Seventh stage:	Dirkou to Termit (583km special)

They were now in the Ténéré region, sometimes known as the 'zone apart', sometimes as the desert within the desert, in the south central Sahara. It's an immense sand plain of more than 154,000 square miles from Niger to Chad. Bandit country: historically, convoys of as many as 10,000 camels moved in convoy across it trading millet for salt and dates. Bandits materialised if any of the convoy became isolated. Might the bandits still be there …?

Eighth stage:	Termit to Agadez (535km special)
Rest day:	3 January, Agadez

Autosport reported that 'the rescue planes were still picking up the last stragglers on the Dirkou-Termit section as the survivors of the Ténéré set off from Agadez for Tahoua. By mid-afternoon all had been found, although as usual the Ténéré had taken its toll. However some, thought to have retired, turned up, among them the incredible Clay Regazzoni.'

Ninth stage:	Agadez to Tahoua (541km, 325 special)
Tenth stage:	Tahoua to Niamey (427km, 220 special)
Eleventh stage:	Niamey to Gao (641km, 495 special)
Twelfth stage:	Gao to Timbuktoo (611km special)
Thirteenth stage:	Timbuktoo to Bamako (881km, 379 special)

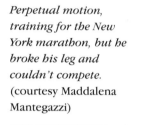

Perpetual motion, training for the New York marathon, but he broke his leg and couldn't compete.
(courtesy Maddalena Mantegazzi)

'We were in Mali and it was a strange day,' del Prete says. 'We started from Timbuktoo, we crossed the desert to a road at a place called Bidonville that comes from the north and goes down to Gao. It's the "road of the oil-drums" – there are 200-litre oil-drums full of sand each 5–10km to show you the right way to go. So you go 300, 350, 400km 270° West till you cross this Bidonville then you go 50, 60km south to Gao. We're in the desert, so I was watching on the compass. We were always a little bit further south than 270° – say 250, 260°. I was thinking *They wanted us to cross the Bidonville just south of the desert sand* – because if you go into the sand it could end your rally. So I was thinking about that.

'I saw a helicopter and I said "Follow it." Clay changed his line. I looked at the compass and it was 320°, meaning we'd moved a lot. We did that for 50km, and then after about half an hour we saw the first tent. We arrived there just after the leading car arrived.'

Del Prete: 'Hey, Clay, today is our day. They started 20 minutes before us.'

Regazzoni: 'Stupid calculations! If you want to win you must arrive in front of them, you must be *physically* in front.'

Del Prete: 'But if we arrive together we win by 20 minutes.'

Regazzoni: 'Not enough for me!'

Both cars moved through the control and del Prete got another rush of impressions. 'We started to fight with the other car side-by-side on this small road – touching. They were surprised by that in a 10,000km rally, but for Clay it was part of the game, again unbelievable. While we were fighting we jumped a little bit wide and I saw one wheel go past.'

Del Prete: 'Clay, that is *our* wheel.'

Regazzoni: 'I know.' (To which del Prete adds this footnote: 'We didn't win that day …')

Fourteenth stage:	Bamako to Labe (852km, 501 special)

Bamako was in Mali, Labe in Guinea. 'From Mali we reached a forest,' del Prete says. 'We went from desert to savannah, which is desert with some trees, to forest. We reached a river and a Nissan was in the water – the river was very high because of rain the week before. The co-driver nearly drowned in this Nissan and everybody was on the bank talking because they couldn't cross. The river was not only high but the water was flowing fast. I said to Clay "Our car is very high. Let me go into the water and check if it's high enough, and if it is I'll show you the way." He said "Bullshit, OK? We go *now*."'

Del Prete got a rush of impressions: full throttle … into the water so fast the current had no time to seize the Mercedes … the water cascading up and over the roof … and a question: how deep is it, one metre, two, more? … then emerging onto the far bank and continuing at full throttle.

'We arrived at the next control and I was talking with the marshal. "How many cars have passed this checkpoint?" He said "Nobody – no cars and no motorcycles." I said "Clay, we're in front." He said "That cannot be. It's a joke." I said "It's true. No one has come through."'

That evening Regazzoni said to del Prete: 'I was watching when the Nissan tried and he went into the water very, very slowly.'

Which was why he hadn't done that, or perhaps ever would have done that.

Fifteenth stage: Labe to Tambacounda
(448km, 380 special)
Sixteenth stage: Tambacounda to Saint-Louis
(512km, 203 special)

'We were running closer and closer to the border,' del Prete says. 'I remember we were on one road and it had a steep camber. The surface was slippery and he was doing 100kmh and I was making sure the four-wheel drive was always on.'

Regazzoni: 'turn it off. I'll do it without.'

Del Prete: 'OK.'

Regazzoni: 'It's better without. No problem.'

Del Prete: 'I have a note in my book: *Very dangerous section, a lot of corners, be careful.* At the side of the road there are termite mounds a metre high and very soft and if we hit one it could be a bad if these termites got into the engine.'

Regazzoni: 'No problem.'

He continued, of course, to drive very fast. 'We touched one of these things, we rolled at 200kmh and that was where I broke my leg. While we were rolling over he was talking explaining *why* and so on. He switched off the engine and then when the rolling had finished we were upside down on the side of the road. The car was completely destroyed. No part of the bodyshell was still on the car. There was fuel all around. I was hanging upside down and he said "Be careful because of the fuel. We have to get out immediately." My arm was trapped by the rollcage. He undid his seat belts and came over me, lifted the rollcage so I could get my arm out. "Now we have to get out." But my leg was broken. I helped him and he helped me and we got 50 metres away.'

They waited for assistance.

Seppi, who arrived much later, remembers 'the road had a steep camber. We went at 120–130kmh,

At the Targa Florio in Sicily, with a Ferrari trophy. (courtesy Maddalena Mantegazzi)

not more. If you were on the right or the left you had the camber. I saw only this red bar [see picture on page 232] and a lot of people. I said to my co-driver "Let's stop a minute." Then I saw it was the Mercedes. I asked the people "What happened?" They said the people in the car were OK but one of them was unable to walk. I knew that was Clay and I knew they were all right.'

Why was he crazy like this?

'I don't know,' Seppi says. 'Maybe because of the accident at Long Beach – he had less to lose – or maybe because he was a driver and all his life was like this. He crashed every time, he never arrived in the rallies. His driving style was too aggressive. He broke the car all the time. He didn't think *I must slow down to finish*, he thought *I'm all right if I'm driving like this*.

'Several times I saw him do things I wouldn't have done. I was behind him, but being behind is very easy because you can see how he jumps and copy him. I thought *How can he maintain this 100 per cent aggression?* If Massimo told him "There's a big hole coming," he'd ask "Are you sure? If you have doubts, I carry on." Ten times you might get away with it but the eleventh time, when the hole *was* there …

'Massimo would come to me. He knew the car very well and he knew that it would break down if it was driven like this. He wasn't afraid of breaking his leg. He'd say "It's a pity to stop on the second day of a rally, because we could have had a good result by going a bit slower." Massimo asked me to talk to Clay because, as a driver, he thought Clay would listen to me more. I'd say "Please Clay, slow down, do it for me" – we were in the same team, we were together, the money was for everybody, but the next day Clay would start off just the same.'

For Regazzoni, the rest of this rally – the seventeenth stage from Saint-Louis to Dakar (257km, 70 special) and the arrival at Dakar on 13 January – became academic. That's a very dry and unsympathetic way of describing a full-frontal assault on a large portion of Africa and, yes, you know the story by now.

He'd be back.

Seppi has a final memory of the rally. He saw Regazzoni at the airport without his wheelchair: it had been broken when the Mercedes rolled. 'Then I saw how helpless he was in this condition, because he couldn't do anything. He was there sitting on all his luggage and if he needed to go to the toilet we carried him.'

He took part in the Targa Florio historic meeting, driving his Lancia Aurelia B-20, and surely that soothed him after the Dakar.

In 1990 he and del Prete 'did the Pharaoh's Rally with the truck in November–December and won.' The fact that Massimo del Prete went with him again tells you a great deal about his courage and his affection for Regazzoni. Very few could stand the rush of impressions on a regular basis and, as we shall see, one man stood it for a very short distance only before fleeing the rally, the area and the country.

Regazzoni took del Prete on the 1990 Paris-Dakar, again in a Mercedes.

'We were in Mali and we took a decision to stop because we had a big accident, went into a big hole and broke a lot of things on the car. It was strange because it didn't happen in a dangerous place. So we broke the car, we lost one day and we decided to go to Dakar a different way to put it on the boat while we flew back.

'We got a little bit lost in Mali between a lot of small villages. We looked at the map and there was a railway which went where we wanted to go. All we had to do was follow that. We went *onto* the railway and I thought that would destroy the car. It was single-track railway and we came to a tunnel.'

Del Prete: 'If we go in and a train is coming the other way …'

Regazzoni: 'Bah! Probably only one train a day.'

Del Prete: 'Yes, but you can't see the end of the tunnel. Let me just check if there's any other way round.'

Del Prete jumped out and at that instant Regazzoni set off into the tunnel. The Mercedes' engine echoed, faded and after a few minutes echoed again as he came back.

Regazzoni: 'It's 400 metres, not more.'

Del Prete: 'Yes … but if you find a train in front of us what are you going to do? There's *nowhere* to go.'

Regazzoni: 'No train here!'

At that moment a train chugged up from behind them and went into the tunnel.

Regazzoni: 'Ah! A train, and it's gone. Won't be another. Now we go.'

They followed the train through and when they reached the far side Regazzoni found to his intense irritation that it was only doing about 40kmh. Del Prete realised that he wanted to *overtake* it. All he could think of saying was 'Clay, *please*.'

By 1992, and almost in the background, the Driving School was organising annual courses on all the Italian circuits, and I must declare an interest here. I was doing a series (*Whatever Happened To?*) for a motoring magazine and Regazzoni was an obvious subject. Touchingly, he faxed me a great deal of information on the School's activities and I gained the impression that of course he welcomed the publicity, but he was proud, too. I gave it all the publicity I could, although whether that really makes any difference the writer rarely discovers. You may think writing is powerful and can reshape the world. Invariably it is impotent and very quickly forgotten. That's just the way it goes, and anyway I insist that giving one handicapped youngster real hope – getting a wonderful, wondrous sparkle in their eye – as they throw a car into a corner for the first time at Vallelunga or wherever, and suddenly sense *I can really live*, is worth more than all the articles I've ever written.

A book has more permanence but a different kind of impotence. You may remember Regazzoni through what you are reading now, but that'll only be because you remember him. You won't remember me and that's as it should be.

Anyway, thanks for the faxes, Clay.

The Paris-Dakar beckoned again, like a constant taunt and temptation, although this year with a trifling difference: it went from Paris to Cape Town, which is, without being pedantic, a little further. Let's say 7,000 miles further.

Massimo del Prete remembers all that. 'It was very dangerous because we were in position six or seven – a good position. We were in Chad and the special stages were very short each day, 200km. The rest was 1,000km in between. We had no back-up truck, no assistance, and I didn't like to continue like that.'

Del Prete: 'Clay, we're in sixth position.'

Regazzoni: 'But with no back-up we're finished.'

Del Prete: 'I'll find a truck with some tyres, don't worry.'

Regazzoni: 'We're already ten hours from the leading cars.'

Del Prete: 'Anything can happen.'

Regazzoni: 'No, I don't want this.'

They'd go home instead. Del Prete is sure Regazzoni's attitude was governed by the fact that he couldn't finish in first position. 'We took the map and we checked. If we got to Dakar (and a boat) we'd have 4,000km to cover, otherwise we could go into the Congo – which is shorter but you have to cross the forest of Congo. Clay said "OK, we go to the Congo."

'So we crossed Cameroon somewhere, we crossed Nigeria and we arrived in the Congo – and in the Congo, before you can cross the forest, there's a gate. There must be at least four cars and you must have at least one guide with a certificate to take you. They stopped us and said "You can't travel alone. You must have a guide and a minimum four cars because it's 400km of forest."'

Regazzoni: 'Bullshit! We have the GPS. Don't worry.'

Congolese gatekeepers: 'No, you cannot enter.'

Regazzoni: 'OK.'

Del Prete remembers that 'we went away and had something to eat.' He remembers much more vividly the fateful conversation flowing from that meal.

Regazzoni: 'Do you think they'll still be there this evening?'

Del Prete: 'No. They'll close the gate and go home.'

Regazzoni: 'Do you think we can cross?'

Del Prete: 'Yes – but they don't want us to.'

Regazzoni: 'Bullshit! 400 kilometres: so if we run at 40kmh, in ten hours we cross the Congo.'

At nine that evening they went back. 'It was a big gate and it was closed,' del Prete says, 'but at the side of it – nothing. So we crossed and we went into the forest at 9:30. It was really difficult and maybe we were doing 10kmh, trees and branches everywhere. We had to cross rivers. We'd done about 190km when we reached a small hill. We drove around it but we were on mud so slippery it was very dangerous. Controlling the car was difficult. Suddenly we were going down backwards and we rolled. The car caught fire.'

Del Prete: 'I can put the fire out.'

Regazzoni: 'Let it burn!'

Del Prete: 'OK, but I'll get our documents.'

The wheelchair was trapped under the car and so was all the luggage. Regazzoni remained perfectly calm (and I asked son Gian Maria how he could have reacted like that. 'Maybe it was part of a fatalistic way of being.') Del Prete 'pulled Clay up the hill but it was slippery – mud everywhere. The car was still burning. We reached the top of the hill.'

Regazzoni: 'You got my wallet with the passport and everything?'

Del Prete: 'Yes.'

Regazzoni: 'Water?'

Del Prete: 'No water.'

Regazzoni: 'But there's a river here so we can have water.'

Del Prete: 'What are we going to do? It's about 210km to the end of the forest and 190 back to the other end.'

Regazzoni: 'No problem. We'll find a way. Now we have to keep quiet and sleep.'

The car stopped burning, although del Prete 'hadn't taken anything from it to start another one and keep us warm. I didn't even have a lighter. I wasn't smoking at the time. I tried to start a fire by rubbing sticks together but I don't know how they do that. I tried with everything, dry wood, green wood – everything. No way.'

Regazzoni: 'Try with stones.'

Del Prete: 'Yes, but you need special stones which make sparks, and you need hay or dry grass.'

Regazzoni: 'Bullshit! Forget all that. It's only in books!"

They went to sleep although del Prete 'was not sleeping really because I could hear animals – *peep, peep, peep, cuuk, cuuk, cuuk, took, took, took* – and you could feel them coming closer and closer. I had a Swiss Army knife and I cut some branches to try and build something to protect us, but it wasn't really going to work. Clay was sleeping. He started snoring very loudly. Then he woke up.'

Regazzoni: 'You're not asleep?'

Del Prete: 'No. Clay, I can hear a lot of animals.'

Regazzoni: 'No animals here!'

Del Prete: 'Clay, to me all the animals *are* here. Maybe *wild* animals. We're in the *jungle.*'

Regazzoni: 'Bullshit! There's nothing. Don't worry. Sleep well.'

With that Regazzoni went immediately back to sleep but, as you can imagine, del Prete didn't. Regazzoni woke between five and six o'clock.

Regazzoni: 'Ah, a good day. The car is burnt. OK, we'll get a new one. You have to go and find help.'

Del Prete: '190km back or 210 forward?'

Regazzoni: "190 no – nothing back there. There must be something in the other direction. I cannot believe it's 210 anyway. It's nothing!'

Del Prete: 'You don't think it might be dangerous?'

Regazzoni: 'Yes, but it's also dangerous for us both to stay here. I'll stay alone. No problem.'

Del Prete started to walk. 'From six o'clock in the morning I walked all day long, all night long, all day long again until the evening. One day and a half without stopping for one second, just walking. I was thinking I'd done 36 hours at something like three kilometres an hour: 100 kilometres probably. Then in the late afternoon – well, the evening – it was starting to get dark again. You don't know where you are. I had the GPS with batteries and sometimes I'd switch it on to see how far I'd gone and to get the right direction. Then I saw a black thing in a tree and I stopped. I didn't move *anything*. I don't know for how long I stood motionless. I didn't know what it was – maybe an ape – but definitely something black.

'Then I saw a man. He was watching me. As soon as he started to come in my direction I started to go in his direction in order to avoid this thing in the tree. He stopped. I stopped. I made a gesture. He made the same gesture. He copied my movements. I said "Hello" and he said "Hello." I said "How are you?" and he said "How are you?"

Then I tried in French. "*Ça va?*" He said "*Ça va?*" He was just like a parrot. He came closer and closer and closer until he was probably ten metres away. I had the Swiss Army knife in my hand, because you don't know what can happen. He looked quiet but his dress was really strange – not really Zulu, just strange. I tried to ask him if there was a village – we were speaking in French because it was a French-speaking country. "*Il y a un petit village la-bas?*" He made a strange noise and I thought he was crazy.

'Then I saw some smoke – a village. I walked towards it and as I got closer I found some people working. I reached the middle of the village: around 50 people, not more. I went to the chief and he spoke a small amount of French. Well, enough French. I explained to him that my friend is one and a half day's back there and he can't move.'

Chief: 'I don't think your friend will be still alive. I'm surprised that *you* are still alive. You are very, very fortunate.'

Del Prete: 'Why?'

Chief: 'The animals are in season and very aggressive. I can send people there from this village – but are you crazy or what, to have come into the forest? Why didn't you stay close to your car?'

Del Prete: 'It's burned!'

That's how matters rested for about an hour, when Del Prete espied a convoy of some ten cars

Blissfully happy, although when Maddalena went rallying with Regazzoni there were strains. (courtesy Maddalena Mantegazzi)

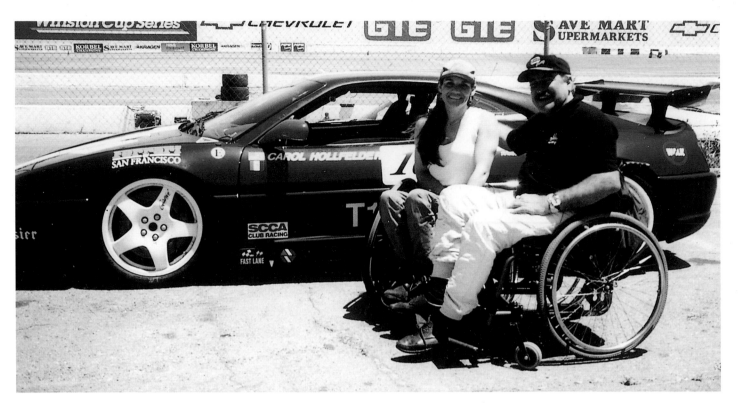

Regazzoni tests Carol Hollfelder's Ferrari at Sears Point. (courtesy Carol Hollfelder)

approaching from the direction he'd just come. 'I stopped the first two and said "Have you seen Clay Regazzoni?" *"Clay Regazzoni?* Where?!?" The third car arrived, then the fourth and he was in it.

Regazzoni: 'What are you doing here?'
Del Prete: 'Nothing!!!'
Regazzoni: 'It's two days I've been there. OK, doesn't matter. Everything is OK. Now this guide will bring us out of the forest, no problem.'

And that's how it happened, although there is a revealing postscript. Maddalena Mantegazzi drove to Nice Airport to pick him up and he came through in a wheelchair – he'd been able to find one – but nothing else except the clothes he wore. 'I said "What happened?" and he replied "It's nothing. The car burned." It wasn't worth asking him more.'

She did rallies with Regazzoni, 'Le Maroc several times, the Isle of Elba and others, but the main one was in 1992. We left Argentina for the Copa America – it was the 500th anniversary of the discovery of America. Buenos Aires to New York! It was hard because it went from Peru to Venezuela in the mountains and the heat, and the engine blew air at us which was not cold. We didn't have any shock absorbers and the Pan American followed the original route, with big holes in the road. He said it's not worth going gently so he went at the maximum, as he always did. We arrived at Lima one evening and I asked myself *How is it possible that Clay can drive this car?* It

was so hard. We had done 11,000km – *how was that possible?*

'Once we did 3,000km through the desert and we had sand inside the car, in our teeth, in our hair, everywhere. Then we were in Washington and it snowed, and in New York it was cold – that was in November. When we got there I was flat out, KO'd. Him? Super strong. The explanation? He *was* strong. I don't think it was anything to do with the wheelchair. He was always like that.

'During the rallies he was hard, although between us we did them for amusement. At San Remo in an historic rally I don't know what he was thinking but he took my notes and everything I had and threw it all out of the window. He said "Go back to your garden with your tomatoes!" I'd made a mistake but afterwards it was forgotten. He laughed. "Maddalena, *I* made a mistake!"

'It's true I wasn't very disciplined with him because somewhere in Morocco I'd say "Look how beautiful it is, Clay" and afterwards "You must take the left hand road now." For me it was a holiday to be with him, to pass time with him. I wasn't so concerned about rallying for myself, frankly. I was pleased when we won some special stages but the result wasn't as important as being with him. For him it was the results which counted. It was always the results – well, it was a holiday when he was with me rather than Claude Valion [another co-driver who could take the rush of impressions and barrel-rolling] or Massimo, where it was competition, but even so it was always a little bit of competition. He would have liked to win. We passed some great moments together rallying.'

Maybe Massimo del Prete sums it up best. 'Once in the desert I said "Oh my God, we're lost," and he said "Don't worry, nothing is finished until the end." For me it was something unbelievable for a man to be able to think like that.'

By the 1990s, Regazzoni lived in a state close to perpetual motion. He'd take part in rallies all over the world, as we're seeing, do some karting and still make his contribution to the driving school. He'd also show that he hadn't forgotten Carol Hollfelder, whose father had written for help so long before.

There are many touching witnesses to all this. Leo de Graffenried is typical of them. 'We [Marlboro] did a kart race in Zurich with him. He did so much you couldn't believe it. He was more active than a normal person. Paralysed people should take him and what he did during his life as an example. Nothing is impossible. He was a kid in his head, he never accepted his age. He'd go to dinner with me in Lausanne and the same night drive to Monte Carlo. He did more after he was paralysed than when he was *not* paralysed.'

He co-drove a Honda Prelude Si (with another paraplegic, Mitch Payton) in a 12-hour endurance race at Sebring, Florida, in March 1993. Although minor, it was what Americans call a 'street stock event'.

He took his Mercedes 600 SC to the Baja Aragon rally in Spain in July – the Baja inspired by the Paris-Dakar and run over 1,000km in the Montegros desert.

Philip Morris, however, were taking a more sanguine view of Regazzoni's desert storms on the Paris-Dakar. Klaus Seppi was invited to their headquarters in Lausanne and was told 'if you convince Clay to be team manager, he can follow the rally on the truck – but not driving. You'll be the driver and Clay will find another driver. He'll have the budget he needs and we will sponsor you.' This would allow Seppi to become a full-time driver for the next four or five years.

'I went to Menton and told Clay the position. He said "If I can't drive I stay at home." I thought it's impossible: they give us a lot of money to get organised and the only thing they want is for nobody to get hurt. "No," he said, "I'll never do it." I couldn't believe this – it was such a lot of money. Three times in Menton I talked to him, and even Maddalena said to him "You must." If he wanted to go to Africa, if he wanted adventure, he could have it, but not driving. I said "Surely, Clay, you're not doing the right thing. You're too egotistical." Our ways parted then, because I found another sponsor and another car.'

In 1994 he authorised the creation of a fan club to raise funds for the Magenta Hospital in Milan which specialised in helping paraplegics, *Aiutiamo la Paraplegia – Fans Club Clay Regazzoni Association*. It was the only club he

Driving lesson from the master. (courtesy Carol Hollfelder)

authorised and the funds – raised by various events – went, at Regazzoni's suggestion, to Magneta's uroparaplegia ward, co-ordinated by Professor Michele Spinelli, which did research and development.

That same year, as Carol Hollfelder remembers, 'my dad got a phone call from Chuck Jones, a very good friend of Clay's.' Jones, of course, had been involved in the Ensign team. 'Chuck said who he was and that he was holding in his hand a photograph of me, because dad had included it in the letter. He said Clay was coming to the United States to compete in the pro-celebrity race at the Toyota Grand Prix at Long Beach, and that he had some technicians with him. If we were still interested they would be happy to install hand controls into a vehicle.

'Of course we were thrilled with that and sure enough Clay showed up at our shop with three chain-smoking Italian technicians and proceeded to put the hand controls from the Guidosimplex company onto my Ferrari. Then Clay Regazzoni proceeded to teach me how to drive on the streets in my home town. That was overwhelming and amazing and emotional and a highlight of my life. He was a charming and wonderful man, intensely competitive and also very kind.

'He drove it first giving me a ride up and down and then I got to drive it, and it was extremely difficult because I had never driven with this kind of hand control before. Also, when you're sitting

Carol Hollfelder, Regazzoni, Chuck Jones and two young mechanics. (courtesy Carol Hollfelder)

next to someone who'd driven at the level that he had, it's a little bit intimidating.

'He made it very easy. I tend to overuse the word with him, but he was extremely charming, very personable. He made people feel very comfortable, and especially women. When I met him he was in his late 50s and he could still make women feel as if they are the most interesting and beautiful person in the room.' (To which Brian Redman adds: 'Carol said he had the art of making you feel like the only woman in the world. Well, a lot of women thought that.')

The Toyota race potentially posed the most obvious emotional problems about returning to the exact place where he had been crippled: the exact place where he walked to the Ensign, got in, and never walked again.

Maddalena Mantegazzi was 'very nervous because I thought *how can he drive the same circuit?* I didn't speak to him about it because I saw him and I saw he was OK. The Grand Prix was the past. He was looking at the present and the future. He always had a lot of programmes for the future, and the past was the past. You only become a racing driver if you have the character, otherwise you don't. Like Gian Maria. He wanted to become a racing driver but Clay didn't want that, because perhaps Clay knew that he couldn't, and it can be dangerous finding out – not like, say, tennis. He didn't help Gian Maria.'

What makes a man need to do this?

'It's not very easy to find out. I don't know what you have inside. Passion? For Clay it was so important to live in the car because even in a wheelchair he was not free, but in a car he was, to go wherever he wanted. That's why he didn't like to take planes. He had to have his car and he was happy to be in the car.'

Such a man was unlikely to be emotional about Long Beach, and wasn't.

Gian Maria 'went to Long Beach and it was no problem, no problem at all. He did the race and he was saying hello to everyone. We were having dinner and the drivers were like kids who'd got back together. You could feel how Formula 1 was. Fittipaldi was in the same restaurant and he came up behind my father pretending he was the waiter with the dish. You could see after years and years they'd stayed the same. My father was laughing …'

Hollfelder says that 'we went as his guests at the Grand Prix at Long Beach at the Toyota pavilion, which was also much fun and excitement. Actually he was very pragmatic about going back to Long Beach. He wasn't, at least from our conversations or my observations, overly emotional about it being essentially the scene of the crime. It was the first time that he had driven there since his injury but he seemed more excited to get back out there in a race car and test the circuit again. That was wonderful, and it was the same kind of attitude that I get from most people who were injured in an accident – so yes, he didn't seem to be overwhelmed by it at all but was excited to be there again.'

Brian Redman 'met him many times after the crash in 1980. We both took part in the Toyota race although of course he had a specially adapted one. I think it wasn't so easy for him. There were four professional drivers: Juan Manuel Fangio the second, a drag racer, myself and Clay. I don't remember racing with him in that race. I think I was probably a little bit ahead of him.

'You find that racing drivers by their nature are adaptable to the circumstances they find themselves in and make the most of them. What else can you do? Clay certainly did that. What's the point of self-pity? When I broke my neck in Canada in 1977 I was in a Montreal neurological institute with eight other people who were either paralysed or had broken necks. I was the only one of the eight who ever regained normality. It's just life, isn't it? What do you say, what do you do? You read the papers every day and you see the most dreadful things, and I don't think there is any real reason for it: you just do the best you can in the circumstances.'

Dan Gurney (who may have competed in that Long Beach race but can't remember: 'I was in quite a few of those!') muses that Regazzoni 'had an inspirational attitude about this thing' – his disability – 'and he still had the racer's passion about racing and automobiles. So he came back to Long Beach and raced a Toyota that was set up with the hand controls, and that was it. Then he just moved on.

'What happened to him, of course, was an abrupt change in his life and essentially there's nothing you can do about it except to accept it, and I thought he did a great job of getting on with it – but there is something out of the ordinary about motor racing people, yes. Otherwise they wouldn't do it in the first place.'

After the Long Beach race fellow drivers signed Regazzoni's helmet. Here is a selection of what they said:

Clay, you made one of my dreams come true. To Clay, you're the best. Clay, you are No 1.

Now I can say we raced together, with a lot of respect and friendship – Fangio

To Clay, a real living legend.

Clay, it was a real pleasure, an honour to drive on the same track.

Well, cheers. (courtesy Carol Hollfelder)

None of them had to do this, and none of them had to say what they said. It seems to have been spontaneous. In any other context, these dedications would be frankly corny, the sort of American schmaltz which cultured Europeans delight in looking down at. In this context, they were entirely sincere and true.

That same year – still 1994 – Gian Maria launched a career as a driver, although, at 23, he was late for that. 'My father said you can do whatever you want. If you want to race you have to find a sponsor. He left me on my own. When I was racing I had problems with my sponsor … I didn't have anything easy. He said "I'm not going to give you any more than the 2,000 francs I gave when you studied."'

He tried, and failed, to qualify for the Formula 3 race that supported the Monaco Grand Prix. Eventually he made his way to the United States, where he earned good money but spent it on the career. At one point it became a question of $8,000 to keep going and Regazzoni was approached. He said 'It's about time you went to work!' Gian Maria returned broke and took a job as a gardener.

He didn't quite understand why his father behaved the way he did – when with a wave of the hand motor sport doors would have opened – but he has grown to understand it, just as he has grown into being a genuine Regazzoni.

You want it, you go out and get it – by yourself.

Notes: *1. Tatra, the Czech Republic truck manufacturer; 2. New York Times; 3. Dick Doughty in 'The Desert Game' on pages 26–33 of the May/June 1990 edition of* Saudi Aramco World; *4. Mercedes-AMG, the high performance division of Mercedes.*

CHAPTER 11

MARATHON MAN

Now Regazzoni decided that he'd enter the London-Mexico Rally 'with my Mercedes 300 SEL/6.3.' The late Nick Brittan had organised the London-Sydney event in 1993 and recounted how, when that was over, many competitors demanded to know 'where do we go next?' The answer was easy enough: the London-Sydney had in fact been a celebration of its 25th anniversary and the 25th anniversary of the London-Mexico fell in 1995. Nine competitors signed up for it on the evening the London-Sydney ended and eventually 59 took part.

It would be run from 22 April to 21 May through 15 countries. Brittan spent some eight months travelling South and Central America to get the route and discover sections used in 1970. The rally went over the Andes from Bolivia to Peru.

That was not the only link. Brittan persuaded Jac Nasser, then Chairman of Ford Europe, to bring the winners of 1970 – Hannu Mikkola and Gunnar Palm – out of retirement and rebuild an Escort like the one they'd used.

Ron Jackson, helping Brittan organise the event, answers the question 'how was Regazzoni allowed in?' by saying 'because he put an entry in and on TWE [Trans World Events] events why not? He had to have a competition licence and he always produced one. I don't know how he got it. He was an asset to the events in every sense. There have been people in this country who are disabled to a certain extent who have licences.'

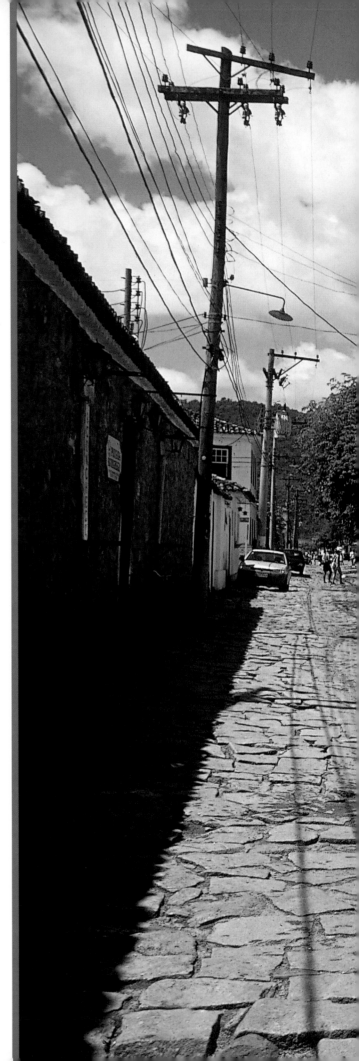

RIGHT *The Inca rally, in 2001, was not for persons of a nervous disposition and it wasn't a scenic tour either.* (Michael Johnson)

And *this* is what the man in the wheelchair faced: 'There was a war going on between Peru and Ecuador,' Brittan remembered, 'but through the British Embassies in both countries we were able to negotiate a six-hour ceasefire for the event to pass through the frontiers. That was pretty impressive. The ship carrying the cars and crews from Cartegena in Colombia to Panama was suddenly put out of service and banned by government from running the route because of the threat of carrying a cattle disease. Again we were able to prevail on the Panamanian government via the Embassy and special permission was given. In Mexico the event was held up for three hours on a bridge in a political demonstration.'

A German, Gunther Stamm, was one of the competitors. 'Clay did it in his Merc with the 6.3 engine – which he destroyed. He bought another car from a guy in Florida! Clay did drive competitively. He was still a very good driver despite his disability and he didn't let the disability stop him doing whatever he wanted to do. Not at all, not at all.

'He tried to find co-drivers who could help him with his wheelchair. They'd fold the wheelchair while Clay stood at the side of the car leaning. They'd put the wheelchair on the back seat and then Clay got in. He had a complete hand and foot control car so that his co-driver could drive the car too, in an emergency. One day on a special stage he overtook me. I knew he was a minute behind me and I thought *Well, he'll get me at some point*. He flew past me, sparks flying everywhere, then he broke the dif because it was a bloody bad road with rocks and everything. He didn't care a bit.'

Jackson remembers Regazzoni did it with 'Claude Valion and he blew the engine. I can't remember the exact location now but what I do remember is he went out into the town and found another Merc which had the same engine as his, found the owner – who at that time was in Florida, I think – and negotiated over the phone for the purchase of this car. He took it away, took the engine out, put it into his rally Merc and had what was left of the one he'd bought shipped back to Monte Carlo. Then he carried on and it was either one or two days later he damaged the sump, damaged the engine and he was out. It was in the middle of South America.'

There's a precious film clip of a very rural stage in Colombia – verdant and almost tropical, the road little more than a dusty track that twists right onto a little straight then left. As the cars come through, churning the dust, locals squeal with pleasure and wave. Then Regazzoni: the Mercedes

The face would always be full of character. (courtesy Dylan Mackay)

seems solid as a fortress, imperious as a battleship. One of the locals seems to shout 'Regazzoni!' as if the name was known even here and the mighty Mercedes has gone fast-fast-fast round the left-hander. It is already moving out of sight.

Jackson says that 'in South America crowds came out to watch the cars and I'm sure they came out to watch Regazzoni because of the tradition of Grand Prix racing on that continent. Although people there are motor sport crazy they may not have known the names from rallying but Regazzoni they did know. Wherever you went people knew him.'

Mikkola and Palm won, Regazzoni and Valion classified 11th.

He went full tilt into 1996, competing in Cuba, winning a couple of kart races and taking part in the historic Mille Miglia again in the Lancia Aurelia with Idris Sanneh from Senegal, a journalist cult figure among immigrants in Italy and also described as a 'superfan' of the Juventus football team. These two figures together on an iconic Italian (described as a 'mobile museum') car provoked purest joy among the crowds as the Thousand Mile event proceeded.

Sanneh described the Aurelia as 'a wonderful car, a true lady of the road.' He said there was in fact only one problem: Regazzoni, who was an Inter-Milan supporter.

'Would,' someone demanded, 'Regazzoni switch his allegiance to Juventus?'

'It is inevitable because we are the perfect team. He is white and I am black!' – the Juventus colours.

In 1997 Regazzoni (and co-driver Erminio Naibo) prepared to contest the Panama-Alaska Rally, from 1 to 25 June, in the Mercedes. He was keen: he had entry number five of the eventual 53 entries in his class, and 90 altogether from 16 countries.

The rally was the direct progeny of the London-Mexico because, as Nick Brittan knew, a strong demand for events like these existed but he'd run out of anniversaries. To solve this particular problem his fertile mind wandered from Panama to Anchorage, Alaska, a distance of some 15,000km through, as he put it, 'the spectacular third world countries of Central America and Mexico, across the back roads of America, through the remote wilderness lands of Canada and the Yukon into the glaciers of Alaska.

'I knew that Central America and Mexico could work and I fancied the challenge of the Baja Peninsula and doing something that no one had done before. A stage rally the length of America and Canada. Something to put into the history books of motor sport.'

Panama - Alaska 1997

Date	Night stops
June	
1st	Panama city, Panama
2nd	San Jose, Costa Rica
3rd	Managua, Nicaragua
4th	San Salvador, El Salvador
5th	Tuxtla, Mexico
6th	Huatulco, Mexico
7th	Acapulco, Mexico
8th	Morelia, Mexico
9th	Mazatlan, Mexico
10th	La Paz, Baja
11th	Loreto, Baja
12th	San Felipe, Baja
13/14th	Las Vegas, Nevada
15th	Page, Arizona
16th	Salt Lake City, Utah
17th	Butte, Montana
18th	Calgary, Canada
19th	Dawson Creek, Canada
20th	Fort Nelson, Canada
21st	Watson Lake, Canada
22nd	Whitehorse, Canada
23rd	Dawson City, Canada
24th	Fairbanks, Alaska
25th	Anchorage, Alaska

The eventual itinerary: Panama City, San Jose in Costa Rica, Managua in Nicaragua, San Salvador in El Salvador, then into Mexico: Tuxtla, a regional capital half in a valley and half spread into the mountains, Huatulco in the mountains, Acapulco on the Pacific, Morelia north of Mexico City and surrounded by hills, a run up the coast through Mazatlán, across the Gulf of California by plane to La Paz, following that coast up to Loreta and San Felipe, across the border into the United States and the flatlands towards Las Vegas, across Arizona to the town of Page, on to Salt Lake City, up to Butte in Montana, into Canada to Calgary, then Dawson Creek in north-east British Columbia, Fort Nelson on the Alaskan Highway, Watson Lake which they call the gateway to the Yukon, then Whitehorse the capital of the Yukon and on the Alaskan Highway, Dawson City in the Klondike, up to Fairbanks in Alaska, down to Anchorage.

Just the sort of thing to lure Regazzoni and his big Mercedes 300, in fact.

Day one: Panama Prologue. Regazzoni was tenth.

Day two: Panama City to San Jose. One car swerved to avoid a lorry in a mountain section and somersaulted into a ravine. Bushes and heavy mud slowed its decent and the three occupants were unhurt. 'The final leg of the long road

Dylan Mackay prepares to get in the car with Regazzoni for the first time.

Regazzoni at the wheel, pensive, as he negotiates the Baja region.

Ignacoio Sunsundegui, completed the first stage and died from a heart attack. In this Regazzoni got the Mercedes up to eighth.

Day four: Managua to San Salvador. Three special stages in three countries. Regazzoni held eighth although 'in Managua I tried to lift the front suspension, the front kept sinking and it hit heavily on the solid bump guard which protected the sump – and troubles were still to come …'

Day five: San Salvador to Tuxtla. A long day: two special stages in El Salvador, then the rally moved through Guatemala to Mexico – 854km and 13 long hours behind the wheel. Thereby hangs a tale, although a tale hung to every moment of all Nick Brittan's historic rallies.

An Opel dealer from Berlin and a very experienced driver, Heidi Hetzer, had been progressing well with her American son Dylan Mackay. She handled the driving – and weakened. 'I made a mistake letting him drive. As a mother I gave up saying no. He was always asking "Mama, when can I drive, mama, when can I drive?" I never give the steering wheel to somebody else but since it was my son I didn't want to fall out with him so I said "OK." Then with no experience he drove. It was in Guatemala and actually for no reason we had a difficult accident. I was sitting on the right side

section was for most run in the dark, the competitors facing the added difficulty of rain-washed roads where potholes, gullies and landslides are common hazards.'[1] Even in these conditions Regazzoni held tenth.

Day three: San Jose to Managua. The second stage, on gravel, had to be cancelled because the riverbed they were to use was washed out and too dangerous. A Spanish competitor, 56-year-old

and wearing his seat belts but he is taller than me. He braked and didn't take his foot off. He made a beginner's mistake. We went in a slide on a corner, we went 150m down a hill and I hit my head on the steering wheel.'

Dylan remembers the descent. 'It was a feeling of constant updates in my mind about whether I was still alive.'

The official report says it was a 'miracle escape after their Opel Kadett plunged off the road and fell 200 metres down a ravine into a river creek. While overtaking a truck Dylan hit a bump in the road, lost control of the car and plunged down the 70-degree slope. Amazingly both escaped with nothing worse than minor cuts and bruises, and were able to scramble up the bank to the road and "hitch" a lift to Tuxtla, Dylan with one of the touring cars and Heidi one of the organisational vehicles.'

Heidi says that 'we left the car there, took our stuff and got a lift with some other people on the rally to Mexico. There they stitched my head and luckily there were four people on the rally as kind of tourists. They hadn't realised how much trouble the rally was or how much work it demanded. They wanted to go home and they were happy that we took their car to Alaska. So we went on in this other car.'

Regazzoni held eighth place. He described the first five days as 'sweaty' and 'noticed that my new co-driver, who paraded calm and reliable by the swimming pool, became untrustworthy when seated behind the Tripmaster. Up to Tuxtla, through well-known landscapes and treacherous gravel roads, everything was under control. I drove with extreme caution and tried not to stress my front suspension too much.'

Day six: Tuxtla to Huatulco. He lost ground to the Porsche in front of him and punished 'his rear tyres too much on the second stage which meant he had to fit two new tyres to the rear of his car for the final stage.'[2]

He explained that 'the front tyres were not very good, so with two new ones on the rear the handling was very strange. It completely changed the balance of my car.'

Day seven: Huatulco to Acapulco. One car – a Porsche – crashed and Regazzoni went off at the same place. 'I swapped my new tyres to the front after the problems yesterday, so this time the back end started to go. I corrected it and then understeered off on the loose edge.' The Mercedes was undamaged.

Day eight: Acapulco to Morelia and disaster just 4km into the second stage. 'A front tyre blew as I went through a corner and the car understeered

This is the view Mackay had. (all courtesy Dylan Mackay)

The cracked oil pan.

Regazzoni directs Mackay as the repairs get under way.

Mackay supplies his own caption: 'Fixed – but it didn't last long …' (all courtesy Dylan Mackay)

into a ditch then into rocks on the other side of the road. A rock smashed the sump and took off the front-right suspension.'

He 'promptly took up traffic duty after his crash in order to warn other competitors about the oil slick he had left on the road.'[3]

The driver Jiri Kotek in the leading Skoda was thankful for that because of the parked Porsche. 'He was sitting by the side of the road and waved us down as we arrived at the blind corner. If he hadn't we would have hit the Porsche head on, because he had spun on the oil and was sitting in the middle of the road.'

The plan was to get the Mercedes towed to Morelia and repair it overnight. 'At this point I discovered the inefficiency and poor mechanical knowledge of my service people. The only competent workshop was already full of vehicles so I had to wait until next day to have my car repaired. Consequently I was out of the race.'[4] To the others it was a rally but not to him, and he'd go flat out to Alaska whether he was still in the thing or not. 'Anchorage was still far away but I wanted to get there.'

As Ron Jackson says, 'he was in a Mercedes again and went off the road, broke the sump. That was his speciality.'

Day nine: 'My co-driver, who was already feeling stressed after the first stages, decided to go back to Italy,' Regazzoni said.

Gunther Stamm remembers that Regazzoni's co-driver 'was fed up after a week because Clay was a competitive driver and that wasn't something his co-driver had expected. In the evening he was pale – no, he was more than pale. He left. Clay had to have another co-driver.

'My wife loved him. She said "He's such a nice guy." I said "Be careful" – to which she said "No, no, no, I am too old for him. Don't worry about that." He really was a very, very charming chap. We often met him and his regular co-driver Claude Valion.'

When the rally reached La Paz in the Baja region Regazzoni invited Dylan Mackay, 'a smart young man,' to take over as co-driver.

Mackay remembers that 'I didn't have any qualms about getting in because I honestly didn't know much about him. I had not really followed Formula 1. I was very young – 24 – and basically on the rally because of my mother's interest in it all. I was pretty much open for anything. I knew he was in a wheelchair because he'd had a racing accident, but racing by its very nature is dangerous and any car that you get into you hope is safe enough that if you have a crash you'll survive it. In fact my mother and I had just survived that very major crash in Guatemala.'

Heidi Hetzer was not so sanguine because she did know about Regazzoni. 'How did I feel letting him get in with Regazzoni? That was the thing. I said "Dylan, you have to decide if you want to go or not. I think it's very interesting but of course I'm also a little bit afraid. Anyway, *you* have to decide."'

Mackay decided. 'We went two or three days together. It was a mix. There are two things that I can remember clearly. One is that his driving was really impressive because it was very, very smooth. It's hard for me to describe what it was that was different about it against being in other cars with other drivers, but it seemed like he navigated the car with a lot of ideas of what was coming up ahead. It was very calm driving and yet it was very, very fast. Really impressive.

'In cruising along Baja's roads – and here I mean the paved parts – it struck me that the line which he drove was perfectly smooth and efficient. The remarkable thing was not so much that he used both our lane as well as the one intended for oncoming traffic – anybody can do that in Mexico – it was more that he recognised exactly how the road was supposed to be driven, and the lines drawn on the asphalt were exposed as meaningless markings made by people who didn't have his grasp of shapes and of motion. It may sound obvious that a Formula 1 driver in his car knows better that the man standing on the road with a paintbrush, but the physical feeling of experiencing it in his car was in fact different than in others, and it actually left a lasting impression with me.

'We were in his Mercedes – the battleship! – but unfortunately, and this is the second thing that I remember, the battleship didn't really withstand Baja's rocks. In fact, the first day that we were driving we hit some rock that the oil pan wasn't protected from and so after the first four or five hours we were stuck at Baja someplace and had to be towed. I never really understood why the oil pan wasn't protected. Usually you have some sort of guard on it or a protection plate. I don't know if something was missing or it was just unlucky.

'We didn't talk much because there was only so much shared language that we had: my Italian-Spanish mix was not really much to communicate to him with and his English was limited but we understood each other well enough to drive together and to tell him what I felt I needed to. I think I understood what he wanted from me. I basically went from what my mother had needed from me as a co-pilot.

'We didn't have any crashes nor did we have any near misses. It was smooth driving most of the

With Heidi at the finish in Alaska. (courtesy Dylan Mackay)

time and waiting around the Baja desert the rest of it. Then he drove on the regular roads up to Las Vegas and they were pretty much empty. I don't think he took the speed limit too seriously but then neither did most people. I never felt unsafe.'

Heidi explains that her son 'said to me "You could feel that he was a very good driver. You could feel that in the way you go into the corners. He didn't have to correct, he knew what he was doing." Then there was a sunset and he couldn't see and they hit a rock. Before that there was a technical problem. Dylan is not a mechanic but he is an intelligent technical person so Clay told him what to do and he had to fix the car.

'They drove all night and arrived early in the morning where I waited. My God, I was so scared – so afraid that something had happened. Then they came and Dylan said "Mama, I think I want to go with you!"

'Clay never gave up whatever happened. At night when we were going to bed you saw him in the hotel in his wheelchair and he'd be headed towards the fax machine trying to get parts so he could start again the next morning. I tell you, the next morning parts were there. I don't know how he did that. We said "My God, when does he sleep?" It was unbelievable.

'I thought: I have to learn from him. For me he was a portrait of what you can do, a symbol you look up to. He *is* a symbol for me and I do look

up. He's not only a symbol, I have used this symbolism practically. He gave me a power to do that and when sometimes I have problems I think *what he did I can do and for me it will be much easier*. It's really something great.'

One of Regazzoni's service crew co-drove up to Alaska. Of this, Regazzoni would say: 'The rest of the rally, although demanding because I had a lot of problems with my car, was a fantastic route through canyons, deserts, rivers and villages where time seemed to have stopped at the beginning of the century.'

Ron Jackson says that 'we were getting up north and the highway is dead straight to Alaska. Of course everybody was speeding. Clay was arrested by the police for that but he talked his way out of it. I imagine they were fairly surprised to see a semi-paralysed man doing those speeds. I always sympathised with his co-drivers because as sure as nuts were nuts he was going to drive off the road somewhere. The old spirit was still there, oh heavens yes. It was amazing.'

Australian Rick Bates, with Brittan's wife Jenny as co-driver, won in a 911 Porsche.

Maddalena Mantegazzi 'joined Clay in Alaska at the end. He told me "OK, you will come to Anchorage on a certain date" – say 11 July, I don't know now. "You will have your hotel and then the next day you'll come to the city and I'll pick you up." I said "OK." I left from Nice, I went there, I had my hotel and next day I took a taxi to the city with my suitcase and he came to pick me up. He knew I could do this trip alone. I hoped he would come because otherwise I'm in Anchorage …

'Then we went on a boat from Alaska to Canada after the rally, a cruise.'

Before these rallies did he get nervous?

'No, never. No, no. When I did rallies with him I was nervous. Do you think a Formula 1 driver gets nervous? I never saw Clay nervous about that – I saw him nervous [agitated] about other things, like the story about the airport. Instead of speaking to him this girl asked me if he needed help to get into the plane. He was nervous because he didn't understand this. "Why do you speak to her and not ask me? Do you think I can't speak?" But nervous in the other sense, about anything – I never saw that.'

(Gian Maria says 'He got angry at airports if they spoke only to Maddalena, but inside, I guess, he was having fun as well when he complained. That was in his character – if he wanted to tell you something it was *boom.*' The meaning: there'd have been *booms* all over airports for a couple of decades if he'd wanted to play it like that.)

In 1998 he entered the 'slalom' at Romont, a celebrated event in a small place near Berne. Drivers negotiated a twisting road with temporary chicanes erected at strategic points – hence slalom. He took his Ferrari F40. It clearly appealed to the driver in him. He also did the Tour of Spain in the Lancia Aurelia. Oh, and the Shield of Africa, another of Brittan's pageants of movement in unlikely settings. Let Brittan describe it himself: 'Starting and finishing in Cape Town, the Shield of Africa was a 21-day event through the six countries of southern Africa. It covered 12,500km over back roads and remote areas taking in 44 timed stages. Namibia, Botswana, Zimbabwe, Swaziland and the tiny mountain kingdom of Lesotho gave the 72 competitors a unique insight into the stunning scenery, primitive lifestyles and great opportunities to see the wild game Africa is famous for. The event attracted drivers from 15 countries and competition was fast and furious over the gravel stages.'

Thereby hangs a tale or two.

Firstly Regazzoni had a co-driver called Mustafa Samel from Ghana and they got so lost on the way to the first special stage that Clay stopped a taxi driver and asked where it was.

Then, Brittan wrote, 'I felt sad for Clay Regazzoni going out on the first day when the transmission of his potent 6.3 Mercedes went pop. Clay is a great competitor. He hasn't changed in the 20-odd years I've known him and he has two speeds. Flat out, or asleep in bed. I have a feeling that the Merc transmission isn't up to putting all that power onto the floor, certainly not with Clay operating the gas pedal. Maybe we should get

At a car show in Lugano with the late, lamented Michele Alboreto. (courtesy Maddalena Mantegazzi)

together and buy him something good and strong for the next event. Like a war surplus Sherman tank perhaps.'

Mustafa Samel could take away one consolation: he hadn't had time to get the rush of impressions.

In 1999 Carol Hollfelder's father invited Regazzoni to come back. 'I started racing in 1998,' Carol says, 'when Ferrari introduced the Formula 1 paddle shifter into their 355. The hand controls that were installed in my street car by Clay and his mechanics were wonderful but they were very unreliable and the only paperwork we had was in Italian, so we didn't have a manual and the company in Europe were not terribly helpful in terms of giving us support. So over the years we always had difficulty with those hand controls and my dad was kind enough, when Ferrari introduced the 355, to think that this would be a car that I could race in. He co-ordinated with the Ferrari factory and got their permission and so on, and I got to race a Ferrari for a while. It was an amazing gift. Most people never get to drive one let alone race one.

'Clay was invited to come and test drive my race car. My dad designed a brake throttle system for it and he wanted to get Clay's input regarding that. Out of anybody in the world Clay had probably driven with more types of hand controls than anyone else and understood them as well.

'We brought Clay up to the San Francisco area and tested the car at Sears Point,[5] then brought him down to Los Angeles, took him out to Willow Springs[6] and drove there. It meant he drove my car at both of those tracks and drove me around at them. Having had Clay show me how to drive a street car was exciting, having him actually take me around a racetrack at speed in a Ferrari was overwhelming.

'One of the things I remember being so shocking at the time was that not only were we going fairly fast but that, even with a handicapped driver using hand controls, if he's got Italian blood in him at all he can still talk with his hands while he's driving! I wanted to take his hand and put it back on the steering wheel – but the driving was so smooth and so precise. It's an honour to be in a car with someone who has that level of skills.

'Whatever the disability happens to be, it directly impacts upon the focus of your life. He struck me as a very pragmatic individual who figured out a way to deal with it, to work with it.

'The hand controls that are available today are in no way a handicap and it has more to do with getting in and out of the car than it does being able to drive it. If Clay had had his accident today the technology would have been so advanced that maybe he could have gotten back into it competitively – certainly not at the Formula 1 level but he was brilliant behind the wheel of a sports car also.'

And surely would …

It's temptingly easy, exploring the rather bizarre world of the rallies – rather like rediscovering the Wild West, only mechanised – to see Regazzoni as, truly, a cowboy on a succession of horses he is constantly trying to tame, and him loving it, expressing the life process itself through it. But there was another Regazzoni, far from this.

'I did the cooking and he liked my cooking a lot,' Maddalena Mantegazzi says. 'He didn't want anybody in the house, not a cleaning lady. It was me and that was all. He broke his femur karting in August 1999. He stayed in the house. He didn't want a nurse and I had to do everything – he just didn't want anybody else. We had a walkie-talkie in the room when he broke his femur. If I wasn't there he'd call me and I'd arrive. (After that we had mobile phones.) That was a month, just us two. One day he began to shout for something and I said "No! Listen, Clay, we've had a month of we two alone. No shouting like that. Quietly, gently!" Then everything was fine.'

London-Sydney Marathon 2000
The Overall Route

London, UK
European Sector
Ankara, Turkey
Chiang Mai, Thailand
Thailand/Malaysia Sector
Johor Bahatu, Malaysia
Darwin, Australia
Australian Sector
Sydney, Australia

He could make great noises, and make cars and trucks make great noises, and he could be silent.

Into the new century, Clay Regazzoni remained in perpetual motion and Nick Brittan had the perfect way of accommodating that.

He put together another re-run of the 1968 London-Sydney Marathon in midsummer 2000 spread over 34 days in three legs. The first took competitors across the Channel into France and Germany and then the Czech Republic. From there it travelled south to Slovakia, Austria and Hungary, across Romania and into Greece. Then it travelled to Turkey, and, as Brittan said 'along to the Mediterranean coast, inland through tiny forgotten hill villages and into the moonscape mountains of remote eastern Turkey.'

Antonov aircraft lifted the cars out overnight to northern Thailand, and then they'd reach Australia.

'The final eight-day leg took the survivors into the deserted outback of the Northern Territory and into the edges of the Simpson Desert where, when the temperature gets above 40 degrees, it's possible to fry an egg on the bonnet of the car,' Brittan wrote.[7] 'The route took in an overnight stop at Alice Springs and then swooped out of the desert into Port Augusta, one of the stopovers on the old '68 event, and then into the spectacularly beautiful Flinders Ranges. Across country to Broken Hill, into the Snowy Mountains to Canberra and its pine forests eventually to finish on the steps of one of the world's most recognisable landmarks, the Sydney Opera House.'

Where else would Regazzoni and the 6.3 Mercedes be?

He lured Pipino back after all these years 'but in a car this time! Clay telephoned and said "I have got a very good car. Come to Sydney." He had a fantastic man who prepared the car and it seemed perfect, but when we started the rally we had a lot of problems.'

Pipino also noticed that 'what annoyed him was getting on a plane. He didn't want to be carried on like a baby, he wanted the proper facilities. He was fighting for things like that and all the things that enable handicapped people to lead normal lives.

'Everywhere he went in the world he had a little bag with playing cards in it and he'd play – on a plane, perhaps – and always he wanted to win. I said to him "You win because you're lucky," but he said "No, I win because I'm the best."'

Mikkola, Stig Blomqvist and Michele Mouton were, of course, part of rallying history and they brought a great legitimacy to the London-Sydney.

The rally got under way by crossing Westminster Bridge with Big Ben and the Houses of Parliament framed in the background. The competitors faced two special stages in England and by the overnight halt in Metz they'd have done 677km. Next day, down to Nuremburg, that would be 600 more kilometres with another two special stages. 'The two 13.5 and 9.4km stages were run through some of the most scenic countryside in France, the 92 remaining competitors that started the day in Metz all enchanted by the rolling countryside that included two thrilling undulating tarmac stages.' Regazzoni, in his 'trusty Mercedes 300,'[8] finished it 23rd overall. Blomqvist moved into the lead.

On day three – to Prague – Mouton won a stage and moved into second place. Meanwhile the official account records 'Clay Regazzoni struck trouble with his Mercedes. The ex-Formula 1 star missed both the stages due to a suspension problem which cost him 64 minutes in road penalty times. Another 36 minutes and he will be excluded from the event.'

Day four – a 'thrilling combination of tarmac and dirt' to Budapest – proved better. He was 'back in action following delays from a leaking fuel tank which kept him out of both stages yesterday. A local Zodiac boat repair man managed to fix it

and he was back in action today with 18th time on the first stage and 36th on the second. "The car was so soft on the gravel it was like driving on ice," said Clay, "but good fun."'

'We'd had fuel inside the car!' Pipino says. 'If there had been a spark – boom! Clay didn't stop. He didn't like to spend money on the best equipment and that was the problem of the leaking tank. It was an old tank. Usually a tank has a certain life but he'd extend it to save money. Imagine the competitors. There were these world champions with Porsche-prepared cars and the competitors really were much better prepared. We stayed with them because of the way Clay drove but it was tense on the special stages. *Was I frightened?* No. Clay's reactions were very fast and there was no comparison with normal people. He had a completely different way of driving.'

He was apt, when confronted by a field of wheat, to enquire where the route went, and if it went round the edge – the long way – he would immediately go straight across, making the Mercedes into a Formula 1 combined harvester.

Day five – to Targu-Jiu, Romania – and Blomqvist was still forging ahead. There was action behind him. 'Many of the competitors found themselves supporting the local economy after being stopped by policemen along the route. Some were bogus

policemen according to those that were stopped, but most ended up supporting the local retirement fund with "donations" ranging from five to one hundred dollars depending how long you were prepared to discuss the point. The big Mercedes of Clay Regazzoni and the Ford Mustang of John Spiers were seen heading for the excellent local service centre laid on by the Romanian Automobile Club. Regazzoni was trying to get his fuel tank fixed after it had sprung a leak again.'

Days six (to Kavala, Greece) and seven (to Canakkale, Turkey) brought them to day eight and more problems with the fuel tank, which needed repairs, so he missed both stages. The tank had to be cleaned because, evidently, it had some contaminated fuel in it. Then they rested for a day before covering 553km to the coastal resort of Alanya past unprotected cliff edges and on loose gravel in boiling temperatures. At the front Blomqvist and Mikkola were trading fastest times.

Three days remained in Turkey and when they'd been completed the 89 remaining competitors out of the 95 who'd started had covered 29 stages totalling 489km – 8,650km in total.

Somewhere in amongst all this Regazzoni wagered another competitor ten cases of champagne that he would be quicker over one of the special stages. To achieve this he drove straight through a wood at racing speed and Pipino got the rush of impressions then, all right. Regazzoni won the bet.

On June 16 the two Antonov freighters flew the cars to Chiang Mai in Thailand for what one of the competitors called 'the most expensive sauna I know'.

They spent four days getting to Sungai Petani. The official report says: 'The French Porsche 911 of Henri Goyunne-Duperat /Claude Valion tumbled down the overall standings from 20th to 48th when they took a slow time on both stages and an added road penalty after the distributor cap came loose and then came off and was eaten up by the car's fan. They had a spare cap on board, but were not able to work out which ignition lead went where in order to get the car going again. They ended their day being towed in by the big Mercedes of Clay Regazzoni.'

As Pipino says, 'at one point we came across a car which had broken down. We gave it a tow and Clay went at 150kmh.'

Next day, working his way through the first stage of 11km, he 'ran out of brakes' and struck a bank, bending the left-front wing of the Mercedes. Next day 'after fixing most of the poor preparation problems on his big Mercedes over the past two weeks, it was almost a relief to have an everyday

London-Sydney Marathon 2000
The Thailand/Malaysia Sector

puncture slow Clay Regazzoni's progress on the first stage, Clay limping to the finish before changing the wheel.'

They flew to Darwin and after seven days were on the Broken Hill to Wagga Wagga section.

One of those days Ron Jackson was running the morning control. 'Clay drove forward right onto my foot. I was screaming – heavy, those Mercs. He rolled forward and rolled back over it again just to complete the job. That was the instant when I decided I was no longer running the morning control but retiring in agony. I was very lucky I didn't break anything. An inch more towards my actual leg and I'd have broken it but the car went more over my toes. I had a nice imprint of a tyre on my foot for a bit, tread and everything. He was so concerned. For days afterwards it was "How is it, how is it? You all right? I'm so sorry."'

Now, heading towards Wagga Wagga, disaster. The official report said: 'The second stage, run mainly over fast flat gravel roads and open flatlands, had a couple of memorable moments including the jump and a mud-hole that caught out several cars, including the fourth placed Escort of Andrew Haddon/Mark Solloway. He spun in the mud, which rammed itself into the car's bell housing and forced the clutch apart. He managed to get going, but lost seven minutes in the incident dropping to fifth overall, now 2m 17s behind the Datsun 240Z of Simon Lingford/David Moir which was pulling 190 kph on some of the long straights!

'The mud-hole also spelt disaster for Clay Regazzoni/Franco Pipino in their big Mercedes. After clawing their way back up the results following several strong days of finishes, they slipped to the back again when Clay spun in the mud and was then hit by the MGB of Henry and Tina Koster who arrived on the scene and could not stop. They hit the Mercedes head on, the big German car coming off worse when it broke the oil and water radiators. The MGB managed to get going again but had no lights and a badly bent front end.'

Henry Koster says 'Forgive me for this mistake! I was running in the special stage and I think it was more than two hours. It was dry weather and everything was dry. My daughter told me – she was my navigator – "Daddy, in 20km there's a mud-hole." I said "Tina, it's not possible. You must be looking at the wrong road atlas. Everything is dry so don't tell me about a mud-hole." She said "And now it's 15km …"

'Suddenly I saw something yellow and I remembered there was one yellow Porsche and I thought maybe it was in a little bit of trouble. Still, everything was dry, no water, nothing. Then I saw a silver car and I remembered that there was only one silver car in the Rally so it must have been Clay in his Mercedes. Clay was still sitting in his car and it had turned round. He was facing me so he'd been in a lot of trouble. I braked and I was completely in this mud-hole. When I braked nothing happened – now everything was mud on the right side and everything on the left side was dry. I tried to get out of the two tramlines which my little MG was in and it wasn't possible. The only thing I could do was keep on braking. The whole time I could see Clay's eyes and he was looking into mine.

'I crashed into him – a great crash – and I tried to reverse for half a metre but nothing happened. My car was OK. I got out into the mud, I went to Clay and asked if I could help try and repair his car. I had pushed my MG into his oil radiator and the oil radiator into the water radiator, so everything was broken: oil and water.

'I'd not met Clay before. He said "I saw everything that you did – I was sitting in the front row! – and I saw it wasn't possible for you to avoid me." We tried for ten minutes to get Clay to continue but we couldn't. Clay said "Stop. There's help on the way." The yellow Porsche towed me out so we could continue.

London-Sydney Marathon 2000
The Australian Sector

'Clay wasn't angry or anything, no, no, no, no. He said "Henry, do me a favour – go, go, go, please go. We've ordered a four-wheel car and he'll be here soon. Then we can continue also." That was a great mistake. They ordered it from a farmer, I suppose by telephone, but there was trouble.'

Gunther Stamm, driving a Mustang, remembers his friend Koster 'could drive away with the MGB but Clay was stuck in the mud. A farmer pulled him out and brought the car to his farm in the middle of nowhere. They phoned for a pick-up guy to get Clay and bring him and the car to the next point. With those rallies that Nick organised you had to be at the start on the next day within 30 minutes of your starting time. Otherwise you were out of the rally. Normally it's not a problem.'

Regazzoni remembered the Mercedes was stuck like in quicksand in a deserted landscape: 'there were Italian immigrants who knew my name. They fed us and gave us their house to wait in, then they went out to a party.'

In fact, the farmer had a picture of Regazzoni in a Ferrari on his wall and, accompanied by his family, proudly brought it to show him. They were all in tears.

Stamm remembers that 'the farmer said to Clay "Look, I've been invited out but the pick-up truck will come some time in the afternoon or evening and take you where you need to go." Hours later the phone rang and a lorry driver said "I'm looking for this bloody farm. Where are you?" Clay said "I have no bloody idea – somewhere in Australia!" The farmer came back early in the morning totally drunk … and it was all a disaster. Clay and the car only reached the start when all the others had left, so he was out.'

To which Regazzoni said: 'The tow truck was supposed to be there at ten o'clock but it came at three in the morning. The Mercedes was taken to a workshop a long way away and repaired so I got it to Sydney.'

Ron Jackson remembers Regazzoni 'sitting outside the hotel after he'd had to retire and he was talking about it: how he'd had an MG impaled on the front of his car. He was sanguine. Clay started five of our events and he retired on all five …'

Regazzoni and Pipino flew back to Nice Airport and parted without saying a word. Pipino is still not sure why. Perhaps there was nothing left to say.

In October 2001 Regazzoni and Valion entered the Inca Trail rally, a big event – 50 historic rally cars and 50 4x4s – and a hard event, although John Brown of the Historic Endurance Rally Organisation, running it, insists that 'our events are much less demanding than the Paris-Dakar but Clay did all kinds of things and it was quite amazing. He was super-active. The first event of ours he did was the Scottish Malts – a fun event. It's a classic car rally round Scotland. We had no

The Inca rally, and still the centre of attraction. (Michael Johnson)

qualms about him entering the Inca, none at all. He was a grown man, you know.'

It's difficult to control 34-odd days of God knows what.

'That's his job and his co-driver's job. He was neither a fool nor a helpless person. He knew we couldn't possibly make special provision for him on an event like that. He just had to go and get on with it and look after himself. If anything went wrong with the car (a) he had an able-bodied co-driver and (b) there are always people willing to help, other participants or whatever. People would always stop for him.'

(Incidentally, Brown had been one of those sharing the London flat with Chris Lambert and Simon Taylor. 'The thing Clay was accused of was basically shoving Chris off and he fell down into the tunnel access road. I never discussed it with Regga. I thought it was a bit sensitive and I didn't think it would be politic. Chris was a racer, Clay was a racer and I think he did push hard. There's no doubt about it: Clay was a pusher.')

Fred Gallagher was by now on conversational terms with him. 'Because I was in the Citroën factory team he would know who you were. I remember doing a Paris-Peking rally. I've no idea why, but we went via Venice airport. We had a special stage down in that bit of northern Italy and he turned up just to watch in his Ferrari. I talked to him then, and on the Scottish Malts. I think he was a brave adventurer because he clearly wasn't doing it to make any money. It was difficult for the rest of us so it was ten times more difficult for him. He was very normal to talk to, no big star side to him whatsoever that I could see.'

'The Inca was a hell of a thing, nearly two months long,' says rally photographer Mike Johnson. 'It started in Rio and finished there too. It went through Bolivia, Peru, Chile, down the western coast skirting backwards and forwards from Chile to Argentina, right down to Piero del Fuego and then back up the east coast through Uruguay or Paraguay, Argentina and back to Rio. There weren't so many flat-out special stages – there were some – but it was more an endurance event. Some of the roads were extremely rough and a lot of people on it spent a lot of time working on their cars. There were quite a mixture of cars, too: one section for 4x4s, another for classic cars – which Clay was in, with the Merc. I think there was another Merc there with a couple of his friends in.

'I was hired by the organiser to photograph the rallies. I had not met Regazzoni before. He was very polite and friendly towards me, obviously very determined. If you think of a man paralysed

The Inca rally, and normal service: flat out. (Michael Johnson)

from the waist down, over 60 and taking on something like that, it's incredible. He seemed to have no fear. I've no idea what he was like before but he didn't let these problems stand in his way. If he wanted to do something he would do it. He had a natural charisma about him.'

A strange story emerged of how at one point he was first to go in a hill-climb stage on what he'd been told was a closed road. The road had bends in it but Regazzoni took the racing line through them and found himself confronted with a red Volkswagen Polo coming down. He took avoiding action but they crashed, damaging the front door of the Mercedes. Another competitor, coming along afterwards, noticed an iguana in the middle of the road ...

'He had an accident on the event because towards the end a local person got onto the stage and he had a head-on. No one was hurt,' Johnson says.

Perpetual motion ...

At a different level he'd compete in the Yaris Stars Challenge in France, using – by definition – Toyota cars. In May he raced at Dijon and put on a spectacular performance to take pole. He made a poor start, however, and was beaten to the first corner. This car and Regazzoni went round the whole of the first lap door-to-door, and you can imagine what that meant. Then he fell back and was even overtaken by Toyota's Dijon concessionaire.

There is no record of what he said about that. Use your imagination.

Notes: 1. The 1997 Panama-Alaska Rally (TWE); 2. Ibid; 3. Ibid; 4. Ibid; 5. Sears Point, a 2.52-mile circuit built in 1968 at Sonoma, California; 6. Willow Springs, a 2.5 mile circuit built in 1953 at Rosamond, California; 7. The 1997 Panama-Alaska Rally; 8. Ibid.

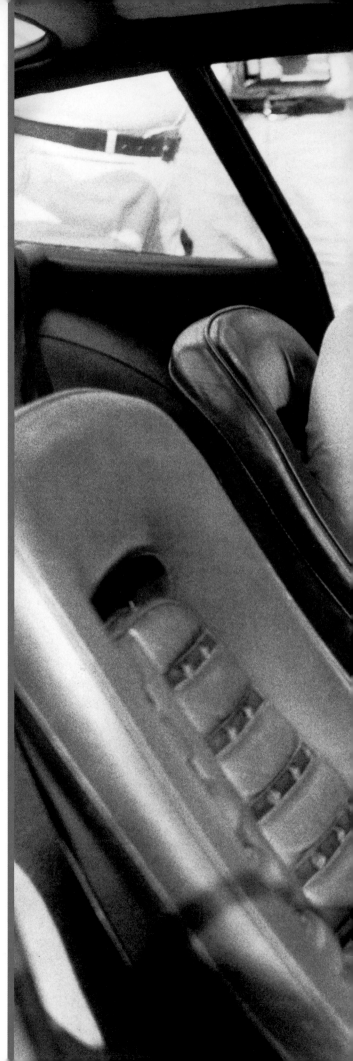

CHAPTER 12

ROCK 'N' ROLL

Alan Barton 'began organising the Targa Tunisia in early 2002 after initial positive meetings with the Tunisian Tourism Board in London and the *Automobile Club de Tunisie* in Tunis. Whilst the Tourism Board were to remain enthusiastic supporters throughout, the AC de T were more interested in personal financial inducements, which I suppose comes with the territory in that part of the world.

'Living in France at the time I made friends with a local rally enthusiast, Henri Goyunne-Duperat, a salesman at the local Peugeot dealership. Henri was good friends with Clay and contacted him to see if was interested in competing. I subsequently spoke to Clay, giving him a comprehensive breakdown of each day of the 12-day event, emphasising the competitive element – over 500km of closed road, timed-to-the-second tests, first-class hotels and a good social atmosphere at the end of each day's competition. By the time we'd finished our chat I could tell he was up for it, especially as I gave him a huge reduction in the entry fee, and we "shook hands" on the deal over the phone. True to his word, a completed entry form arrived shortly afterwards.

'A couple of weeks later I received a call from Jose "Zica" Capristano, a Portuguese guy I had originally met on the Round the World in 80 Days Rally, who informed me he was going to co-drive for Clay. Whilst I was delighted to have "Zica" on board – knowing he enjoyed the social side of

RIGHT *As the years went by, Regazzoni would master the art of driving with hand controls so completely that even passengers hardly noticed.* (LAT)

rallying – I was none too sure of his prowess as a co-driver, but I assumed from what he told me that he and Clay would be a combination hard to beat in Clay's Mercedes [280SE].

'I met Clay later that year at the *Circuit des Ramparts* event in Angoulême where he was holding court in the *Chez Paul* restaurant with Henri and their mutual friends. He was an extremely likeable chap who obviously enjoyed the good things in life, never being far from a glass of wine, a cigar and with a twinkle in his eye for the passing ladies. It was clear motor sport was nowadays a means to an end, an opportunity to socialise with friends whilst still breathing in the fumes of Castrol R and reminiscing of good times past. It was also clear he still had a competitive streak and as more than one person commented, "He could probably get round the circuit quicker in his bloody wheelchair than some of those buggers!"

'Nine months later I saw him again on the quayside in Marseilles, where competitors and officials met for our overnight journey across the Mediterranean courtesy of CTN ferries. The crossing was enlivened by a superb dinner where everyone got to know one another, Clay being the centre of attention for much of the evening as he regaled fellow competitors with tales of derring-do when Formula 1 was "real racing" and drivers where "real men".'

Mike Johnson went on the Targa Tunisia. Compared to the Inca, this was 'more of a faster paced, special stage rally for more modern cars with proper special stages. It was a smaller entry, something like 18 cars. He was very quick.'

Regazzoni was an old man now. He just didn't accept it, here in deepest Tunisia or anywhere else. (Michael Johnson)

The 500km of special stages and 2,600km on linking public roads went 'down alongside the Algerian border to Tataouine at the Sahara, and then up the east coast back to Tunis 12 days later. Scrutiny was on the quayside in Marseilles in sunshine on Thursday 9 October, at the tail end of the traditional "Mistral winds" [down the Rhône-Saône valley], which are of gale force proportion.'[1]

Martin Taylor, a rally man from Dublin, 'first came across Regazzoni in the UAE Desert Challenge in 1994 when he went out there in his Mercedes. Apparently he had a bit of a name for this, but he started that event and he fell out with the co-driver. He kicked him out. I think they'd started taking bets on the boat to Tunisia as to how long the co-driver would last this time.'

The official report of the rally says 'although we were late arriving the crowds were out in force in the *Avenue Bourguiba* as the Mayor of Tunis Mr Mohsen and the British Ambassador Robin Kealey flagged cars away at the start of our ten day adventure.'[2]

Taylor remembers Regazzoni as a 'terribly nice man. I think he liked signing autographs. He was good fun. The first night in one of the hotels over there he went off and he bought the Arab headgear like a big tea towel – and everybody else was wearing baseball caps or something like that. He had the full gear!'

Barton remembers 'arriving in Tunis the following day there were more than a few thick heads and thousands of very noisy, enthusiastic locals. Two fantastic tarmac tests took crews to Tabarka only 5km from the Algerian border on the north coast. Chatting to Clay that evening he said how good the roads had been and would there be more of the same on the days ahead? "It gets better as we go along," I replied. "Oh good," he said, "all I need now is a new co-driver." Already the cracks were appearing as it seemed 'Zica' had found the navigation and timing difficult to master, especially as the last section had been in the dark but, as I said, no one ever said it was going to be easy.

'Whilst "Zica" was not proving the best co-driver in the world, it also appeared that Clay was a little lax when it came to car preparation. His only concession to checking the Mercedes had been to fill it with petrol for the drive from Italy to Marseilles, blowing the dust and cobwebs off en route! He reckoned it was a Mercedes and would easily get round a little bit of desert. After all, he said, "Rommel achieved pretty much the same 60 years ago!"

'The next day was a long, demanding section down to Kairouan in central Tunisia with four

cracking, timed-to-the-second tests en route. Clay's rally started to go wrong here with a puncture, then the first of many brake problems which, with his disability and "Zica's" lack of mechanical knowledge, was a recipe for disaster. Fortunately the rally had excellent officials and two mechanics ready to help any competitor who struck trouble. Between them they were able to get Clay and "Zica" into Kairouan that evening. The next day was a difficult loop into the maze of olive groves between Kairouan and El Jem: four tests totalling more than 60km of competitive driving which would decide the fate of many and were not an attractive proposition for a crew with dodgy brakes and an equally dodgy co-driver.

'Whilst Clay clearly enjoyed the tests it was obvious that "Zica" was suffering and he looked unwell at that night's overnight halt back in Kairouan. The car had a thorough makeover that evening and both Clay and "Zica" put a brave face on things, but rumours were rife of a serious rift. One thing that had become established right from the outset was that the French contingent of officials and marshals, plus Clay and the Italian film crew (the attractive female producer was well known to Clay), always ate together. There was no fraternising with Les Anglais. This doesn't mean there wasn't a great atmosphere on the rally – there was, and everyone got on very well together, but the French and Clay always stuck together.'

Day five comprised, as Barton says, 'a 400km run down to Tozeur on the edge of the Sahara desert with one very long all-tarmac test over the mountains to the north of Sbeilta which Clay thoroughly enjoyed as the Mercedes was running OK and the navigation was simple. As he said to me, "If we had the time I'd have gone round again and had another go."

'That night in the five-star Palm Beach Hotel in Tozeur (nearest beach 500km away) crews relaxed around the pool and compared tales of the "we were flat in sixth when we came over a crest to find a herd of camels in the road" variety. The exception was "Zica", who came to my room to tell me he was unwell, having been bitten by some dreaded Tunisian fly that had caused him to feel so ill he was going to return to his native Portugal for medical attention. When I asked him what Clay was going to do he said, "I think he will carry on, by himself if necessary." Naturally I was disappointed but I understood there had been tensions. I decided to leave it until the following day to resolve the issue of Clay disappearing off into the desert by himself – after all, look what eventually happened to Rommel.

'Ferocious sandstorms the day before our arrival into Tozeur had completely obliterated much of the rally route and we had to undertake a major re-route to get any competitive mileage that day. It meant an afternoon session only but at least crews had the morning off to laze around the pool. This gave me an opportunity to talk to Clay and clear up what he was going to do.

'As the organiser I couldn't allow him to continue alone because it was simply too dangerous. That really wasn't an option, despite his enthusiasm. One of the French rally officials, Claude Valion, a close friend of both Henri Goyunne-Duperat and Clay, was also a qualified co-driver so the logical solution was to ask him to step into the co-driver's seat whilst we covered his official duties. Clay obviously relished having Claude alongside and by the time the rally reached Tataouine two days later – and despite the Mercedes suffering from brake and suspension problems – he was a changed man.

'A day off at the beautiful Sango Privilege Hotel in Tataouine put everyone in an even better mood, if that were possible, because by now competitors had also become friends, a sense of camaraderie had been established, and more than one competitor commented that the tests were as good, if not better, than many on the World Rally Championship series. And they still had another four days to go.

'Clay did a long interview sat by the pool with the Italian television crew, extolling the virtues of the rally and telling everyone to come to Tunisia, a place he'd never been to before and wished he had done. "The people, the scenery, the food and the wine were all excellent," he said. He was a real ambassador for the event and for Tunisia.

'The Sango Privilege was a unique hotel built into the red rock of the hillside and each room was reached via twisting paths through gardens rich in bougainvillea, jasmine and wild roses, quite beautiful but not designed for anyone in a wheelchair. We had reserved the room closest to the bar and restaurant for Clay, which still meant he faced a short obstacle course getting to the bar but he didn't complain once, although, at the end of each evening, he always had a willing band of unsteady helpers to get him back to his room.'

Ron Jackson remembers the hotel 'didn't have any disabled facilities at all and was on a hillside with steps down. Regazzoni came down them in his wheelchair by himself. He was dependent on a lot of people, obviously, to get him back up the steps but that didn't deter him at all. You never knew what he was thinking, from his face you could never tell about that, but he could make that wheelchair go!'

Running repairs. Regazzoni constantly surprised people by what he could do from the wheelchair. (Michael Johnson)

Alan Barton explains that 'now his rally was about to take yet another twist. Valion, a customs official, had to leave the rally unexpectedly due to official business. Once again Clay was without a co-driver. Fortunately a solution was at hand. Julian Morris and Jim Baynam were competing in a Mk 1 Escort and thoroughly enjoying themselves until they broke the diff, and although they were having another one flown out from the UK it wouldn't arrive until the rally was back in Tunis. It was decided that Julian would get the car taken back to Tunis by truck whilst Jim stepped into the breach and co-drove Clay for the next few days. This was quite a move – Jim's first ever rally. However, as it turned out the pair hit it off from the start.'

Baynam confirms this. 'Our car was *hors de combat* and Clay was driving on his own. Basically they would allow him to do the road sections but they wouldn't allow him the stage sections. The guy who was running the rally said to me "Look, this is simple: would you like to co-drive with Clay Regazzoni?" I said "Oh, go on then" – having been a circuit racer for over 20 years, I thought *Wow, yes, not half!*'

Baynam was about to get the full rush of impressions. 'We had met once or twice because there weren't a lot of cars on that rally, a disappointing entry. I'm a circuit racer not a rally driver so it was a new thing for me. I was taken over to him and it was "Well, let's have a chat."

'He was quite jovial and amenable, and we had a laugh. I'm a big guy, six foot one, and I said with a big smile on my face, because it's my style,

"Look, let's get one thing straight here. If I do this we're going to enjoy it. We're not going to fall out – because I'm bigger than you!" I said one or two other things I can't remember but he absolutely roared with laughter. He looked at me, he put his hands out and said "I am a gentle man." I said "Right, you'd better be. I'm not standing for any tantrums." He roared with laughter again and shook my hand.

'So off we went. He was driving it with hand controls, obviously, and it wasn't a problem to him. It was no surprise to me because I had seen the car during the course of the event and I was intrigued to know how he did it only with hand controls.

'I wouldn't say I was in awe of him but there was something special about the man. He had an amazing aura and presence about him, and I was pleasantly surprised at his knowledge of all aspects of motor sport. He was genuinely interested in the cars that I raced in the UK and the circuits we raced on there. There was certainly something special about sitting there with someone like that. We'd be driving down a 50-mile road section chatting away about all sorts of motor racing things. To be sitting next to someone relating first-hand stories about Frank Williams, Niki Lauda and so on was just amazing. He was genuinely interested in the TVR and MGB I raced at that time. We talked and we chatted. Most of Regga's stories were hilarious.

'We hadn't got far down the road in this huge lump of a car he was driving and we were chattering away. We were on a dual carriageway but he was a really eccentric driver and seemed to prefer the hard shoulder. He certainly didn't have too much respect for other road users.

'In racing, you must have confidence in people's ability and I certainly did. He was very hard on the brakes and I asked what kind he was running. He said "Oh, on the back we have the one brake." I thought *I don't know much about Mercedes* and for one stupid minute I thought *Well, how does that work?* Then I thought *That's ridiculous, you can't have only one brake.* He said "Ah, the brake on the left-hand side has been broken and we've had to send for spare parts." I know rally drivers are slightly mad, and while I could cope with going round corners at crazy angles I questioned the wisdom of being in a car with only one rear brake.

'The main job of the navigator is to work the Halda. This is a very accurate meter which measures distance and time. I'd never used one before but I soon got the hang of it and realised how important it is when you're navigating in an area with few landmarks.

'At the start of the rally the Halda is calibrated on a precise measured mile, then zeroed at the start of every stage. The stage notes will tell you, for example, to turn right after 1,550 metres. The Halda acts as a very accurate tripmeter and when it reads 1,550 metres there should be a road to turn onto!

'Given that there are no signposts, the Halda *has* to be precisely calibrated. Equally important is to remember to reset it at every marker point, or you just don't know where the hell you are. The Halda is hugely important and it's almost impossible to run a fast stage without it.

'With a few minute of starting on the first stage we were hurtling down the road and it became very apparent that the Halda in the Mercedes wasn't working properly. Given Regga's "Mr Angry" reputation, I was more than a little concerned but clearly I had to raise the matter.'

Baynam: 'Clay, we seem to have a problem with the Halda.'

Regazzoni: 'Ah yes! It doesn't work properly when we go over 80kmh.'

Baynam: 'Er, does that mean we have to stay below 80kmh?'

Regazzoni: '!'

Baynam: 'Well, how do I know when to turn off?'

Regazzoni: 'You must be joking. I want to win this [expletive] rally.'

Baynam: 'So what do I do?'

Regazzoni: 'You have to make a lot of very good guesses!'

Baynam thought *No wonder his original navigator went home. Here I am sitting next to a grumpy old man in a car with dodgy brakes and a Halda that isn't working.* In fact, however, Baynam's fears proved baseless because 'despite having an extremely competitive nature Regga had quite a soft side and we got on really well together.

'We came in at the end of the first day and I lifted the wheelchair out. When we met up in the evening the results came out. He looked across at me and he had the biggest grin you could ever see. He just put his thumbs up and he said "We are quickest!" We'd got the fastest time of the day despite only having one brake. It was mostly sandy stages that day but he drove the thing like a bloody hooligan. Typical rally driver, I guess.

'The next day, the penultimate day of the rally, we were heading off for a stage – and this was a serious stage, a proper, full-blown thing – about ten miles long through hills and low level mountains. The guy who'd organised the rally said "It's a straight road and there's not a lot of navigating, in fact there's not an awful lot for the co-driver to do here except to sit back and hope for the best. It's straight road." There were no turn-offs, you just followed the track in front of you, which was loose tarmac. We went hurtling down this track and we were getting higher and higher. We got these views over vineyards and goodness knows what else, and it was all rather lovely.

'He slammed the brakes on to a right-hander and, with only one rear brake working, the car turned sharp left. It hit a small earth bank and it took off. This was one big, heavy car and it was one high mountain but the front of the car went up and I could see the sky. We were belted in but no crash helmets. It sounds a bit dramatic but for someone who'd been around the circuits for a long time I thought [expletive], *this is going to hurt.* We were sitting high up and you couldn't see. In an instant the car landed pointing down a slope which was pretty bloody steep, I can tell you. The Mercedes went hurtling down the hill, crashing and bashing through bushes and branches and scrub and God knows what. Somehow or other it stayed upright and stopped. I thought *Christ, that was serious.* It was the biggest fright I've had in those 20-plus years' racing.

Regazzoni always respected motor racing history. Here he is happy to pose in front of a giant photograph of Juan-Manuel Fangio. (Michael Johnson)

'In circuit racing, when you do go four wheels off on the grass at high speed – at somewhere like Oulton Park – your first reaction is *How am I going to get back on the track?* If that doesn't work, the next stage is to plan the path of least destruction, but initially you don't think about the consequences, only how quickly you can get back and how few places you can lose.

'Having got over the initial shock – and we'd realised we still had four wheels on the ground – our first thought was how on earth could we turn the car round, get back up the hill and back onto the track. We found a bit of flat ground at the bottom of the hill. Regga did a neat handbrake turn to spin the car round and he stuck it in first gear. We hurtled back up the hill, scattering more bushes on the way before going airborne yet again. We landed back on the road with a huge crash and carried on at unabated speed. At the end of the stage he leaned across, shook my hand and he said "Now we need a drink." He had a couple of thermos flasks and I reached down and picked one of them up. He said "No, no, not this one, take the other one." I opened it and it was whisky. We had a drink …

'Clay was actually quite shaken after what was a very close call. A stiff drink from the thermos flask calmed us both down. We talked about the incident and he said to me something along the lines of "Your reaction was that of a racer, you didn't panic and you just wanted to get back on the track as fast as possible, and get racing again." All the same, it was a scary moment.

'He had no real fear while competing. He acknowledged the risks but his view was that everything in life has a risk attached to it so let's just enjoy doing what we love. He was typical of the drivers from that generation. He could be difficult and abrasive but he also had a wicked sense of humour and could be incredibly charming. A good-looking woman brought a twinkle to his eye.

'He was a humble man in many ways although quite brash and arrogant. We had long chats because there were two hours between stages. We talked very openly and I almost wish I'd been able to tape some of the stories. He told me word for word what happened the whole day at Long Beach, how it happened, he told me where he lost the World Championship. You read about these things but to have it first hand is a very special memory.'

Barton remembers Baynam 'saying "I've really, really enjoyed the rally, the route was fantastic, the country and the people have been outstanding and it was always going to be something I would look back on and say *I'm glad I did it*, but that was even before I got in with Clay. Of course, I never ever expected anything like that and it really has proved to be the icing on the cake. He was the perfect gentleman and proved just what a driver he must have been at his peak. To see him throw that Mercedes around some of those roads with total commitment is something I'll never forget."

'I think that encapsulates what we all thought on meeting Clay. He didn't tolerate fools gladly, that's for sure, but why should he? He was the perfect gentleman, polite and courteous to a fault, and even though he knew within a few days he was never going to win the event he kept his competitive spirit going right to the end.'

The official report said: 'Day 8. Clay Regazzoni pronounced himself more than happy with his new co-driver Jim Baynam. With the replacement diff that Julian Morris was hoping would arrive today to get him and Jim back in the rally in the RS2000, still being stuck in Brussels, it looks as if Jim will continue with Clay for the rest of the rally.'

In fact the spare parts arrived in time for Morris and Baynam to return to the rally in their Escort for the final day. Regazzoni couldn't get a replacement co-driver and whilst he wasn't allowed to do the final times stages he completed the road stages to be classified as a finisher.

Martin Taylor confirms that Regazzoni made it to the end because 'we were outside the hotel and he was just starting to push himself along to go and have a look at the wrecked car. There was a big hill. I said to him "Do you want a push?" and he said "Yeah, yeah."'

He telephoned Barton 'a few weeks after the rally to thank me personally and to wish me well for the future, promising to see me on the next

Regazzoni plus Yaris. He could make that go too.

Targa Tunisia or whatever I was going to organise. As long as there was a strong competitive element, good food and wine and good companionship, he said he'd be there. Sadly I never got the chance to take him up on his offer but at least I can say I met him, and like Jim Baynam and the others from Targa Tunisia, I'm richer for it.'

Perpetual motion?

In September he drove in the Yaris Stars Challenge at Lédenon and the drivers – including 'elderly' Regazzoni, as one report put it – 'all tried to give the best of themselves, in good spirits and joy with one common objective: to transmit that.'

It had always been like that.

Gian Maria found himself racing against his father in a Yaris round at Albi. Gian Maria had been due to co-drive a Ferrari Modena in a different race but 'I was there for nothing. It could have been the worst weekend of my life – my team-mate broke the car. My father had had his birthday a couple of days before. The Yaris people said "As a present we'd like to give your son this race." So we had practice and on race day I made a good start. My father was in front of me and I went to overtake. He closed the door! Into the next chicane I was faster than him. I locked wheels, I went sideways on the grass but I managed to pass. After the race he never mentioned I'd overtaken him. I had a couple of contacts with other cars – lucky contacts – and I won. I wasn't supposed to [as a birthday guest]. I was sitting with him at

lunch and he said "How did you do?" I said "I won." He was smiling, he was so happy. People were complaining about the way I drove. He said "Tell them it was to maintain the family name …"'

In November he took part in the Tour of Spain Lancia Classic in the Aurelia B-20 and the car was described as one of the main attractions. Of the 146 entrants 102 made the finish – Regazzoni fourth.

Perpetual motion?

'He did so much for disabled people,' Derek Bell says, 'and he obviously had adequate funds behind him, which was nice because a lot of guys come out with sweet FA. He always seemed to have wealth and he'd been earning reasonably well. He had such enthusiasm and such drive, and he was at every event. I was with him a lot in the last three years in the karts. We raced in Bogotá together, we raced in Uruguay together. He was [expletive] good in them. They were charity kart Grands Prix – Juan-Pablo Montoya raced in them – around the southern hemisphere raising money for kids. They were fun but serious: nothing too crazy, despite Regga being in it.'

At the start of one of these seasons:

Bell: 'How have you been the last year?'

Regazzoni: 'Fine, fine, but I broke my leg.'

Bell: 'What do you mean, you broke your leg?!'

Regazzoni: 'I had a crash in a car and smashed my legs up.'

Bell did not inquire about the details of the crash because, as he knew from personal

Grand Prix racing would always guard precious memories of Regazzoni. The rally community would always guard other precious memories, like this one in Tunisia.
(Michael Johnson)

experience, Regazzoni had spent the whole of his adult life crashing, although there was the amusing (if you can put it like that) notion that 'of course it didn't matter because he couldn't feel any pain – but, I mean, that was Clay. What an amazing man, and he always had that smile. Clay was perfect except for his legs. I met him at Ferrari events because we were Ferrari drivers, but I saw more of him in the last few years and I just adored him. I mean that sincerely. He had a real talent. If he hadn't, they'd have said "Oh, he's a crasher, forget him."'

Speaking of karting, Nino Fiorello 'did some with him in Portugal. We did it for fun but he wanted to win, he *always* wanted to win.'

Mario Andretti remembers a kart race at Homestead.[3] 'It was like a 45-minute race, and there were two drivers in each team – you each did a stint. Clay and I teamed up, but obviously he had to have his own kart, fitted with hand controls, so the understanding was that we would have a ten-second penalty at changeover time, because we weren't actually switching drivers – we were switching *karts*. So he was supposed to wait ten seconds before he left, but of course as soon as I pulled in, off he went! And of course we won the race. Some guys like Arturo Merzario were bellyaching away about it and Clay, of course, thought that was hilarious. Boy, there was a guy who knew how to have fun.'[4]

In 2004 he took part in the Great Tour of China with Valion. John Brown says it 'started in Beijing and went all the way across China diagonally through Xi'an, where we looked at the Terracotta Army. We went across to the northern point of Tibet, down through Tibet to Lhasa, out to the Everest base camp, back to Lhasa and down through a horrendous stretch of road for four or five days – they were building it – through the Yunnan Province, the one that runs closest to the Myanmar border [Burma] – through all the river gorges there – and across to Hong Kong, where it finished. It was 11,000km over 30-odd days and Regga did it in a 4x4.

'I spent a lot of time with him during that event. His co-driver was a great cook and we would stop and have lunch with them until they ran out of Italian food. There were always girls there, too – the ladies' crews always stopped there to see Regga.'

On the Tibetan border he and Valion decided to have a barbeque – that is to say, barbeque a whole yak. They bought one, which was not a problem, but kindling was and they had to travel some distance to find any. They overcame the trifling problem of not having a barbeque by buying several dozen metal coat hangars and fashioning them into a grille. Unfortunately they couldn't get enough heat to cook the yak properly, although the bits they did eat tasted … well, OK.

'He was a very nice guy, very affable,' Brown says. 'What amazed me was how little he complained and how he just got on with things. He never moaned about being disabled. We always tried to get him rooms on the ground floor and all that kind of thing but he was not a moaner if he didn't have everything he wanted. I think he accepted, when he came on events like ours, that they weren't designed for disabled people. Of course he got a lot of help lifting his wheelchair up steps.

'He enjoyed the company of people. I think he didn't really think about the fact that he was disabled. He was disabled, he accepted the fact and any disabled person needs to be able to do that, in the same way as if you're bald or short-sighted. It's not quite the same, I know, but he did accept it and got on with his life. I wouldn't pretend to know the psychology of it – whether he needed that or whatever – but I think he did need company and things to do, like everybody else. He was just part of the company, and of course the fact that he was a famous Formula 1 driver helped in the company he was moving in anyway. He was a celebrity there already.'

Then there'd be the historic Targa Florios in 2004 and 2005. Listen:

'Imagine a beautiful island with rugged scenery, the air full of the perfume from wild flowers and surrounded by a sparkling blue sea. All this bathed in early summer sunshine. Sounds idyllic, doesn't it? Ah, but to make it perfect you would want a wonderful selection of classic cars to drool over, wouldn't you?

'Well there is such a place. It's Sicily during the first week of June when the Giro di Sicilia – Targa Florio takes place. Organised by the Veteran Car Club Panormus each year the Giro takes these cars on a circuit of the island over a period of five days. With a history going back almost one hundred years it claims to be the oldest motoring event still in existence.'[5]

Vic Elford remembers 2004. 'I got to know him a little through sports car racing because he was racing with Ferrari as well, but I didn't really know him well. I got to know him better afterwards because for three or four years in a row I went to Sicily for the Targa Florio reunion meeting. Clay was always there with one of his own cars – he had a Ferrari Daytona, which he drove with the hand controls, and then he had another one, a 250 or 275 that he took one year.

'We used to talk quite a lot there. I'm one of those odd people who wakes up and gets up early, because I like it. Clay was the same. In the hotel at our overnight stays, or before we were going anywhere in Sicily, I would be up around seven, go downstairs and have a cup of coffee. Invariably he'd be there too, in his wheelchair. So we'd have the coffee and chat while everybody else was still sleeping. We talked about things in general: a little bit about racing, and who was doing what. I think we talked about politics and the world in general, the sort of thing that two reasonably intelligent people talk about when they get together. That doesn't have to be just motor racing. Far from it.

'He was still an intensely active man. He was always smiling, always cheerful, always ready to swear if somebody upset him. Apart from the fact that you could see it, you couldn't believe that he was in a wheelchair. There was no self-pity, none at all. Oh, no. Absolutely none.'

Photographer Roger Dixon remembers 2005. 'The event was the Giro and Targa combined so it was over about five days. Each day was part of the Giro of Sicily and then the last day, or sometimes

it's the first day, they do a lap of the small Targa circuit and then another of the medium Targa circuit. Regazzoni did all three. He was quick. He usually used to come through first out of anybody, didn't hang about. Even in his wheelchair he didn't hang about. He scooted around. He could

The Targa Florio in 2005. Relaxing before the start, and letting the Ferrari devour the road. (Roger Dixon Photography)

really make it move and he was like this in the Piazza Verdi in Palermo where all the people had their cars and they all chatted to each other. It's a great event because it starts off with nobody really knowing anybody else and by about the third day, when they've all shared the same hotels and breakfast tables, everybody's "Borrow this from me" and "Can I borrow that from you?" You get a huge camaraderie, but he was doing it on the first day. Obviously people knew *him*.'

Dixon started 'in the mid-1960s and worked my way into doing Formula 1 and sports car races until about the mid-'70s. Then I decided to get married and settle down so I got a proper job. I did newspaper photography on local papers. Later on, about ten to fifteen years ago, I got back into doing motor sport.

'Because of my previous life, shall we say, historics suited me well: a lot of the cars I'd photographed when they were original. I started off by going to Goodwood and eventually, after

The rare photograph, as Regazzoni himself pointed out: he's not in the wheelchair. (Roger Dixon Photography)

two days, I'd bumped into so many people I'd known in years gone by that things developed almost instantly.

'So I went to do the Giro Targa Florio in 2005 and by coincidence Regazzoni was driving in that. Obviously when you're on the scene and taking photographs of people – which I'd been doing all those years ago – you get to be a nodding acquaintance. I wouldn't say I knew him. We had faces which each other knew. You take a photograph and people look at you and give you a second to take the photograph. I'd give them a nod and say "Thank you for that" or something similar, and this happened over the years. I've found that that little nod, that little "Thank you," that "Good morning" when you pass them, is enough to build up a relationship. However, even in those days people were wary of getting too involved, for obvious reasons. They didn't want somebody like a photographer following them 24/7.

'At the Targa he said to me "I know you from somewhere. Your face looks familiar. Have we met before?" The whole thing was far more relaxed than Formula 1 had been, of course. I said "Yes, I used to do Grands Prix way back." He'd remembered the face. I'm an ugly bastard so I suppose that makes sense! You are, however, talking 30 years.

'We chatted on the odd occasion and he was very, very enthusiastic while he was there. One particular time I remember at the beginning of the event. It started in the Piazza Verdi, all the cars together for a couple of hours. The public were there looking and he was scooting round in his wheelchair, peering under the bonnets of people's cars and chatting to them and generally thoroughly enjoying himself.

'He was very approachable, very relaxed about it. I saw him in action driving a Ferrari on the northern road and he was going fast. One particular time – and this is typical of the way he was – it was a lunch stop and again on the northern end of the island. It was right down by the sea, a little fish restaurant called *La Baya* in S Agata Di Militello on the northern coast of Sicily. He got out of his car into his wheelchair and we all sat there and had about a five-course fish lunch – the courses coming up and coming up and coming up – and we all enjoyed ourselves. When we looked round Regga's fast asleep. He just sat there in the chair and snored away for half an hour, woke up, had a glass of water – having already consumed quite a drop of wine – jumped in his Ferrari and did the afternoon section.'

Classic Driver[6] carried a feature in which the reporter said that of the entry of 44 'the sound of

Clay Regazzoni's Ferrari Daytona as he accelerated along Via Liberta' was one of the factors that made the whole trip worthwhile.

Roger Dixon remembers an Historic Monaco when 'one of the marshals said to me "Could you take my photograph with Regga and send it to me?" I said "Yes, sure!" Regga posed and the guy's got his arm round him and I sent a copy to the chap. So my recollection of Regga – certainly in those days – is very amiable, full of vigour and energy, and happy just to be back.'

Dixon remembers Regazzoni at Goodwood. 'Literally somebody lifted him out of the car and they sat him on this little stone seat while they got the wheelchair out and ready for him. He's sitting there as if he was as he was before Long Beach. I said "May I take your photograph?" and he said "Yes, no problem." He sat there and looked at me, got himself together and I took the shot. He said to me "That's a very unusual photograph" – because he wasn't in his wheelchair.'

In August 2005 he was a guest of honour during a sailing day for the disabled at Trapani, Sicily, featuring Andrea Stella and his unique catamaran *The Spirit of Stella*. It was run at the same time as the America's Cup.

Regazzoni was officially described as a 'godfather' and exceptional driver 'whose name was so closely associated with the world of disability – where the victim can be a champion. The aim of the day was to attract the media and thousands of guests to see that a wheelchair is not the equivalent of house arrest.'

The Stella story: he'd spent his vacation 'in Florida when I was 24 years old and now [in 2007] I'm 31. I'd left my car in a private road in Fort Lauderdale and when I came back some people were trying to steal it. I didn't react to what they were doing, I didn't speak. They shot me. If they'd asked for the keys I'd have handed them over but they didn't ask, just shot. They were probably full of drugs. I don't know.

'I was in depression although I was supported by my family and my girlfriend. After some months I came back to sailing, because I'd had a boat before. I tried to find a boat that was accessible – all round the world, at any price – but I couldn't find what I was looking for. I built the catamaran, at 56 feet, and I thought *Ah, this is better for everyone* – not only the disabled. I thought *If I can do anything with my catamaran, why in Italy can't I move round the cities. Why can't I move easily in Milan or Rome? Why? Why?* I crossed the Atlantic Ocean from Genoa to Miami and it was easier than crossing Milan by bus.

'I created a foundation which is called *Lo*

Spirito di Stella and we take 600 people every year, completely free of charge, to do a trip for one day in a boat. I give lessons and I give classes in university speaking about it.

'I met Clay at different times of my life – in Vicenza, for example – because he was part of a group of people, handicapped and non-handicapped, who drove. I spent two very intensive days when he sailed with me. I don't think he was an expert sailor but I think he liked the sailing life. He was very impressed by the catamaran. We spoke about the problems of being disabled. I can control my catamaran by hand.

'I think exactly like Clay: people are disabled if their environment puts them in the position of being disabled, so when I don't find toilets are accessible then I am disabled. If you're put in an environment where it doesn't matter you become normal again. He drove a Ferrari at Monte Carlo [where he lived] but in Italy it was not possible for disabled people to drive. He put up a very strong fight for the disabled to have the opportunity to drive every type of car. I think he was a great man because, with his money, he could have stayed at home and found whatever pleasure he wanted but he spent so much of his time helping other people and changing the mentality of society.'

Thereby hangs a delightful tale.

Alice Widdows is 'very much involved in the sailing world and for the past four years I've been working on the America's Cup project, running a Superyacht – the large private yachts that come and visit and support the racing around the America's Cup, from 25m and above. It's the private side of the America's Cup. One of our events took place down in Sicily in 2005. It was called the Louis Vuiton Act Eight and Nine, in a little fishing port, Trapani. I was managing the berthing for the Superyachts, inviting clients to come down and watch the racing, hosting them and looking after them.

'One of my clients was the specially-rigged catamaran sailed by Andrea Stella. He has become a well-known figure on the sailing circuit but also within the handicapped world. He was working very closely with organisations and charities to encourage handicapped children. In each city they visited he encouraged handicapped children on board.

'So Andrea was my client and we became good friends. He'd ask me what I was doing, and the fact that my father had been a racing driver in Formula 2 and Formula 1 came up in conversation. Andrea mentioned this to Clay, who was on board sailing with him during this event in Trapani. I'm not sure in what capacity Clay was there – as a supporter, a spokesperson or bringing clients down. Anyway, Andrea mentioned this to Clay. Before I knew it – in the middle of this major event, which is rather like being in the pit lane at Formula 1 and there I am in the thick of it – I suddenly hear this commotion. It's Clay approaching in his wheelchair saying "You must be Robin's daughter!"

'To be honest, I didn't have a huge memory of him. He finished racing in 1980 and I'm 32. He was so thrilled to have found pops basically through me. We called on a mobile back to my father at home so that the two of them could talk. It was a really special moment. They came across as very good friends.'

He had met charming ladies before …

'I was nothing new! [*chuckle*] He was a gentleman in the old-fashioned sense of the word and I was bowled over by exactly that: this gentleman who'd sought me out in the middle of a very, very crowded event to pass on his regards – and literally his love. It really was passionate of him. He sort of fell upon me because he was so delighted to have found pops. He was still a very handsome man, absolutely charming and always surrounded by beautiful Italian girls. He had lots of girls very willing to push his chair.'

To which Robin Widdows says: 'My daughter rang me and said "There's a racing driver here that knows you!" It was Clay – helping people who'd had accidents to go sailing.'

To which Andrea Stella says merrily: 'She met Clay on my boat before the America's Cup and they spoke. He said "I know your father very well!"'

He did.

Perpetual motion …

From 26 January to 1 February 2006 some 300 entries took on the Monte Carlo Historic Rally. Interesting entries, too: Jean-Pierre Nicolas of Peugeot Sport, former Grand Prix driver Erik Comas, David Hallyday, son of the pop star Johnny – and Regazzoni in the Lancia Aurelia with Valion.

Vic Elford did the Targa Florio in 2006 – 'the hundredth anniversary, but two separate groups decided they were running the anniversary and the group with whom I normally went didn't want to pay for my fare and everything, so I went with another group. I think Clay was with the other lot. It meant the last time we were together there was 2005 – and that was the third time.'

This marshal at Historic Monaco in 2002 asked Roger Dixon if he'd mind taking a photograph of himself and Regazzoni. Lots of people liked being pictured with him.
(Roger Dixon Photography)

Ron Jackson remembers that Regazzoni 'had a bit of time off from us but he came back in 2006 for the last of Nick's events, the Carrera Sud Americana, which he did with Claude Valion again.' He drove an IKA Torino.

This rally lasted 21 days and moved across Argentina, Bolivia, Peru and Ecuador with closed-road special stages – some days two, some days three ranging from 10 kilometres to 30. 'The route combines great motoring roads, spectacular scenery and, with planned rest days, the opportunity to spend time in some of the world's most spectacular, heritage-preserved, 15th-century cities, Sucre and Potosi in Bolivia, and Machu Picchu, the Lost City of the Incas, in Peru.'[6]

On day two the official report says: 'The water-filled fords were a source of amusement and entertainment for spectators. Clay Regazzoni stalled with water-saturated ignition. Next man on the scene was Norwegian Vidar Christensen who steered his Peugeot around the banking [in a] wall-of-death style to a safe landing on the other side and continued unabated.'

Regazzoni continued abated – eventually – too and by day five the official report recorded: 'Favourites with the crowd were Regazzoni and the magnificent shoulder-high open Bentley of Gerry and Helen Leumann.'

Regazzoni was 21st but on day nine joined the retirements, 'the engine of his Argentine-built IKA Torino having blown itself up.' That was at La Paz, but he 'found a novel way of following the event to the finish. By taxi! Yes, you read that right. He investigated what Mr Avis and Mr Hertz had to offer but it was all too complicated and expensive. So he found a willing taxi driver who offered to take him three days up the road and then introduce him to fellow drivers who would take him all the way to the border with Ecuador. Costs were around US $75 per day.'

Please remember the man doing this was now 65 and a pensioner.

In a very poignant sense, however, he was no longer young. 'I was afraid because in the last years – and I tried to tell him, but he didn't want to listen – I told Alessia I'm worried about your father because in the night it was as if he was drowning, not breathing,' Maddalena Mantegazzi says. 'I worried about this because, I have now discovered, if you don't breathe during the day properly you don't have enough oxygen, and during the day you're very tired, which means you can go to sleep while you're driving. I saw that he was very tired. At night he snored but he didn't breathe. It is very, very dangerous.

'When we were together in the car and I saw him like this, even in the mornings, I tried to stop him. I'd say "Shall we take a taxi or do you want me to drive?" He'd say "No, no, no, it's OK. Have a coffee and I'll have a coffee too." The last time I saw him very tired I told him "OK, Clay, you have a coffee but please let me drive. I'm tired but I will wake up." "OK, you can." He slept and I drove.

'This was not the first time it had happened, although with Clay it wasn't easy to say "You're tired. Stop and I will drive." You had to have tactics – but in everything in my life with Clay, to live with him was a tactic. You can't say "Well, why don't you do this?" or "Why do you say this?" or "You don't have to say this, you don't have to do this." No!

'For me it wasn't frustrating because, as I've said, it was a lesson to try to understand somebody else and to try to do your best, so that the relationship worked well, and that's why I'm happy because I know in my soul that I did a lot of work.

'He needed to have people around him like, I think, every star. He *needed* to have them because it's love. Love comes to you in this way – but sometimes it was too much. He wanted at least to have a break, although in general he was happy when people went to him.

'You know, once – I can't remember whether it was in Miami or New York – we were in a restaurant with friends and a man came up. He took his wallet out and inside he had a one-dollar bill with Clay's signature from 20 years before. He said to Clay "Please can you sign it again?" That was fantastic. He'd carried this dollar for 20 years and he had absolutely no idea he'd bump into Clay that day. Clay was happy and proud.

'I think he became more famous after the crash because he had such a strength, such a power, that everyone admired it.'

Why did he really do the Paris-Dakar? For the adventure or to win?

'He always said "I like the desert because I like solitude" but I'm not sure that he did 100 per cent. I think it was the silence of the desert he liked, because sometimes he had need of that, but he also had need of his house, the garden, and he had a lot of modesty. So it was the silence of being alone with himself and the peace of being at home – he had need of both. You've heard about when the television people came to the house ...'

A TV company were making a documentary and wanted to interview him. He wanted to be left alone but they were not to be dissuaded. Before they came he was very grumpy – irascible is perhaps a better word. When they arrived he gave

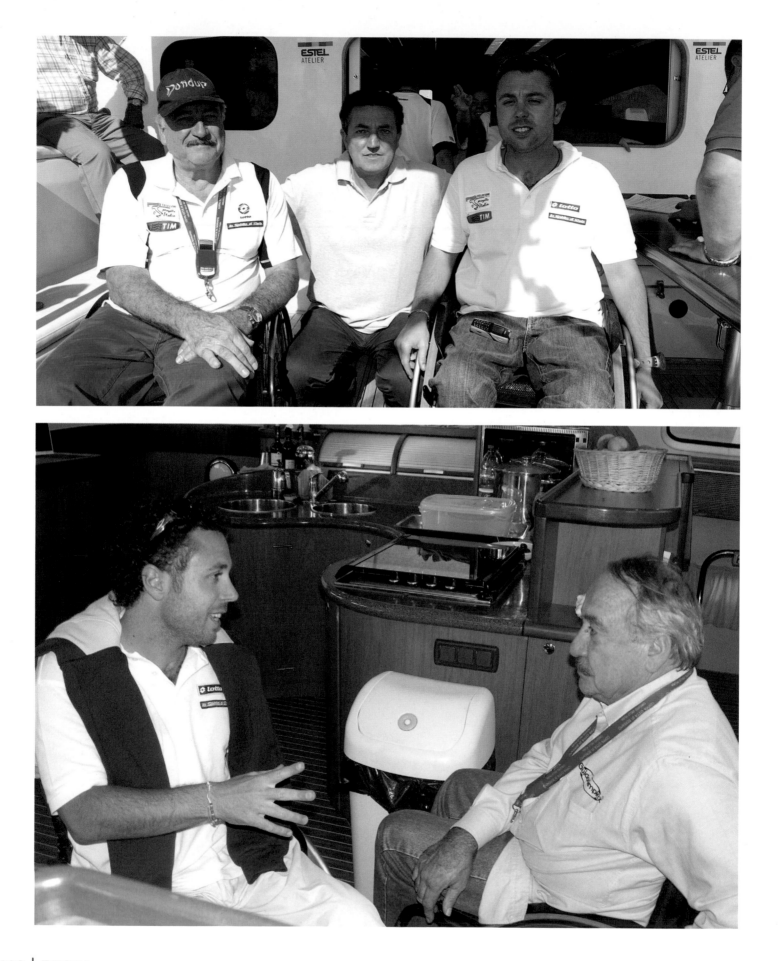

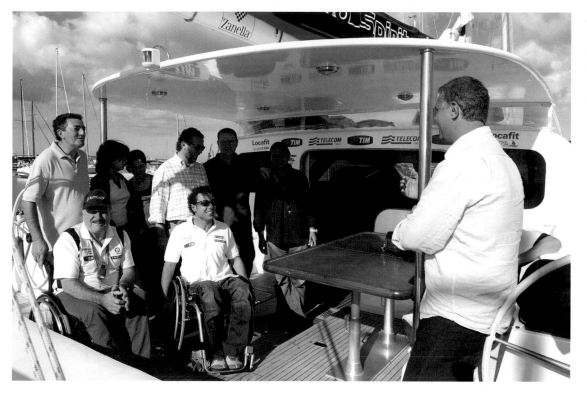

Regazzoni meets a kindred spirit, Andrea Stella, and they discuss sailing with hand controls. (courtesy Andrea Stella)

a consummate performance for them, turning it on and turning it off when the interview was over.

He didn't act like a star.

He was a star.

'He liked the unknown,' Maddalena says. '"What will happen tomorrow?" It was adventure and the unknown, I think, which appealed to him as it appeals to a child. Behind our house was a small path where you could walk, and he wanted to know what there was along this path. I said "Clay, we can't go. There are steps to get down to it. It's impossible." "No, no, let's go." I was frightened. I turned him in the wheelchair and I went down first so that if he fell he'd fall on me. He *had* to see what was there – but only this once. Once he'd seen, that was fine. To see it was enough.

'I don't know if he had a need to be recognised by other people but I do think he got pleasure from talking, from discussion with the women who came. He had a lot of patience but there were times when it was too much, although he had a need to be loved by women. Ah, yes. By women and by friends.'

There'd be a final rush of impressions. Stefano Venturini of Guidosimplex went on the Barcelona-Dakar, as it was, in 2005. 'We'd programmed this for a long time and finally we started this adventure. Although I was the navigator, I asked also for an international driving licence so I could drive if necessary, although I didn't have to drive even 100 metres. He was unbending … never

tiring, never uncertain … driving at the maximum possible … not his maximum, but the car's.'

He wanted to do an historic Paris Dakar. 'He was talking with my mother,' Massimo del Prete says, 'because my first answer was "Clay, I'm involved in the A1GP" at the moment and I don't have time to work on your car and prepare everything." He said "You must help." Then he started to call my mother so that she would *tell* me to go with him.'

Regazzoni: 'I want to do this Paris-Dakar for the last time but I don't want to go there with someone I don't know.'

Del Prete: 'It's not the time for us now, it's different.'

Regazzoni: 'No, no, we have to go and I go only if you come with me. I don't want any other co-driver.'

Regazzoni continued the bombardment. Del Prete would 'get home and my mother would say "I've been talking with Clay again. I don't know what I'm supposed to say." He was ringing twice a day. He said "You have to come. We will be doing something beautiful, something unbelievable. Because this is the Historical Paris-Dakar only a certain number of people can take part, the people who went before like Jacky Ickx and Patrick Tambay. So I said "Clay, I will try."'

It didn't happen.

People were saying goodbye but they didn't know it.

Sir Jackie Stewart last saw him 'at the Geneva Motor Show and he was on this motorised thing going along. I swore at him as he passed me going too fast – as a joke, of course – and the next minute the brakes screeched, he spins it round and comes back! It was nice. He was just a very gregarious man, having known life as he knew it, and he was a boy, you know, a lad.'

Lauda saw him for the last time during the Monaco Grand Prix in May. 'I was always surprised by his positive thinking, his incredible desire for life. He loved smiling and that day we spent some hours together amusing ourselves talking about old times. Clay was a big driver.'

Some time that late summer, as Zunino says, 'Clay came to Argentina but I had no opportunity to see him at that time. I'm in a place just at the foot of the Andes.'

The lost opportunity would now be forever.

In the autumn, Rainer Küschall 'sponsored the World Handicapped Table Tennis Championship in Montreux and Clay was a guest. We were together for two days. An old girlfriend came who he'd known 20 years before – so everywhere in the world he somehow had a link to a woman.'

Leo de Graffenried was there, 'the last time I saw him.'

That autumn Henry Koster, who'd had the full-frontal experience with Regazzoni in Australia on the London-Sydney marathon, met him at the Klausen hill climb in Switzerland.

Koster: 'Clay, I have only three questions and maybe you can answer them. The first is do you remember me?'

Regazzoni: 'No, I'm sorry, I don't.'

Koster: 'That's not a problem. The second question is do you know – I'm sorry for asking you this – my good-looking young daughter Tina?'

Regazzoni: 'I'm sorry, sir, I know it doesn't sound good for me but I don't remember your young daughter.'

Koster: 'OK, now the third question. Do you remember the MG?'

Regazzoni: 'Ah, Henry!'

In early December Massimo Del Prete met him at an historic race at Santa Monica (the Misano circuit) after a typically brusque, forceful telephone conversation.

Regazzoni: 'Where are you?'

Del Prete: 'I'm at home.'

Regazzoni: 'I'll be in Santa Monica tomorrow. Will you come?'

Del Prete: '"Sure!'

So del Prete went because, as he says, although the last events they'd done together were in the early 1990s 'we stayed friends. Sometimes we used to meet in Lugano and our relationship was perfect until the end.

'He was driving a Mustang in an historic race. I adjusted his brake because it was not working properly. He was like a child in karting for the first time. You could see it in his eyes: a child.'

On 12 December Regazzoni drove to Lugano for a meeting with brother Dodo about karting. Dodo was (and is, at 55 in 2008) an active kart driver and they were discussing future projects. 'He'd just come back from Argentina and he looked in very good condition. He was happy. The problem I saw in the last year was that the travelling could make him very tired, and he was always busy. He felt that if your body and your mentality were OK, the age of the body was not very important. Every time you met him he was younger.'

Dodo means young at heart, never mind the tiredness.

They never met again.

Gian Maria records how 'there had been a change between me and my father and the relationship was really growing. Once, ten years before, we'd had a really bad fight when I stopped racing and I'd sent him to hell – we didn't speak for a couple of weeks, but we needed this. I found my own way in life and he was happy about anything I wanted to do.

'In Menton you are not allowed to light fires in back gardens at certain times because it can be very, very dangerous [in hot summers]. He had his own incinerator but even that wasn't allowed. He'd wait until it was a cloudy day then he'd say "Come over, we're going to light it." If the police came he'd pay the fine. One night I was waiting and waiting for the police to come and they didn't. It was nice. There was just the two of us looking into the fire without saying one word.'

Gian Maria remembers taking one of the cars across to Venice to have the electronic controls fixed for his father and then ringing him.

Regazzoni: 'What are you doing?'

Gian Maria: 'I'm just coming back.'

Gian Maria did set off back, sensed Regazzoni was proud and, anyway, 'it was nice because usually he'd have dinner, watch TV and in half an hour he'd be snoring – but this time my phone rang.'

Regazzoni: 'Where are you?'

Gian Maria: 'Just down the hill in Menton ten minutes away.'

At which point Regazzoni called up to Maddalena, who was asleep: 'Wake up, wake up. Gian Maria is back! You have to cook something for him!'

Gian Maria remembers 'he was always working, in the garden or decorating. He had a particular thing about the roses. He was a handyman, good with his hands, and he could make things for the garden out of wood – like a miniature house.

'We'd have different opinions about how to do things and it was amazing because when you did something wrong it would be "Ah! Look at that!" *but* when he made mistakes he would say nothing. He would never give *you* the chance to say "Ah!" No way!'

'He was very romantic. He enjoyed nature so much. That's a simple pleasure. He enjoyed the last race he did, in Argentina, not only the driving but all that went with it. He loved to meet different people. There was a weird thing about Argentina because he hadn't been there for seven or eight years and a friend gave him land. It was like 1,500 miles from where he was. He said "I want to go see the land" and he drove there. Why was he given the land? I don't know.'

In the house in Menton some tiling needed doing and tiling is like the roses, you need patience. Regazzoni had that. Gian Maria says 'When he was in company he was talking to anybody, always laughing. When he was on his own he could spend a whole day and not need to talk to anyone, and I understand because I'm a little bit the same. I enjoy having my space.'

Anyway, Father & Son 'went to the do-it-yourself the day before and I said "Dad, you have the tubes of grouting, ready mixed, and you just put it on." But no, he wanted to buy the powder and add the water.'

This is the traditional way and, as anyone who has tried it will tell you, getting the consistency right – not too thick, not too runny – is damnably elusive, because if you add even a tiny amount more water than you need it's like sludge, so you add more powder and you have the equivalent of chewing gum, so you add more water …

Father & Son had a very predictable exchange, centred around 'You have to put some more water in' followed by 'No, there's water enough.'

Gian Maria took a little brush and showed Regazzoni the modern way to apply the powder. 'He looked at me and it was the first time ever that he said "You're right." He was a very difficult man – the whole family are not easy – so when he said it I had to call my wife! I am *right*! That, to me, was like when you get a diploma. You have passed.

'Then the last dinner we had: that's another thing that makes me feel good. He forgot he had a dinner with all his friends, and everybody kept on calling him, but he wanted to stay with us. So he turned the phone off. He'd never done this before. Never. I would have understood if he'd

known it would be the last dinner, but he didn't know that. It was weird.'

Gian Maria remembers how dad 'turned and said "You're exactly like me." He'd never said anything like that before.'

On 15 December, Giacomo Tansini received a call from Regazzoni, using his mobile from the *autostrada*. He was on his way to the annual meeting of the *Club Italia* at the Regio Theatre in Parma.

'"We start at half past seven. Come!" I said "No, I'm tired. Please." Clay was terribly angry and said "You must come" then he rang off. I thought *Well, Clay wants to meet me there so I'll go.* I phoned his mobile but he was engaged so I left a message: *OK, Clay, I'll be there.*'

They never spoke again.

Fifty minutes later Regazzoni was dead. He'd reached a bridge over the River Taro near a village called Fontevivo, almost at the point where the La Spezia *autostrada* branches off. He was overtaking a lorry and, it seems, brushed against it. That was enough to pitch him into a skid. The Chrysler struck the Armco and turned over. A reconstruction by the police said the weather was fine, the road dry and he wasn't driving fast. Some witnesses suggested he lost control before he brushed the lorry, which implies plain fatigue.

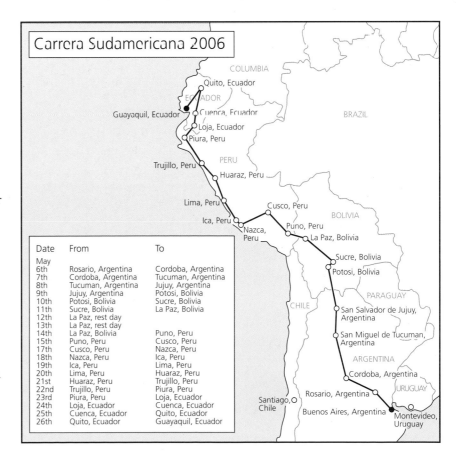

Carrera Sudamericana 2006

Date May	From	To
6th	Rosario, Argentina	Cordoba, Argentina
7th	Cordoba, Argentina	Tucuman, Argentina
8th	Tucuman, Argentina	Jujuy, Argentina
9th	Jujuy, Argentina	Potosi, Bolivia
10th	Potosi, Bolivia	Sucre, Bolivia
11th	Sucre, Bolivia	La Paz, Bolivia
12th	La Paz, rest day	
13th	La Paz, rest day	
14th	La Paz, Bolivia	Puno, Peru
15th	Puno, Peru	Cusco, Peru
17th	Cusco, Peru	Nazca, Peru
18th	Nazca, Peru	Ica, Peru
19th	Ica, Peru	Lima, Peru
20th	Lima, Peru	Huaraz, Peru
21st	Huaraz, Peru	Trujillo, Peru
22nd	Trujillo, Peru	Piura, Peru
23rd	Piura, Peru	Loja, Ecuador
24th	Loja, Ecuador	Cuenca, Ecuador
25th	Cuenca, Ecuador	Quito, Ecuador
26th	Quito, Ecuador	Guayaquil, Ecuador

The picture which distils the whole of his rallying career: big speeds big consequences. This is the Paris-Dakar, the one he never beat. (DPPI)

Leo de Graffenried was 'driving from Cannes to Lausanne and Jacques Deschenaux called to tell me. I think Clay was too tired, recently he was doing too many things. After the Table Tennis he went with his Ferrari to a hill climb, one which my father had done. I said to Clay "Listen, my friend, you're doing too much. You'd better calm down a little bit because you're not 20 any more and you have to be careful" – but he was always motivated

to do things. That was his life. He didn't make a mistake, I'm sure, in the accident. I think he fell asleep and that caused it.'

Massimo del Prete 'received a call from a friend who said "Have you seen the television?" "No. What's happened?" "One of your big friends has lost his life."

'You know, I did the Paris-Dakar a lot of times, I did a lot of rallies, and the main problem is the

moment you don't have everything under control *you* will be the problem. For Clay, in each situation he was calm, he was thinking, he was deciding what to do – but there is another problem. At 67 your reflexes are not the same. The *mind* is still the same but it's the reflexes.'

The autopsy, conducted at the Medicine Legal Institute in Parma, excluded illness as a cause. There were no signs of coronary or other physical problems. The involvement of a third party was also excluded.

His body left Parma for Lugano, and was to be buried in a private ceremony.

Niki Lauda, Emerson Fittipaldi and Peter Sauber, who once ran the Swiss Formula 1 team that bore his name, were among the 1,000 mourners at the main basilica in Lugano. Stewart describes it as 'an immense event. I didn't get to Seppe's funeral but I did Clay's. He was a great Swiss hero there and everybody loved him. In the car he was a bit difficult and wild at the start but he was a real gent out of the racing car, very good company, very well mannered and he carried himself and represented himself as well as his country very well.'

Leo de Graffenried 'didn't go to the funeral because I think he was with me and I was with him.'

How many people across the world felt the same?

We can go some way to answering that by citing just one instance. A year later there was what has been described as a 'moving' day of commemoration of him: Holy Mass with all his family attending in a small local parish church then, in the afternoon, an historic car meeting. That attracted around 50 entries, including a Ferrari Daytona that had belonged to him.

The last postcards he ever signed were carefully given out.

Everything after that was memories.

Gian Maria 'never wanted to know the reason for the accident. He had this problem that at night you stop breathing. You could see the effects. Maybe after lunch with friends he'd fall asleep although his driving was OK, you know. He was driving so slowly in the accident that I thought maybe he was in the slow lane, maybe he felt dizzy. I wonder, because he was just a couple of miles away from the exit. People were saying "Ah, he might have fallen asleep," but my father used to cover so many miles and drove so much and he was never tired. He'd wake up in the morning in Monte Carlo, come to Lugano for a meeting and in the night go back to Monaco.

'He felt that to live life you have to move and move. I saw an interview – I guess the last one he gave – and in it he said that life is beautiful but at the same time it is short, so you have to live it all the time.'

It is exactly what he had done.

Notes: 1. TargaTunisia.com; 2. Ibid; 3. Homestead, a 1.5-mile Florida circuit built in 1995; 4. Talking to Roebuck; 5, www.girodisicilia.com; 6. Carrera Sud Americana official report; 7. A1GP, a series contested by 22 national teams without, as it says, 'financial or technological advantage.'

CHAPTER 13

SIMPLE TRUTHS

'Clay Regazzoni could not exist today,' Vic Elford says, very precisely and very deliberately. 'I was thinking who in Formula 1 would be most like him and nobody came close – nobody. Well, Montoya while he was there, driving and the rest, inasmuch as he was allowed to be. He was certainly a Regazzoni-like character: if you don't like it, stuff it. In his driving Hamilton is a little bit like that but he sure as hell doesn't have the character to go with it.

'The world is a bit grey, particularly Europe, and particularly the United Kingdom. It's become so bloody politically correct it is nonsensical. It's unreal. I've seen a politically correct calendar – nothing to do with motor racing! – and it has so much unbelievable crap on it I was falling about laughing when I read it.'

We wonder what Regazzoni would have made of the calendar and we could both, I think, hear a thundering noise coming down from the Alps and through Lugano.

'Bullshit!'

Jochen Mass takes a slightly different view. 'He was not a man from another era, he was a man from *our* era. There were quite a few of those then, although he was an exceptional character.'

Vic Elford has said he couldn't imagine Regga in Formula 1 now.

'Well,' Mass responds, 'times would have shaped him differently, his education and other things would have been different, so probably he

RIGHT *A career is a sequence of precious memories for drivers and spectators. This is vintage 1968 at Vallelunga, showing the speed he adored so much.*

The old master preparing to drive fast in a new century. Tunisia, 2003. (Michael Johnson)

would have portrayed a different character under the light of modern money and pressures, this and that – *but* he had something in him which made him always outstanding. I think he still would have been like that today, still a different person to many other people.'

Nino Fiorello takes up the comparison with the modern era. 'When he was in the wheelchair people would ask him all the time about Schumacher and Ferrari. He'd say "What are you talking about? Schumacher *ching chung chang, ching chung chang*" – all Schumacher had to do was press the buttons to drive the car.'

Gian Maria feels that 'in the 1970s everybody had their own character and there were so many special people. Now they're all the same. These days he would have said "It's bullshit!" and gone go-kart racing instead. He would never drive those cars [with all their electronic aids] and he would never have done what they wanted him to do – sit here, wear this sponsor's hat, say this, say that. But he was in a privileged position. He could afford to do a little bit of what he wanted to do. Now things are more strict. I used to say that in his day it was the Wild West, and he had his own law.'

John Wayne would certainly have understood. You'll see why in a moment.

Who was Regazzoni? It's time to listen to a chorus of voices because each has something valuable to say and, taken together, they make a beautiful sound.

'His weakness was racing,' Massimo del Prete says, quickly and volubly. 'All his life was racing, just racing.'

I wondered how it was possible to continue being his co-driver knowing that, on the law of averages, more crashes were coming. I prefaced this by asking del Prete how many accidents he'd had. He replied by rolling up his sleeve to show a deep scar and said softly 'Two times I went into hospital with something broken. I was worried about it each day but at the same time I was happy to be a co-driver with Clay Regazzoni. I will remember all my life each kilometre of the Paris-Dakar.

'I didn't ever meet Alain Prost or, I don't know – George Bush! – I didn't meet everybody, but that would have made no difference. In my heart I am sure Clay is the only one I will never forget.'

Luca di Montezemolo: 'He was unique inside and outside racing and we have so much to remember him by. For Clay, racing was daring and a challenge, of going to the limit from the first lap to the last one.'

Mario Andretti: 'I don't think he had an enemy in the world. He was one of those rare individuals who it was always a pleasure to be with. I struck an immediate friendship with him the first time I met him. That was the just the way he was, a character you can talk about for the rest of your life. Clay was flat out always, wasn't he? The racer's racer.'[1]

Carol Hollfelder: 'I've heard a quote attributed to him, something along the lines of *I don't race to challenge death, I race to experience life.*'

Klaus Seppi: 'He was very, very good to other people. I saw that he always had time if somebody asked him for something, especially people in wheelchairs. We had a Yaris presentation, I called him, he came and signed autographs. He was very patient but also very hard. He could have come from the South Tyrol, from the mountains[2] – they say that people with mountains around them are hard. I never had problems with him. Whatever he said was honest.'

Ricardo Zunino: 'I drove with him in Formula 2 and of course in Formula 1 and the problem is that when you're in that kind of sport you look into the eyes of the other guy and you can only *feel* if he likes you. I felt Clay did. For me, Clay was a great personality, a great driver and very tough guy. (He once spent 19 hours in a car during a rally.) He had a lot of accidents in his life and he was still pushing as hard in the last race as he was pushing in his first race.

'I met him after the accident here in San Juan [in Argentina]. We talked about many things but we didn't talk about the accident. If you go motor racing you have to accept that these things can happen. I didn't bring the matter up and he didn't. There was nothing to say.'

Hans Stuck: 'There was always much smiling when he appeared, due to *his* smile and the personality he presented to the public. Clay was that kind of person, a friendly guy who had a nice word for everybody. I see him now exactly in front of me with his moustache. He always called me *Hanslie*. *H-a-n-s-l-i-e!* he'd say, very affectionate, but on the other hand I tell you, if somebody got into a problem with him he could get very angry. Believe me.'

Leo de Graffenried: 'He was a lovely man, charming man. He wore his heart on his sleeve. He was maybe *too* nice and that was his problem. If he'd won the Championship I don't think it would have changed his life at all. I always think of Sir Jackie Stewart who was World Champion. It never changed him, either. '

Keke Rosberg: 'Clay was one of the nicest … he and Mario … the rest, average!'

Sir Frank Williams gives a final perspective in response to the question *Do you regret those old, buccaneering days – the Regazzoni days – are gone?* 'Not at all. If you're a Formula 1 racer you always want to go faster, always want to go better and to do that you have to compete, have to move on. All that really matters is not falling off your perch.'

And Gareth Rees, the outsider: 'What made Regazzoni special for me? I never met him, so all my impressions are just those of an observer. He always seemed to get on with the job and never make a big fuss when things weren't going his way. It was as if he was just glad to be able to race cars, and he knew that sometimes it went well and sometimes it didn't. He rarely seemed to smile, or even talk much. It's funny, but during all those years when he was racing I don't recall reading *one* interview with him and I read lots of magazines! His presence added tangibly to the glamour of Formula 1 in the 1970s and yet this apparently just happened on its own and not due to any obvious self-publicity on his part. Of course, just the sound of that name, *Clay Regazzoni*, must have helped and, usually, being in a Ferrari helped too. Was there ever a better name for a racing driver?

'When, at the end of 1979, Williams, with their new-found competitiveness, wanted to sign the two fastest drivers they could find, Regga, for the second time in his career, had to watch Carlos Reutemann waltz in and take over his car. Again, as at the end of 1976, he accepted the team's decision graciously and headed back to a warm welcome at Ensign and the rear end of the grid. It would have been the ideal time to retire but he liked racing too much and probably didn't know

what else to do anyway. His good grace and lack of self-pity was horribly put to the test after Long Beach.

'Regazzoni perhaps wasn't quite World Champion material, but few really are. He was

Reggazoni's son, Gian Maria, at the family house in Lugano, surrounded by memorabilia. (Author)

always as good as his cars and he contributed more than his fair share of excitement to the world of Formula 1 for ten whole years. As far as I know, all his team-mates had a special affection for him and, in the cases of Lauda and Jones, both spoke out against their teams when he was replaced – even if doubtless partly motivated by their shared dislike of Reutemann!

'In modern Formula 1 it's easy to take the cynical view and say "Yes, it's not surprising they liked Regga because he was relatively easygoing and no regular threat to stars like Ickx, Lauda and Jones" – all of whom he partnered at their peaks. Maybe so, but to my mind there's something honourable in a Grand Prix driver who could deal with that and then just calmly get on with his work. These days the media would be constantly trying to talk down such a driver and a team might soon be under pressure to replace him. It's good that Regazzoni raced when he did. With that moustache and flat cap, he was marketable in a way that suited the early commercial era of Formula 1 – but he might not have met all the sponsors' criteria nowadays …'

That brings us back to the roaring noise from the Alps and the politically correct calendar.

A racer's racer? A man's man, too. 'He liked to drink,' Rainer Küschall says. 'When he visited me in Locarno on holiday, ten o'clock in the morning I'd say "Let's have a coffee," and he'd turn around and take Cognac.'

A woman's man, as well. 'Naughty things?' Jochen Mass muses about that. 'It depends how you define naughty. Of course he was a woman's man and he liked girls, let's put it that way. If you want to call that naughty, yes, then he probably was, but he wasn't overly so, not openly, not vulgar. Whatever he did, it was discreet enough.

'Talking about sex appeal, I have a picture of him standing in the water knee-deep and naked somewhere in the Virgin Islands – lovely shot of him, wonderful picture.[3] It was too funny for words. I had it blown up quite big and I kept it for years and years, didn't give it to anybody. Then he was sat in the wheelchair in Monaco in the paddock and his daughter was there. I said "Hey, Clay, I've always forgotten to give you something – here it is." He looked at it and he nearly fell out of his chair. His daughter blushed and said "But papa, papa!"

'We don't just remember him from the wheelchair, we remember him from the pre-wheelchair days, how good-looking he was. That made this man: his physical charisma, his mental charisma. He had a smile for everybody. He came up to you and he always smiled, he always had friendly words and there was never any misgiving about anything.'

One highly relevant way of answering *Who was he?* is to examine what he did beyond the public gaze, going about his everyday business unobserved, specifically on the *autostradas* when he had no need to impress anybody and could proceed like any other law-abiding citizen. If I tell you that the speed police across northern Italy came to know him and his Ferrari F40 intimately you'll be getting the answer already.

Del Prete offers a neat preface to the subject by saying that 'on the *autostrada*, *nobody* overtook him *ever*. Impossible. I-m-p-o-s-s-i-b-l-e. IMPOSSIBLE.' Del Prete reinforces this with a revealing little anecdote.

Traffic policeman: 'Don't you realise the speed limit on the *autostrada* is 130 kilometres an hour? You were doing 200.'

Regazzoni: '200? Bullshit! I was doing 250 …'

Gian Maria points out in nice contradiction that if Regazzoni was in his Chrysler Voyager 'and came across a Ferrari or a Porsche he couldn't hold them.' Without getting too deep into such matters, the Chrysler's top speed is about 185kmh but I leave it entirely to your imagination to create pictures of what Regazzoni might have made it do when a Ferrari or Porsche had the impertinence to try and go by. Think *boom*. Keep thinking *boooom*.

If you work in imperial measures, to help you appreciate the sort of speeds we'll be talking about. here is a simple guide:

kmh	mph
100	62
130	80
150	93
200	124
250	155
300	186
320	198

Let's begin with a revealing example of how Regazzoni *thought*. It happened on the *autostrada* between Florence and Bologna. 'He looked in his mirror and saw a police car, and the blue light came on for him to stop so (naturally) he accelerated,' del Prete says. 'The policeman telephoned ahead to another patrol and said "A Ferrari will arrive at high speed. Stop him. We're unable to stay with him." The patrol ahead blocked the road, both lanes, but not the hard shoulder so (naturally) he went onto the hard shoulder and kept on going at full speed. So they called a patrol further ahead and they blocked the *whole* autostrada with cones, forcing all the traffic into a petrol station. They stopped him there and pointed out what the speed limit was.

'When something went wrong it was always *your Italy*, when it was good it was *our country*. He said to the policeman "*Your* stupid country. You sell cars that reach 300kmh then you have a speed limit of 130. Stupid! Why do you take my money for a car that can do 300 and then want me to drive it in second gear? The law is wrong! Don't you understand that?" And they let him go …'

(Gian Maria, who seems to have inherited a large measure of this, was taking the Ferrari down to Rome 'to have the hand controls fixed' and was doing 320kmh. 'You have to look ahead because as soon as you see a truck which is only a point in the distance, you have to start slowing down.')

There are dark tales of another police chase that Regazzoni shed. They called in a helicopter and he tried to outrun that. He failed. Once they'd stopped him they said 'Ah, *Regazzoni*,' and they let him go …

He had a stock of photographs for just such eventualities and would sign them for the police. He had T-shirts too. Usually, no doubt, an autograph sufficed. This even reflected on Gian Maria. 'In Italy they'd stop me, see who I was and it was no problem. I remember they once caught me going to Monte Carlo on my own. As soon as they stopped me I showed them my documents. The policeman said "Are you?" and I said "Yes!" He laughed. "We used to stop your father very often." He'd not even get fined.'

There's another revealing example of Regazzoni's thoughts. Gian Maria explains that in Switzerland 'there are roads with no hard shoulder so the speed limit is 80kmh rather than the usual 120. We were doing 240 and my sister said "But it's 80." My father said "Yes, but it's 80 each."'

Gian Maria insists, however, that to Regazzoni '200 was driving normally – "It's safe." I believe the same if you know what you're doing. You just keep your eye on the road. I felt safe with him all the time because you had the feeling he did know what he was doing. And, anyway, you were used to it. He didn't drive like a criminal and you could tell he was in control. Of course, for regular people he was, like [*laughter*] … Well, it's a piece of cake for a professional at those speeds, it's natural.'

Nino Fiorello says gently that 'being in a car with him, you had to be careful what you said. You had to remember that he was a big champion. You couldn't be like him and he couldn't understand

that not everybody was like him. It all depended on if the night before had been good.'

In other words, it might not be a good idea to point out to him that he was driving like a hooligan or even that he was going too fast, just in case that made him go *much* faster. As for the events of the night before, I leave that to your imagination. The central point, however, is that you cannot tell whether these incidents happened before he became handicapped or not. It simply didn't, and doesn't, matter.

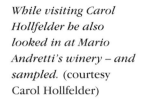

While visiting Carol Hollfelder he also looked in at Mario Andretti's winery – and sampled. (courtesy Carol Hollfelder)

Memories: Regazzoni in the BRM in 1973. (courtesy Gareth Rees)

There are dark tales of him holding driving licences for several countries so that if he lost one through a speeding ban he'd use one of the others.

'His style was what we call "the dying leaf" – moving from side to side. He always drove like that,' del Prete says. 'He'd do 250 in the F40: right-left, right-left, overtaking on the left, on the right – on the hard shoulder a lot of times.

'Once in the old days there was a party near Rimini. I don't know what the car was. Clay was driving at maximum speed, Elio de Angelis, Teo Fabi and Piercarlo Ghinzani the passengers. Outside Rimini was a tunnel. There were two trucks, one overtaking the other. Clay arrived and went onto the hard shoulder to overtake both just before the tunnel. He was doing maybe 180kmh and at the time that was very high. The hard shoulder ended at the tunnel entrance – the road finished! Everybody in the car was screaming "Stop!" Ghinzani told me "I was sure I was going to die." Still full throttle, Clay pulled back in front of the trucks. Ghinzani said "I'm sure there were not more than 5cm between us and the tunnel and truck." Regazzoni said "Hey, it

was nothing. What are you guys doing? You're racing drivers!"

'I worked for the Minardi Formula 1 team because Clay rang up and said "Take this guy, he's very good with suspensions." The first thing that Giancarlo Minardi said to me was "You're crazy to be Regazzoni's co-driver. I'll *never* go in a car with him! You know what he did one time to me?" Minardi was driving a very fast Fiat and Regazzoni was in the passenger seat reading a newspaper. He looked at the speedometer and asked "Why are we going so slowly?" – Minardi had the car at the maximum. Minardi said "This *is* the maximum speed." Regazzoni put the newspaper in front of Minardi's face and began to put the handbrake on ...'

Alex Zanardi, an open admirer of Regazzoni for several reasons, remembers driving in fog and Regazzoni going past at some 200kmh. A few kilometres further on Zanardi pulled into a petrol station and found him there.

'Clay, are you crazy? You passed me at 200!'

'Look, I have a theory. Fog is so dangerous that the less time I spend in it the better.'

These days the Italian police are enforcing the *autostrada* speed limit with a kind of calculated ferocity and if you do these big speeds you risk having your car confiscated on the spot. It's a moot point whether *any* policeman would have dared to do this to Regazzoni, a notion compounded by the fact that they'd be leaving him on the hard shoulder in a wheelchair.

There are dark tales of him coming up behind a Citroën Deux Cheveux at traffic lights and, when they changed, pushing the little car up the hill ahead. It involved a sequel and at the same place: Gian Maria driving, Regazzoni in the front passenger seat, Maddalena in the back. Regazzoni could be surprisingly sanguine and, as Gian Maria came upon a car that wouldn't let him through, slept. Gian Maria tried to overtake on the right – the inside – 'and the guy accelerated so I clipped him a little bit on the bumper.'

To which Maddalena said '*Touche!*' – meaning *You too!*

There was the ploy for defeating the barriers on motorways at toll booths, which, as Klaus Seppi says, was a kind of game. How did he do it? 'I don't know!' Well, it may have been done like this: one car (with a racing driver in it) reaches the booth and pays. The second car (also with a racing driver in it) is directly behind. The instant the barrier goes up, both drivers react as if from a grid and both get through before the barrier comes back down again. Seppi thinks it more likely that Regazzoni used the lane reserved for *Telepass* – the automatic electronic toll collection system that you just drive through. We may conclude that

a) he didn't have a *Telepass* and

b) he went through flat out

Then there was a race at Paul Ricard that involved the Regazzoni Mercedes which Gian Maria was to drive back from the circuit. When it reached the circuit it was fitted with slick racing tyres, but for a technical reason these were impossible to take off prior to departure so Gian Maria embarked along the ordinary roads with them. In a little village he did what a Regazzoni was always going to do and overtook about six or seven cars, something that caught the interest of the *gendarmerie*. They summoned a tow truck to remove this illegal vehicle but Gian Maria pointed out that the tyres were so low profile it wouldn't go up the ramp. At this point Regazzoni arrived, said the equivalent of *What the hell have you done here?* and sped off. The Mercedes didn't go onto the truck so the police took Gian Maria to a garage where eventually the tyres were changed. Then he had to go back to the police and pay the fine. He got home about three in the morning.

No doubt Regazzoni had been sleeping soundly for several hours.

On the road, Poltronieri proclaims, Regazzoni was at the cutting edge (a 'battle-man'!) between real drivers and those foolish people who imagine they can drive at the limit without risk. 'He was rushing at the cars in front of him and brushing bumpers. If a poor man didn't move, he overtook him on the right!' – that's inside, and just as illegal as you imagine it to be. 'It seemed that every time we talked on the phone he was saying "I've had another three fines for overtaking on the right".'

The poor Swiss drivers weren't so poor (in the vulnerable sense) because, prim little spies that they were, they reported him to the police, and the police, themselves paragons of primness, Were Not Amused.

When he and Maria Pia split up, she kept the number plate of the Ferrari Daytona but he made a copy of the document for it – so amateurish that you could see it was simply laid at an angle over another piece of paper and photocopied. As Gian Maria says, 'he didn't even care about trying to make it look authentic. He drove all those years in the Daytona with this. He made his last licence plate in the garage with plastic stripes which didn't even *look* original. He got that car into Morocco with it.'

Before we leave the subject, Stefano Venturini gives a glimpse of exactly what Fiorello means when he says you couldn't be like Regazzoni behind a wheel, although this happened on a circuit not the *autostrada*. 'I was in an Alfa Romeo GTU with Clay at Mugello. His driving was clean and very quick yet everything seemed planned. When he accelerated the car didn't leap forward and didn't swerve around. I have always thought I could drive … then I saw him going round the track without using the brakes …'

Brakes? Bullshit! You don't need them if you know what you're doing, and he did.

The accident in 1980 did not alter the man.

'I met him many times after Long Beach,' Frank Dernie says. 'He always used to greet me as a long-lost friend because, of course, we'd worked together so many years before. I was pleased to see him, he was pleased to see me, we'd have a brief chat and move on, because we never worked together again. It only happened when we bumped into each other in the pit road so it was a typical paddock relationship. I now find that, after all the years I've done, if I go to a test as I walk down having a look at what people are up to I find that it takes me about an hour and a half to get from one end of the pit road to the other because there are so many people who come whizzing out of the garage to say "Hello, how are you?" That was the sort of Regazzoni relationship as well.'

Neil Oatley 'probably saw him a couple of times a year at Grands Prix and certainly in later years I used to bump into him at historic meetings. He'd always be there and on occasion he'd take part in them too. He was still the bloke I remembered. His character hadn't really changed. He didn't feel sorry for himself and he always seemed reasonably happy, quite switched on to what was happening in the sport at the time. He didn't have any side to him. What you saw was what you got. He was a very straightforward individual, very apolitical in motor racing terms – unusual for an Italian! He was a real racer and he had a real racer's name, hadn't he? The name just rolls off the tongue.'

Brian Hart 'raced him in Formula 2 when he was in the Tecno. We did one or two engines for them because Brian Hart Limited started in 1967. Then he got to Ferrari and it all became a bit legendary. You wouldn't forget Clay Regazzoni because of his name and winning the Italian Grand Prix in 1970. He didn't change at all during those years although possibly he carried on in Formula 1 longer than he should have done. However, those men that were racing drivers then couldn't stop, they just carried on and if he hadn't had the accident he'd have carried on till he was about 45. He just loved racing cars. I met him when he was in the wheelchair. I didn't find it difficult because I'd had several friends hurt car racing and you just had to face up to the fact that they'd been hurt. Like Frank. It doesn't affect me if I talk to him. What these people have is a mental attitude and you can compare them to Douglas Bader [the WW2 British fighter pilot who lost both legs and flew in combat again]. They won't accept their disability. Not only that, they believe there's a possible way to continue living as they want – just because I've smashed my legs or whatever isn't going to stop me.'

Quite unprompted, Sir Jackie Stewart makes the same comparison in answer to the question: *Frank, Streiff, Regga – is there something in motor racing that people just don't give in?*

'I always think some of the racing drivers, particularly of that period, were kind of Douglas Bader-type people. They were World War 2-type people. It was the same when we lost friends. We saw so much grief that we got used to it and it was just like what pilots must have felt. It's not a fair comparison because they were fighting for their country and we were getting paid to do our job, but it's a similar thing. We were doing it because we wanted to do it, not because we were paid to

do it, but we saw such a lot of grief and such a lot of pain in those days. There were serious accidents and somehow or other the racing driver mentality is get up and go. Clay was a striking example of that because he kept racing. He had these Alfa Romeos with hand controls, a big Merc, Ferraris, everything. I think that's synonymous with the sport, if I might say.

'He was really active and he was a great example to other people with similar disabilities. I think that's what made him what he was, his character. He was amazingly gregarious, even in his motorised wheelchair. To begin with it wasn't motorised, and then it was.'

And then he could really make it go.

Tim Parnell insists that 'whatever he did in life he'd got no regrets and the way that he adapted his life after his accident was wonderful. Magnificent.'

He was certainly entitled to a measure of self-pity in that the accident was not of his making and was compounded by circumstances beyond his control: the two parked cars, the shortness of the escape road.

However, as Brian Redman says, 'in the old days it was extremely dangerous and every time you left home you didn't know whether you'd see your family again. It was extremely difficult. You didn't really consciously think about it, you just hoped it would never happen to you. I was extremely fortunate in that I had three really bad accidents and I survived. Many, many of my friends only had one accident and they were dead. Of course, Clay had a lot of accidents but he only got hurt once. The irony is that it wasn't his fault, but that was what motor racing was like in those days. The cars weren't strong, the safety precautions weren't as good, there shouldn't have been a parked car in that escape area – well, two.'

To which Derek Bell adds: 'The shunts and the bloody incidents we had were unreal. He was my real problem, he really caused havoc for me. We had some wonderful bloody races but you could never trust him, that was the trouble.' After a race when there'd been an incident Bell would seek Regazzoni out.

Bell: 'Clay, what the hell were you doing?'

Regazzoni: 'What do you mean? What did I do?'

Bell: 'Well, you [expletive] had me on the grass coming down to the *Parabolica*.'

Regazzoni: 'Oh, really?'

Bell adds: 'It's funny, but when you get to my age I'm sure there's a story to be written about the guys who survived and what they're like now – what they do and what their personalities are like. How have they changed, and even have they changed? Are they bastards or more humble? I meet them all the time at the driver get-togethers. Yesterday I was sat doing stuff with Roger Penske.[4] What a man! He's worth $2.8 billion. He's still walking round motor shows with his book under his arm. His son is there with him and they're signing up people. He's got 300 car dealerships. Clay couldn't have vegetated. Like Frank Williams, they're not that breed.

'It was difficult to talk to Clay about his driving [after the accident] because what he was doing was quite natural to him. You couldn't say "Clay, you're a bloody miracle. Great stuff, Clay, great drive." You couldn't say "You'd have been better if you'd had your legs" – because he was bloody good anyway. He was more Italian than Swiss – no, totally Italian, and of course the Italians loved him with a name like that. A cracking guy, one of the best. He was a hero.'

Patrick Tambay nicely contradicts Bell's notion of Regazzoni being only Italian. 'The Swiss loved him. They *loved* him. He had all the personalities of the Swiss people in him, Swiss-Italian, French-Swiss, maybe not so much the German-Swiss. They were very proud of him. You can talk to Jacques Deschenaux and he's very much a Siffert man.'

Regazzoni's impact on the world of the handicapped is hard to assess with any accuracy, as these things invariably are, although Aleardo Buzzi, once of Marlboro and a firm friend, points out that 'he was able to get a law allowing handicapped people to be able to drive, which was impossible before. It's possible now in Italy, and this is thanks to Mr Clay Regazzoni. That's an absolutely wonderful thing to have done.'

Meanwhile, Giacomo Tansini – the fan who became a friend – 'finally persuaded Clay to agree to help in setting up a paraplegic movement. I convinced him. I organised charity events, Clay's friends helped and Clay decided who the money went to.' This was 1994, and as we've seen, the money went to the uroparaplegic ward at the Magenta Hospital in Milan, creating a research and development centre to help paraplegics. They're reportedly making real progress.

The movement was in fact a club, called *Aiutiamo la Paraplegia – Fans Club Clay Regazzoni Association*, simplified two years later to *Club Clay Ragazzoni* when it sharpened and intensified its activities. The Club has ten directors, 900 registered members and remains the only one authorised by Regazzoni himself.

Tansini explains that the Club organised special days for Ferrari owners, who got to meet

Regazzoni, got to have a ride with him and, entering the spirit of the whole thing, towns would happily close their streets so that the days could happen. 'People who took part had to make donations. Everybody wanted to meet Clay Regazzoni so the events were successful. There was one at Lodi on a Saturday and we collected eight million lire [very approximately £3,500].'

It also arranged highly successful dinners. 'Clay was always wonderful because if people liked meeting him he liked meeting people.' The dinner in early 2008 raised a truly astonishing € 43,000,

Memories: he never refused an autograph request, all the way through his career. (courtesy Gareth Rees)

and in the Club's 14 years of existence such dinners have raised over €540,000. That's serious money, and it's augmented because Clay Regazzoni watches have been marketed for a long time. If you buy one, some of the price goes to the Club and the hospital.

Cumulatively it's quite an epitaph all by itself.

Rainer Küschall, the insider (who I suspect is proud – or, rather, professionally satisfied – that Regazzoni 'got so used to using the wheelchair' he made, 'because it was so super light, that I never had to modify it'), kept a steady eye down the years and does a nice line in controversy. Regazzoni 'was never good in the Paris-Dakar. I know a polio guy who was ten times better than him and he was winning and that was such a shock that the newspapers avoided writing about it. Things are relative.'

Yes, well … what about Regazzoni? 'First, racing drivers must be extremely egotistical. Second, they want to be better than the others – that he didn't lose. It's in your blood or not. Most racing drivers are slim and at least not tall. He's controlling a powerful car and we think *That's strength – he's got guts, he's a real man*, but in truth maybe they're scared about simple things, so it's very, very difficult to understand the reality of a person like that.

'My experience of life has taught me that if you're trying to sum someone up you can't do it by making just one point. You learn that when you open a door you have another door behind it which you have to open. Maybe an onion is a better example. You peel it and peel it. He seemed strong, indestructible, had great energy, and stupidity – because he might do something which seemed crazy but *intellectually* was stupid. That's why we love heroes. I'd rather see a racing car

This is Tansini's visiting card … the rear cover of his pocket notebook … and Tansini's impression of Regazzoni's impression of Lauda's autograph. Regazzoni forged them profusely, to meet demand! (all courtesy Giacomo Tansini)

Aiutiamo la paraplegia

CLUB CLAY REGAZZONI onlus

Giacomo Tansini
Presidente

Sede a Paullo c/o Tansini Giacomo
Via Mazzini, 74
20067 Paullo Milano
Tel. e Fax 02.90630113
Cel. 338 -2705227

with smoking tyres, like Regazzoni, than one which looks slow – like Alain Prost used to drive them.

'Clay felt very comfortable everywhere he went and he had a kind of security because he'd have one of his friends with him, looking after him, carrying the bags. The word relative is very important [in discussing handicapped situations]. I remember his team bosses from Formula 1 gave him a Jaguar already adapted to hand controls. He got in and straight away drove at 200kmh on the highway. Everywhere he went it was organised and he was welcome: the go-karts were already modified when he arrived to drive them, and that's why it's relative. On the other hand, it was nice because he was still a hero and provided a kind of a public image for wheelchair people.'

Küschall, who knew him so well, still has many questions about who he was. 'Everyone has a perception of a picture, but if you go further, or deeper, suddenly you see a different kind of person. You [the author] say he had two lives. OK, that's a very quick way to analyse it, but what about maybe his third life? How was he really? There are a lot of boxes you could put him in but which is the real box in the end is the difficult question.'

Let's tackle this by listening, by way of introduction, to Dodo Regazzoni talking about Maddalena Mantegazzi.

'Maddalena stayed with Clay through the good times and the bad,' Dodo says. 'She understood him and that was very important for Clay. Sometimes he told me how important. In a wheelchair you have many problems with everything – when you wake up each morning you start another very hard day – and for the woman it's not too easy either. Maddalena was like my mother: a woman who gave her life to her man but stayed at a distance, in the sense that Maddalena didn't like the publicity. She preferred the home.'

Now Maddalena herself.
What did he like to watch on television?
'Lieutenant Colombo, John Wayne – he adored John Wayne – and any kind of sport, tennis, skiing, all of them. I think he liked John Wayne because in another life he was John Wayne; in another life he wanted to be a cowboy!

'He cared about politics and he had big discussions with friends about Italy, about France, about Switzerland. He always said that people should try to work. He was hard: everybody should work. Here in France when they cut the working week to 35 hours he agreed with that for certain jobs although not all.'

That means you're on the left, he on the right?
'[*Chuckle*] Me, I think we should stop this left and right, it's now a question of the planet. He was rigid. Sometimes discussing politics irritated him. When he was on holiday he'd take a book to read, but latterly he was finished with reading newspapers, perhaps because it was always the same thing. Before, he'd read what was happening in the world and all the sport but that diminished.'

You lived with him for 19 years, you saw him like nobody else. Did he ever feel sorry for himself?
'No. I think that … it's not easy because I saw him a few times when he was in the garden and he looked into the emptiness of the sky with his thoughts, but he was discreet [kept his thoughts to himself] and had a certain *pudeur* [modesty]. I didn't want to disturb him. For me, it was his moment and his thoughts. Maybe he felt regret. The accident was not his fault but the decision to have the career of a racing driver was, therefore I think he had to accept it. He did a lot of things but he never spoke of his suffering. Never, neither physically nor from the point of view of morale.

'When I met him he took a lot of pills for spasms, for many things, but afterwards he stopped gradually, because he, like me, thought that a human being can find the strength to surmount obstacles by him or herself without medication and pills. He showed a lot of strength in that. He knew that a human being is capable of many things, that you have forces which you don't know *but* which you can discover. I am sure that I gave him that, too. I think he learnt a lot of things from me even if he didn't say so. He pushed me to discover a lot of things about myself and I worked a lot on that. He saw me change a little but the change which I made in myself was to understand him. I think he understood that, but you know, he never said that to me. He didn't want to speak about certain things – because he knew and I knew, and because he was extremely intelligent. He understood people. He understood everything. It was why I stayed all those years with him, because he had had a lot of women in his life. Why me and not somebody else? Once he told me something. He told me *Someone has put you on my route.* That was at the beginning. That was clear. It was not necessary to ask why.

'I took account of the fact that he didn't talk a great deal but we understood each other and now, when I'm with someone who talks a lot, it throws me. It's funny, isn't it? I talk a great deal because I'm talking about him, but with him it was as if sometimes words were not necessary.

'From time to time it got on my nerves because I'd have liked more, although it wasn't necessary. I understood that it was not in his character. When he was tranquil at the house and his friends called he might signal "No, I don't want to talk." He just didn't want to. You have to be very hard with yourself to behave like that. I don't mean to say that if his best friend rang he wouldn't talk to him – so if Valion rang, he would, because Valion had a good character. Valion never tried to criticise or examine Clay. Never. He accepted Clay as he was and, me, I accepted him like that too.

'He brought back little souvenirs from South Africa but a burning car meant nothing. Why? The souvenirs were for me and the house. The car or the lorry were his work. When I moved something in the house he – a traditionalist – would say *When you've put something somewhere, it should stay there.*

'When he went to China he sent me a postcard which said "Me and the Dalai Lama!" on it because he knew I was interested in Buddhism – all religions. He hadn't met the Dalai Lama! I'm Catholic and he was Catholic, but I think that was through the education he received. Afterwards he didn't practise.

'We have a rake for the lawn, a little one, on the little tractor that he used in the garden. He loved to work the ground with his hands, he loved his roses. He always had his secateurs with him. He'd say "Maddalena, I've left the rake near the tree. Can you go and get it?" Or "I've left it in the garage. Can you go and get it?" For me it was a souvenir better than jewellery – it was something important. The other day in the garage I saw it there. I picked it up and it was necessary to get rid of it, to create some distance, to understand that it's finished. And I began to cry, because getting rid of this tool was a finality. I asked myself why I was reacting like that, because I have a lot of souvenirs of our time together. I think it was because the tool was an everyday thing, a souvenir of my stable life with him.'

Perhaps the rake is more than symbolic. Perhaps it answers Rainer Küschall's fundamental dilemma about the boxes and how many of them Gianclaudio Giuseppe Regazzoni fits into: it was nothing as complicated as that. He found the elixir of life in speed, in racing, in being a racer, and Maddalena Mantegazzi needs only five words to express it.

'He was a simple man.'

Once upon a time Roland Ratzenberger's father Rudolf and I were standing beside his grave in a churchyard at Salzburg.[5] Rudolf suddenly said: 'My

He cast a giant shadow.
(Michael Johnson)

The passion never went away. This is Monaco, 2002. (Roger Dixon Photography)

has lived a life." Then I realised, now that I'm 40, that at that age you're still so young. My father was very strong. He tried to walk again and then after that he just turned the page. My only regret is that I can never know where our relationship would have reached in another ten years, but I can live with the feeling that things were going well.'

Here is Gian Maria's rush of impressions. 'He would never throw money away ... I never saw him do that ... my wife used to tell him things about me and he'd be laughing ... he was very fatalistic, *When your time comes, that's it ...* he didn't even know what class I was in at school, never ... many times he wasn't there when I got my report ... he kept on saying "School's not worth it," because now you find so many students who finish university and have no job, nothing, so my father never studied ... it wasn't material things that he cared about – new cars, new television ...

'He could – how would you say it? – go anywhere, in any kind of milieu, and he was still fine ... kings or ordinary people, made no difference ... that's what I mean. He would be comfortable. The real man? He'd be sitting there playing cards with his friends ... or cheating at backgammon ... simple pleasures because he really was simple.'

Quite unprompted, the television man Mario Poltronieri, who'd followed him through all of his career and shared some of it, said: 'His motivating spirit was simple. He always loved going back to his small town close to Lugano to play cards with his childhood friends and the companions of his nice and beloved father.'

That one word – simple – keeps returning us to the beginning of our story because, again quite unprompted, Dodo Regazzoni used it about Pio and Bruna when he was describing what they were like and what the family was like.

It doesn't say everything – nothing can ever do that – but it says enough.

son lived into his 70s.' I pointed out that Roland was 32 when he was killed at Imola. 'Oh yes, yes, correct,' Rudolf said, 'but in motor racing Roland filled every day of his life so full that it would have taken a normal man at least 70 years to do the same. My son had a long and fulfilling life, but not on your timescale.'

I mentioned this to Gian Maria because it seemed appropriate. We'd been standing beside Regazzoni's grave in a little churchyard high above Lugano and overlooking it. The headstone is imposing and adorned by a sculpture of a head with, wreathed round it, what appears to be a crown of thorns. Without being sacrilegious, it ought to have been a helmet.

This is what Gian Maria said, accepting the comparison with Ratzenberger: 'Even if it had been worse at Long Beach he'd still had a very full life. At 40, he was already the equivalent of 70. At 67 he was 167.

'I was 12 so my father was old to me and one thing I remember is that I used to say "At least he

Notes: 1. Talking to Roebuck. Andretti also said: 'I was just thinking a second ago, here we are, talking ... it's a terrible, tragic, day, and here we are, reminiscing, smiling at all the stories about this man. Says everything, doesn't it? That's what it's all about – that's how he'll be remembered. We should raise a glass to him tonight ...'; 2. South Tyrol, the area of northern Italy that borders Austria and looks astonishingly Austrian; 3. A Winston Churchill anecdote (which Regga would have loved) seems entirely appropriate here. Someone asked him if he knew where the Virgin Islands were. 'No,' he said, 'but I bet they're a long way from the Isle of Man ...'; 4. Penske, an American businessman who owns a racing team; 5. Roland Ratzenberger, an Austrian rookie (although aged 31), was killed when his Simtek crashed during Saturday qualifying for the 1994 San Marino Grand Prix. He was the first man to die in a Formula 1 car since Elio de Angelis in 1986.

STATISTICS

These statistics are confined to races in championships. Regazzoni did a lot of racing, some of it obscure, in the early part of his career. To keep that manageable, only top-six finishes are given. All his Grands Prix, and other major events, follow.

dq = disqualified; r = retired; nc = not classified; nq = did not qualify

1963
Austin Sprite 950 (3 Kandersteg; 3 Marchairuz)

1964
Mini Cooper S (1 Monte Ceneri; 2 Payerne; 3 Kandersteg; 3 Marchairuz; 3 Schauinsland)

1965
De Tomaso – Formula 3 (6 Magny-Cours)
Brabham – Formula 3 (5 Rouen)
Honda 600 (2 Slalom Agno)

1966
Brabham – Formula 3 (2 Vallelunga; 3 Vallelunga; 7 Pau)
Brabham – Formula 2 (6 Eifel)
Honda 600 (1 Monza 4 Hours)

1967
Tecno – Formula 3 (1 Madrid; 2 Hockenheim; 6 Mar del Plata)

1968
Tecno – Formula 3 (1 Vallelunga; 1 Hockenheim; 2 Monza)
Tecno – Formula 2 (3 Crystal Palace; 4 Buenos Aires; 4 Cordoba; 4 Enna; 5 Madrid; 6 San Juan; 6 Pau)

1969
Tecno – Formula 2 (4 Enna)

1970
Tecno – Formula 2 (1 Hockenheim; 1 Paul Ricard; 1 Enna; 2 Crystal Palace; 2 Rouen; 2 Hockenheim)
Ferrari 512 – Le Mans 24 Hours (r)

Ferrari 312B – Formula 1

21 June	Holland	Zandvoort	4
19 July	Britain	Brands Hatch	4
2 August	Germany	Hockenheim	r
18 August	Austria	Österreichring	2
6 September	Italy	Monza	1
20 September	Canada	Mont-Tremblant	2
4 October	USA	Watkins Glen	13
25 October	Mexico	Mexico City	2

Championship: third (33 points)

1971
Ferrari 312 – Sports Prototype (1 Kyalami 9 Hours; 2 Brands Hatch 1,000 km)

Ferrari 312B – Formula 1

6 March	South Africa	Kyalami	3
18 April	Spain	Montjuich	r
23 May	Monaco	Monte Carlo	r
20 June	Holland	Zandvoort	3
4 July	France	Paul Ricard	r
17 July	Britain	Silverstone	r
1 August	Germany	Nürburgring	3
15 August	Austria	Österreichring	r
5 September	Italy	Monza	r
19 September	Canada	Mosport Park	r
3 October	USA	Watkins Glen	6

Championship: seventh (13 points)

1972

Ferrari 312 – Sports Prototype (1 Monza 1,000 km;
1 Kyalami 9 Hours; 2 Buenos Aires; 2 Spa; 4 Daytona)

Ferrari 312B – Formula 1

23 January	Argentina	Buenos Aires	4
4 March	South Africa	Kyalami	12
1 May	Spain	Jarama	3
14 May	Monaco	Monte Carlo	r
4 June	Belgium	Nivelles	r
30 July	Germany	Nürburgring	2
13 August	Austria	Österreichring	r
10 September	Italy	Monza	r
24 September	Canada	Mosport Park	5
8 October	USA	Watkins Glen	8

Championship : joint sixth (15 points)

1973
BRM P160 – Formula 1

28 January	Argentina	Buenos Aires	7
11 February	Brazil	Interlagos	6
3 March	South Africa	Kyalami	r
29 April	Spain	Montjuich	9
20 May	Belgium	Zolder	r
3 June	Monaco	Monte Carlo	r
17 June	Sweden	Anderstorp	9
1 July	France	Paul Ricard	12
14 July	Britain	Silverstone	7
29 July	Holland	Zandvoort	8
5 August	Germany	Nürburgring	r
19 August	Austria	Österreichring	6
9 September	Italy	Monza	r
7 October	USA	Watkins Glen	8

Championship: joint seventeenth (2 points)

1974
Ferrari 312B3 – Formula 1

13 January	Argentina	Buenos Aires	3
27 January	Brazil	Interlagos	2
30 March	South Africa	Kyalami	r
28 April	Spain	Jarama	2
12 May	Belgium	Nivelles	4
26 May	Monaco	Monte Carlo	4
9 June	Sweden	Anderstorp	r
23 June	Holland	Zandvoort	2
7 July	France	Dijon	3
20 July	Britain	Brands Hatch	4
4 August	Germany	Nürburgring	1
18 August	Austria	Österreichring	5
8 September	Italy	Monza	r
22 September	Canada	Mosport Park	2
6 October	USA	Watkins Glen	11

Championship: second (52 points)

1975
Ferrari 312B3, 312T from South Africa – Formula 1

12 January	Argentina	Buenos Aires	4
26 January	Brazil	Interlagos	4
1 March	South Africa	Kyalami	r
27 April	Spain	Montjuich	nc
11 May	Monaco	Monte Carlo	r
25 May	Belgium	Zolder	5
8 June	Sweden	Anderstorp	3
22 June	Holland	Zandvoort	3
6 July	France	Paul Ricard	r
19 July	Britain	Silverstone	13
3 August	Germany	Nürburgring	r
17 August	Austria	Österreichring	7
7 September	Italy	Monza	1
5 October	USA	Watkins Glen	r

Championship: fifth (25 points)

1976
Ferrari 312T – Formula 1

25 January	Brazil	Interlagos	7
6 March	South Africa	Kyalami	r
28 March	USA West	Long Beach	1
2 May	Spain	Jarama	11
16 May	Belgium	Zolder	2
30 May	Monaco	Monte Carlo	r
13 June	Sweden	Anderstorp	6
4 July	France	Paul Ricard	r
18 July	Britain	Brands Hatch	r/dq*
1 August	Germany	Nürburgring	9
29 August	Holland	Zandvoort	2
12 September	Italy	Monza	2
3 October	Canada	Mosport Park	6
10 October	USA East	Watkins Glen	7
24 October	Japan	Fuji	5

*Disqualified after retirement for restarting race in spare car
Championship: fifth (31 points)

1977
Ensign N177 – Formula 1

9 January	Argentina	Buenos Aires	6
23 January	Brazil	Interlagos	r
5 March	South Africa	Kyalami	9
3 April	USA West	Long Beach	r
8 May	Spain	Jarama	r
22 May	Monaco	Monte Carlo	nq
5 June	Belgium	Zolder	r
19 June	Sweden	Anderstorp	7
3 July	France	Dijon	7
16 July	Britain	Silverstone	nq
31 July	Germany	Hockenheim	r
14 August	Austria	Österreichring	r
28 August	Holland	Zandvoort	r
11 September	Italy	Monza	5
2 October	USA East	Watkins Glen	5
9 October	Canada	Mosport Park	r
23 October	Japan	Fuji	r

Championship: joint seventeenth (5 points)

1978
Shadow DN8/ DN9 from Monaco – Formula 1

15 January	Argentina	Buenos Aires	15
29 January	Brazil	Rio de Janeiro	5
4 March	South Africa	Kyalami	nq
2 April	USA West	Long Beach	10
7 May	Monaco	Monte Carlo	nq
21 May	Belgium	Zolder	r
4 June	Spain	Jarama	r
17 June	Sweden	Anderstorp	5
2 July	France	Paul Ricard	r
16 July	Britain	Brands Hatch	r
30 July	Germany	Hockenheim	nq
13 August	Austria	Österreichring	nc
27 August	Holland	Zandvoort	nq
10 September	Italy	Monza	nc
1 October	USA East	Watkins Glen	14
8 October	Canada	Montréal	nq

Championship: sixteenth (4 points)

1979
Williams FW06, FW07 from Spain – Formula 1

21 January	Argentina	Buenos Aires	10
4 February	Brazil	Interlagos	15
3 March	South Africa	Kyalami	9
8 April	USA West	Long Beach	r
29 April	Spain	Jarama	r
13 May	Belgium	Zolder	r
27 May	Monaco	Monte Carlo	2
1 July	France	Dijon	6
14 July	Britain	Silverstone	1
29 July	Germany	Hockenheim	2
12 August	Austria	Österreichring	5
26 August	Holland	Zandvoort	r
9 September	Italy	Monza	3
30 September	Canada	Montréal	3
7 October	USA East	Watkins Glen	r

Championship: fifth (32 points, 29 counting)

1980
Ensign N180 – Formula 1

13 January	Argentina	Buenos Aires	nc
27 January	Brazil	Interlagos	r
1 March	South Africa	Kyalami	9
30 March	USA West	Long Beach	r

INDEX